CliffsTestPrep®

FTCE: General Knowledge Test

by

By Jeffrey S. Kaplan and Sandra Luna McCune

WILEY

Wiley Publishing, Inc.

About the Authors

Jeffrey S. Kaplan, Ph.D., is an Associate Professor of Educational Studies in the College of Education at the University of Central Florida in Orlando. He has spent thirty years in education in the state of Florida. Dr. Kaplan has authored many publications on teacher preparation and lectures widely at state and national professional conferences.

Sandra Luna McCune, Ph.D., is Regents Professor and math specialist in the Department of Elementary Education at Stephen F. Austin State University in Nacogdoches, Texas. Dr. McCune is a nationally recognized author of teacher education test preparation review materials.

Publisher's Acknowledgments

Editorial

Project Editor: Suzanne Snyder

Acquisitions Editor: Greg Tubach

Copy Editor: Kelly Henthorne

Technical Editor(s): Tom Page

Production

Proofreader: Christine Pingleton

Wiley Publishing, Inc. Composition Services

CliffsTestPrep® FTCE: General Knowledge Test

Published by:
Wiley Publishing, Inc.
111 River Street
Hoboken, NJ 07030-5774
www.wiley.com

Copyright © 2005 Wiley, Hoboken, NJ

Published by Wiley, Hoboken, NJ
Published simultaneously in Canada

Library of Congress Cataloging-in-Publication Data

Kaplan, Jeffrey S., 1951
   CliffsTestPrep FTCE : general knowledge test / by Jeffrey S. Kaplan and Sandra Luna McCune.
     p. cm.
   ISBN-13: 978-0-7645-8948-5 (pbk.)
   ISBN-10: 0-7645-8948-2
   1. Teaching—Florida—Examinations—Study guides. 2. Teachers—Certification—Florida.
 I. McCune, Sandra L. II. Title.
LB1763.F6K36 2005
371.12'09759—dc22

2005018889

Printed in the United States of America

10 9 8 7 6 5 4

1B/SU/QY/QV/IN

For general information on our other products and services or to obtain technical support, please contact our Customer Care Department within the U.S. at 800-762-2974, outside the U.S. at 317-572-3993, or fax 317-572-4002.

Wiley also publishes its books in a variety of electronic formats. Some content that appears in print may not be available in electronic books. For more information about Wiley products, please visit our web site at www.wiley.com.

WILEY

Acknowledgments

Dr. Kaplan gratefully acknowledges Dr. Sandra Robinson, Dean of the College of Education at the University of Central Florida, and his department chair, Dr. Karen Biraimah, Professor, Educational Studies for their allowing him the time and resources to complete this teacher test preparation guide. Special thanks must be made to Grace Freedson of Grace Freedson Publishing who initiated this project, Suzanne Snyder, the editor at Wiley Press who carefully reviewed the many drafts of this text, and Dr. Sandra McCune, colleague and friend who ushered this text to its eventual fruition. Finally, he also deeply thanks his parents, James and Anita, his daughter Lauren, and his dear wife, Renee, for whom this book would not be possible without their loving guidance and support.

Dr. McCune would like to express her sincere gratitude to Grace Freedson of Grace Freedson Publishing for involving her in this project and to Jeff Kaplan, her co-author, for working with her on it. She would like to thank the editors at Wiley Press, especially Suzanne Snyder, for their patient guidance and expert assistance. She would like to thank her husband, Donice, and their children for their loving support. Finally, she would like to say a very special thank-you to her parents, Joe and Kathryne Luna, for giving her a thirst for knowledge and understanding.

Table of Contents

PART III: TWO FULL-LENGTH PRACTICE TESTS

Introduction

General Description

The Florida Teacher Certification Examination (FTCE) General Knowledge (GK) Test is designed to assess basic skills in reading, writing, and mathematics. The test is composed of four subtests:

- Subtest I—Essay Writing
- Subtest II—English Language Skills
- Subtest III—Mathematics
- Subtest IV—Reading

You will have 3½ hours to complete the test.

For the essay question, you choose from two prompts. The answer booklet includes lined paper for your essay.

Each multiple-choice question will contain three or four response options. You will record your answer choice in the separate answer booklet by filling in the space corresponding to **A, B, C,** or **D.** No penalty is assessed for wrong answers (you score a zero for that test question). For the Mathematics Subtest, the test center provides a 4-function calculator and a mathematics reference sheet.

Format of the Examination

Format of the Examination			
Subtest Competencies and Skills	**Number of Multiple Choice Questions**	**Number of Essay Questions**	**Time Allowed**
Subtest I: ESSAY			
Essay		1	
Subtest Total		**1**	**50 minutes**
Subtest II: ENGLISH LANGUAGE SKILLS			
Organization and Concept Skills	4		
Word Choice Skills	6		
Sentence Structure Skills	6		
Grammar, Punctuation, and Spelling	24		
Subtest Total	**40**		**40 minutes**

(continued)

Format of the Examination *(continued)*

Subtest Competencies and Skills	Number of Multiple Choice Questions	Number of Essay Questions	Time Allowed
Subtest III: MATHEMATICS			
Numeration and Operations	8		
Measurement	10		
Geometry	9		
Algebraic Reasoning	9		
Probability and Data Analysis	9		
Subtest Total	**45**		**80 minutes**
Subtest IV: READING			
Literal Comprehension Skills			
Inferential Comprehension Skills			
Subtest Total	**40**		**40 minutes**

The Role of the FTCE General Knowledge Test in Teacher Certification

The FTCE GK Test is one of the state-mandated teacher certification tests in Florida. If you want to teach in a Florida elementary, middle, or secondary public school, you have to take and pass at least three tests: the FTCE GK Test, the FTCE Professional Education Test, and a subject area examination (SAE) in the field in which you want to be certified. The tests and the testing program that goes with them are the result of legislation passed by Florida in 1980. For the FTCE GK Test, you have to demonstrate basics skills in reading, writing, and mathematics, which is what this book is designed to help you do. The FTCE Professional Education Test assesses your knowledge about learning, teaching, and professional conduct. The subject area test covers the content that you are required to teach. Elementary teacher education candidates take the FTCE Elementary Education K-6 test, and middle grades candidates take the Middle Grades Integrated Curriculum test as their subject area test. The purpose of the certification program in Florida is to ensure that certified teachers possess sufficient professional knowledge and skills to perform their roles as teachers in Florida schools effectively.

Statewide committees of subject area specialists identified and validated the content of the FTCE GK Test. The committee members consisted of public school teachers, district supervisors, and college faculty with expertise in the subject areas—with public school teachers comprising the majority of the committees. Selection to committee membership was based on recommendations by professional organizations, subject area experts, and teachers' unions. The test development process involved an extensive literature review, interviews with selected public school teachers, a large-scale survey of teachers, and pilot testing.

Questions Commonly Asked About the FTCE General Knowledge Test

Q. What is the FTCE General Knowledge Test?

A. The FTCE GK Test is the required basic skills test adopted by the Florida Legislature for assessing reading, writing, and mathematics skills of applicants for the Florida Teacher Certification license. It replaces the College Level Academic Skills Test (CLAST).

Q. Who administers the Florida Teacher Certification Examination?

A. The FTCE is part of the Florida Teacher Certification program, which is administered by the Florida Department of Education. A committee of experts in teacher education and specialists in specific subject areas draws up the guidelines for the FTCE examination.

Q. When and where is the Florida Teacher Certification Examination given?

A. Currently, the FTCE is administered four times a year (usually in October, January, April, and July) at locations throughout the state. Four additional supplemental testings (usually in December, February, May, and September) are administered in four cities only: Jacksonville, Miami, Orlando, and Pensacola. You can find information on test dates, site locations, fees, registration procedures, and policies in the current *Registration Bulletin* available through the University of South Florida's (USF) Certification Examinations for Florida Educators Web site (www.cefe.usf.edu/Default.aspx) and on the Florida Department of Education FTCE Web page (www.firn.edu/doe/sas/ftcehome.htm). You should check the FTCE and University of South Florida's Web sites and the FTCE Bulletin for updated information regarding changes in tests and application procedure.

Q. How do I register to take the test?

A. You must complete and send an official application (FTCE Form CG-20-04) to the address on the envelope enclosed with your registration application. Mail all FTCE test registration applications for test administrations in April, May, July, and September of 2005 to:

FTCE/FELE Registration
P.O. Box 17900
Tampa, FL 33682-7900

Exception: To send an application via an overnight carrier such as Federal Express that does not deliver to P.O. boxes, or to deliver the application in person, use the following address:

Institute for Instructional Research and Practice
University of South Florida
4202 East Fowler Avenue, HMS 401
Tampa, FL 33620

Your application must be received at the FTCE Tampa address at least 50 days prior to the examination date for regular administrations. Applications can be ordered through the University of South Florida's Certification Examinations for Florida Educators Web site (see previous question/answer for the Web address) or by writing to:

Florida Teacher Certification Examinations
Florida Department of Education
325 West Gaines Street, Suite 414
Tallahassee, FL 32399

You can also call (850) 245-0513 to order an application. Applications and registration bulletins are available from Florida school district offices and education departments at Florida colleges and universities. You must use the official application to register to take tests. You cannot register by telephone or online.

Registration deadlines are strictly enforced. Late registration requires an additional fee ($30 in 2005). If you really get in a bind and miss the regular registration deadline *and* the late registration deadline, you can call (813) 974-2400 and "late register" for a charge of $125 in addition to all other fees, including late fees. To emergency register, you must pay by Visa or MasterCard (American Express is not accepted) on the day you call.

Q. What is the fee for the test?

A. The current fee (in 2005) for regular registration is $25. The fee for late registration is an additional $30 charge. If you fail to meet either the regular registration deadline or the late registration deadline, an additional charge of $125 is assessed for emergency registration.

Q. What should I bring to the test site?

A. After you mail your registration form, you should receive an admission ticket by one week before your scheduled test date. If you have not received your admission ticket by this time or if you have lost your admission ticket, call the Florida Department of Education at (850) 245-0513. Your admission ticket will include your name, the tests you are registered to take, the test date, the test site address, the reporting time, and a reminder of what to bring to the test site. Check the information on your admission ticket to make sure that it is correct. You will not be allowed to make changes at the test site.

The day of the test, you *must* bring your admission ticket, and *two* positive identification forms, including one that is government issued with a recent photo and signature. You may be refused admission to the testing room without your valid admission ticket or proper identification. In addition, you should bring several sharpened Number 2 soft lead pencils with good erasers and a watch to help pace yourself during the exam. You are *not* allowed to bring calculators or calculator watches, watches that beep, photographic or recording devices, audiotapes, highlighters, dictionaries, spell checkers, slide rules, briefcases, backpacks, packages, cellular phones, beepers, notebooks, textbooks, scratch paper, or any other aids inside the testing room. Also, you are *not* allowed to eat, drink, or smoke inside the testing room.

Q. Are special testing arrangements available?

A. If you have a disabling condition (visual, physical, hearing, or so on), special testing arrangements and test materials can be made available for you. You have to fill in the oval in Block 20 of the registration application and send in the following two items with your application:

1. A letter stating the specific accommodation that you are requesting.
2. A letter on official letterhead stationery from a medical doctor, a licensed psychologist, or a university official documenting the specific disability indicated. This documentation cannot be older than 3 years.

If you are unable to take the test on Saturdays because of your religious convictions, you can request an alternate test day (usually a Sunday or Monday) by filling in the oval in Block 21 of the registration application. A letter from your clergy on the clergy's letterhead, verifying the religious basis for your request, must be included with your registration application.

You should write your name, social security number, and phone number on all correspondence to ensure proper handling of your documentation. Don't forget to make copies of everything before you mail it in.

Q. May I change my registration if I need to?

A. Yes, you may change tests, test sites, or transfer registration to a later test date by sending a letter requesting the change(s) to:

FTCE/FELE-USF
University Center for Business
10500 University Center Drive, Suite 270
Tampa, Florida 33612

Your letter must be received *at least* 30 days before regular administration test dates or 15 days before supplemental administration test dates.

Q. When will I get my score report?

A. For regular test date administrations, unofficial online pass/fail scores may be viewed approximately 30 days after the test administration date at www.cefe.usf.edu. This service is available free of charge, 24 hours a day, 7 days a week until 7 weeks after the test administration date. For supplemental test administration dates, unofficial online pass/fail scores are available approximately 15 days after the test administration date. Official paper score reports are mailed approximately 30 days after regular test date administrations, and approximately 2 weeks after supplemental test date administrations.

Q. What is the passing score?

A. The passing score for the FTCE GK Test is a scaled score of 200 or higher.

Q. How long are my subtest scores good?

A. Passing scores must be applied toward a credential within five years of the test date on which the scores are earned.

Q. What is included in the FTCE General Knowledge Test?

A. The sections of the FTCE GK Test include four subtests: Essay, English Language Skills, Mathematics, and Reading.

Q. How much time do I have to complete each subtest?

A. Three and one-half hours are given to complete all four subtests. For the Essay subtest, you are given 50 minutes to prepare, write, and edit your response. The English Language Skills and Reading subtests are each 40 minutes long. The Mathematics subtest is 80 minutes.

Q. If I pass part of the test, do I have to retake the whole test?

A. After you pass a subtest, you do not have to retake that subtest. You need to retake only the subtests that you did not pass. However, the fee for the FTCE GK Test is $25, regardless of the number of subtests you are taking. Also, you will not be given extra testing time when you are retaking subtests. The time allotted for a subtest is the same as that given when you take the entire test.

Q. Do I need to take all the subtests at one time?

A. The FTCE GK Test is an all-day test. Candidates may take the Essay subtest of the FTCE GK Test and the Professional Education Test on the same date. Other FTCE GK subtests (English Language Skills, Reading, and Mathematics) cannot be taken or retaken on the same test date as the Professional Education Test.

Q. How many times may I retake the test?

A. You may retake the entire test or a subtest as many times as is necessary to pass, but you must wait 31 calendar days before retaking the test. Also, you must submit a new registration application form and pay the full fees every time you retake the test or one or more subtests.

Q. What other tests must teacher candidates take?

A. Candidates applying for a Professional Teaching Certificate must take the FTCE GK Test and the FTCE Professional Education Test. In addition, candidates applying for a Professional Certificate and those adding a subject area to a Professional Certificate may need to pass a subject area examination (SAE) in a field in which they are seeking certification.

Q. Can I take all my teacher tests on one day?

A. Candidates may take the Professional Education Test and one (1) subject area exam, except Elementary Education K-6, on the same test date. Candidates may take the Professional Education Test and the Essay subtest of the FTCE GK Test on the same test date.

Q. Should I guess on the test?

A. Yes! Because no penalty is charged for guessing, guess if you have to. On the multiple-choice section, first try to eliminate some of the choices to increase your chances of choosing the right answer. But don't leave any of the answer spaces blank. On the essay response section, be sure to write a complete and logically constructed essay.

Q. May I write on the test?

A. Yes! No scratch paper is provided. You must do all of your work in the test booklets. Your answer sheet for the multiple-choice section, however, must have no marks on it other than your personal information (name, registration number, and so on) and your answers.

Q. **Is computer-based testing for the FTCE GK Test available?**

A. Computer-based testing for the FTCE GK Test, except for the Essay, is available. You can obtain complete registration and fee information by clicking on Computer-Based Testing at www.cefe.usf.edu. The number of test items and the time allowed are the same as for the paper and pencil test. Registration is online only, and you must pay online by credit card or electronic check at the completion of your online registration. You will receive an unofficial score on the screen at the end of your test. Two official score reports will be mailed to you two weeks after the test administration.

Q. **How should I prepare for the FTCE GK Test?**

A. Using this test prep book is your best preparation. This study guide gives you insights, reviews, and strategies for the question types. Some universities offer preparation programs to assist you in attaining a passing score. Check with them for further information.

Q. **How do I get more information about the Florida Teacher Certification Examination?**

A. Check the Florida Department of Education Website at www.fldoe.org. As new information on the developing program becomes available, it is posted on this site.

How to Use This CliffsTestPrep Book

This book is organized around the reading, writing, and mathematics competencies and skills of the FTCE GK Test. It includes a thorough review and study strategies for the test, a diagnostic test, and two full-length practice tests. When you read through the list of competencies and skills covered on the FTCE GK Test, you may feel overwhelmed by the task of preparing for the test. Here are some suggestions for developing an effective study program using this book.

1. To help you organize and budget your time, set up a specific schedule of study sessions. Try to set aside approximately 2 hours for each session. If you complete one session per day (including weekends), it should take you about 5 to 6 weeks to work your way through the review and practice material provided in this book. If your test date is coming up soon, you may need to lengthen your study time per day or skip sections that cover topics that you feel you already know fairly well. Nonetheless, be cautious about deciding to skip sections. You could find yourself struggling through material that would be easier to master if previous sections had been reviewed first. Particularly, be wary of skipping math topics, which are usually highly dependent on previously learned skills.

2. Choose a place for studying this book that is free of distractions and undue noise, so that you can concentrate. Make sure you have adequate lighting and a room temperature that is comfortable—not too warm or too cold. Try to have all the necessary study aids (paper, pen, 4-function calculator, and so on) within easy reach, so that you don't have to interrupt your studying to go get something you need. Ask friends not to call you during your study time.

3. Don't make excuses. Studying for the FTCE GK Test must be a priority. It will require a lot of time and a conscientious commitment on your part. Think of it as a job that you must do. In reality, studying for the FTCE GK Test is one of the most important jobs you will ever do. The outcome of the test can determine your future career opportunities. Do not avoid studying for it by making excuses or procrastinating.

4. Take the Diagnostic Test in Chapter 1 before you begin your study program. For the essay question, try to see where your answer might have failed to adequately address the given prompt. Of course, you have to judge the quality of your response based on the scoring criteria explained in Chapter 2 and in comparison to the sample response given in the answer explanations. For the multiple-choice questions, carefully study the answer explanations for *all* the questions, not just the ones you missed, because you might have gotten some of your correct answers by guessing or by using an incorrect method. Plan your study program so that you can concentrate first on topics that your diagnostic test results indicate are weak areas for you. If you did fairly well in mathematics and writing but poorly in reading, then you should begin your FTCE GK Test preparation with the reading review in Chapter 5.

5. Carefully study the review chapters, being sure to concentrate as you go through the material. Don't let yourself be diverted by extraneous thoughts or outside distractions. Here are some study strategies:

   • Monitor yourself by making a check mark on a separate sheet of paper when your concentration wanders. Work on reducing the number of check marks you record each study session.

   • Take notes as you study, using your own words to express ideas.

   • Leave ample room in the left margin, so that you can revise or make comments when you review your notes. Extract key ideas and write them in the left margin to use as study cues later.

   • Make flashcards to aid you in memorizing key ideas and keep them with you at all times. When you have spare moments, take out the flash cards and go over the information you've recorded on them.

   • Set aside certain days to review material you have already studied. This strategy will allow you to reinforce what you have learned and identify topics you may need to restudy.

   • If possible, set up a regular time to study with one or more classmates or friends. A good way of learning and reinforcing the material is to discuss it with others.

6. When you complete your review, take Practice Test 1 in Chapter 6. Use a timer and take the test under the same conditions you expect for the actual test, being sure to adhere to the time limits for each subtest. When you finish taking the test, as you did for the diagnostic test, carefully study the answer explanations for *all* the questions.

7. Analyze the results of the practice test, then go back and review again any topics in which you performed unsatisfactorily.

8. When you complete your second review, take Practice Test 2 in Chapter 7 under the same conditions you expect for the actual test; adhere to the time limits for each subtest. When you finish taking the test, carefully study the answer explanations for *all* the questions and do additional study, if needed. After completing your study program, you should find yourself prepared and confident to achieve a passing score on the FTCE GK Test.

How to Prepare for the Day of the Test

There are several things you can do to prepare yourself for the day of the test.

1. Know where the test center is located and how to get there.
2. Make dependable arrangements to get to the test center in plenty of time and know where to park if you plan to go by car.
3. Keep all the materials you will need to bring to the test center—especially, your admission ticket and two forms of identification—in a secure place, so that you easily find them on the day of the test.
4. Go to bed early enough to get a good night's rest. Avoid taking nonprescription drugs or alcohol, as the use of these products may impair your mental faculties on test day.
5. On the day of the test, plan to get to the testing center early.
6. Dress in comfortable clothing and wear comfortable shoes. Even if it is warm outside, wear layers of clothing that can be removed or put on, depending on the temperature in the test center.
7. Eat a light meal. Select foods that you have found usually give you the most energy and stamina.
8. Drink plenty of water to make sure that your brain remains hydrated during the test for optimal thinking.

What to Do during the Test

Here are some general test-taking strategies to help maximize your score on the test. You are given content-specific strategies in the review chapters: Chapters 2, 3, 4, and 5.

1. During the test, follow all the directions, including the oral directions of the test administrator and the written directions in the test booklet. If you do not understand something in the directions, ask the test administrator for clarification. The test administrator will indicate how you are to ask for assistance.

2. Move through the test at a steady pace. Work as rapidly as you can without being careless, *but do not rush*. Use your watch to check the time occasionally.

3. Try to answer the questions in order. Skipping around can waste time and may cause mistakes on your answer sheet. However, if a question is taking too much of your time, place a large check mark next to it in the test booklet (*not* on the answer booklet), mark your best guess in the answer booklet, and move on.

4. Read each question entirely. Skimming to save time can cause you to misread a question or miss important information.

5. Mark in the test booklet. Circle or underline important information and lightly cross out answer choices you've eliminated. On the math subtest, mark on diagrams, draw figures, and do calculations in the test booklet. Remember, however, to mark your answer choice in the separate answer booklet. Answers marked only in the test booklet are not scored.

6. Read all the answer choices before you select an answer. You may find two answers that sound good, but one is a better answer to the question.

7. Try to eliminate at least two answer choices. Before you make your final choice, reread the question (Don't skip doing this!) and select the response that best answers the question.

8. Change an answer only if you have a good reason to do so. Be sure to completely erase the old answer choice before marking the new one.

9. If you are trying to recall information during the test, close your eyes and try to visualize yourself in your study place. This may trigger your memory.

10. Remain calm during the test. If you find yourself getting anxious, stop and take several deep, slow breaths and exhale slowly to help you relax. Do not be upset if the student next to you finishes, gets up, and leaves before you do. Keep your mind focused on the task at hand—completing your exam. Trust yourself. You should not expect to know the correct response to every question on the exam. Think only of doing your personal best.

11. Record your answers in the answer booklet carefully. The multiple-choice items are scored electronically, so it is critical that you mark your answer booklet accurately. As you go through the test questions, circle the letters of your answer choice in the test booklet. Then mark those answers in the answer booklet in bunches of five to ten (until the last minutes of the time allotted, when you should start marking answers one by one).

12. Before turning in your answer booklet, be sure you have marked an answer for every test question. You are not penalized for a wrong answer (you score a zero for that test question), so even if you have no clue about the correct answer, make a guess. Also, erase any stray marks in the answer booklet and brush off any loose eraser dust.

13. As you work through the diagnostic and practice tests provided in this book, consciously use the strategies suggested in this section as preparation for the actual FTCE GK test.

You will benefit greatly from this CliffsTestPrep book. By using the recommendations in this chapter as you complete your study program, you will be prepared to walk into the testing room with confidence. Good luck on the test and on your future career as a teacher!

PART I

DIAGNOSTIC TEST

Answer Sheet for FTCE General Knowledge Diagnostic Examination

(Remove This Sheet and Use It To Mark Your Answers)

Diagnostic General Knowledge Test: Essay

Write your essay on lined paper.

Diagnostic General Knowledge Test: English Language Skills

1 Ⓐ Ⓑ Ⓒ Ⓓ	11 Ⓐ Ⓑ Ⓒ Ⓓ
2 Ⓐ Ⓑ Ⓒ Ⓓ	12 Ⓐ Ⓑ Ⓒ Ⓓ
3 Ⓐ Ⓑ Ⓒ Ⓓ	13 Ⓐ Ⓑ Ⓒ Ⓓ
4 Ⓐ Ⓑ Ⓒ Ⓓ	14 Ⓐ Ⓑ Ⓒ Ⓓ
5 Ⓐ Ⓑ Ⓒ Ⓓ	15 Ⓐ Ⓑ Ⓒ Ⓓ
6 Ⓐ Ⓑ Ⓒ Ⓓ	16 Ⓐ Ⓑ Ⓒ Ⓓ
7 Ⓐ Ⓑ Ⓒ Ⓓ	17 Ⓐ Ⓑ Ⓒ Ⓓ
8 Ⓐ Ⓑ Ⓒ Ⓓ	18 Ⓐ Ⓑ Ⓒ Ⓓ
9 Ⓐ Ⓑ Ⓒ Ⓓ	19 Ⓐ Ⓑ Ⓒ Ⓓ
10 Ⓐ Ⓑ Ⓒ Ⓓ	20 Ⓐ Ⓑ Ⓒ Ⓓ

Diagnostic General Knowledge Test: Mathematics

21 Ⓐ Ⓑ Ⓒ Ⓓ	31 Ⓐ Ⓑ Ⓒ Ⓓ
22 Ⓐ Ⓑ Ⓒ Ⓓ	32 Ⓐ Ⓑ Ⓒ Ⓓ
23 Ⓐ Ⓑ Ⓒ Ⓓ	33 Ⓐ Ⓑ Ⓒ Ⓓ
24 Ⓐ Ⓑ Ⓒ Ⓓ	34 Ⓐ Ⓑ Ⓒ Ⓓ
25 Ⓐ Ⓑ Ⓒ Ⓓ	35 Ⓐ Ⓑ Ⓒ Ⓓ
26 Ⓐ Ⓑ Ⓒ Ⓓ	36 Ⓐ Ⓑ Ⓒ Ⓓ
27 Ⓐ Ⓑ Ⓒ Ⓓ	37 Ⓐ Ⓑ Ⓒ Ⓓ
28 Ⓐ Ⓑ Ⓒ Ⓓ	38 Ⓐ Ⓑ Ⓒ Ⓓ
29 Ⓐ Ⓑ Ⓒ Ⓓ	39 Ⓐ Ⓑ Ⓒ Ⓓ
30 Ⓐ Ⓑ Ⓒ Ⓓ	40 Ⓐ Ⓑ Ⓒ Ⓓ

Diagnostic General Knowledge Test: Reading

41 Ⓐ Ⓑ Ⓒ Ⓓ	51 Ⓐ Ⓑ Ⓒ Ⓓ
42 Ⓐ Ⓑ Ⓒ Ⓓ	52 Ⓐ Ⓑ Ⓒ Ⓓ
43 Ⓐ Ⓑ Ⓒ Ⓓ	53 Ⓐ Ⓑ Ⓒ Ⓓ
44 Ⓐ Ⓑ Ⓒ Ⓓ	54 Ⓐ Ⓑ Ⓒ Ⓓ
45 Ⓐ Ⓑ Ⓒ Ⓓ	55 Ⓐ Ⓑ Ⓒ Ⓓ
46 Ⓐ Ⓑ Ⓒ Ⓓ	56 Ⓐ Ⓑ Ⓒ Ⓓ
47 Ⓐ Ⓑ Ⓒ Ⓓ	57 Ⓐ Ⓑ Ⓒ Ⓓ
48 Ⓐ Ⓑ Ⓒ Ⓓ	58 Ⓐ Ⓑ Ⓒ Ⓓ
49 Ⓐ Ⓑ Ⓒ Ⓓ	59 Ⓐ Ⓑ Ⓒ Ⓓ
50 Ⓐ Ⓑ Ⓒ Ⓓ	60 Ⓐ Ⓑ Ⓒ Ⓓ

CUT HERE

CUT HERE

General Knowledge Diagnostic Test: Essay

This section of the examination involves a written assignment. You are asked to prepare a written response for *one of the two topics* presented. Select one of these two topics and prepare a 300–600 word response. Be sure to read both topics very carefully to make sure that you understand the topic for which you are preparing a written response. Use your allotted time to plan, write, review, and edit what you have written for the assignment.

Topic 1

A place you would like to visit

Topic 2

An invention that changed the world

Be sure to read the two topics again before attempting to write your response. Remember to write your answer on the space provided in the examination booklet.

Your essay is graded holistically, meaning only one score will be assigned for your writing—taking into consideration both mechanics and organization. *You will not be scored on the nature of the content or opinions expressed in your work.* Instead, you are graded on your ability to write complete sentences, to express and support your opinions, and to organize your work.

At least two evaluators review your work and assign it a score. Special attention is paid to the following more specific indications in your writing.

- Does your writing demonstrate a strong definitive purpose?
- Is there a clear thesis or statement of a main idea?
- Are your ideas organized?
- Do you support your thesis with clear details?
- Are effective transitions present?
- Do you demonstrate an effective use of language?
- Are a variety of sentence patterns present?
- Is there a consistent point of view?
- Are the conventions of standard American English used?

Before you begin, be sure you plan what you want to say. Organize your thoughts and carefully construct your ideas. This should be your original work, written by your own hand, and in your own voice.

As you write your piece, you may cross out or add information as necessary. Although handwriting does not count, be sure to be legible in your response.

For those individuals who cannot physically write, you can arrange for a proxy to do your writing. Please contact the Florida Certification office before you take the examination to make the necessary accommodations.

General Knowledge Diagnostic Test: English Language Skills

Directions: For items 1 and 2, read the entire passage carefully and then answer the questions. Please note that intentional errors have been included in this passage. This passage is designed to measure both the identification of logical order in a written passage and the presence of irrelevant sentences.

(1) If you traveled in America's heartland—the great American West—you would see large tracts of land with very few people, homes, or businesses. (2) For the most part, you would travel through large stretches of America's great landscapes, used primarily for ranching and farming. (3) Generally, the people who live in America's West do the work that best supports the land on which they live. (4) In fact, some places exist where there are less than two people per square mile. (5) For the most part, people living in the West farm or ranch. (6) Los Angeles is a very busy place with a high population density. (7) For example, farmers in Idaho grow potatoes; Washington is known for its apples; and California alone grows more than half the fruits and vegetables raised in the United States. (8) Much of the land in the West is rugged, however, and on this land, the landowners raise cattle.

1. Select the arrangement of sentences 2, 3 and 4 that provides the most logical sequence of ideas and supporting details in the paragraph. If no change is needed, select Choice A.

   A. For the most part, you would travel through large stretches of America's great landscapes, used primarily for ranching and farming. Generally, the people who live in America's West do the work that best supports the land on which they live. In fact, some places exist where there are less than two people per square mile.

   B. For the most part, you would travel through large stretches of America's great landscapes, used primarily for ranching and farming. In fact, some places exist where there are less than two people per square mile. Generally, the people who live in America's West do the work that best supports the land on which they live.

   C. Generally, the people who live in America's West do the work that best supports the land on which they live. In fact, some places exist where there are less than two people per square mile. For the most part, you would travel through large stretches of America's great landscapes, used primarily for ranching and farming.

   D. Generally, the people who live in America's West do the work that best supports the land on which they live. For the most part, you would travel through large stretches of America's great landscapes, used primarily for ranching and farming. In fact, some places exist where there are less than two people per square mile.

2. Which numbered sentence is LEAST relevant to the passage?

   A. Sentence 5
   B. Sentence 6
   C. Sentence 7
   D. Sentence 8

Directions: For questions 3–17, select the answer choice that corrects an error in the underlined portion. If there is no error, choose **D** indicating "No change is necessary."

3. Everyone <u>accepted</u> the presents from the
   [A]

   <u>principle</u> and the members of the school <u>board</u>.
   [B]   [C]

   A. excepted
   B. principal
   C. bored
   D. No change is necessary.

4. My father, <u>Doctor</u> Leonard Pitts, teaches <u>English</u>
   [A]   [B]

   to foreign-born students, every <u>spring</u> academic
   [C]

   term.

   A. doctor
   B. english
   C. Spring
   D. No change is necessary.

5. In the book *Gone With the Wind*, <u>author</u>
   [A]

   Margaret Mitchell writes about the life and times

   in the <u>South</u> during the <u>civil war, this</u> was a
   [B]   [C]

   time of great strife in American public life.

   A. Author
   B. South
   C. Civil War. This
   D. No change is necessary.

6. Formerly, science was taught by the textbook
   <u>method, now</u> it is taught by the laboratory
   method.

   A. method; now it is
   B. method. While now it
   C. method while now
   D. No change is necessary.

7. The <u>alternate</u> plan <u>is</u> a good substitute for
   [A]   [B]

   <u>affecting</u> a change in his personality.
   [C]

   A. alternative
   B. was
   C. effecting
   D. No change is necessary.

8. <u>When</u> the students were on the field trip to the
   [A]

   <u>museum they</u> took notes in <u>their</u> journals.
   [B]   [C]

   A. Whenever
   B. museum, they
   C. there
   D. No change is necessary.

9. The professor felt <u>badly</u> about giving a failing
   [A]

   grade on the <u>English</u> paper to the son of the <u>dean</u>
   [B]   [C]

   of the College of Fine Arts.

   A. bad
   B. english
   C. Dean
   D. No change is necessary.

10. I am <u>concerned because</u> the relationship between
    [A]

    <u>you and I</u> is <u>definitely</u> unfriendly.
    [B]   [C]

    A. concerned, because
    B. you and me
    C. definately
    D. No change is necessary.

11. My son, <u>who</u> is a star basketball player, is <u>much</u>
    [A]   [B]

    taller than <u>me</u>.
    [C]

    A. whom
    B. more
    C. I
    D. No change is necessary.

12. Each of the women gave <u>their</u> account of <u>what</u>
    [A]   [B]

    caused the accident <u>between</u> the pickup truck and
    [C]

    the luxury vehicle.

    A. her
    B. whatever
    C. among
    D. No change is necessary.

13. Through a survey of the student population, we
    [A]   [B]
obtained data that show strong support for the
                 [C]
new school logo.

    A. Threw
    B. population we
    C. shows
    D. No change is necessary.

14. Because the teacher had assigned a number of homework problems, the students should have began the assignment before they left class.

    A. should of began
    B. should have begun
    C. should of begun
    D. No change is necessary.

15. When I was a student, I had made very good grades.

    A. have made
    B. made
    C. had been making
    D. No change is necessary.

16. My children had some old toys that were still in
                                [A]
good condition, so I gave them to a local charity.
[B]   [C]

    A. are
    B. well
    C. the toys
    D. No change is necessary.

17. The principle reason I am not supporting that
         [A]
candidate is that he has been dishonest with the
           [B]   [C]
taxpayers.

    A. principal
    B. because
    C. have been
    D. No change is necessary.

18. Michael, leader of the student prom committee and a high school senior, is speaking to the faculty of his high school, requesting that juniors and seniors be allowed to leave early on the day of the prom. Choose the most appropriate opening statement.

    A. "My esteemed colleagues and learned teachers, before we digress, let us consider the delicate issue of leaving class early on the days of joyous occasions. The need to leave our halls of academe. . ."
    B. "As you know, nothing really happens in class on the day of the high school prom! So, why not let us go home early?"
    C. "Good afternoon. Before I begin, let me say that many students—juniors and seniors, in particular—have been working very hard on this year's high school prom. We are very much looking forward to attending."
    D. "Hey! Don't you think seniors deserve a break? Why not let them skip school on the day of this year's prom?"

19. Choose the sentence that is punctuated correctly.

    A. After hearing the two customer's complaints about being overcharged, the store manager gave each of them a $10 gift certificate.
    B. After hearing the two customer's complaints about being overcharged the store manager gave each of them a $10 gift certificate.
    C. After hearing the two customers' complaints about being overcharged, the store manager gave each of them a $10 gift certificate.
    D. After hearing the two customers' complaints' about being overcharged, the store manager gave each of them a $10 gift certificate.

20. Choose the sentence in which the modifiers are placed correctly.

    A. Driving along the highway, Paul was surprised by a sudden noise coming from the trunk of the car.
    B. Paul was surprised by a sudden noise coming from the trunk of the car driving along the highway.
    C. Coming from the trunk of the car, Paul was surprised by a sudden noise driving along the highway.
    D. Driving along the highway, coming from the trunk of the car, Paul was surprised by a sudden noise.

General Knowledge Diagnostic Test: Mathematics

Mathematics Reference Sheet

Area

Triangle

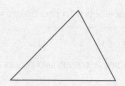

$A = \frac{1}{2} bh$

Rectangle

$A = lw$

Key	
b = base	d = diameter
h = height	r = radius
l = length	A = area
w = width	C = circumference
S.A. = surface area	V = volume
	B = area of base
Use π = 3.14 or $\frac{22}{7}$	

Trapezoid

$A = \frac{1}{2} h (b_1 + b_2)$

Parallelogram

$A = bh$

Circle

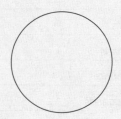

$A = \pi r^2$
$C = \pi d = 2\pi r$

Surface Area

1. Surface area of a prism or pyramid = the sum of the areas of all faces of the figure.

2. Surface area of a cylinder = the sum of the two bases + its rectangular wrap.

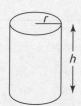

$S.\, A. = 2(\pi r^2) + 2(\pi r)h$

3. Surface area of a sphere: $S.A. = 4\pi r^2$

Volume

1. Volume of a prism or cylinder equals (Area of the Base) times (height): $V = Bh$

2. Volume of a pyramid or cone equals $\frac{1}{3}$ times (Area of the Base) times (height): $V = \frac{1}{3} Bh$

3. Volume of a sphere: $V = \frac{4}{3} \pi r^3$

CUT HERE

Mathematics Reference Sheet, continued

Pythagorean Theorem: $a^2 + b^2 = c^2$

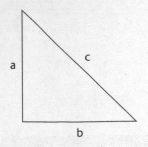

Simple Interest Formula: $I = prt$

I = simple interest, p = principal

r = rate, t = time

Distance Formula: $d = rt$

d = distance, r = rate, t = time

Given a line containing points

(x_1, y_1) and (x_2, y_2),

- Slope of line = $\dfrac{y_2 - y_1}{x_2 - x_1}$

- Distance between two points =

$$\sqrt{\left(x_2 - x_1\right)^2 + \left(y_2 - y_1\right)^2}$$

- Midpoint between two points =

$$\left(\dfrac{x_1 + x_2}{2}, \dfrac{y_1 + y_2}{2}\right)$$

Conversions	
1 yard = 3 feet = 36 inches	1 cup = 8 fluid ounces
1 mile = 1,760 yards = 5,280 feet	1 pint = 2 cups
1 acre = 43,560 square feet	1 quart = 2 pints
1 hour = 60 minutes	1 gallon = 4 quarts
1 minute = 60 seconds	1 pound = 16 ounces
	1 ton = 2,000 pounds
1 liter = 1000 milliliters = 1000 cubic centimeters	
1 meter = 100 centimeters = 1000 millimeters	
1 kilometer = 1000 meters	
1 gram = 1000 milligrams	
1 kilogram = 1000 grams	

Note: Metric numbers with four digits are written without a comma (e.g., 2543 grams).

For metric numbers with more than four digits, a space is used instead of a comma (e.g., 24 300 liters).

CUT HERE

Directions: Read each question and select the best answer choice.

21. Perform the indicated operations: $-9(5) - 18 \div 3^2$

    A. -3
    B. -7
    C. -47
    D. 47

22. In 1965, the tuition at a certain university was $5 per semester credit hour. In 2005, the tuition had increased to $80 per semester credit hour. What is the increase in tuition cost for a 15 semester-credit-hour course load?

    A. $75
    B. $1200
    C. $1125
    D. $1275

23. Which of the following expressions is NOT equivalent to the others?

    A. $3^3 \times 8^2$
    B. $2^6 \times 9 \times 3$
    C. 32×54
    D. 9×16

24. Perform the indicated operations: $\dfrac{54 \times 10^{12}}{6 \times 10^4}$

    A. 9×10^{-8}
    B. 9×10^8
    C. 9×10^3
    D. 9×10^{-3}

25. If 12 of the 150 fans who attended a football game on a particular Saturday were parents of students, what percent of the fans were students' parents at the game on that Saturday?

    A. 0.08%
    B. 8%
    C. 12%
    D. 80%

26. If $x = -2$ and $y = -10$, then $x - y =$ what?

    A. 8
    B. -8
    C. 12
    D. -12

27. Which of the following statements is true?

    A. $\dfrac{4}{7} > \dfrac{5}{9}$
    B. $0.5 < 0.35$
    C. 5% of 60 < 10% of 20
    D. $-18 > -5$

28. In right triangle ABC, the length of side AB, the hypotenuse of the right triangle, is $\sqrt{41}$. What is the approximate value of $\sqrt{41}$?

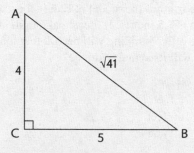

    A. Between 4 and 5
    B. Between 5 and 6
    C. Between 6 and 7
    D. Between 36 and 49

29. The distance from the Earth to the Sun is approximately 93,000,000 miles. Which of the following numbers shows the approximate distance from the Earth to the Sun in scientific notation?

    A. 9.3×10^8
    B. 9.3×10^7
    C. 9.3×10^{-8}
    D. 9.3×10^{-7}

30. A fitness club charges its members a $300 annual fee plus $5 every time a member brings a guest to the club pool. The fitness club charges no other additional fees. Donna was charged a total of $385 last year in membership fees to the fitness club. How many times did she bring a guest to the fitness club pool?

    A. 77
    B. 60
    C. 27
    D. 17

31. An artist cut out a circular piece of stained glass with a radius of 4.1 centimeters. The artist then calculated the area of the piece of glass. Which of the following is a reasonable estimate for the artist's calculation of the area of the piece of glass?

   A.   25 cm^2

   B.   50 cm^2

   C.   160 cm^2

   D.   200 cm^2

32. An architect built a scale model of an office building to show her client. The front of the office building will have a rectangular shape. The length of the front of the model is 12.5 inches, and its width is 7.5 inches. If the actual length of the front of the office building will be 100 feet long, how wide will its actual width be?

   A.   60 feet

   B.   75 feet

   C.   166 feet

   D.   750 feet

33. Determine which of the following ordered pairs satisfies the given system.

$$3x + y = 2$$
$$x + 2y = 9$$

   A.   (–1,–5)

   B.   (1,–5)

   C.   (1,5)

   D.   (–1,5)

34. A 13-foot piece of lumber is leaning against the wall of a building. The bottom of the piece of lumber is 5 feet from the base of the wall. How high up the wall does the piece of lumber reach?

   A.   18 feet

   B.   14 feet

   C.   12 feet

   D.   8 feet

35. A spinner for a board game has 4 red sections, 3 yellow sections, 2 blue sections, and 1 green section. The sections are all of equal size. What is the probability of spinning yellow on the first spin and blue on the second spin?

   A. $\dfrac{3}{50}$

   B. $\dfrac{2}{25}$

   C. $\dfrac{3}{10}$

   D. $\dfrac{1}{5}$

36. Which of the following statements is always true about parallelograms?

   A.   All angles are 90°.

   B.   All sides are congruent.

   C.   Opposite sides are parallel.

   D.   The diagonals are perpendicular to each other.

37. A student needs an average of at least 90 on four tests to earn an A in a college course. The student has grades of 87, 91, and 83 on the first three tests. What is the *lowest* grade the student can make on the fourth test and still receive an A in the course?

   A.   90

   B.   95

   C.   96

   D.   99

38. The graph shows a budget for a monthly salary after taxes.

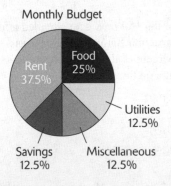

Monthly Budget

If the monthly salary is $2,800, how much money is budgeted for rent?

   A. $105

   B. $350

   C. $700

   D. $1,050

39. Kathryn runs 5 kilometers each day for 7 days and records the following running times: 24 minutes, 21 minutes, 21 minutes, 25 minutes, 21 minutes, 22 minutes, 27 minutes. What is the median running time for the 7 days?

    A. 21

    B. 22

    C. 23

    D. 25

40. For lunch Richard can choose from three types of sandwiches: ham, turkey, or peanut butter. He can choose from two drinks: milk or juice. How many possible combinations of sandwiches and drinks can Richard choose for lunch?

    A. 4

    B. 5

    C. 6

    D. 7

General Knowledge Diagnostic Test: Reading

Directions: Please read the following passages carefully. Each passage in this section is followed by questions based on the passage's content. After reading each passage, answer the questions by choosing the best answer from among the four choices given. Be sure to base your answers on what is *implied* or *stated* in the passage.

Passage 1

Los Angeles

(1)   Los Angeles, California, is a fascinating place to live and work. There are many exciting venues to explore and enjoy. Home to more than twelve million people, Los Angeles and its surrounding suburbs teem with people from all walks of life who are engaged in all sorts of conventional and unconventional activities and employment. Thus, given its population size and metropolitan allure, Los Angeles has become a mecca for young people seeking to make their fortune in this growing and tantalizing economy. For even though the Los Angeles community is an expensive place to live, the return on one's investment in both real estate and vocational possibilities can be endless and substantial.

(2)   Like many places in the United States, Los Angeles has much to offer its people. It has beautiful, sandy beaches that stretch endlessly along its sun-drenched west coast. Sports fans can be entertained by baseball games at Dodger Stadium and football games at the Memorial Coliseum. If they prefer to play instead of watch, recreational enthusiasts can find any number of outdoor facilities, including sports fields, golf courses, tennis courts, hiking and jogging paths, and horseback riding trails. For cultural enthusiasts, the Los Angeles community offers a plentitude of venues to suit every artistic need and desire imaginable. Plays, concerts, operas, ballets, choirs, and orchestras can be enjoyed at the Los Angeles' Music Center for the Performing Arts or any of the dozens of other venues situated throughout this highly artistic community. And if reading is your hobby, the Los Angeles Public Library is the third largest library in the United States, housing more than five million books.

(3)   To be sure, newcomers to the Los Angeles area have little problem finding good times. Often times, though, they have trouble finding affordable housing. Los Angeles and its surrounding community have little land left on which to build homes. In fact, new homes are usually built on land once occupied by older homes, or large, towering apartment buildings are constructed, designed to house a maximum number of people within a small, confined erect space. The result is that living space in Los Angeles is at an all-time premium. Consequently, many people who can afford to do so move to houses in the suburbs, or even miles away in surrounding communities. Once there, they make the long daily commute to their places of work in Los Angeles proper. For these traveling commuters, Los Angeles is the home to more than 750 miles of freeway, which to the delight of its many commuters is toll free.

(4)   Rapid growth, like elsewhere, has created its share of problems for the Los Angeles community. Exhaust fumes from vehicles and smoke from working factories continue to create their share of air pollution. And although governmental regulations in recent years have cut down on some potential environmental damage, there is still a considerable health hazard for those who live in this densely populated and congested community. Besides tackling these environmental concerns, the city is also working to improve transportation, build affordable housing, construct world-class public schools, and provide for its growing number of indigent and poor. Moreover, Los Angeles, like most of California, has a burgeoning immigrant population. These foreign-born nationals come with their own set of concerns and issues, but nothing Los Angeles cannot handle. Los Angeles—despite all its problems—is one of the most exciting cities in the world to visit, and—if you are lucky enough—to live and work in as well.

41. The main idea of this passage is

A. Los Angeles is a thriving metropolitan community.

B. Los Angeles is an expensive place to work and live.

C. Los Angeles is a city of immigrants and natives.

D. Los Angeles is a city both in transition and stasis.

42. In paragraph 2, the author is telling the reader

 A. about Los Angeles' rich, cultural offerings.
 B. about Los Angeles' leading economic indicators.
 C. about Los Angeles' diverse cultural venues.
 D. about Los Angeles' social restorative powers.

43. As implied in this passage, Los Angeles is experiencing

 A. the implicit consequences of urban sprawl.
 B. a dramatic increase in affordable living space.
 C. tension between urban and rural environments.
 D. tension between diverse races.

44. Overall, the author's tone is

 A. cautiously pessimistic.
 B. decisively sarcastic.
 C. implicitly realistic.
 D. deliberately noncommittal.

45. In the first paragraph, the word *mecca* means

 A. melting pot.
 B. transition.
 C. retreat.
 D. destination.

Passage 2

A Simple Token System for David

(1) David, an eight-year-old boy in a regular second-grade classroom, was brought to see the elementary school guidance counselor because his parents were having difficulty managing his behavior at school and at home. David is an only child and functions in the type of home environment that "only children" usually have. He has doting and overprotective parents and little, if any, conflict over sharing his toys and possessions. Still, like many young children, David has a persistent stubborn streak. At home, he does what he wants to do when he wants to do it. Driving his parents crazy seems to be David's favorite pastime. He does not stay in his bed at night, does not follow directions, and only eats certain foods. His deliberate defiance also is beginning to appear in his second-grade class where he does not pay attention, complete his assignments, or stay put in his chair. He is beginning to annoy the other children and distract them from their work. Naturally, his parents, his teacher and his counselor are upset and desire to change his behavior.

(2) David's elementary school guidance counselor suggests that David's parents faithfully observe and record their son's behaviors, so that—in time—they can make necessary modifications. Agreeing that they should limit their observations to just one behavior problem, David's parents decide that getting out of bed at night is the most troublesome behavior he exhibits at home and should be handled first.

(3) Soon, their observations give way to a solution. After discussing several possible strategies to keep David from leaving his bed at night, his parents agree to use a simple token system. David is shown a chart and told that if he stays in his bed from the time he is tucked in at night until the next morning, he will get a star to paste on his chart. Five stars collected in a row means that David can select a small toy as a reward. In addition, his parents will give him lots of praise that next morning.

(4) To his parent's surprise, almost immediately, David's behavior dramatically reverses. Within days of initiating this behavior modification system, David stays in bed all night. Translating their success into other concerns, David's parents begin to keep behavior modification charts to monitor David's other problems. Quickly, David begins to comply, and soon, he is following directions, eating all his meals, performing well in school, and acting as a healthy and happy eight year old. Instituting a simple token system to modify noncompliant behavior proved to be the remedy for improving young David's home and school performance. Thus, this case demonstrates how guidance counselors can effectively help parents and teachers shape children's behaviors.

46. The *simple token system* is a method that best fits within the larger context of

 A. behaviorism.
 B. humanism.
 C. constructivism.
 D. essentialism.

47. In the first paragraph, the author implies that

 A. David's issues are insolvable.
 B. David's parents are indifferent.
 C. David's counselor is naive.
 D. David's problems are typical.

48. Implicit in this passage is the belief

    A. that learning is developmental.

    B. that learning is predetermined.

    C. that learning is self-centered.

    D. that learning is mechanistic.

49. In the second paragraph, the author speaks of *necessary modifications*, meaning

    A. self-examining internal strife and external conflicts.

    B. reviewing personal motivations, ambitions and goals.

    C. making changes that are warranted.

    D. monitoring prescribed actions and outside force.

50. The author of this narrative would most likely concur with which one of the following statements?

    A. Radical change occurs exponentially.

    B. Self-defeating behavior is irreversible.

    C. Developmental needs are predetermined.

    D. Narrowing issues is reasonable.

Passage 3

Anne Frank: The Power of the Living Word

(1) The story of Anne Frank is the story of one family's struggle to survive one of the most unthinkable horrors of the twentieth century—the Holocaust. A Jewish family forced into hiding to escape Nazi persecution, the Franks are today remembered not because they were unique, but because young Anne kept a diary of her and her family's experiences. At the conclusion of the Second World War, her diary was found, published, and widely read throughout the world, making Anne one of the most renowned victims of the Holocaust. Her diary has been made into plays and movies, and—in many cases—is required reading in schools and universities throughout the world. The Frank family tragedy has become the living symbol for the triumph of the written word and courage over human despair and tragedy.

(2) Anne Frank was born in Frankfurt am Main in Germany in 1929. Soon afterward, in 1933, the anti-Jewish National Socialist Party led by Adolph Hitler came to power. Fortunately for Anne, her parents Otto and Edith had decided shortly after Anne's birth that there was no future for them in Germany, so they fled to the Netherlands, eventually settling in Amsterdam, Holland. There, Anne lived a relatively carefree childhood until she turned 11 years old; however, in 1940, the Netherlands became occupied by Germany, and the protection that Holland provided for the Jewish people came to an abrupt end.

(3) Soon, Anne's life—as well as the lives of all Jewish families living under Nazi occupation—became increasingly restricted by Hitler's Jewish decrees. Beginning in 1942, Hitler ordered all Jews to report to so-called "work camps." Refusal to comply meant being sent to a prison camp. Having no choice, the majority of Jews complied and were shipped off to places where they were eventually tortured and killed.

(4) Sensing this fate, Anne's parents decided to escape Nazi persecution by going into hiding. Since fleeing the Netherlands was near impossible, the Frank family chose to hide in the attic of a building near Otto Frank's place of work in Amsterdam. With the aid and the ever-protecting vigilance of their friends, the Frank's extended family—Anne's parents, Anne, her older sister, a Jewish dentist, and another Jewish couple and their teenage son—lived inside a cramped second-story space for slightly more than two years, from July 9, 1942, to August 4, 1944.

(5) During these years, Anne wrote in a diary that had been given to her on her thirteenth birthday. Writing in Dutch, Anne described her fears of living in hiding; her awakening feelings for Peter (the teenager living with them); the conflicts of living in such closed quarters; and her aspirations of becoming a writer. In fact, she even rewrote some of her diary in the hopes of publishing her work after the war.

(6) Sadly, Anne would never live to see the worldwide acclaim of her published diary. After more than two years in hiding, a tip from a Dutch informer led the Gestapo, the Nazi police, to their hiding place. Arrested and deported, Anne and her family were transported to concentration or "death camps" where all but Otto Frank, Anne's father, perished. It is now known that Anne and her older sister, Margot, were sent to Auschwitz, but eventually died at the Bergen-Belsen camp of typhus in March, 1945.

(7) Fortunately, Miep Gies, one of the Frank family friends who cared for them during the hiding years, found Anne's diary and saved it. When Anne's father was released from the concentration camp, Miep Gies gave him Anne's diary, and—although at first reluctant—her father edited it for publication under the title *The Diary of Anne Frank*. Almost immediately, Anne's dream to become a world-renowned writer became reality. A testimony to the triumph of the human spirit during Hitler's oppressive regime, Anne's words show how one voice—one lone, distinct, vibrant voice—can record and influence our own perception of history.

51. After reading this passage, an individual might think

    A. that human beings are unforgiving.

    B. that individual differences are insurmountable.

    C. that human indifference is pervasive.

    D. that tenacious spirits endure.

52. More than likely, Otto Frank initially published an edited version of Anne's diary because

    A. he cherished her memory and did not want to reveal family secrets.

    B. he did not value writing and thought Anne had wasted her time.

    C. he loved writing, but felt Anne's thoughts were untrue and uninteresting.

    D. he didn't agree with the beliefs Anne expressed in her diary.

53. By escaping into hiding, the Frank family

    A. were able to continue working at Frank's factory.

    B. were able to live two more years in isolation.

    C. were able to enjoy the fruits of their labor.

    D. were able to prepare themselves for the inevitable.

54. Miep Gies can best be described as

    A. altruistic.

    B. solipsistic.

    C. narcissistic.

    D. recalcitrant.

55. The best phrase to describe the tone of this narrative is

    A. beleaguered cynicism.

    B. cautious optimism.

    C. divine inspiration.

    D. inspired revisionism.

Passage 4

An Unexpected Snowfall: The Teachable Moment

(1) During the middle of March, a funny thing happened in Georgia. It snowed. School was closed for a day while roads were cleared and transportation problems were solved. Snow in the middle of March in Georgia is unexpected. Thus, when students returned to school, they were doubly excited about their unexpected day off, and of course, for many, their first chance to see snow. Georgia teachers, especially in the elementary and middle school grades, responded to their students' enthusiasm by encouraging them to discuss their experiences with their classmates. Naturally, they were eager to do so.

(2) In one particular middle school classroom, a seventh-grade science teacher took it upon himself to structure an entire lesson around his students' first-time experience with snow. Taking his seventh graders outside, he found one flake of snow and placed it upon a thin piece of transparent plastic that had been chilled on top of the snow. The middle school youngsters then looked at the snowflake through a hand lens. They were amazed at what they saw.

(3) Expecting to see a simple nondescript blob, the seventh graders, instead, saw a delicate structure. When the snowflake melted, the science teacher told his students to place another snowflake on the thin sheet of chilled plastic and then describe this snowflake as well. To their amazement, they saw a different structure under their hand lens. The snowflake was similar in delicate design to their first viewing, but yet, totally different. Repeating this experiment several times, these middle school students soon realized that all snowflakes have six sides, but that no two snowflakes look alike.

(4) Following their observations, the seventh graders left the freezing cold of the Georgia outdoors and went back into the classroom. There, under the guidance of their middle school science teacher, they discussed their observation of snowflakes. They marveled at how different each snowflake they observed was and how this phenomenon is multiplied countless times wherever and whenever it snows.

(5) Their scientific discussion soon led to a conversation about how life in this central Georgia community had radically changed as a result of this sudden and unexpected snowfall. The youngsters shared stories of playing in the snow, of slipping and sliding everywhere, and of the difficulty many of their parents were having with stalled cars and hazardous roads. This tangent in the discussion took the class outside again. This time they did experiments to investigate why the city had spread sand on the streets and walkways after it snowed.

(6) In the end, what teacher and students learned is that scientific experiments, especially unexpected ones, make the best teaching moments. This middle school teacher took advantage of an unexpected event to teach his students scientific principles using the inquiry method. This act alone provided his students with both a positive experience and the

impetus to learn about science and its relationship to their daily lives. Indeed, this teacher took advantage of a teachable moment that will stay with his students for the rest of their lives.

56. According to the passage, one way in which this seventh-grade science teacher motivated his students is by

   A. following a prescribed lesson.
   B. engaging his students' interests.
   C. sharpening his students' study skills.
   D. increasing his students' workload.

57. As used in the fourth paragraph, the word *phenomenon* most nearly means

   A. occurrence.
   B. illusion.
   C. principle.
   D. opinion.

58. Which sentence best states the main idea of this passage?

   A. Teaching is often best when the learning is unexpected and unplanned.
   B. Teaching is often best when the learning is prescribed and deterministic.
   C. Teaching is a complex task that is more science than art.
   D. Teaching is best when the teacher takes students outside to learn.

59. Identify the relationship between the following two sentences in the fifth paragraph:

"Their scientific discussion soon led to a conversation about how life in this central Georgia community had radically changed as a result of this sudden and unexpected snowfall. The youngsters shared stories of playing in the snow, of slipping and sliding everywhere, and of the difficulty many of their parents were having with stalled cars and hazardous roads."

The second sentence

   A. contradicts the first.
   B. restates the first.
   C. supports the first.
   D. redirects the first.

60. For this passage, the author uses an overall organizational pattern that

   A. summarizes contrasting uses of teachable moments.
   B. contrasts teaching styles and instructional methodologies.
   C. outlines specific procedures for impromptu instruction.
   D. provides illustrations that support spontaneous instruction.

Diagnostic Test Answer Key

General Knowledge Diagnostic Test: English Language Skills

1. B	8. B	15. B
2. B	9. A	16. C
3. B	10. B	17. A
4. D	11. C	18. C
5. C	12. A	19. C
6. A	13. D	20. A
7. A	14. B	

General Knowledge Diagnostic Test: Math Skills

21. C	28. C	35. A
22. C	29. B	36. C
23. D	30. D	37. D
24. B	31. B	38. D
25. B	32. A	39. B
26. A	33. D	40. C
27. A	34. C	

General Knowledge Diagnostic Test: Reading

41. A	48. A	55. B
42. C	49. C	56. B
43. A	50. D	57. A
44. C	51. D	58. A
45. D	52. A	59. C
46. A	53. B	60. D
47. D	54. A	

General Knowledge Diagnostic Test: Essay Explanation

In this section of the examination, you were asked to prepare a written assignment on one of two topics.

Topic 1

A place that I would like to visit

Topic 2

An invention that changed the world

You were asked to write a 300–600 word response that would be well written, organized, and defined. You were also informed that your writing would be graded holistically, taking into consideration both mechanics and organization.

What follows are examples of a weak and strong response to both prompts.

Topic 1—A Place That I Would Like to Visit

Weak Response

There are so many places that I would like to visit that I cannot even name them all. I like to travel and I have had the chance but I have not been too many exotic places. I have been to Washington, D.C. on a school trip in the seventh grade and there I saw many exciting things. I saw museums, statues, and even famous people. I remember that as our bus was driving past the White House we saw a limousine leaving the gate and I am sure that I saw President Bush wave. It was the first President Bush, not the second, and I am certain that I saw both him and his wife, Barbara, wave. As seventh graders, we were terribly excited and this made our trip to Washington even more special. I look forward to going again one day and of course to making many more wonderful trips across the world.

Strong Response

Of all the world's destinations, none is more desirable to me than Washington, D.C.— our nation's capital, long the home of the world's most powerful leaders and influential figures. There, amidst our nation's legacy of recorded and memorialized history, stand living, breathing governmental bodies that decide the fate and destiny of countless millions of individuals every year. And there, in the halls of the White House, Congress, and the Supreme Court, work the individuals with whom we trust our most sacred treasure—the lives of our fellow human beings. No other place on earth has such a mixture of old and new, of tradition and experimentation, of history and modernity.

Washington, D.C is our nation's capital and the seat of our nation's power. There, the President of the United States resides and governs. In the White House, the President lives with the First Family, and presides over both ritual and government with equal importance and magnitude. As president, this chief executive officer determines the direction of the course of world events for not only the term that he or she serves, but, often, for many years to come. This is why visiting Washington, D.C. is such a driving and powerful desire for me. I long to visit a place where great decisions are made daily. I long to see where our governmental leaders, particularly the president, live and work. I long to experience the wonderment of how they manage to get so much done in a place that seems, at first glance, so overwhelming.

Our nation's capital, as mentioned, is a place that is both historical and contemporary. It is not only the seat of great governmental power, but also the home to some of the world's most fascinating and intriguing museums and memorials, such as the Smithsonian, the Air and Space, and the Holocaust museums. The Smithsonian Museum is actually a number of buildings that house everything our nation considers to be precious and historical—from historical artifacts to television memorabilia. At the Air and Space Museum, visitors can get a firsthand glimpse at our nation's aviation history: everything from the Wright Brothers' first plane, the Kitty Hawk, to our nation's early space capsules. And at the Holocaust Museum, individuals from all walks of life can learn firsthand just what it was like to be a Jewish person caught in the throes of the Nazis' horrifying regime.

Finally, our nation's capital is the home to sophisticated and trend-setting modern elements as well. Those privileged to live in and near this bustling city can partake of its many cultural events, fine eateries, and exciting happenings. Cultural events include original plays at the Arena Theatre, musical and dramatic events at the Kennedy Center, and numerous outdoor concerts. Dining options range from some of the country's most sophisticated restaurants (where famous politicians and entertainers can regularly be seen) to local eateries specializing in all sorts of ethnic cuisines. And special happenings include monthly events held on the Washington Mall (especially during the warmer months) where vendors and entertainers delight visitors and natives with their special talents and wares.

In conclusion, Washington, D.C. is the one place that I would love to return to year after year. It is one place on the face of the earth where richness never wears out its welcome. This is a living breathing entity of the old and the new, the powerful and the rich, the traditional and the experimental that makes for a continually fascinating and intriguing arena in which to live and thrive. I love visiting there. And who knows? Maybe, someday, I will call it home.

Topic 2—An Invention That Changed the World

Weak Response

Some discoveries change the face of the world because they bring to everyone a new invention that makes our lives better and more comfortable. Inventions like the phone, the computer, and the laptop have changed the way we live and work and made everyday living so dramatically different. One discovery, though, that comes to mind that has changed the world as we know it is the mass production of the powerful antibiotic, penicillin. This discovery might not seem as dramatic as the computer or the laptop, but, to be sure, it has changed the face of the globe. Penicillin has helped eliminate world disease in all type and fashion. No longer are people getting sick for no apparent reason other than they are catching all sorts of diseases because of poor sanitation. Penicillin made life easier for countless thousands of people and for that, we will be forever grateful.

Strong Response

Can you imagine life without penicillin? Can you imagine a life without a powerful drug used to treat infections caused by bacteria? For millions of Americans prior to the 1940s, life without penicillin was an everyday reality. Simply put, there was no available drug to treat serious diseases in human beings. Not until the discovery and widespread use of penicillin in the mid-1940s did a miracle drug play a significant role in changing the face of the world. For the first time, human beings had a chance to escape the ravages of serious and often fatal illnesses.

In 1928 a British scientist, Sir Alexander Fleming, discovered penicillin when he noticed mold growing in a lab dish containing common bacteria. Fleming noticed that the bacteria around the mold had died. Fleming made note of this discovery and a few years later, other British scientists capitalized on Fleming's work and writings and began their own experimentation. Soon, they had developed a small strain of penicillin and began using it on patients to treat deadly infections. What they soon discovered is that the patients would do well until they needed more penicillin and none was to be found. There and then, British scientists and physicians realized the power of this new miracle-inducing drug.

During the 1950s, researchers found ways to produce large quantities of penicillin. Soon, doctors had at their disposal a number of strains of penicillin that could be used to play a large role in treating such previously deadly diseases as pneumonia, rheumatic fever, scarlet fever, and other serious illnesses. The development of penicillin had a tremendous impact on medicine and encouraged research that led to the discovery of many other antibiotics. For their work, Fleming and his associates were awarded the Nobel Peace Prize in Medicine.

As with any medicine, though, there are often unanticipated side effects. Some people who take penicillin suffer allergic reactions. These reactions are usually minor, causing fever or rashes. Yet, for a few, life-threatening reactions involving shock and breathing difficulties may occur. And usually, patients allergic to one form of penicillin will likely react to all forms. Fortunately, such patients can more than likely be treated with antibiotics that are similar to penicillin and have been used since the 1960s.

Penicillin is known as the "wonder drug" of modern medicine. Until the discovery and widespread use of penicillin and similar antibiotics, people often died of bacterial illnesses. The number of deaths, though, caused by meningitis, pneumonia, tuberculosis, and scarlet fever changed dramatically after antibiotics became available. In addition, antibiotics are also used to treat infectious diseases in animals. Thus, the world is a much healthier and happier place to live since the discovery and use of penicillin. Indeed, it is difficult to imagine a life without this wondrous drug of modern medicine.

General Knowledge Diagnostic Test: English Language Skills Answers and Explanations

1. **B.** The question deals with conceptual and organizational skills, which fall under English Language Skills. Thus, the primary focus of the question is Competency 1: Identify logical order in a written passage. Sentences arranged in the following order—(2), (4), (3)—complete the paragraph's thought pattern. This is the most logical order of progression, allowing the reader to follow the author's train of thought from a general conclusion to logical supporting detail. Choices **A, C,** and **D** do not present the material in a logical fashion.

2. **B.** Sentence (6) is the sentence that is LEAST relevant to this paragraph. The sentence speaks about the city of Los Angeles, whereas the remainder of the paragraph speaks about America's West. There is no logical explanation for inserting information about the city of Los Angeles when the remainder of the paragraph speaks about the vastness of the America's western landscape and its land use for primarily farming and ranching.

3. **B.** The question deals with word choice skills, which fall under English Language Skills. Thus, the primary focus of the question is Competency 2: Choose the appropriate word or expression in context. In this sentence, the misused word is "*principle*." The word should read "*principal*." The word *principle* means main idea. The word *principal* means the administrative leader of a school. The other words in the sentence, *accepted* and *board,* are used correctly.

4. **D.** The question deals with sentence structure skills, which fall under English Language Skills. Thus, the primary focus for the question is Competency 4: Identify standard capitalization. No change is necessary. The word *doctor* is capitalized when referring to a specific doctor, as in *Doctor Leonard Pitts*. The word *English* is capitalized because it is referred to as a language. The word *spring* is not capitalized because the names of seasons—*spring, summer, winter,* and *fall*—are always written in lowercase, unless the reader is using it in a poetic form.

5. **C.** The question deals with sentence structure skills, which fall under English Language Skills. Thus, the primary focus for the question is Competency 4: Identify standard capitalization. *Civil War* should be capitalized because it is the name of a specific event, place, or thing. In the remainder of the sentence, the word *author* is used correctly because there is no need to capitalize the word author before Margaret Mitchell's name. Finally, the word *South* is correct, because it is referring to a specific geographical region in an historical context.

6. **A.** The question deals with sentence structure skills, which fall under English Language Skills. Thus, the primary focus for the question is Competency 4: Identify standard punctuation. The correct choice should read, "*by the textbook method; now it is. . . .*" A semicolon is needed between the two main clauses (Choice **A**). The remaining choices are grammatically incorrect and inappropriate in sentence construction.

7. **A.** The question deals with word choice skills, which fall under English Language Skills. Thus, the primary focus for the question is Competency 2: Recognize commonly confused or misused words or phrases. The word *alternate* should be substituted for the word *alternative*. *Alternate* means to take turns, whereas *alternative* means or implies a choice between two things. In the remainder of the sentence, the word *is* is appropriately used, referred to the singular noun *plan*. The word *affecting* is used appropriately as well. *Affect* is a verb meaning to have an "influence upon" and *effect* is a noun meaning "result."

8. **B.** The question deals with grammar, spelling, capitalization and punctuation skills, which fall under English Language Skills. Thus, the primary focus for the question is Competency 4: Identify standard punctuation. A comma is needed following the introductory clause. The word *When* at **A** is correct and makes sense in the sentence. The possessive pronoun *their* at **C** is correct.

9. **A.** The question deals with grammar, spelling, capitalization and punctuation skills, which fall under English Language Skills. Thus, the primary focus for the question is Competency 4: Identify the correct use of adjectives and adverbs. In this sentence, the word following the verb *felt* at **A** modifies the subject (a noun). The word *badly* is an adverb. It should not be used to modify a noun. The adjective *bad* should be used instead. The word *English* at **B** is a proper noun, so it should be capitalized. The title *dean* at **C** should not be capitalized. Titles are capitalized when they precede proper names, but as a rule are not capitalized when used alone.

10. **B.** The question deals with grammar, spelling, capitalization and punctuation skills, which fall under English Language Skills. Thus, the primary focus for the question is Competency 4: Identify agreement between pronoun and antecedent. The word *between* at **B** is a preposition. The object of a preposition should be in the objective case. Change *I* to *me* to make the sentence grammatically correct. No comma is needed at **A.** The word *definitely* at **C** is spelled correctly.

11. **C.** The question deals with grammar, spelling, capitalization and punctuation skills, which fall under English Language Skills. Thus, the primary focus for the question is Competency 4: Identify agreement between subject and verb. The word *I* at **C** is the subject of the verb *am* (which is understood) and, thus, should be in the subjective case. Change *me* to *I* to make the sentence grammatically correct. The pronoun *who* at **A** is correct because it is the subject of the subordinate clause it introduces. The adjective *much* at **B** is correct and makes sense in the sentence.

12. **A.** The question deals with grammar, spelling, capitalization and punctuation skills, which fall under English Language Skills. Thus, the primary focus for the question is Competency 4: Identify agreement between pronoun and antecedent. The word *Each* is the singular antecedent of the pronoun at **A.** Use *her* instead of the plural pronoun *their* to refer to the singular antecedent *Each.* The word *what* at **B** is correct and makes sense in the sentence. The preposition *between* at **C** is correctly used to indicate a relationship involving two people. The preposition *among* is used when the relationship involves more than two people or things.

13. **D.** The question deals with word choice skills, which fall under English Language Skills. Thus, the primary focus for the question is Competency 2: Choose the appropriate word or expression in context. This sentence is correct as written. The preposition *Through* at **A** is spelled correctly and makes sense in the sentence. The comma at **B** following the introductory prepositional phrase is correct. The plural verb *show* at **C** is correct because the word *data* is a plural noun.

14. **B.** The question deals with grammar, spelling, capitalization and punctuation skills, which fall under English Language Skills. Thus, the primary focus for the question is Competency 4: Identify standard verb forms. The past participle for the verb *to begin* is *begun.* Note that "should of" in **A** and **C** is an error for "should have."

15. **B.** The question deals with grammar, spelling, capitalization and punctuation skills, which fall under English Language Skills. Thus, the primary focus for the question is Competency 4: Identify standard verb forms. The past perfect form *had made* is used to indicate an action took place before another action in the past occurred. In the sentence given there is no reference to a prior action. The simple past tense *made* is all that is needed here.

16. **C.** The question deals with grammar, spelling, capitalization and punctuation skills, which fall under English Language Skills. Thus, the primary focus for the question is Competency 4: Identify agreement between pronoun and antecedent. Does *them* at **C** refer to *children* or *toys*? Change *them* to *the toys* to avoid ambiguity. The verb *were* at **A** is in agreement with the plural noun *toys* (the antecedent of the pronoun *that*). The adjective *good* at **B** is correct.

17. **A.** The question deals with word choice skills, which fall under English Language Skills. Thus, the primary focus for the question is Competency 2: Choose the appropriate word or expression in context. The word at **A** should be an adjective because it modifies the noun *reason.* The word *principle* is a noun. Change *principle* to *principal* to make the sentence grammatically correct. The word *that* at **B** is correct. It would be redundant to use *because* at **B** because the word *because* means *for the reason that.* The singular verb *has been* at **C** is in agreement with its singular subject *he.*

18. **C.** The question deals with word choice skills, which fall under English Language Skills. Thus, the primary focus for the question is Competency 2: Recognize diction and tone appropriate for a given audience. The most appropriate expression is the one that is formal, polite, and respectful. The other choices—**A, B,** and **D**—are inappropriate, impolite, and disrespectful.

19. **C.** The question deals with grammar, spelling, capitalization and punctuation skills, which fall under English Language Skills. Thus, the primary focus for the question is Competency 4: Identify standard punctuation. All punctuation in sentence **C** is correct. In sentences **A** and **B,** the word *customer's* is punctuated incorrectly. To form the possessive of a plural noun ending in *s*, put an apostrophe after the *s*. Sentence **B** also needs a comma following the introductory phrase that begins the sentence. In sentence **D,** the apostrophe in *complaints'* should be deleted.

20. A. The question deals with sentence structure skills, which fall under English Language Skills. Thus, the primary focus for the question is Competency 3: Recognize correct placement of modifiers. The modifiers in sentence **A** are placed correctly. The participial phrase *Driving along the highway* modifies *Paul,* the noun subject of the main clause of the sentence, and should be close to it. In choices **B** and **D,** *Driving along the highway* is separated from the noun *Paul,* resulting in ambiguity. Choice **C** is an example of a dangling participle because the participial phrase *Coming from the trunk* seems to modify the noun *Paul,* which does not make sense.

General Knowledge Diagnostic Test: Mathematics Answers and Explanations

21. C. Follow "Please Excuse My Dear Aunt Sally."

$-9(5) - 18 \div 3^2 =$

$-9(5) - 18 \div 9$ There are no parentheses, so do exponentiation first.

$-45 - 2$ Multiply and divide from left to right, next.

$-45 - 2 = -45 + -2 = -47$ Then subtract, yielding the answer in Choice **C.**

Choice **A** results if you work the problem in order from left to right without following the order of operations. Choice **B** results if you fail to follow the order of operations and make computational errors as well. Choice **D** results if you make a sign error in the computation of $-45 + -2$. This occurs if you use an incorrect sign rule for the sum of two negative numbers. The sum of two negative numbers is negative, not positive.

22. C. Three steps are needed to solve the problem:

Step 1. Find the cost for a 15 semester-credit-hour (s.c.h.) course load in 1965:

$\dfrac{\$5}{\text{s.c.h.}} \times 15$ s.c.h. = \$75 in 1965. (Hint: Quantities following the word "per" should be written in the denominator of a fraction.)

Step 2. Find the cost for a 15 semester-credit-hour (s.c.h.) course load in 2005:

$\dfrac{\$80}{\text{s.c.h.}} \times 15$ s.c.h. = \$1200 in 2005.

Step 3. Find the difference in cost between the two years:

$1200 - \$75 = \$1125$, Choice **C.**

Choice **A** is the difference in tuition for one semester credit hour, not 15 semester credit hours. Choice **B** is the tuition for 15 semester credit hours in 2005, not the difference between the two years. Choice **D** is the sum of the two tuitions, not the difference.

23. D. The simplest way to work this problem is to compare the expressions by performing all the indicated operations:

Choice **A:** $3^3 \times 8^2 = 3 \times 3 \times 3 \times 8 \times 8 = 1{,}728$

Choice **B:** $2^6 \times 9 \times 3 = 2 \times 2 \times 2 \times 2 \times 2 \times 2 \times 9 \times 3 = 1{,}728$

Choice **C:** $32 \times 54 = 1{,}728$

Choice **D:** $9 \times 16 = 144$

Choice **D** is *not* equivalent to the other choices, so it is the correct response.

24. B. Work the problem in two parts as follows:

$\dfrac{54 \times 10^{12}}{6 \times 10^{4}} = \dfrac{54}{6} \times \dfrac{10^{12}}{10^{4}} = 9 \times 10^{12-4} = 9 \times 10^{8}$, Choice **B.**

In the first fraction, divide 54 by 6 to obtain 9. In the second fraction, you have two exponential expressions that have the same base. To perform the division, keep the same base and subtract the denominator exponent, 4, from the numerator exponent, 12, as shown. Choice **A** occurs if you subtract the exponents in the wrong order. Choice **C** occurs if you mistakenly divide the exponents instead of subtracting. Choice **D** occurs if you mistakenly divide the exponents instead of subtracting and you make a sign error.

25. **B.** To solve the problem, you must answer the question: 12 is x (%) of 150?

Method 1: Write an equation and solve it:

$12 = x$ times 150 Hint: The word "of" is "times" when it occurs between two numbers.

$12 = x150$

For convenience, you should rewrite the expression on the right of the equation as $150x$:

$12 = 150x$

You are solving for x, so divide both sides of the equation by 150, the coefficient of x:

$$\frac{12}{150} = \frac{150x}{150}$$

$0.08 = x$

Change 0.08 to a percent by moving the decimal point 2 places to the right and adding a percent sign:

$x = 8\%$, Choice **B.**

Method 2: Set up a percent proportion and solve it:

$$\frac{x}{100} = \frac{12}{150}$$

Multiply 12 by 100 and then divide by 150:

$x = \frac{12 \times 100}{150} = 8$, $\frac{8}{100} = 8\%$, Choice **B.**

Choices **A** and **D** result if you make a decimal point mistake. Choice **C** occurs if you analyze the problem incorrectly.

26. **A.** Substitute into the expression, being sure to enclose the substituted value in parentheses:

$x - y = (-2) - (-10) = -2 + 10 = 8$, Choice **A.**

Choice **B** occurs if you make a sign error. Choices **C** and **D** result if you deal with the subtraction incorrectly.

27. **A.** Check each choice to determine the correct response:

Checking Choice **A:** Find a common denominator of 63 and rewrite the fractions as equivalent fractions with denominators of 63:

$\frac{4}{7} = \frac{36}{63}$ and $\frac{5}{9} = \frac{35}{63}$, so $\frac{4}{7}$ is greater than $\frac{5}{9}$ because $\frac{36}{63}$ is greater than $\frac{35}{63}$. Therefore, Choice **A** is true.

In a test situation, you could stop without checking the other choices since you have obtained the correct answer. If you are running short of time, you should go on to the next question. If not, you may want to take the time to check the remaining choices to make doubly sure that your answer choice is correct.

Checking the remaining choices, you would find:

Choice **B** is false because 0.5 = 0.50 which is greater than 0.35.

Choice **C** is false because 5% of 60 = 0.05 × 60 = 3, which is not less than 10% of 20 = 2.

Choice **D** is false, because –18 lies to the left of –5 on the number line, which means –18 < –5.

28. C. To approximate the value of $\sqrt{41}$, find two consecutive integers such that the square of the first integer is less than 41 and the square of the second integer is greater than 41. Since Since 6^2 is $36 < 41$ and 7^2 is $49 > 41$, the approximate value of $\sqrt{41}$ is between 6 and 7, Choice **C**. Choice **A** results if you mistakenly use the length of the legs of the right triangle to approximate $\sqrt{41}$. Choice **B** results if you underestimate $\sqrt{41}$. Choice **D** results if you mistakenly use the squares of the consecutive integers 6 and 7 to estimate $\sqrt{41}$.

29. B. A number written in scientific notation is written as a product of two numbers: a number that is greater than or equal to 1, but less than 10, and a power of 10. The number 93,000,000 is greater than 10, so the decimal point must be moved to the left to make the first factor greater than or equal to 1 but less than 10. If the decimal point is moved 7 places to the left, the first factor will be 9.3.

$$93,000,000 = 9.3000000 \times 10^7 = 9.3 \times 10^7$$

Since the decimal point was moved to the left 7 places, the exponent for the power of 10 is 7. The exponent needs to be positive 7 so that when you convert back to the original number, the value is the same. The number 93,000,000 is written as 9.3×10^7 in scientific notation, Choice **B.** You can check your answer by quickly performing the indicated multiplication.

$$9.3 \times 10^7 = 9.3 \times 10,000,000 = 93,000,000. \ \checkmark$$

Choice **A** results if you incorrectly count the number of decimal places moved. Choices **C** and **D** result if you incorrectly use a negative exponent on the power of 10. Negative exponents are used in scientific notation when you are writing very small numbers that are between 0 and 1. For example, 0.00000005 is 5×10^{-8} in scientific notation.

30. D. Write an equation that can be used to find the total annual cost of belonging to the fitness club and bringing pool guests. Let n equal the number of times Donna brought a guest to the club pool. If it cost $5 every time a member brings a guest to the pool, then $5n$ represents the guest pool charges for the year. The annual membership charge is $300. The total annual cost ($385) is the annual fee ($300) plus the guest pool charges ($5n$). Write this statement as an equation and solve it, omitting the units for convenience:

$$385 = 300 + 5n$$

$$385 - 300 = 300 + 5n - 300 \quad \text{Subtract 300 from each side.}$$

$$85 = 5n$$

$$\frac{85}{5} = \frac{5n}{5} \quad \text{Divide each side by 5.}$$

$$17 = n, \text{ Choice } \mathbf{D.}$$

Donna brought a guest to the club pool 17 times last year.

Choice **A** results if you incorrectly figure out the problem by dividing 385 by 5. Choice **B** results if you incorrectly figure out the problem by dividing 300 by 5. Choice **C** results if you make a mistake when dividing 85 by 5.

31. B. First sketch a diagram to illustrate the problem:

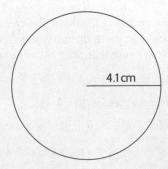

4.1 cm

The formula for the area of a circle is $A = \pi r^2$. (You can look up the formula on the mathematics reference sheet provided.) To decide which answer choice is reasonable, estimate the area of the piece of glass. Round the radius to 4 centimeters and plug this value into the formula.

$A = \pi r^2$

$A = 3.14(4 \text{ cm})^2$

$A = 3.14(16 \text{ cm}^2)$

$A = 50.24 \text{ cm}^2$

The area of the circle is approximately 50.24 cm², so 50 cm² (Choice **B**) is a reasonable estimate. Choices **A** and **D** result if you use the wrong formula for the area of a circle. Choice **C** results if you mistakenly multiply 3.14 times 4 before squaring when calculating the area.

32. **A.** First sketch a diagram to illustrate the problem. Of course, you can't draw it exactly to scale, but the sketch will help you "see" the situation:

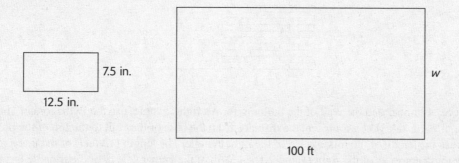

Let w = the width of the front of the actual office building. The fronts of the model and building can be represented with two rectangles. The rectangles are similar figures, so the measurements of their corresponding sides are proportional. That is,

$$\frac{\text{length of the model}}{\text{actual length of the building}} = \frac{\text{width of the model}}{\text{actual width of the building}}$$

Plug in the values from your diagram. Be sure to check to make sure the units match up correctly.

$\dfrac{12.5 \text{ in.}}{100 \text{ ft}} = \dfrac{7.5 \text{ in.}}{w\,(\text{ft})}$ Check: Both ratios have inches in the numerators and feet in the denominators.

For convenience, omit the units while you solve the proportion:

$\dfrac{12.5}{100} = \dfrac{7.5}{w}$

Multiply 100 by 7.5, then divide by 12:

$\dfrac{100 \times 7.5}{12.5} = 60 \text{ feet}$

The width of the front of the actual office building will be 60 feet, Choice **A**.

You should eliminate choices **C** and **D** right away because these answers are not reasonable. The width of the model is shorter than its length, so the width of the actual building should be shorter than its length. Choice **B** results if you make a computation error when solving the proportion.

33. **D.** To determine which ordered pair satisfies the system, you will need to find the ordered pair that makes *both* equations true. Check each ordered pair by substituting the x and y values into the two equations, being careful to enclose the substituted value in parentheses.

Checking **A:** $3x + y = 3(-1) + (-5) = -3 + -5 = -8 \neq 2$. Since $(-1,-5)$ doesn't work in the first equation, you don't have to try it in the second equation. Eliminate **A**.

Checking **B:** $3x + y = 3(1) + (-5) = 3 + -5 = -2 \neq 2$. Since $(1,-5)$ doesn't work in the first equation, you don't have to try it in the second equation. Eliminate **B**.

Checking **C:** $3x + y = 3(1) + (5) = 3 + 5 = 8 - 2$. Since $(1,5)$ doesn't work in the first equation, you don't have to try it in the second equation. Eliminate **C.**

By elimination, you know that Choice **D** is the correct response. You can check it to convince yourself.

Checking **D:** $3x + y = 3(-1) + (5) = -3 + 5 = 2$ ✓; $x + 2y = (-1) + 2(5) = -1 + 10 = 9$ ✓.

34. C. First sketch a diagram to illustrate the problem:

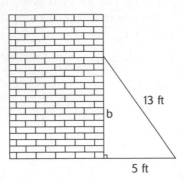

Since the piece of lumber and the wall of the building form a right triangle, use the Pythagorean Theorem to find the length of the missing side. Let b represent the distance from the base of the wall to the top of the piece of lumber. This distance is the length of the missing leg of the right triangle. The length (13 feet) of the piece of lumber is the length of the hypotenuse, c, of the right triangle. The length of the known leg, a, of the triangle is 5 feet. Substitute these values into the Pythagorean Theorem:

$a^2 + b^2 = c^2$

$5^2 + b^2 = 13^2$

$25 + b^2 = 169$

$25 + b^2 - 25 = 169 - 25$ Subtract 25 from both sides.

$b^2 = 144$

$\sqrt{b^2} = \sqrt{144}$ Take the square root of both sides.

$b = 12$ feet, Choice **C.**

The piece of lumber reaches 12 feet up the wall. Choice **A** results if you mistakenly decide to solve the problem by adding the lengths of the hypotenuse and known leg to find the length of the missing leg. Choice **B** results if you make a computation error. Choice **D** results if you mistakenly decide to solve the problem by finding the difference between the lengths of the hypotenuse and the known leg to find the length of the missing leg.

35. A. The outcome of the first spin has no effect on the outcome of the second spin. Therefore, this is a compound event made up of two independent events. To find the probability of spinning yellow on the first spin and blue on the second spin, multiply the probabilities of these two events: P(yellow) · P(blue).

First, calculate the probability of spinning yellow on the first spin. There are 3 yellow sections on the spinner, out of a total of 10 sections: $P(\text{yellow}) = \frac{3}{10}$.

There are 2 blue sections on the spinner, out of a total of 10 sections: $P(\text{blue}) = \frac{2}{10} = \frac{1}{5}$.

To find the probability of spinning yellow on the first spin and blue on the second spin, multiply the probabilities:

$P(\text{yellow}) \cdot P(\text{blue}) = \frac{3}{10} \cdot \frac{1}{5} = \frac{3}{50}$, Choice **A.**

Choice **B** results if you multiply the two probabilities incorrectly. Choice **C** is the probability of spinning a yellow only. Choice **D** is the probability of spinning a blue only.

36. **C.** Check each statement.

Checking **A:** False. Rectangles and squares are special parallelograms in which all angles are 90°. This is *not* true of all parallelograms.

Checking **B:** False. Squares and rhombuses are special parallelograms in which all sides are congruent. This is *not* true of all parallelograms.

Checking **C:** True. Parallelograms are quadrilaterals in which opposite sides are parallel. This is true of all parallelograms.

Checking **D:** False. Squares and rhombuses are special parallelograms in which the diagonals are perpendicular to each other. This is *not* true of all parallelograms.

37. **D.** A quick way to work this problem is to check the answer choices—a good test-taking strategy for multiple-choice math tests.

Checking **A:** $\dfrac{\text{sum of 4 test grades}}{4} = \dfrac{87 + 91 + 83 + 90}{4} = \dfrac{351}{4} = 87.75 < 90$.

Checking **B:** $\dfrac{\text{sum of 4 test grades}}{4} = \dfrac{87 + 91 + 83 + 95}{4} = \dfrac{356}{4} = 89 < 90$.

Checking **C:** $\dfrac{\text{sum of the test grades}}{4} = \dfrac{87 + 91 + 83 + 96}{4} = \dfrac{357}{4} = 89.25 < 90$.

Checking **D:** $\dfrac{\text{sum of 4 test grades}}{4} = \dfrac{87 + 91 + 83 + 99}{4} = \dfrac{360}{4} = 90$, correct.

38. **D.** From the pie chart, you can see that 37.5 percent of the monthly salary is budgeted for rent. To answer the question, you must find 37.5 percent of $2,800.

Method 1: Change 37.5% to a decimal fraction and multiply:

37.5% of $2,800 = 0.375 × $2,800 = $1,050, Choice **D.**

Method 2: Set up a percent proportion and solve it:

$\dfrac{37.5}{100} = \dfrac{x}{2,800}$

Multiply 37.5 times 2,800, then divide by 100:

$\dfrac{37.5 \times 2,800}{100} = \$1,050$, Choice **D.**

Choice **A** results if you make a calculation error. Choice **B** results if you solve the problem incorrectly by finding 12.5 percent of $2,800. Choice **C** results if you solve the problem incorrectly by finding 25 percent of $2,800.

39. **B.** In an ordered set of numbers, the median is the middle number if there is a middle number; otherwise, the median is the arithmetic average of the two middle numbers. First, put the running times in order from smallest to largest:

21 min., 21 min., 21 min., 22 min., 24 min., 25 min., 27 min.

Since 22 minutes is the middle number, it is the median running time (Choice **B**). Choice **A** is the mode running time. Choice **C** is the mean running time. Choice **D** results if you forget to put the running times in order first.

40. **C.** Use the Fundamental Counting Principle to work this problem. First, decide how many tasks are involved. Richard has two tasks to perform. His first task is to choose a sandwich. After he completes that task, his second task is to select a drink. The number of ways the second task can happen does not depend on the outcome of the first task. To find the possible combinations for the two tasks, multiply the number of ways the first task can occur by the number of ways the second task can occur: (number of ways Richard can select a sandwich) · (number of ways Richard can select a drink) = 3 · 2 = 6 ways, Choice **C.** Richard can select 6 different combinations of sandwiches and drinks for lunch. Choices **A** and **D** result if you analyze the problem incorrectly. Choice **B** results if you add the number of ways each task can occur, instead of multiplying.

General Knowledge Diagnostic Test: Reading Skills Answers and Explanations

41. A. The main idea of this passage is that Los Angeles *is a thriving metropolitan community*, rich in business, cultural, and recreational venues to explore and enjoy. Choices **B** and **C** are certainly correct but are not the main idea of this passage. Choice **D** is a vague and contradictory statement that has no relation to the paragraph's central narrative or main idea.

42. C. In the second paragraph, the author is telling the reader about Los Angeles' many cultural and recreational venues. Choices **A** and **B** are only briefly discussed in the second paragraph, and Choice **D** is not mentioned at all.

43. A. The implication of this passage is that the city of Los Angeles and its surrounding community is experiencing the consequences of urban sprawl, which occurs when a multitude of individuals in a specific region begin to move to outlying areas. Choice **B** is contradictory to what the passage states; the amount of affordable homes is on the decrease. There is no mention of Choice **C** or Choice **D** in this passage.

44. C. The author's tone is *implicitly realistic*, meaning the author matter-of-factly states the obvious and then underscores both the positives and negatives. Choices **A, B,** and **C** are not relevant to this passage. The author writes enthusiastically about the prospects of living in and around Los Angeles and is never negative or cynical in her writing.

45. D. In the first paragraph, the word *mecca* means a *desired destination*. Choices **A, B,** and **C** are inappropriate definitions.

46. A. The *simple token system* is a method that fits within the larger context of *behaviorism*. Behaviorists believe that individuals learn through a system of rewards and punishments. Choice **B** is incorrect because *humanism* is the learning philosophy in which one treats the whole individual instead of isolated events in their behavior. Choice **C** is incorrect because *constructivism* is the theory that individuals learn to construct their own reality from a given set of constructs and circumstances. And Choice **D** is incorrect because *essentialism* is the teaching philosophy that says all learning should be based on what is essential or basic for all students to know.

47. D. In the first paragraph, the author clearly implies that while David's problems are certainly exasperating, they are indeed typical. Choice **A** is incorrect because at no time does the author state that David's problems are insolvable. Choice **B** is incorrect because the author implies that David's parents are concerned and loving. And Choice **C** is incorrect because David's elementary counselor's suggestions were shown to be practical and effective in solving David's problem and modifying his behavior.

48. A. Implicit in this passage is the belief that learning (*all* learning, whether it is the ABCs, or correct behavor) is *developmental*. Although the author writes about a token system of reinforcement for correcting inappropriate behavior, the author's implied message is that all learning needs to be appropriate to the individual and compassionately enforced. Choices **B, C,** and **D** are incorrect because at no time does the author underline that learning is predetermined, self-centered, or mechanistic.

49. C. In the second paragraph, the phrase *necessary modifications* means *making changes that are warranted*. Choice **B** is incorrect because the author makes no mention of anyone's reviewing young David's personal motivations, ambitions, or goals. Choice **A** is incorrect because again, the author makes no mention of anyone imploring David or his parents to *self-examine internal strife and external conflicts* surrounding David's inappropriate behavior. Finally, Choice **D** is incorrect because *necessary modifications* mean more than monitoring prescribed actions and outside forces. It means taking action to change the observed behavior.

50. D. The author of this narrative would most likely concur that when dealing with behavior problems, *narrowing issues is reasonable*. Choice **A** is incorrect because the narrative speaks of gradual, not radical change. Choice **B** is incorrect because the narrative does not speak about the nature of self-defeating behaviors. Choice **C** is incorrect because the narrative does not speak of developmental needs as predetermined needs.

51. D. After reading this passage, the phrase *an individual might think that tenacious spirits endure* is the correct choice. The story of the Frank family, with Anne's diary as the centerpiece, is truly the story of individual will and the human spirit triumphing over unspeakable atrocities and horror. Choices **A, B,** and **C** are worthy of consideration but do not accurately reflect the tenor and tone of this passage.

52. A. As implied in this passage, Otto Frank more than likely initially published an edited version of Anne's diary because he cherished her memory and did not want to reveal family secrets. Choices **B, C,** and **D** are incorrect because at no time does the narrative imply that Otto Frank did not value Anne, her writing, or her beliefs. After all, he knew Anne was writing in her diary and that she wanted to share her thoughts with the world at the conclusion of the war.

53. B. By escaping into hiding, the Frank family *members were able to live two more years in isolation*. The Franks knew very well that the days of Jewish people under Hitler's regime were numbered and that any moments they had together were to be treasured. They went into hiding—with a few friends—to find a respite from the drumbeat of war and persecution just outside their door. Choice **A** is incorrect because the Franks were unable to work while they hid in the attic. Choice **C** is incorrect because they had to rely on the kindness of their protectors for daily sustenance. And Choice **D** is incorrect because they had no possible way of preparing themselves for the unspeakable horror that awaited them upon their capture.

54. A. As implied in this passage, Miep Gies can best be described as *altruistic*. She was selfless in her devotion to others as she protected the Frank family at great personal cost. Choice **B** is incorrect because *solipsistic* means to be concerned with only one's own affairs. Choice **C** is incorrect because *narcissistic* means to be deeply in love with oneself. And Choice **D** is incorrect because *recalcitrant* means to be reluctant.

55. B. The best phrase to describe the tone of this narrative is *cautious optimism*. The narrative readily acknowledges the cruelties and horrors of war and unspeakable tragedies. Yet, the narrative also shows how a single diary can be a source of inspiration to countless individuals who will long remember the atrocities of Hitler's bloody regime. Choices **A, C,** and **D** are inappropriate for the tone and tenor of this piece.

56. B. According to the passage, the one way in which this seventh-grade science teacher motivated his students is by *engaging his students' interests*. Using a teachable moment, the teacher capitalized on the fact that his seventh graders had never seen snow before and then proceeded to create a lesson from the snow on the ground outside their classroom door. Choices **A, B,** and **C** are incorrect because these activities were not mentioned in the narrative as techniques to engage student learning.

57. A. As used in the fourth paragraph, the word *phenomenon* most nearly means an *occurrence*. Choices **B, C,** and **D** are inappropriate definitions for the word *phenomenon*.

58. A. *Teaching is often best when learning is unexpected and unplanned* is the sentence that best states the main idea of this passage. The value of the teachable moment is the central theme of this descriptive narrative about teaching seventh-grade science on a March day in central Georgia. Choices **B** and **C** are incorrect because they represent the opposite conclusion of this paragraph's main idea that teaching is at its best when it is spontaneous. Finally, Choice **D,** that teaching is best when students go outside to learn, represents a single idea of this paragraph and not the main idea.

59. C. In the fifth paragraph, the *second sentence supports the first sentence*. The second sentence adds more detail to the first sentence, thus clarifying the actions of the class lesson in greater detail. Choices **A, B,** and **C** are simply incorrect.

60. D. For this passage, the author uses an overall organizational pattern that *provides illustrations that support spontaneous instruction*. The author clearly provides vivid examples of classroom instruction to support the central thesis that teaching is best when it is spontaneous. Choices **A, B,** and **C** are inappropriate choices because they do not nearly approximate the organizational pattern of this particular narrative. In this passage, there is no comparison of teaching styles or delineation of specific procedures to follow to implement impromptu instruction. There is simply a strong narrative outlining two examples of teachable moments used effectively.

PART II

REVIEW OF EXAM AREAS

Review for the GK Essay Subtest

The Essay subtest of the FTCE GK Test consists of a choice between two topics, one of which you must select and write an essay about in 50 minutes. The allotted time is for preparing, writing, and editing your essay. Your work will be scored holistically by two judges. "Holistically" means that your essay will receive only one score for both content and mechanics. The personal views you express in your essay are not an issue; you are judged only on the style in which you present your views. Specifically, your essay is evaluated on the logic of your arguments and the degree to which you support your position in a reasonable and coherent manner. The topic may ask you to take a position or develop an argument, but you will be graded on your writing skills, not on your personal beliefs or your knowledge of any particular subject or area. You cannot bring written notes or scratch paper into the testing center. You have to write in your test booklet when working out problems.

The Essay Review in This Study Guide

This chapter contains a review of how to write an essay, both in general and for this specific examination. The review sections present writing-skill concepts with examples and explanations, as well as "Test Yourself" exercises. These exercises give you an opportunity to practice what you just learned. When doing the "Test Yourself" exercises, you should write in response to the questions. Then, if possible, have someone proof your writing for content, style, and grammar. The sample essay questions are similar to what you might expect to see on the FTCE GK Test. A sample essay question and response is provided immediately after the writing-skills review exercises.

Also, included in this section are "General Strategies for Writing the Essay for the General Knowledge Test" and the "Scoring Criteria for the General Knowledge Essay" as found in the *Competencies and Skills Required for Teacher Certification in Florida, Ninth Edition* (www.firn.edu/doe/sas/ftce/ftcecomp.htm).

Essay Skills

As listed in the *Competencies and Skills Required for Teacher Certification in Florida, Ninth Edition* (as mentioned above), the Essay competencies/skills you should be able to do are the following:

- Determine the purpose for writing.
- Formulate a thesis or a statement of a main idea.
- Organize ideas and details effectively.
- Provide adequate, relevant supporting material.
- Use effective transitions.
- Demonstrate a mature command of language.
- Avoid inappropriate use of slang, jargon, and clichés.
- Use a variety of sentence patterns effectively.
- Maintain a consistent point of view.
- Observe the conventions of standard American English.

Determine Your Purpose for Writing

Writers write for many reasons. Some write to inform, others to share, and still others to explain. Whatever the need, you need to **determine your purpose for writing** before you begin. Knowing your purpose will help clarify your message.

Four common purposes for writing are as follows:

- self-expression–to express a desire or personal feeling
- exposition–to transform information from writer to reader
- entertainment–to arouse the interest of the reader
- persuasion–to share a point of view

The more clearly you know what you want to accomplish, the better equipped you will be to write your essay. You will be able to make the proper choices to sharpen your writing and perfect your message.

Tip: You also need to know the audience for whom you are writing. Knowing your audience will help you clarify your purpose for writing.

If you are writing to a friend, you might write in a open and informal style. "Hey, Steve! What's up? What are ya doin' this summer? Want to have a blast? I know a great summer camp. . . ."

If you are writing to a general audience, you might write in a more formal style. "The following information is intended to help undecided voters select the candidate who most nearly represents their views and interests."

Finally, if you are writing to a well-defined audience, you might write in a style that reflects their level of expertise. "The high cost of medical insurance reflects the ever demanding and volatile relationship between the real and actual cost ratio factors of doing business in the transactional universe of medical liability."

Look at the examples of these following topics and then ask yourself what might be your purpose for writing in each case and what style of writing you might use.

- **A.** The High Cost of Medical Insurance
- **B.** The Decline in Moral Values
- **C.** My Beloved "Talking" Dog
- **D.** Six Easy Ways to Invest Your Money
- **E.** Eat Right! Eat Healthy!

Now that you have had a chance to read these topics, here are some possible reasons or purposes for writing the essays to accompany these titles and also some styles that you might use.

A. The High Cost of Medical Insurance

Your purpose for writing could be how escalating expenses are harming the individual's ability to receive proper medical care. You might use an *exposition* style to communicate facts to the reader about the rising cost of medical insurance and expound upon ways this issue can impact the reader's life.

B. The Decline in Moral Values

Your purpose for writing may be because you perceive a decline of civility and decency in today's confusing and conflicting cultural landscape. You might use a *self-expressive* style to personally state your own feelings.

C. My Beloved "Talking" Dog

Your purpose for writing might be to share the happy and fun-filled misadventures of your beloved "talking" dog, a pet who seems to have a mind of its own. You might use an *entertaining* style to delight and amuse your readers.

D. Six Easy Ways to Invest Your Money

Your purpose for writing could be to encourage readers to invest their money in profitable ventures that are reasonably guaranteed to provide a safe return on their investment. You might use a *persuasive* style in writing this essay.

E. Eat Right! Eat Healthy!

Your purpose for writing might be to encourage your readers to eat a healthy, low-fat diet so that they increase their chances of living a long, illness-free life. You might use a *persuasive* style to motivate your readers to make this change in their lifestyles.

Formulate a Thesis or a Statement of a Main Idea

Formulating a thesis or statement of a main idea involves two factors–the subject on which you are writing and your attitude or opinion toward that subject. Focusing your attitude or opinion in a single direction gives you a defined purpose for your writing. And since your attitude or opinion may not necessarily be shared by your reader, you need to explain the reasons for your choice.

In all good writing, the reader should know by the end of your first paragraph your thesis statement or main idea. They should have a strong idea of what you are writing about. A good thesis statement helps not only the reader but also helps the writer remain focused on what she is supposed to be writing.

Using the previously listed sample topics, here are some sample thesis statements:

A. The High Cost of Medical Insurance

Given the escalating costs of today's medical care, it is no wonder that the price of medical insurance continues to rise. Because fewer and fewer individuals can afford to pay for basic health insurance premiums, clearly something must be done.

B. The Decline in Moral Values

As I look around my world, I feel disheartened and disappointed at the lack of real civility and decency in today's confusing and conflicting social arena.

C. My Beloved "Talking" Dog

Believe it or not, I have a dog that manages to get everything he wants by talking in a language all his own.

D. Six Ways to Invest Your Money

Money schemes come and go, but after reading this essay, you will walk away with a clear understanding of how to invest your money in safe, reasonable, and risk-free accounts, guaranteed to yield a modest return.

E. Eat Right! Eat Healthy!

With the variety of foods available to eat, it is more important than ever to know which foods are healthful and which might lead to health problems in years to come.

These five are sample thesis statements. Notice that each thesis statement names the subject of the essay and provides a clear point of view or opinion about that subject. These are the hallmarks of a strong thesis statement.

Organize Ideas and Details Effectively

After constructing a strong thesis statement, you need to begin **organizing ideas and details effectively.** With a sharply defined and well-written thesis statement, your ideas and details should flow naturally. You should be able to list fairly rapidly the essential reasons for defending and defining your thesis statement.

Before you begin, it is always best to set up a plan of action. A plan insures a better-finished product, as your ideas will flow with greater logic and clarity. There are several different ways to write an essay, but one of the ways involves the following steps:

1. Write down all the possible ideas you can think of on the essay's topic.
2. Circle the ideas you think are the most important and that you can write about most effectively.
3. Group the ideas that you have circled into possible paragraphs.
4. Organize the groups into possible ways to answer the essay's topic.

Many writing projects can be organized into three parts: 1) the introduction, 2) the body, and 3) the conclusion. In the introduction, you briefly state your topic, presenting your reader a preview of what is to come. The body of the paper—the main and longest portion of your paper—provides the facts and examples that support the main idea expressed in the introduction. The conclusion summarizes and restates the main idea.

The three parts to your essay should work together to make an effective and cohesive whole. Your introduction should be an attention-grabbing device that will "pull" the reader into your essay. In the body of your essay, make sure that every point is relevant to the subject you are discussing. Avoid irrelevant or extraneous information that does not relate to your main topic. Finally, your conclusion should be a strong ending that restates your thesis statement.

A simple technique to remember is to tell the reader what you are going to say, say it, and then, tell the reader what you said. Keeping this rule in mind will help you considerably as you write your impromptu essay. For example, suppose you were asked to write an essay on the following: Choosing a career.

1. Allowing a few minutes to think, you might write something like this:

   Interests, money, location, college, courses, preparation, skills, talents, hobbies, schooling, time, travel, passion, income, standard of living

2. Next, circle the ideas you think are the most important and that you can write about most effectively. Remember, you cannot write about everything you can imagine; you will only have time to explore a few key points.

3. Now, group the items you have selected into possible paragraphs. Your essay might look like this:

   - Personal interests

     Talents, hobbies, passion

   - Preparation for career

     Schooling, time, college, courses

   - Financial considerations

     Money, income, standard of living

4. After you have grouped ideas into similar sections, you can organize your groups into an outline. Outlines are an easy way to organize your thoughts and prepare your essay. For example, an outline for an essay on "choosing a career" might look like this:

   I. Introduction—There are many reasons for choosing a career

   II. Personal Interests

      A. Talents

      B. Hobbies

      C. Passion

   III. Preparation for Career

      A. Schooling

      B. Length of study

      C. Money to study

   IV. Financial Considerations

      A. Potential income

      B. Standard of living

   V. Conclusion—Reiterate reasons for choosing a career

When organizing your essay's ideas and details, it is important that you follow a few guidelines. They are as follows:

- **Determine the amount of background information required.** Does your reader know your material? Do you have to provide background information?

- **Define required terminology.** Does your reader need to know technical terms? If so, which terms?

- **Define the tone of your discussion.** Should you write in a formal or casual style? Which would be most effective?

- **Determine the number of examples required.** Should you include many examples to define your thesis? If so, how many? Which ones?
- **Determine the organizational pattern to use.** What organizational pattern should you use to explain your thesis? Which style is most effective?

Organizing your ideas and details to explain your thesis statement takes a good understanding of your subject matter. Thus, when writing an essay, be sure to select a topic for which you know much about; otherwise, you will be struggling to add strong details to your writing.

Provide Adequate, Relevant Supporting Material

To develop an effective essay, you must provide your reader with **adequate and relevant supporting material.** The information that you select to include in your essay must meet the needs of not only you as the writer, but should directly pertain to the needs of your reader. Otherwise, your writing serves no real purpose.

To make sure that your writing provides strong and relevant supportive material, always be mindful of your reader and ask yourself some basic questions. They are as follows:

- Do all your sentences help develop your thesis statement?
- Do your sentences follow a logical and clear sequence of ideas?
- Do you include all relevant detail?
- Do you write with a controlled voice?
- Do you answer all the reader's questions?
- Do you include vivid examples to define your point of view?

The following is an example of a passage in which the writer's thoughts are not connected in a coherent, logical, unified, and well-ordered manner:

> I like animals, especially, dogs. Sometimes, I like cats. Most dogs are enjoyable to have as pets, yet sometimes, they can be most difficult, especially when you want to take long trips. I once had a dog who loved to bark all night. Taking a dog on a summer road trip is never easy. You must bring along lots of food and water. I remember a trip we once took in the dead of winter, which made traveling with our family pets exceptionally hard. I do not know what I would do without my favorite dog, Millie.

How much better would the above paragraph be if it were written like the following?

> Keeping animals happy and healthy involves five simple rules. The first rule is to keep your pets' food dishes clean. Wash them thoroughly every day. This will help prevent the spread of bacteria and other diseases from infecting your pets. The second rule is to make sure your pets eat right. A balanced diet is necessary if your pets are to be healthy. If you are unsure what your animals should eat, check with a veterinarian. Also, buy prepared foods for most kinds of pets. By using these foods, you can be sure that your pet receives the right amounts of vitamins, minerals, and proteins for their nourishment. The third rule is to never overfeed your pets. Give your animals as much food as they will eat without leaving any food behind. If your pets leave the dish before emptying it, be sure to take the dish away. This will insure that your pets do not overeat and next time, you will know to feed them less. Feeding animals the right food at the right time prevents sickness. The fourth rule is that all pets must have good houses. Whether the house is a cage or a pet bed, make sure that it is dry, warm, and suitable in size for the animal to live comfortably. Finally, the fifth rule is to make sure pets are checked regulary by trained veterinary doctors and given all the required vaccinations. A sick animal cannot only harm itself, but could infect others—including people in some cases. By following these five simple rules, you can help your pets to enjoy good health and a long life.

As you can tell, the second paragraph contains relevant and supporting details presented in a logical, coherent, and organized manner.

Use Effective Transitions

Good writers make **use of effective transitions.** They use transitional words or phrases to connect ideas and thoughts. Transitional words also provide for a logical sequence of ideas.

Look at the following list of transitional words and phrases. By adopting these words and phrases into your own writing, you can begin to develop a writing style that is clear and unifying for your readers.

again	conversely	in any case	namely	therefore
also	finally	in any event	nevertheless	thereupon
as a rule	first of all	in brief	of course	thus
as usual	for example	in essence	rather	to sum up
besides	for instance	in short	secondly	
briefly	furthermore	in the long run	similarly	
by and large	generally	instead	that is	
consequently	however	moreover	then indeed	

Many other transitions are available, but you will find that the preceding list will serve you well. Using these words to connect your thoughts will significantly improve your writing style and fluency.

Look at some examples of how these transitional words can be used:

- Learning to laugh at one's mistakes, therefore, can bring a whole new perspective on one's life.
- Briefly, the three main points of this essay are . . .
- In short, I intend to run for president of the senior class and win.
- Consequently, the politician had little to say when he was indicted on charges of election fraud.
- The construction crew worked tirelessly; however, they did not manage to finish the Robertsons' brand new home in time for the start of the Robertsons' summer vacation.
- The President ignored his own good judgment; therefore, the military mission was an abysmal failure.

Demonstrate a Mature Command of Language

Writing a strong and effective essay requires the ability to **demonstrate a mature command of language.** Writers must be able to articulate their thoughts in a clear and logical fashion so that all may read and understand their thoughts easily and readily. Any confusion evidenced by the writer's handling of language will result in the reader's misinterpretation of the material. Thus, to avoid such confusion, good writers should do the following:

- Write with a clear and resonant voice. Be sure all your words are chosen to convey the most precise and logical analysis of your argument or thesis statement.
- Use paragraph breaks to divide your thought patterns and make your essay easier to read.
- Use transitions and related word links to connect your thoughts and ideas.
- Provide a sound and logical conclusion to your essay that summarizes your key ideas and thoughts.
- Avoid spelling and mechanical errors. Proofread your work.
- Avoid wordiness. It is always best to use fewer words to express a difficult idea or thought.
- Avoid repetition. Always state enough ideas to make your point but not so much as to bore the reader.
- Avoid oversimplification. It is always wise to clarify your ideas with the words *often, usually,* and *sometimes.*
- Write simply. Often a simpler word is an effective substitute for a more difficult word. By writing simply, you can help clarify your thoughts.

As an example of the need to write simply, examine these two sentences.

1. Joe Smith is responsible.
2. The undersigned official assumes responsibility.

Which do you prefer? Obviously, the first choice conveys the meaning of the sentence simply and directly. The second choice, however, is obtuse and may imply another agenda other than simply stating the truth.

As an example of a longer passage, examine these two examples.

Passage #1

Bungee jumping was inspired many, many years ago by the celebrated vine jumpers of the world-famous Pentecost Islands in Vanuatu (formerly the New Hebrides) in the vast stretches of the Pacific Ocean, where it is understood by all the inhabitants and natives that bungee jumping is doubly a rite of passage into manhood and a fertility rite performed to ensure a good and plentiful yam harvest. Modern bungee jumping began with four simultaneous jumps off the renowned Clifton Suspension Bridge in Bristol, England, on the very first day of April in 1979. Today, bungee jumping is a sporting event that is practiced all over the world, almost everywhere that people can ever imagine.

Passage #2

Bungee jumping was inspired by the Pentecost Island vine jumpers. There, natives bungee-jumped as a rite of passage into manhood. It was also considered a fertility rite to ensure a strong yam harvest. Modern bungee jumping began with four simultaneous jumps from the Clifton Suspension Bridge in Bristol, England on April 1, 1979. Today, bungee jumping is practiced worldwide.

As you can see, the second example dispenses with unnecessary wordiness. Following the preceding rules will help you demonstrate a mature command of language and write with proficiency and efficiency.

Avoid Inappropriate Use of Slang, Jargon, and Clichés

When writing an essay, you would be wise to purposely avoid the inappropriate use of slang, jargon, and clichés. This use of common sayings and expressions might be appropriate for creative writing; however, it is inappropriate for formal essay writing. Thus, it is wise to keep your writing to standard English usage and style.

Slang is street language. It is the highly informal language that is perfectly suited for conversations among friends, but highly inappropriate for formal writing. Slang is sometimes referred to as "colloquial," a word meaning language that is spoken by everyday people.

Some common slang words and their meanings are as follows:

airhead—stupid person

*Dave is a real **airhead**.*

armpit—dirty, unappealing place

*His bedroom is a regular **armpit**.*

awesome—great and impressive

*Hey, man, that roller coaster ride was **awesome**!*

bling-bling—fancy or showing off

*Oh, look, at Mr Fancy wearing all his **bling-bling** and driving his new car.*

booze—alcohol

*Dan is tired because last night he drank too much **booze**.*

bread—money

*Hey, ask your old man if we can borrow some **bread**.*

cheesy—cheap, outmoded, out of date

*My boyfriend was wearing such **cheesy** clothes.*

chick flick—a movie primarily of interest to females, often a love story or heavy emotional drama

*Last night, my wife went out with her girl friends to see the latest **chick flick** at the movies.*

dorky—strange, peculiar (socially weird)

*Gee, your friend is such a **dorky** guy.*

fab—look grand, fabulous

*Wow, you are just **fab**.*

flick—movie

*Hey, wanna see a **flick**?*

hairy—difficult

*Driving super fast, Arnie took some **hairy** turns.*

idiotsyncrasy—a strange personal mannerism

*Yeah, he's picking at his ear again; it is just one of his crazy **idiotsyncrasies**.*

lip—fast, cheap talk

*The students in fourth period always give their substitute teacher **lip**.*

mickey-mouse—unimportant, time wasting

*This math exercise is such a **mickey-mouse** assignment.*

paws—hands

*Get your **paws** off my girlfriend!*

rug rat—child

*My brother has a couple of **rug rats** running around his house.*

scarf—to eat fast

*Rushing off to school, I **scarfed** down my breakfast as I headed out the door.*

threads—clothing

*Willie bought a whole new set of **threads**.*

tie one on—to get drunk

*In celebration of their last final, the fraternity boys are going to a local bar to **tie one on**.*

turkey—failure, flop

*The movie was a real **turkey**.*

umpteen—countless times

*If I have told you once, I have told you **umpteen** times, "Don't wear your shoes inside the house!"*

wheels—car, motor vehicle

*I took off on the open road in my brand new set of **wheels**.*

whitebread—plain, boring; white, suburban, middle class.

*The TV talk show host had never met a guest that was so **whitebread**.*

*Outside the inner city, the **whitebread** community of upper-mobile adults was one of the most affluent communities in the country.*

zero—unimportant person

*He is such a real **zero**!*

Jargon is the specialized language of a discipline or a profession. Individuals involved in a particular discipline, job, or profession use the same words, or jargon, frequently, and usually, only the individuals intimately connected to the words know of their meaning. Nothing is wrong with jargon; it must be used judiciously so that its meaning is clear to all involved.

Tip: When in doubt, always use a simple word. Simplicity breeds understanding, and understanding means clarity in thought and reason.

Clichés are overused expressions that lack originality. When writing, use clichés when necessary—when they add punch to your writing style–and not when a more apt word or phrase will do. It is always better to use fresh, original expressions to define your writing. Some common examples of clichés are as follows:

A chicken in every pot

A penny for your thoughts?

Agree to disagree

As old as dirt

Bug off

Close only counts in horseshoes and hand grenades

Cut bait and run

Don't rock the boat

Easy pickings

Exception that proves the rule

In any way, shape, or form

In close quarters

Last but not least

Life's a long hard climb

No rest for the wicked

On the rocks

Stay the course

The ball's in your court

The worm turns

Through thick and thin

Venture a suggestion

Worse for the wear

Again, these colorful expressions are fun to say, but avoid them in formal writing.

Use a Variety of Sentence Patterns Effectively

Using a variety of sentence patterns effectively is essential to good writing. A paper that has all the required information, but is uninteresting to read will either bore the readers or leave them more confused than when they started to read. Thus, a good technique to improve your writing is to vary your sentence patterns.

Look at the following example of how sentences may be constructed into interesting patterns:

First, a sentence, by definition, is an **independent clause.** An independent clause is a group of words that contains a subject and a verb and expresses a single thought. An example of an independent clause is

I went to the movies.

Second, a sentence can be enhanced by adding a **dependent clause.** A dependent clause is a group of words that contains a subject and a verb but does not express a single thought. Thus, it is **not** a complete sentence. An example of a dependent clause is:

When Lauren was done

Often a dependent clause is marked by a **dependent marker** word. A dependent marker word is added to the beginning of an independent clause. When this occurs, the independent clause becomes a dependent clause. Some common dependent markers are:

after, although, as, as if, because, before, even if, even though, if, in order to, since, though, unless, until, whatever, when, whenever, whether, and *while.*

Third, independent and dependent clauses can be connected by **coordinating conjunctions** and **independent markers.** Coordinating conjunctions include

and, or, but, nor, so, for, and *yet*

Independent markers include

also, consequently, furthermore, however, moreover, nevertheless, and *therefore*

Also, when the second independent clause in a sentence begins with an independent marker word, a *semicolon* is needed before the independent marker word. For example:

I went to the movies; however, I went when Lauren was finished with her homework.

Knowing this, here are some examples of how two sentences can be combined:

I went to the movies. I went when Lauren was finished with her homework.

I went to the movies; I went when Lauren was finished with her homework.

I went to the movies, but I went when Lauren was finished with her homework.

I went to the movies; however, I did not go until Lauren was finished with her homework.

When Lauren was finished with her homework, I went to the movies.

I went to the movies when Lauren was finished with her homework.

Keep these sentence variations in mind when you write your essays.

Maintain a Consistent Point of View

Maintaining a consistent point of view is the hallmark of strong writing. A good writer maintains consistency in style, content, and theme throughout a piece. To maintain such consistency, it is best for writers to adopt one voice throughout their work.

As a writer, you can choose from three points of view to write your pieces. These points of view are **first, second** and **third person.** Each one has specific responsibilities, characteristics, and effects for both you as the writer and the reader. Here are examples of how each point of view may be used in your essay.

The **first person point of view** is a narrative written with the word "I," which makes it highly personalized. Use this point of view when you want to cultivate a sense of closeness with your readers or when you want the readers to identify or sympathize with you. An example of a first person point of view is as follows:

I went home around 2 o'clock yesterday morning and checked my refrigerator. Nothing was there to eat. So, hungry, I walked over to my neighbor's apartment and asked whether she would like to go out to grab a snack with me. We knew each other well enough to do those fun things on the spur of the moment, so off we went.

The **second person point of view** is when the narrator addresses the protagonist as "you." Often, second person point of view is used when the narrator is speaking to a younger or less experienced reader. Before writing in second person, the narrator should clarify for the reader just who is talking to whom. As you can tell, though, much of the text in this book is written in second person. The reason is that second person is commonly used in technical and reference writing in which a process or technique is being explained. The reader is thought of as a less-experienced version of the author and someone for whom the writer must carefully explain each and every step required to learn a new procedure or method.

Here's our earlier example adapted to second person point of view:

You went home around 2 o'clock yesterday morning and checked your refrigerator. You found nothing there to eat. So, being hungry, you walked over to your neighbor's apartment and asked her whether she would like to go out to grab a snack with you. You know each other well enough to do those fun things on the spur of the moment, so off you went.

The **third person point of view** is when the narrative is told by a supposedly objective voice (see discussion below) not directly involved in the story. The narrator is the voice of authority and should be telling the story without noticeable prejudice or bias. Third person point of view is most present in non-fiction works such as research reports and newspaper articles.

> **When writing in the third person, be careful to keep your voice objective. It is very easy to let subjectivity or bias slip into your narrative. See the discussion of objective and subjective voice below.**

An example of third person point of view is as follows:

> He went home around 2 o'clock yesterday morning and checked his refrigerator. He found nothing there to eat. So, being hungry, he walked over to his neighbor's apartment and asked her whether she would like to go out and grab a snack with him. They knew each other well enough to do those fun things on the spur of the moment, so off they went.

Finally, when writing, there are two kinds of voices in which a narrative may be written. They are objective and subjective voice.

- Objective voice is when the writer leaves herself out of her writing. Objective writing focuses on external things and events, without referring to the personal prejudices or emotions of the writer. News writing is an example of nonfiction objective writing.

- Subjective voice is when the writer leaves herself in her writing. Subjective writing focuses on internal things and events, presenting reality as the writer sees and interprets it, referring continually to the expression of personal thoughts, impulses, and feelings. Editorials, opinion pieces, and personal narratives are examples of nonfiction subjective writing.

When writing, it is imperative that you select a voice and a point of view that is consistent throughout your essay. Knowing what you want to say and how you want to say it are the two key ingredients in any successful writing endeavor. Failure to follow this format will result in poor, unfocused writing.

Observe the Conventions of Standard American English

Finally, when writing your essay, you must always **observe the conventions of standard American English.** Although this might sound simple to do, it is easy to rush your essays and write poorly.

Here, then, are some tips to follow when writing to observe the conventions of standard American English:

1. **Use active voice.**

   In sentences written in active voice, the subject performs the action expressed in the verb. For example,

   "The dog bit the child." (active voice)
   "The child was bitten by the dog." (passive voice)

   "Everyone who attended the housewarming party had a great time." (active voice)
   "A great time was had by everyone who attended the housewarming party." (passive voice)

2. **Be plain spoken.**

   Always say what you mean simply and plainly.

3. **Write in complete sentences.**

   Always makes sure your sentences have a subject and a verb.

4. **Be sure your subject and verb agree.**

   Always make sure that your subjects and verbs agree in number and tense.

5. **Be sure your nouns and pronouns agree.**

   Always make sure that your pronoun references are in agreement with the subjects of your sentences.

6. **Use clear descriptions.**

   Always be careful that your nouns and descriptors agree and are connected.

7. **Use proper grammar symbols.**

   Always be sure that you punctuate your sentences correctly.

8. **Check spelling.**

   Always proofread your papers for common spelling errors.

These writing tips will help you avoid common grammatical errors and adhere to the conventions of standard American English. Also, please note that since you will be writing your essay by hand, you will not have access to spelling and grammer checkers. Thus, avoid words and phrases that are unfamiliar to you to avoid costly errors and mistakes.

General Strategies for Writing the Essay for the General Knowledge Test

As listed in the *Competencies and Skills Required for Teacher Certification in Florida, Ninth Edition* (see the Web address in the first section of this chapter), the General Strategies for Writing the Essay for the General Knowledge Test are the following:

1. **Watch the time.**

   Take a few moments at the beginning of the period to plan your essay and at the end to proofread or revise your work. Use *all* your time wisely. You should not run out of time before you are done; nor should you write an incomplete essay because you did not use all the time allowed. *Note:* You do not have time to write a rough draft and then completely rewrite it. Spend your time writing and editing your final essay.

2. **Read the instructions carefully and select one of the topics.**

   Determine what the topic is asking. Think of how the topic relates to what you know, what you have learned, and what experiences you have had, so you can provide concrete details rather than vague generalities.

3. **Take a few minutes to prewrite.**

   Jot down your first ideas (some you might like; others you might discard). Sketch a quick outline or group your ideas together with arrows or numbers. By prewriting, you can "see" your essay taking shape—even before you start writing.

4. **Write a thesis statement that provides a clear focus for your essay.**

   State a point of view in your thesis that guides the purpose and scope of your essay. Consider the point you are trying to convey to the reader and what you want the reader to understand about the topic. Avoid a thesis statement framed as a statement of fact, a question, or an announcement.

5. **Develop the essay according to your purpose.**

   Develop paragraphs fully to give the reader examples and reasons that support your thesis. Indent each new paragraph. Note that a good essay for the General Knowledge Test might be longer or shorter than the basic five-paragraph format of some short essays. Do not limit yourself to an arbitrary length. The key is to develop a topic by using concrete, informative details.

6. **Tie your main ideas together with a brief conclusion.**

   Provide a concluding paragraph that ties together the essay's points and offers insights about the topic. Avoid a conclusion that merely restates the thesis and repeats the supporting details. Check your time. If the writing period is almost over, wrap up quickly, so you can proofread or revise.

7. **Revise/proofread the essay to conform to standard American English usage.**

   Look for particular grammatical or spelling errors you tend to make. Read each sentence from the last sentence to the first. Mark out errors and correct them. On the FTCE GK, you are not penalized for clearly crossing out errors. Look for words, sentences, or even paragraphs that need changing. Write legibly so that the reader knows what you have written.

Scoring Criteria for the General Knowledge Essay

As listed in the *Competencies and Skills Required for Teacher Certification in Florida, Ninth Edition* (see the Web address in the first section of this chapter) for the "Scoring Criteria the General Knowledge Essay" are the following:

Scoring for the FTCE GK Essay	
Score of 6	The paper has a clearly established main idea that the writer fully develops with specific details and examples. Organization is notably logical and coherent. Point of view is consistently maintained. Vocabulary and sentence structure are varied and effective. Errors in sentence structure, usage, and mechanics are few and insignificant.
Score of 5	The paper has a clearly established main idea that is adequately developed and recognizable through specific details and/or examples. Organization follows a logical and coherent pattern. Point of view is mostly maintained. Vocabulary and sentence structure are mostly varied and effective. Occasional errors in sentence structure, usage, and mechanics do not interfere with the writer's ability to communicate.
Score of 4	The paper has an adequately stated main idea that is developed with some specific details and examples. Supporting ideas are presented in a mostly logical and coherent manner. Point of view is somewhat maintained. Vocabulary and sentence structure are somewhat varied and effective. Occasional errors in sentence structure, usage, and mechanics may interfere with the writer's ability to communicate.
Score of 3	The paper states a main idea that is developed with generalizations or lists. The paper may contain occasional lapses in logic and coherence, and the organization is mechanical. Point of view is ambiguous. Vocabulary and sentence structure are repetitious and often ineffective. A variety of errors in sentence structure, usage, and mechanics sometimes interfere with the writer's ability to communicate.
Score of 2	The paper presents an incomplete or ambiguous main idea. Support is developed with generalizations and lists. Organization is mechanical. The paper contains occasional lapses in logic and coherence. Point of view is confusing and distracting. Word choice is simplistic, and sentence structure is disjointed. Errors in sentence structure, usage, and mechanics frequently interfere with the writer's ability to communicate.
Score of 1	The paper has no evident main idea. Development is inadequate and/or irrelevant. Organization is illogical and incoherent. Point of view has not been established. Vocabulary and sentence structure are garbled and confusing. Significant and numerous errors in sentence structure, usage, and mechanics interfere with the writer's ability to communicate.

Test Yourself–Essay Writing

This section of the examination involves a written assignment. You are asked to prepare a written response for *one of the two topics* presented below. Select one of these two topics and prepare a 300–600 word response. Be sure to read both topics very carefully to make sure that you understand the topic for which you are preparing a written response. Use your allotted time to plan, write, review, and edit what you have written for the assignment.

Topic 1

My teaching philosophy

Topic 2

A sport I like to watch

Be sure to read the two topics again before attempting to write your response. Remember, you will write your essay on the space provided in the examination booklet. Your essay also must be on only one of the topics presented, and it must provide complete coverage of the topic.

Your essay is graded holistically, meaning only one score is assigned for your writing—taking into consideration both mechanics and organization. *You are not to be scored on the nature of the content or opinions expressed in your work.* Instead, you are graded on your abilities to write complete sentences, to express and support your opinions, and to organize your work.

At least two evaluators review your work and assign it a score. Special attention is paid to the following more specific indications in your writing:

- Does your writing demonstrate a strong definitive purpose?
- Is there a clear thesis or a statement of a main idea?
- Are your ideas organized?
- Do you support your thesis with clear details?
- Are effective transitions present?
- Do you demonstrate an effective use of language?
- Are a variety of sentence patterns present?
- Is there a consistent point of view?
- Are the conventions of standard American English used?

Before you begin, be sure you plan what you want to say. Organize your thoughts and carefully construct your ideas. This must be your original work, written by your own hand, and in your own voice.

As you write your piece, you may cross out or add information as necessary. And although quality of handwriting does not count, be sure to be legible in your response.

Sample Answers—Essay Writing

Following are some sample essay answers to the preceding topics. For each topic, there is an example of a poorly written essay and a well-written essay.

Choice 1–My Teaching Philosophy

A weak response

My Teaching Philosophy

My teaching philosophy? I believe that all children can learn and if you try hard enough, you can teach most everybody. Young children, especially, love to learn and grow and therefore, teachers should try their hardest to make sure that they get all the knowledge and skills that they need to grow and become. Teaching is a tough job and I am sure that I as grow in this worthy profession, I will learn much about what it means to be a good teacher. For now, though, I am happy just to work with young children, giving them everything they need to know to become successful in their lives.

A strong response

My Teaching Philosophy

Since I was a youngster, I have always wanted to teach. I have wanted to become a teacher because I love school and I want to help young children learn and succeed. I want to develop a relationship with the students that I teach that will encourage them to come to me with their problems and concerns. This is my guiding philosophy of education—to nurture others to become the best they can possibly be. This philosophy will guide me in the following ways: 1) to encourage the potential in all young people, 2) to encourage strong study and work habits, and 3) to encourage young people to make wise and purposeful decisions. The following paragraphs will explain.

First, as an adult, I believe that all young people have the potential to become anything they want. Given the right push and proper conditions, I believe that young people can mature into healthy, responsible adults, capable of figuratively moving mountains and changing seasons. They possess the potential within to blossom into productive and engaged citizens who attack life with a passionate zeal and purpose that defies all expectations. All they need is the gentle guidance and polite push of a respectful and caring educator who will recognize their capabilities and highlight their strengths. And a nudge is often the spark they need to begin their journey. This nudge can come in many shapes and sizes, most notably direct praise for assignments and jobs well done. Teachers who take the time to listen and talk to their students—about their schoolwork and personal lives—can do much to demonstrate to their students that a caring and compassionate hand can alleviate most any burden. Taking time from a busy schedule to attend to students' immediate concerns can do much to inspire them to achieve any goal they can imagine.

Second, as a teacher, I hope to encourage young people to develop smart study and work habits. By providing them with a recognizable routine in our daily class assignments, I intend to model for my students how they too should perceive and organize their own studies. A teacher who demonstrates good work habits and a steady and recognizable routine can do much to improve the lives of often distracted and unfocused youngsters. After all, I know what it is like to be confused and dazed; I was once a kid myself and I appreciated the many teachers that I had who helped me organize my work and learn my school material. Directly and indirectly, they provided me with many useful suggestions and tips for completing my class assignments and arranging my notes into recognizable and coherent patterns. Once done, I was able to streamline my study time and thus, learn my material quickly and efficiently. When I teach, I hope to model and inspire my students to do the same.

Finally, as a teacher, I hope to encourage young people to make wise and purposeful decisions. I know, of course, that a teacher cannot save the world. They cannot help every child in their care make sound choices, but they can role model for them how one does make wise decisions. By providing young people with lessons in decision-making, I intend to demonstrate simple steps that everyone can take when deciding a course of action. Too often, young people make rash choices without thinking about the consequences of their actions. The result is often near fatal errors that can cause much pain and harm to all involved. Thus, I believe that lessons in decision-making—how best to decide on a course of action, given a set of circumstances and concerns—is the best remedy for helping young people become responsible adults. Whether the decisions be as simple as how to behave on the playground to something more complex like deciding whether to drink and drive, young people need a way to safely and calmly decide how best to behave in a given situation. As a teacher, I can do much to provide lessons in which young people can learn decision-making skills.

Thus, my decision to become a teacher is predicated on the fact that I have always wanted to become a role model for young people. I love school and I want to continue my life as a public school teacher who inspires young people to become equally responsible adults. As a teacher, I believe it is my duty and responsibility to help all young people to achieve their dreams, no matter how difficult and faraway they might initially seem. Once a teacher, I can accomplish my goals by encouraging young people 1) to develop their potential, 2) to improve their study and work habits, and 3) to hone their decision-making skills. By following these precepts, I intend to become the best teacher that I can possibly become.

Choice 2–A Sport I Like to Watch

A weak response

A Sport I Like to Watch

I like to watch many sports. I especially like to watch basketball, tennis and hockey. Each sport is fun to watch both in person and on TV. In fact, I can spend most of the day in my den just lying on the couch and watching cool sports on the tube. Nothing could be better. Except if I am playing a game myself. Sometimes, my buddies and I go out to the neighborhood park and shoot some hoops. Sometimes we play one on one for hours on end. The exercise is good and the sweat I build up helps me lose some of those extra pounds. Of course, snacking in front of the TV watching my favorite sport shows does not help either. But, what are you going to do? I am just addicted to watching sports on television and with so many great sports and games to choose from, it is a wonder that I ever get anything done.

A strong response

A Sport I Like to Watch

Watching sporting events—whether on television or in person—is for me the next best thing to heaven itself. I am a huge sports enthusiast, and in my house, I am always tuned into the latest game or sports show. I like being in the know and cannot wait to learn who is winning, losing, and just plain outshining the competition. I love competition, especially in sports—whether it be college or pro—and I cannot wait to hook into the latest matchup to see how my favorite and least favorite teams are doing. Yet, of all sports to watch, I have a special fondness for golf. I love to watch professional golfers play for many reasons but, especially, for three reasons: 1) relaxation, 2) excitement, and 3) instruction. Simply, I love to watch golf pros at the top of their game.

I love to watch the game of golf, especially as broadcast on television. Every weekend, you can probably find me nestled into my easy chair, soft drink in one hand, television remote in the other, flipping channels, watching professional golfers do "their thing." As an avid golfer, I have a special fondness for watching others maneuver themselves on some of the world's greatest golf courses. I enjoy watching golfers walk the green, size up their shots, and compete with their opponents. Calmly and precisely, they position themselves to be the best they possibly can in this most gentlemanly of sports. True, golfers can be and are fiercely competitive, but their anger and drive hardly ever spills out onto the course. Instead, what I see at home is a nice leisurely walk, interrupted by long shots and inspired swings, all making for a most enjoyable and relaxing sport to watch from the comforts of my living room.

This is not to say golf is a dull sport. If anything, I find it to be the most exciting of sports. You never know what is going to happen. Each weekend, I find myself sitting on the edge of my chair in anticipation of what each golfer will bring to their game. Some begin strong and end weakly. Others are the reverse. And still others have strong games from beginning to end. What is most exciting is to watch golfers sink or nearly sink long putts. Standing far off to the side of the green, these professional golfers manage to make putts or near putts that I can hardly imagine. To be sure, I am an amateur golfer with an equally high handicap. I cannot imagine a golfing game where you compete with such skill and precision. Their sheer power and talent makes for an invigorating and engaging sport to watch.

Finally, I watch professional golf for the instruction. As a viewer, I learn how to improve my stance, my swing, and my follow-through by simply watching professional golfers at work. Fortunately, television broadcasters supplement their golf programs with lessons about how to improve one's game. Complete with instructional video clips, these brief, but informative golfing lessons are just the thing to help me improve my game. Often, I find myself glued to my television, trying to absorb the latest golfing advice from a recognized and established pro. Easy, cheap, and useful, these golfing lessons help me improve my game, keep me interested and involved in the sport, and provide useful information to share with my fellow golfers. After all, you are never too old to learn.

Thus, watching professional golf on television, and if I am lucky, in person, is one of my most pleasurable activities. I enjoy the pleasantness of this most peaceful and relaxing of sports and I relish the quiet time that I have in front of my television watching true professionals display their natural talent. Moreover, I learn to improve my own game while reveling in the heated excitement of a close and competitive round. To the untrained eye, golf is simply hitting balls into a faraway hole, but to me, golf is a beautiful walk, highlighted by great highs and lows, each one bringing its own engagement and insight into a game that I have long cherished for the ease and calmness it brings to my life.

Review for the GK English Language Skills Subtest

The English Language Skills subtest of the FTCE GK test consists of 40 multiple-choice questions, which you must complete in 40 minutes. Each test question requires that you choose among four answer choices labeled **A, B, C,** or **D.** You must fill in the space corresponding to your answer choice in a separate answer booklet. The only materials that you are permitted to use when taking the test are pens, pencils, and erasers. You cannot bring written notes or scratch paper into the testing center. You will have to write in your test booklet when making notes.

The English Language Skills Review in This Study Guide

The English Language Skills review in this CliffsTestPrep book is organized around the four language-skill areas tested on the FTCE GK test:

- Conceptual and Organizational Skills
- Word Choice Skills
- Sentence Structure Skills
- Grammar, Spelling, Capitalization and Punctuation Skills

Each area has a general review and sample questions. The review sections present language skill concepts with examples and explanation for each area. "Test Yourself" exercises are found throughout the review sections. These sample questions are similar to what you might expect to see on the FTCE GK Test, and give you an opportunity to practice what you just learned. The answers to the "Test Yourself" exercises are found immediately following the set of exercises. When doing the "Test Yourself" exercises, you should cover up the answers. Then check your answers when you've finished the exercises.

Conceptual and Organizational Skills

As listed in the *Competencies and Skills Required for Teacher Certification in Florida, Ninth Edition* (available at www.firn.edu/doe/sas/ftce/ftcecomp.htm), the English language competencies/skills you should have mastered for this area are the following:

- Identify logical order in a written passage.
- Identify irrelevant sentences.

Identify Logical Order in a Written Passage

Every written passage should present its information in a **logical order.** A sentence that is **not presented in logical order** is a sentence that is out of order or does not relate to its accompanying sentences. Look at this example of a written passage with sentences that are not in logical order.

> Starving, Rover ate quickly from his favorite dish. We were relieved to have Rover home. Yet, no matter where we looked, we could not find our beloved pet. Quickly, we notified our neighbors that Rover was missing. Last week, we discovered our dog, Rover, was missing. Soon, everyone was looking for Rover. Finally, after a long, tiring week, Rover came home, hungry, but healthy.

The passage is confusing because the sentences are not presented in a logical order. The way the passage is written is confusing to the reader. You must rearrange the sentences in your mind before the passage begins to make sense.

You can correct the confusion by revising the passage like this:

> Last week, we discovered our dog, Rover, was missing. Quickly, we notified our neighbors. Soon, everyone was looking for Rover. Yet, no matter where we looked, we could not find our beloved pet. Finally, after a long, tiring week, Rover came home, hungry, but healthy. Starving, Rover ate quickly from his favorite dish. We were relieved to have Rover home.

Identify Irrelevant Sentences

Every written passage should contain a main idea accompanied by supporting details. All sentences in this passage must relate to the main idea. When a passage contains material that has little or no connection to the main idea (or the connection is not clear), the sentences containing such material are **irrelevant.** Find the irrelevant sentence in this written passage.

> The winter months are the harshest for people living in our uppermost northern states near Canada. There, in places like Maine, Vermont, Minnesota, Michigan, Wisconsin, and North Dakota, winter stays for days on end, making life outside a burden for all who must travel to and from work or to run errands. Days are spent shoveling snow, starting cold engines, and just keeping warm and safe. Sometimes, violent storms wreak havoc on roads and homes, causing days of endless cold snaps and lost electricity. Hawaii is pleasant during this time of the year. On such days, northerners learn to bundle up, enjoy what food items they have stored for safekeeping, and just enjoy each other's company. Harsh winters are simply a fact of life for those who dwell near the Canadian border.

This passage is confusing because it contains an irrelevant sentence (*Hawaii is pleasant during this time of year*). Although the sentence relates to the passage's main idea, it is irrelevant to the passage's logical progression of ideas.

You can correct the confusion by revising the passage like this:

> The winter months are the harshest for people living in our uppermost northern states. There, in places like Maine, Vermont, Minnesota, Michigan, Wisconsin, and North Dakota, winter stays for days on end, making life outside a burden for all who must travel to and from work or to run errands. Days are spent shoveling snow, starting cold engines, and just keeping warm and safe. Sometimes, violent storms wreak havoc on roads and homes, causing days of endless cold snaps and lost electricity. On such days, northerners learn to bundle up, enjoy what food items they have stored for safekeeping, and just enjoy each other's company. Harsh winters are simply a fact of life for those who dwell near the Canadian border.

Test Yourself

Directions: For items 1 and 2, read the entire passage carefully and then answer the questions. (Note: Intentional errors have been included in this passage.)

(1) Florida's citizens face many serious socio-economic problems that may leave the state with fewer resources in the twenty-first century. (2) Each day, individuals from across the globe descend upon Florida's large coastal cities—Miami, Tampa, Jacksonville—seeking work and a place to live. (3) First, Florida is the home to many immigrant populations. (4) They come with the promise of finding a new life in America, having been led to believe in their native lands that America is the land of richness and opportunity. (5) And although some find untold riches, many find only minimum-paying jobs and unaffordable housing. (6) Second, with this constant influx, Florida's eligible school population rises exponentially. (7) As more families arise, the demand for better and improved entertainment venues—from theme park to restaurants and rodeos—becomes ever more demanding. (8) Moreover, Florida, like elsewhere in the country, faces a growing teacher shortage that dramatically impacts the quality of the state's education program. (9) Finally, the gravest socio-economic problems facing Florida are its serious environmental problems that will threaten proper growth and development. (10) Burgeoning populations mean a greater drain on fewer natural resources and less suitable land upon which to grow. (11) For example, drying up swampland for irrigation of farmland and proper disposal of litter become a constant concern as Florida's population increases uncontrollably. (12) Thus, unless Florida's citizens and leaders come to terms on how best to deal with these serious socio-economic problems, Florida will soon find itself in a crisis for which there is no immediate solution.

1. Select the arrangement of sentences 1, 2, and 3 that provides the most logical sequence of ideas and supporting details in the paragraph. If no change is needed, select Choice A.

    A. Florida's citizens face many serious socio-economic problems that may leave the state with fewer resources in the twenty-first century. Each day, individuals from across the globe descend upon Florida's large coastal cities—Miami, Tampa, Jacksonville—seeking work and a place to live. First, Florida is the home to many immigrant populations.

    B. First, Florida is the home to many immigrant populations. Florida's citizens face many serious socio-economic problems that may leave the state with fewer resources in the twenty-first century. Each day, individuals from across the globe descend upon Florida's large coastal cities—Miami, Tampa, Jacksonville — seeking work and a place to live.

    C. Each day, individuals from across the globe descend upon Florida's large coastal cities—Miami, Tampa, Jacksonville—seeking work and a place to live. First, Florida is the home to many immigrant populations. Florida's citizens face many serious socio-economic problems that may leave the state with fewer resources in the twenty-first century.

    D. Florida's citizens face many serious socio-economic problems that may leave the state with fewer resources in the twenty-first century. First, Florida is the home to many immigrant populations. Each day, individuals from across the globe descend upon Florida's large coastal cities—Miami, Tampa, Jacksonville—seeking work and a place to live.

2. Which numbered sentence is LEAST relevant to the passage?

    A. sentence 7

    B. sentence 8

    C. sentence 9

    D. sentence 10

(1) A zoo is a place where animals—both wild and domesticated—arc shown in captivity. (2) In such a special place, animals can be given the kind of care and nurturing that is possible in less protected and more natural preserves. (3) Most zoos show animals of all kinds and types, but in recent years, a few zoos have become more specialized in their approach. (4) Known for its many family-fun animal shows, Sea World is a leading pioneer in marine life re-search, nurturing and saving many sea animals throughout the world. (5) For example, Sea World, not known formally as a zoo, is an attraction that is open to the public and pri-marily specializes in taking care of marine life. (6) In Canada, there is African Lion Safari in which visitors travel in their cars over a 50 acre reserve, where in excess of 1000 animals of over 100 species roam freely. (7) From the closeness of their vehicles, visitors see wild life up-close and personal. (8) And in Miami, Florida, one can find Parrot Jungle, a home for 1.100 tropical birds, all flying freely within the confines of the exhibit. (9) There, visitors can enjoy a leisurely lunch and listen to tourists complain about Miami's crowded beaches and roads. (10) Each of these specialized venues demonstrates how the concept of zoo has changed dramatically in the twentieth century.

3. Select the arrangement of sentences 4, 5, and 6 that provides the most logical sequence of ideas and supporting details in the paragraph. If no change is needed, select Choice A.

    A. Known for its many family-fun animal shows, Sea World is a leading pioneer in marine life research, nurturing and saving many sea animals throughout the world. For example, Sea World, not known formally as a zoo, is an attraction that is open to the public and primarily specializes in taking care of marine life. In Canada, there is African Lion Safari in which visitors travel in their cars over a 50 acre reserve, where in excess of 1,000 animals of over 100 species from freely.

    B. For example, Sea World, not known formally as a zoo, is an attraction that is open to the public and primarily specializes in taking care of marine life. Known for its many family-fun animal shows, Sea World is a leading pioneer in marine life research, nurturing and saving many sea animals throughout the world. In Canada, there is African Lion Safari in which visitors travel in their cars over a 50 acre reserve, where in excess of 1000 animals of over 100 species roam freely.

    C. In Canada, there is African Lion Safari in which visitors travel in their cars over a 50 acre reserve, where in excess of 1000 animals of over 100 species roam freely. For example, Sea World, not known formally as a zoo, is a leading pioneer in marine life research, nurturing and saving many sea animals throughout the world. Known for its many family-fun animals show, Sea World is a leading pioneer in marine life research, nurturing and saving many sea animals throughout the world.

    D. Known for its many family-fun animal shows, Sea World is a leading pioneer in marine life research, nurturing and saving many sea animals throughout the world. In Canada, there is African Lion Safari in which visitors travel in their cars over a 50 acre reserve, where in excess of 1000 animals of over 100 species roam freely. For example, Sea World, not known formally as a zoo, is an attraction that is open to the public and primarily specializes in taking care of marine life.

4. Which numbered sentence is LEAST relevant to the passage?

   A. sentence 1
   B. sentence 8
   C. sentence 9
   D. sentence 10

Answers to Test Yourself

1. **D.** For this paragraph, Choice **D** shows the arrangement of sentences 1, 2, and 3 that provides the most logical sequence of ideas and supporting details. Choices **A, B,** and **C** reflect an arrangement of sentences that are disconnected in thought and thus, are not logical choices.

2. **A.** In this paragraph, Choice **A** or sentence 7 is the sentence that is least relevant to this passage. The sentence about Florida's lack of entertainment venues does not make sense in a paragraph whose discussion is centered on Florida's ever-increasing socio-economic needs.

3. **B.** For this paragraph, Choice **B** shows the arrangement of sentences 4, 5, and 6 that provides the most logical sequence of ideas and supporting details. Choices **A, C,** and **D** reflect an arrangement of sentences that are disconnected in thought, and thus, are not logical choices.

4. **C.** In this paragraph, Choice **C** or sentence 9 is the sentence that is least relevant to the passage. The sentence about sitting at Parrot Jungle and eating a leisurely lunch and listening to tourists complain about Miami's crowded beaches and roads does not make sense in a paragraph whose discussion is centered on innovative venues to preserve wildlife animals.

Word Choice Skills

As listed in the *Competencies and Skills Required for Teacher Certification in Florida, Ninth Edition* (see the first section in this chapter for the Internet address), the English language competencies/skills you should master for this area are the following:

- Choose the appropriate word or expression in context.
- Recognize commonly confused or misused words or phrases.
- Recognize diction and tone appropriate to a given audience.

Choose the Appropriate Word or Expression in Context

Choosing the appropriate word or expression in context is essential to all good writing. When an inappropriate word or expression is chosen to complete a sentence, then the meaning of the sentence can be obstructed. Look at this example of a sentence with an inappropriate word choice.

Steven has the addiction of eating with his mouth open.

The sentence is poorly written because the word *addiction* is an inappropriate choice for this sentence. The way the sentence is written, it sounds like eating with your mouth open is a severe and debilitating ailment that requires medical and psychological help, which clearly is not the intent of the writer.

You can correct this confusion by revising the sentence like this:

Steven has the habit of eating with his mouth open.

Recognize Commonly Confused or Misused Words or Phrases

Often, writers include **commonly confused or misused words or phrases** in their writing. These are words that may sound appropriate because they are used frequently in everyday language and written text; however, the use of an inappropriate word or expression in a sentence can obstruct the meaning of the sentence. Find the commonly confused or misused word in this example.

> The mechanic will access the car's apparent engine trouble.

The sentence is poorly written because the word *access* is an inappropriate choice for this sentence. The writer meant to use the more appropriate word *assess*. The word *access* means the ability to enter or leave an area; the word *assess* means to be able to evaluate a problem or concern.

You can correct the confusion by revising the sentence like this:

> The mechanic will assess the car's apparent engine trouble.

Here is a list of some words or phrases that are commonly confused or misused.

accede—to agree with.

> *The lawyers will **accede** to the judge's request for more time for the defendant to prepare his case.*

concede—to yield, to compromise, or to grant, but not really agree

> *I **concede** that I lack the strength to become an Olympic runner, but I still intend to try.*

exceed—to be more than

> *Daily, my intake of vitamins **exceeds** the minimum daily requirement.*

access—to be available

> *The small crowd assembled at the Vatican was given **access** to see His Holiness, the Pope.*

excess—to have too much

> *Our monthly grocery bill is far in **excess** of the money we have allotted to spend.*

accept—to take or to receive

> *I will **accept** only a handful of people onto the varsity tennis team.*

except—to exclude (preposition)

> *They did not leave the house **except** to buy groceries, get the mail, and walk the dog.*

except—to leave out (verb)

> *Everyone was charged admission to the park, but the children were **excepted**.*

except—to object (verb)

> *The lawyer **excepted** to the judge's ruling that the witness be allowed to testify.*

adapt—to modify or to change

> *Most of my colleagues can **adapt** to sudden mood changes of our boss.*

adopt—to take on or to assume

> *The young couple decided to **adopt** a baby from China.*

adept—to be skillful or to have aptitude

> *The star athlete was **adept** at playing many sports, most notably football, hockey and baseball.*

affect—to influence

> *The cold wind and rain will **affect** your health.*

effect—to have an influence (noun)

> *The **effect** of the last hurricane is still felt among the residents of the badly damaged village.*

effect—to cause change or accomplish (verb).

*The unexpected blizzard **effected** a dramatic lack of activity at the ski resort; patrons wanted to ski, but were stuck inside for several days until it became safe to go out upon the slopes.*

all ready—to have everyone or everything together and prepared

*The students were **all ready** to take the examination when the teacher arrived.*

already—to have come before or to have happened previously

*The dancers had **already** been practicing their routines when their director entered the room.*

all right—to be acceptable or to be agreeable

*As long as you practice for an hour, going to the movies is **all right** with me.*

(alright is not a word; alright is always spelled as two words, **all right.)**

all together—to include everybody or everything

*At the end of the campfire, the two competing camp tribes sang the closing songs **all together**.*

altogether—to be totally inclusive

*Without a doubt, I was **altogether** confused by his sudden change of mood.*

all ways—to include every possible way imaginable

*To our chagrin, the laziest student was in **all ways** amenable to doing the least amount of school work.*

always—to happen at all times

*His sense of humor was **always** present when he was around a crowd of people.*

a lot—to include a large number

*There were **a lot** of people at tonight's ice-hockey game.*

(alot is not a word. It is always spelled as two words, **a lot.)**

among—refers to two or more people or things

*At the end of the day, the grandfather made sure that his hugs and kisses were evenly distributed **among** his four grandchildren.*

between—refers to only two people or things

*I had to decide **between** going to the movies or staying home and watching television; I stayed home.*

amount—refers to large quantities that cannot be counted by hand

*We had a large **amount** of grain stored in a bin to be used during the long winter months.*

number—refers to smaller quantities that can be counted by hand

*I counted the **number** of bags of candies, and they were approximately 36; one for each child present.*

as—refers to a similarity or the same extent; it is always followed by a adjective

*The film wasn't nearly **as** bad as you made it out to be*

like—to resemble something or to be similar to; it is <u>not</u> followed by a verb

*They quarrel so much that they are **like** an old-married couple.*

both—refers to two things considered together

***Both** of them were up for the high school honor award.*

each—refers to only one of two or more things.

*The wrestling coach made sure that **each** member of the team wrestled in the competition.*

can—to be physically able to complete a task

*The little boy **can** tie his shoes without his mother's help.*

may—to ask (or be given) permission to complete a task

*"**May** I leave my dessert and go out and play?" the young girl asked her grandmother.*

*"You **may** be seated," said the pastor to the congregation.*

capital—refers to the city, the town wherein resides the seat of government

*This vacation, we are visiting the old and beautiful town of Albany, the **capital** of New York.*

capitol—refers to the building; the building that houses the United States Congress

*All eyes were on the Washington **Capitol** as the nation awaited to hear the vote on the impending legislation.*

cease—to end or to bring to a conclusion

*Soon, the army will **cease** its fire and set camp for the night.*

seize—to take hold of or to capture

*In short order, the detectives will **seize** the unsuspecting man and bring him into the police station for questioning.*

cite—to summon to court; to quote; to mention in a citation

*The officer **cited** the suspect for breaking and entering.*

*Responsible writers **cite** the sources of their material.*

sight—to glimpse or view with the eyes or mind (or something glimpsed or viewed).

*The balloon rose higher and higher until it disappeared from **sight**.*

*Listening to Paul's defense of his actions caused Sheila to lose **sight** of her original complaint.*

site—the place where something is, was, or will be.

*Gettysburg National Military Park in southeastern Pennsylvania is the **site** of the Battle of Gettysburg.*

coarse—vulgar or unduly rude

*His **coarse** mannerisms were repulsive to the ladies sipping tea and waiting patiently in the garden.*

course—a path

*Looking straight ahead, the captain told his assistant to steer the ship on a **course** heading due North.*

course—prescribed studies

*After looking at the schedule, I have decided to take another geometry **course**.*

complement—to complete a part or to bring to perfection

*Your brand new black and white checked shirt **complements** your black Bermuda shorts.*

compliment—to praise or to show admiration for

*I paid my sister a **compliment** for the wonderful love and care she gives my new baby boy.*

desert—a dry arid piece of land

*The army heads to the **desert**, equipped with plenty of water, sunscreen, and dark glasses.*

desert—to abandon or to leave behind

*When we go to the mall, my mother always **deserts** us and heads right for the latest sales.*

dessert—the final course of a meal

*My favorite **dessert** is a strawberry ice-cream sundae, complete with real ice cream, whipped cream, and a cherry.*

disinterested—to be impartial or without judgment

*The bystander served as a **disinterested** witness to the accident.*

uninterested—to show no interest or fondness for

*Jack and Barbara are **uninterested** in anything Mary and Bill do or say.*

either . . . or—to be used when referring to choices

*"**Either** we go to the Grand Canyon **or** we explore the Rocky Mountains this summer," my father said emphatically. "We cannot do both."*

neither . . . nor—to be used when referring to two unacceptable choices

***Neither** you **nor** I have any real chance of winning the position of Student Council President.*

eligible—to be acceptable or chosen

*Lauren's winning ticket number makes her **eligible** to become the next recipient of an all-expense paid vacation to Hawaii.*

ineligible—to be unacceptable or not chosen

*Since she was under twelve, Marie was **ineligible** to ride on the high-speed roller coaster by herself.*

illegible—to be difficult or near impossible to read or understand

*The doctor's handwriting was **illegible** making it difficult for the pharmacist to read the prescription.*

emigrate—to leave one's native country for a new country

*Most of America's Jewish people **emigrated** from Eastern Europe prior to the start of World War II.*

immigrate—to enter and live in a new country

*In June, I will **immigrate** to South Africa to live with my uncle and aunt.*

elicit—to call forth or draw out

*My shocking red hair always **elicits** the strangest looks.*

illicit—to be not sanctioned by custom or law; to be unlawful

*What my brother does with my baby sister is **illicit;** he enables her to participate in underage drinking.*

fewer—refers to people and things that can be counted by hand

*There are **fewer** people on hand for the store's grand opening than were anticipated.*

less—refers to people and things that are usually considered in mass numbers

*I have **less** gas than I imagined.*

formally—to be considered in an official and dignified manner

*When we went to see the Justice of the Peace, my boyfriend was **formally** dressed.*

formerly—refers to an earlier time or position

***Formerly** a member of the United States Congress, my uncle now teaches at Harvard.*

if—introduces a conditional statement

***If** I exercise regularly, I will certainly lose weight.*

whether—refers to introducing a decision or choice

***Whether** you win or lose depends not on how hard you practice, but how lucky you prove to be.*

weather—refers to the general climate

*When we were in Arizona, the **weather** was hot but dry; there was little humidity.*

imply—to suggest, to hint, or to indicate indirectly

*By asking you about your hair color, I did not mean to **imply** that I thought you dyed it.*

infer—to deduce, to conclude, or to conclude from evidence

*"Are we to **infer** that you simply do not care about your schoolwork?" the desperate mother asked her tenth-grade son when he showed his parents his poor report card.*

incite—to provoke and to urge on

*"The politician's inflammatory language is sure to **incite** the crowd to riot," thought the policeman standing watch.*

insight—the ability to discern the true nature of something

*The news commentator had much **insight** into why the President was so reluctant to tell the nation the truth.*

peak—the highest part of anything

*Climbing to the **peak** of Mount Everest is considered to be a great feat of courage and determination.*

peek—to glance or look quickly, to look furtively from behind or through something.

*Toto gave Dorothy, the Scarecrow, the Tin Man, and the Lion more than just a **peek** at the so-called wizard.*

persecute—to torture or to make life horrible for someone

*We should not **persecute** people whose beliefs are different from ours.*

prosecute—to conduct a criminal investigation or to take legal action against someone

*After much deliberation, the district attorney decided to **prosecute** the accused for manslaughter.*

precede—to come before

*We will **precede** the marching bands and floats as we lead the Christmas parade down Main Street.*

proceed—to move on ahead

*After being given the proper verification, we will **proceed** with the experimentation of the new cancer drug.*

supersede—to replace or to take the place of

*It is more than likely that our initial discovery will **supersede** in knowledge and importance all our latest discoveries.*

principal—refers to the head or main leader of an organization; the first thing

*After school, the new **principal** was introduced to the anticipating faculty.*

principle—refers to a basic and fundamental truth, value or belief

*The **principle** belief of all major religions is to treat every individual with kindness and respect.*

respectably—acting in a decent and moral manner

*"When attending a formal function, you should dress **respectably**," admonished my socially conscious Mother.*

respectfully—marked by a proper manner

*Despite sitting in the cramped and crowded gym bleachers for over an hour, the students listened **respectfully** to the school assembly's guest speaker.*

respectively—refers to the order mentioned or designated

*The two teenage girls were called Jan and Jill **respectively**.*

their—is the possessive form; refers to belonging to a group of people

Their plane arrived late because of inclement weather.

there—is the directional; refers to a specific place

*I saw my many friends from school walk over **there** by the ice-cream store.*

they're—is the contraction; refers to the two words, "they are"

*After the movies, **they're** coming with us to the diner for dinner.*

then—is used to refer to time or consequence

*After holding up the convenience mart, John was **then** tried, found guilty, and incarcerated.*

*If this is true, **then** the man with the limp must be the murderer.*

than is used to compare or contrast things

*He is smarter **than** his younger brother.*

two—is the number 2

*To my surprise, the teacher had only **two** tickets left for the field trip to the ballet.*

to—is the directional word

*I went **to** the grocery store to buy my mother's favorite cookie.*

too—means more than or also

*When all was said and done, the young campers wanted to go hiking in the mountains, **too**.*

your—is the possessive form; refers to belonging to one person

*"I am sure **your** mother will not want you to sleep in the backyard without a sleeping bag," my best friend's mother said to me just before our sleepout.*

you're—is the contraction; refers to "you are."

*When **you're** ready, we will leave for the train station.*

Recognize Diction and Tone Appropriate to a Given Audience

In any given passage, the words you choose must be appropriate to the audience for which the passage is meant. Would you talk to police officers and attorneys the same way you would to a group of four-year-olds in a pre-school? **Recognizing diction and tone appropriate to a given audience** is essential to good writing. When diction or tone for a given sentence is inappropriate, the intent of the author's meaning can be unclear to the reader. Look at this example of a sentence that is inappropriate in its diction or tone.

As the new student body president, Michael addressed his high school teachers during the faculty meeting by shouting, "Hey, teachers! What's up?"

Clearly, Michael should not have addressed his high school teachers in such a loose and cavalier fashion (*"Hey, teachers! What's up?"*) Michael's teachers are not his friends or relatives.

You can correct this inappropriate diction and tone by revising the sentence like this:

As the new student body president, Michael addressed his high school teachers during the faculty meeting. "Good afternoon ladies and gentleman, I, as the new student body president, would like to tell you. . . ."

Test Yourself

For questions 1-3, choose the most appropriate word to complete the sentence.

1. After the football game, the players on the losing team _____ their mistakes and discussed how they could improve their game.

   A. reviewed
   B. reminded
   C. received
   D. relished

2. With seconds left, the frightened family _____ quickly into the shelter, hoping to escape the path of the oncoming storm.

   A. ambled
   B. sauntered
   C. scurried
   D. meandered

3. Filled with trepidation, the little child stepped _____ onto the waiting roller coaster ride.

   A. eagerly
   B. hurriedly
   C. gingerly
   D. willingly

For questions 4 -13, choose the option that corrects an error in an underlined portion. If no error exists, choose "No change is necessary."

4. The <u>principle</u> talked to <u>everyone,</u> <u>except</u> the
   [A]   [B]   [C]
   misbehaving boys' parents.

   A. principal
   B. every one
   C. accept
   D. No change is necessary

5. "Either <u>you</u> <u>go</u> to school <u>nor</u> stay home," said the
   [A] [B]   [C]
   child's father.

   A. you're
   B. goes
   C. or
   D. No change is necessary

6. After <u>their</u> school day, the talented young boys
   [A]
   <u>took</u> an extra <u>coarse</u> in math.
   [B]   [C]

   A. they're
   B. have taken
   C. course
   D. No change is necessary

7. Upon finishing their <u>dessert</u>, the two lovers
   [A]
   <u>preceded</u> to walk home, enjoying the cool
   [B]
   <u>weather.</u>
   [C]

   A. desert
   B. proceeded
   C. whether
   D. No change is necessary

8. <u>Their</u> <u>insights</u> about the upcoming elections
   [A]   [B]
   <u>were</u> most appreciated by the graduate students
   [C]
   in political science.

   A. They're
   B. incites
   C. was
   D. No change is necessary

9. <u>Your</u> brother is more helpful <u>then</u> everyone
   [A]   [B]
   <u>all together.</u>
   [C]

   A. Your'e
   B. than
   C. altogether
   D. No change is necessary

10. Only thirteen years old, he <u>is</u> <u>ineligible</u> <u>to</u> play
                            [A] [B]   [C]
    varsity baseball.

    A. are
    B. uneligible
    C. too
    D. No change is necessary

11. Despite the great <u>weather</u>, we were <u>disinterested</u>
              [A]   [B]

in sitting <u>among</u> the team players and watching
      [C]

the game.

- **A.** whether
- **B.** uninterested
- **C.** between
- **D.** No change is necessary

12. All afternoon, everyone <u>except</u> <u>Mother</u>
                      [A]   [B]

<u>complemented</u> me on my new dress.
   [C]

- **A.** accept
- **B.** mother
- **C.** complimented
- **D.** No change is necessary

13. <u>We'll</u> need to decide <u>among</u> two places <u>to</u> visit.
    [A]   [B]   [C]

- **A.** Will
- **B.** between
- **C.** too
- **D.** No change is necessary

For question 14, choose the most appropriate option to answer the question.

14. Angelo, president of the student debate team, is speaking to his community's civic club about the need for the debate team to raise money for their trip to participate in the national debate championship. Choose the most appropriate opening statement.

- **A.** My friends and fellow citizens, please attend to the following observations as I proceed to enumerate the many substantial reasons that you should choose to sponsor the illustrious debate team's winning journey.
- **B.** As you are well aware, the high school debate team plays a vital role in helping students understand today's social issues.
- **C.** Hey, have you noticed? The debate team has no money.
- **D.** The debate is lots of fun. Would you be willing to give us some money so we can go to the championship game?

Answers to Test Yourself

1. A. In this sentence, the missing word is *reviewed* (Choice A), meaning to evaluate or assess, as in "the losing team reviewed their mistakes." Choices **B, C,** and **D** are not logical selections, given the context of this sentence. Choice **B** is the word *reminded,* and you would not write "the losing team reminded their mistakes. Choice **C** is the word *received,* and although you might write "the losing team received their mistakes," it is not the most logical choice. Choice **D** is the word *relished,* meaning "to enjoy." Clearly, a losing team would not enjoy reviewing their mistakes.

2. C. In this sentence, the missing word is *scurried* (Choice C), meaning to dash or rush as in "the frightened family scurried into the shelter." Choices **A, B** and **D** are not logical selections, given the context of this sentence. Choice **A,** *ambled,* means to stroll or wander, and you would not write "the frightened family ambled into the shelter." Choice **B,** *sauntered,* means to amble or walk, and you would not write "the frightened family sauntered into the shelter." Choice **D,** *meandered,* means to ramble or roam, and you would not write "the frightened family meandered into the shelter." Clearly, a frightened family would scurry in the face of an impending storm.

3. C. In this sentence, the missing word is *gingerly* (Choice C), meaning cautiously or tentatively, as in "the little girl stepped gingerly onto the roller coaster." Choices **A, B** and **D** are not logical selections, given the context of this sentence. Choice **A,** *eagerly,* implies enthusiastically and you would not write "Filled with trepidation (or fear), the little girl stepped enthusiastically onto the roller coaster." Choice **B,** *hurriedly,* implies quickly and you would not write "Filled with trepidation, the little girl stepped hurriedly onto the roller coaster." Choice **B,** *willingly,* implies without hesitation, and again, you would not write "Filled with trepidation, the little girl stepped willingly onto the roller coaster." Clearly, the word *gingerly* is the most logical choice to demonstrate the little girl's fear.

4. A. In this sentence, the word *principle* (Choice **A**) should be replaced with the word *principal*. The word *principle* means a standard or a belief, whereas the word *principal* means a school administrator. In Choice **B,** the word *everyone* is used as a pronoun, and thus, is spelled correctly. In Choice **C,** the word *except*, meaning *to leave out*, is used correctly.

5. C. In this sentence, the word *nor* (Choice **C**) should be replaced with word *or. Either. . . or* is used when referring to choices; *Neither. . . nor* is used when referring to negative choices. In Choice **A,** the pronoun *you* is used correctly. In Choice **B,** the correct form of the verb *to go* is used correctly.

6. C. In this sentence, the word *coarse* (Choice **C**) should be replaced with the word *course*. The word *coarse* is an adjective meaning rough or abrasive. The word *course*, though, is a noun of which one of its meanings is a lesson or a class. In Choice **A,** the word *their*, meaning to indicate possession, is used correctly. In Choice **B,** the word *took*, the correct verb form of the word *taken*, is used correctly.

7. B. In this sentence, the word *preceded* (Choice **B**) should be replaced with the word *proceeded*. The word *preceded* means *to come before,* whereas, the word *proceeded* means *to go ahead*. In Choice **A,** the word *dessert*, meaning a sweet dish served after a meal, is used correctly. In Choice **C,** the word *weather* is used correctly.

8. D. In this sentence, no changes are necessary. Choices **A, B,** and **C** are used correctly.

9. B. In this sentence, the word *then* (Choice **B**) should be replaced with the word *than*. The word *then* refers to *time or consequences*; the word *than* refers to *comparing and/or contrasting things*. In Choice **A,** the word *your*, the possessive form of *you*, is used correctly. In Choice **C,** the word *all together*, meaning everybody or everything, is used correctly.

10. D. In this sentence, no changes are necessary. Choices **A, B,** and **C** are used correctly.

11. B. In this sentence, the word *disinterested* (Choice **B**) should be replaced with *uninterested*. The word *disinterested* means *impartial*; the word *uninterested* means *not interested*. In Choice **A,** the word *weather* is used correctly. In Choice **C,** the word *among*, a word used when referring to more than two people or things, is used correctly.

12. C. In this sentence, the word *complemented* (Choice **C**) should be replaced with the word *complimented*. The word *complemented* means *a completing or finishing part*. The word *compliment* means *an expression of admiration*. In Choice **A,** the word *except*, meaning *excluding*, is used correctly. In Choice **B,** the word *Mother* is used correctly because the name refers to a specific person in the family.

13. B. In this sentence, the word *among* (Choice **B**) should be replaced with the word *between*. The word *among* is used when referring *to more than two people or things*; the word *between* is used when referring to *only two people or things*. In Choice **A,** the word *We'll*, the contraction of *we will*, is used correctly. In Choice **C,** the word *to,* meaning *in the direction of*, is used correctly.

14. B. In this question, the most appropriate opening statement is Choice **B.** The high school student speaks in a reasonable voice and tone. Choice **A** reflects a ponderous and obsequious tone of voice. Choice **C** is much too casual for a high school student speaking to their school faculty. Choice **D** is not as casual as Choice **C,** but still seems to lack the dignity and respect that a student should demonstrate to a high school faculty.

Sentence Structure Skills

As listed in the *Competencies and Skills Required for Teacher Certification in Florida, Ninth Edition* (see earlier in this chapter for Internet address), the English language competencies/skills you should be able to do for this area are the following:

- Recognize misplaced modifiers.
- Recognize faulty parallelism.
- Recognize fragments and run-on sentences.

What Are Misplaced Modifiers?

A **modifier** is a word or group of words that convey information about another word or word group. To avoid confusion, modifiers should be placed close to the word or words they modify. A modifier is a **misplaced modifier** when it is placed in the sentence in such a way that the intent of the writer is unclear to the reader. Look at this example of a misplaced modifier.

> The photographer saw several black bears driving through the woods.

This sentence is confusing because the modifier (*driving through the woods*) is not close to the word it modifiers (*photographer*). The way the sentence is written, it sounds like the bears are driving through the woods, which clearly is not the intent of the writer.

You can correct the confusion by revising the sentence like this:

> Driving through the woods, the photographer saw several black bears.

What Is Faulty Parallelism?

The ideas in sentences should be **parallel**. This means they should be expressed in the same way. For instance, you might write, "I like sunbathing, but I don't like swimming." Your ideas on sunbathing and swimming are expressed using the same type of grammatical construction: in this case, a gerund, the –ing verb form used as a noun. **Faulty parallelism** occurs when the ideas in a sentence are not parallel. The result is an awkward construction, the meaning of which is often unclear. Look at this example of faulty parallelism.

> My son's chores consist of putting the dishes in the dishwasher at night, taking out the trash every day, and to mow the lawn once a week.

This sentence sounds awkward because the ideas are not expressed in the same way. The words *putting, taking*, and *to mow* do not have the same grammatical construction. You can correct the problem by revising the sentence like this:

> My son's chores consist of putting the dishes in the dishwasher at night, taking out the trash every day, and mowing the lawn once a week.

What Are Fragments and Run-On Sentences?

A **clause** is a group of words that contains a subject and a verb. An **independent or main clause** can stand alone as a sentence. A **dependent clause** begins with a subordinating conjunction (e.g., *because, if, when*, etc.) or a relative pronoun (e.g., *who, whom, that*, etc.) and can *never* stand alone.

A **simple sentence** is an example of an independent clause. It has a subject and a verb and expresses a complete thought. Look at this example.

> My favorite subject is history.

A **fragment** is a group of words that looks like a sentence, but does not express a complete thought. A fragment is missing something. Sometimes it is missing a subject. Look at this fragment.

> Didn't run fast enough.

This fragment needs a subject. Who or what didn't run fast enough? To make this fragment into a sentence, you can add a subject.

> Jamie didn't run fast enough.

Sometimes a fragment is missing a verb. Look at this fragment.

> Hundreds of screaming fans.

This fragment needs a verb. What did the hundreds of screaming fans do? To make this fragment into a sentence, you can add a verb.

> Hundreds of screaming fans rushed through the gates.

Sometimes a fragment has a subject and a verb, but it still does not express a complete thought. This often occurs when the fragment is a subordinate clause. Look at this fragment.

> Because I've always liked reading about real events.

To make this fragment into a sentence, you can add a main clause.

> My favorite subject is history because I've always liked reading about real events.

> Because I've always like reading about real events, my favorite subject is history.

A **run-on sentence** is two independent clauses joined without a proper punctuation mark or word to separate them. Look at this run-on sentence.

> Your first test in geometry is tomorrow you'd better study.

A run-on sentence in which the two sentences are joined (spliced) *only* with a comma is called a **comma splice.** Look at this comma splice.

> The test was very hard to finish in the time allotted, it had too many questions on it.

Run-on sentences and comma splices can usually be corrected in one of three ways:

1. Insert a period or a semicolon between the two independent clauses.
   > Your first test in geometry is tomorrow. You'd better study.
   > The test was very hard to finish in the time allotted; it had too many questions on it.
2. Insert a comma and a connector word (e.g., *and, but, or, so,* etc.) between the two independent clauses.
   > Your first test in geometry is tomorrow, so you'd better study.
3. Make one clause subordinate to the other.
   > The test was very hard to finish in the time allotted because it had too many questions on it.

Test Yourself

Directions: For questions 1-2, choose the most appropriate word to complete the sentence.

1. My daughter's homework assignment in English consists of writing her spelling words, memorizing her vocabulary word definitions, and _____ her favorite things to do.

   A. to list
   B. must list
   C. listing

2. My children like to help out at <u>home</u> <u>by</u> washing clothes and occasionally _____ dinner.

   A. cook
   B. cooking
   C. to cook

3. Choose the sentence in which the modifiers are placed correctly.

   A. Drifting down the river in a raft, the girls spotted a deer feeding her young fawn.
   B. Feeding her young fawn, the girls spotted a deer drifting down the river in a raft.
   C. The girls spotted a deer feeding her young fawn drifting down the river in a raft.

4. Choose the option that is punctuated correctly.

   A. Of course, you should take your allergy medicine, your doctor told you that it would relieve your symptoms.
   B. Of course, you should take your allergy medicine your doctor told you that it would relieve your symptoms.
   C. Of course, you should take your allergy medicine. Your doctor told you that it would relieve your symptoms.
   D. Of course you should take your allergy medicine your doctor told you that it would relieve your symptoms.

Answer Explanations for Test Yourself

1. C. In this sentence the missing word is in parallel with the words *writing* and *memorizing*, so it needs to have the same grammatical construction. The correct form is *listing* (Choice **C**). Choices **A** and **B** result in faulty parallelism.

2. B. In this sentence the missing word is in parallel with the word *washing*, so it needs to have the same grammatical construction. The correct form is *cooking* (Choice **B**). Choices **A** and **C** result in faulty parallelism.

3. A. The modifiers in sentence **A** are placed correctly. The participial phrase *drifting down the river in a raft* modifies *girls* and should be close to it. In choices **B** and **C**, *drifting down the river in a raft* is separated from the noun *girls* resulting in ambiguity. Additionally, the participial phrase *feeding her young fawn* modifies the noun *deer* and should be close to it. In Choice **B** the participial phrase *feeding her young fawn* is separated from the noun *deer,* resulting in ambiguity.

4. C. All punctuation in sentence **C** is correct. Choice **A** is incorrect because it is a run-on sentence. It is two complete sentences connected by only a comma. Choices **B** and **D** are also run-on sentences. Each of these sentences is two complete sentences joined without a word to connect them or a proper punctuation mark to separate them. Further, in Choice **D** a comma is needed to set off the introductory element *of course.*

Grammar, Spelling, Capitalization, and Punctuation Skills

As listed in the *Competencies and Skills Required for Teacher Certification in Florida, Ninth Edition* (see earlier in this chapter for Internet address), the English language competencies/skills you should be able to do for this area are the following:

- Recognize subject-verb agreement.
- Recognize standard verb tenses.
- Recognize faulty tense shifts.
- Recognize pronoun-antecedent agreement.
- Recognize faulty pronoun shifts.
- Recognize clear pronoun references.
- Recognize proper pronoun case forms.
- Recognize the correct use of adjectives and adverbs.
- Recognize appropriate comparative and superlative degree forms of adjectives and adverbs.
- Recognize standard spelling.
- Recognize standard punctuation.
- Recognize standard capitalization.

What Is Subject-Verb Agreement?

Subject-verb agreement means a singular subject must have a singular verb and a plural subject must have a plural verb. If the subject is singular, the verb will end in *–s* or *–es* (*the dog barks, the bird flies*). If the subject is plural, the verb will <u>not</u> have an *–s* or *–es* ending (*the dogs bark, the birds fly*).

Errors in subject-verb agreement may occur when other words in the sentence separate the subject and verb. Look at this example of an error in subject-verb agreement.

> A chorus of cheers were heard from the crowd.

The verb must agree with its singular noun subject *chorus*, not the plural word *cheers*. Change *were* to *was* to make the sentence grammatically correct.

> A chorus of cheers was heard from the crowd.

To help with recognizing errors in subject-verb agreement, read the sentence without the intervening words. Try this example.

> The president of the club, as well as the other officers, feel that the membership dues need to be raised.

The subject of the verb is *president.* Does *The president . . . feel* sound correct to you? Change *feel* to *feels* to make the sentence grammatically correct.

> The president of the club, as well as the other officers, feels that the membership dues need to be raised.
> It should be noted that if the sentence began with "The president and the other officers of the club. . . ," the verb would be *feel.*

> The president and the other officers of the club feel that the membership dues need to be raised.

> The reason for using the word *feel* in this example is that "the president and the other officers of the club" is regarded as a plural subject and thus requires a plural verb to complete the sentence.

When two or more subjects are joined by the words *or* or *nor*, the verb agrees with the noun that is closest to the verb. Look at these examples.

> The woman's children or her husband has the videotape of the event.

> Neither the teacher nor the students care that the bell has rung.

Most indefinite pronouns (e.g., *each, everyone, everybody*) take singular verbs. Look at this example.

> Everybody needs to bring a sack lunch to the picnic.

For further clarification, see the section on pronoun-antecedent agreement.

What Do You Need to Know About Verb Tenses?

Verbs have different forms called **tenses**. The tense of a verb in a sentence tells you when the action of the verb takes place. The verb tenses you will need to know for the FTCE GK test are the **simple tenses** and the **perfect tenses.**

The simple tenses are the **present tense** (*I work, he writes*), the **past tense** (*I worked, he wrote*), and the **future tense** (*I will work, he will write*).

The perfect tenses use a form of the helping verb *to have* in their construction. The perfect tenses are the **present perfect** (*I have worked, he has written*), which indicates a past action that is ongoing, the **past perfect** (*I had worked, he had written*), which indicates a past action that occurred before a previous past action, and the **future perfect** (*I will have worked, he will have written*), which indicates a past action that will occur before a future action.

Principal Parts

All six tenses of a verb are formed using its three **principal parts:** the **infinitive** (to work), the past (worked), and the past participle (worked). For **regular verbs,** the past and past participle are formed by adding *–ed*. Some verbs do not form their past and past participle this way. These verbs are called **irregular verbs.** Table 3.1 lists the principal parts of 27 frequently used irregular verbs that you should memorize in preparation for the FTCE GK test.

Table 3.1: Principal Parts of 27 Frequently Used Irregular Verbs								
Infinitive	to begin	to break	to bring	to catch	to choose	to come	to do	to drink	to drive
Past	began	broke	brought	caught	chose	came	did	drank	drove
Past participle	begun	broken	brought	caught	chosen	come	done	drunk	driven
Infinitive	to eat	to fall	to get	to give	to go	to grow	to know	to lose	to ride
Past	ate	fell	got	gave	went	grew	knew	lost	rode
Past participle	eaten	fallen	gotten	given	gone	grown	known	lost	ridden
Infinitive	to rise	to run	to see	to sing	to speak	to swim	to take	throw	to write
Past	rose	ran	saw	sang	spoke	swam	took	threw	wrote
Past participle	risen	run	seen	sung	spoken	swum	taken	thrown	written

Faulty Tense Shifts

Sometimes a writer will start a sentence with one tense and shift to another tense for no logical reason. This is called a **faulty tense shift.** Look at this example of a faulty tense shift.

> My fearless sister walks up to the tiger and quickly took a picture.

This sentence starts off in the present tense, but then shifts to the past tense for no reason. This shifting of tenses is distracting and confusing to the reader. Revise the sentence by using the same tense for both verbs:

> My fearless sister walked up to the tiger and quickly took a picture.

What Do You Need to Know About Pronouns?

A **pronoun** stands for or refers to a person, place or thing whose identity is made clear earlier in the text. For example, when you read

> *They* **say** that chewing gum is bad for **your** teeth.

They is a pronoun referring to someone, but the reader does not know who. In this example, the writer *might* mean "a group of dentists."

Types of Pronouns

The types of pronouns you need to know for the FCTE GK Test are

- personal
- demonstrative
- indefinite
- relative
- reflexive
- intensive
- interrogative
- reciprocal

A **personal pronoun** is a specific person or thing and changes its form to indicate person, number, gender and case. There are three kinds of personal pronouns. They are *subjective*, *objective* and *possessive*:

A **subjective personal pronoun** indicates the pronoun is acting as the subject of the sentence. Subjective personal pronouns are *I, you, he, she, he, it, we, you,* and *they*.

An **objective personal pronoun** indicates that the pronoun is acting as the object of a verb, compound verb, preposition, or infinitive phrase. Objective personal pronouns are *me, you. her, him, it, us, you,* and *them*.

A **possessive personal pronoun** indicates that the pronoun belongs to someone and defines who owns it. Possessive personal pronouns are *mine, yours, his, hers, its, ours,* and *theirs*.

A **demonstrative pronoun** points to and identifies a noun or a pronoun. Demonstrative pronouns are *this, these, that,* and *those*.

An **interrogative pronoun** is a pronoun used to ask a question. The interrogative pronouns are *who, whom, which, what,* and the compounds formed with the suffix *ever.* They are *whatever, whomever, whichever,* and *whatever*.

An **indefinite pronoun** refers to an identifiable but not specified person or thing. The most common indefinite pronouns are *all, another, any, anybody, anyone, anything, each, everybody, everything, few, many, nobody, none, one, several, some, somebody,* and *someone*.

A **relative pronoun** links one phrase or clause to another phrase or clause. The relative pronouns are *who, whom, that,* and *which,* and their respective compounds: *whoever, whomever,* and *whichever.*

A **reflexive pronoun** refers back to the subject of the clause of the sentence. The reflexive pronouns are *myself, yourself, himself, herself, itself, ourselves, yourselves,* and *themselves.*

An **intensive pronoun** is a word used to refer to its *antecedent* or the word that comes before the pronoun.

For example,

> The president himself said he would sign the bill into law. (*Himself* is an intensive pronoun that refers to the president.)

Intensive pronouns are identical in form to reflexive pronouns.

A **reciprocal pronoun** expresses a mutual feeling or relationship between the individuals indicated in the plural subject. Reciprocal pronouns are *each other* and *one another.*

Pronoun-Antecedent Agreement

A pronoun must agree with its antecedent, the noun it replaces. If the antecedent is singular, the pronoun must be singular. If the antecedent is plural, the pronoun must be plural.

Errors in pronoun-antecedent agreement make it difficult for the reader to understand what the writer means. Look at this example.

> A woman who works hard to achieve success may find they are not accepted as equals in certain situations.

The pronoun *they* does not agree with its singular antecedent, *woman.* Change *they are* to *she is* to make the sentence grammatically correct. Also change *equals* to *an equal.*

Most indefinite pronoun antecedents (e.g., *each, everyone, everybody*) take singular pronouns. Look at this example.

> Each of the girls needs to obtain her parents' permission to go on the trip.

For further clarification, see the section on subject-verb agreement.

Pronoun Reference

When a writer uses a pronoun, it should be clear to the reader what the antecedent for the pronoun is. When it is unclear, the reader may find the sentence ambiguous. Look at this example.

> My mother removed the roses from the two vases and threw them in the trash.

What did the mother throw in the trash? the *roses* or the *vases*? The pronoun *they* does not have a clear reference. You can revise the sentence like this:

> My mother removed the roses from the two vases and threw the flowers in the trash.

Pronoun Shifts

The **person** form tells you whether the pronoun is the speaker (**first person**—*I talk; we talk*), the person spoken to (**second person**—*you talk*), or the person spoken about (**third person**—*he, she, it talks; they talk*).

Pronouns should have the same person as their antecedents in a sentence. When a writer fails to do this, the resulting faulty construction is called a **pronoun shift.** Look at this example of a pronoun shift.

> If one studies hard for the test, you will make a good grade.

The sentence goes from third person (*one*) to the second person (*you*). You can revise the sentence like this:

> If you study hard, you will make a good grade.

Pronoun Case

Case shows the function of a pronoun in a sentence. The form the pronoun takes tells you whether the pronoun is a subject (**subjective case**—I, you, he, she, it, we, they, who, whoever), an object (**objective case**—me, you, him, her, it, us, them, whom, whomever), or shows ownership (**possessive case**—my, mine, yours, her, hers, its, our, ours, your, yours, their, theirs, whose).

Use the subjective case when the pronoun is the subject of a verb or has an antecedent that is the subject of a verb. Look at these examples.

> My husband and I often travel abroad.

The pronoun *I* is in the subjective case because it is part of the subject of the verb *travel*.

> The coach gave tickets to whoever arrived first.

The relative pronoun *whoever* is in the subjective case because it is the subject of the verb *arrived*.

Use the objective case when the pronoun is the object of a verb or a verbal (a verb form used as a noun, adjective, or adverb), the object of a preposition, or the subject of an infinitive. Look at these examples.

> Ask whomever you want.

The relative pronoun *whomever* is in the objective case because it is the object of the verb *want*.

> I hope there will be no secrets between you and me.

The pronoun *me* is in the objective case because it is the object of the preposition *between*.

> I could not believe that the committee invited her to serve as master of ceremonies at the banquet.

The pronoun *her* is in the objective case because it is the subject of the infinitive *to serve*.

Use the possessive case when the pronoun shows ownership or if it precedes a gerund (the –ing form of a verb used as noun). Look at these examples.

> Her jewelry is exquisite.

The pronoun *her* is in the possessive case because it shows ownership of the noun *jewelry*.

> His interrupting every few minutes is becoming annoying.

The pronoun *his* is in the possessive case because it precedes the gerund *interrupting*.

What Do You Need to Know About Adjectives and Adverbs?

Adjectives and adverbs are modifiers that describe things or actions in a sentence. **Adjectives** modify nouns or pronouns. **Adverbs** modify verbs, adjectives, or other adverbs.

Correct Usage

To decide whether a word used as a modifier is an adjective or an adverb, ask yourself what word the modifier describes. If it describes a noun or pronoun, it is an adjective. If it describes a verb, adjective, or other adverb, it is an adverb. Look at these examples.

> The <u>rotten</u> fruit smells <u>bad</u>.

In this sentence the word *rotten* describes the noun *fruit,* so *rotten* is an adjective. The word *bad* following the verb *smells* also tells you something about the noun *fruit*—that it has a bad odor. Therefore, the word *bad* is an adjective describing the noun *fruit.*

The racer drove <u>slowly</u> as he passed the accident on the track.

In this sentence the word *slowly* following the verb *drove* tells how the racer drove, so slowly is an adverb describing the verb *drove.*

On the FTCE GK test, you will need to recognize incorrect use of adjectives or adverbs. Be wary when the verb in the sentence is based on one of your senses (*feel, taste, smell, look, sound*) or is a form of the verb *to be.* Usually, adjectives should follow such verbs. Here are examples of incorrect constructions.

I feel <u>badly</u> that I missed your graduation from college.

The modifier after the verb *feel* describes the pronoun *I,* so it should be an adjective, not an adverb. Replace *badly* with *bad* to make the sentence grammatically correct.

I feel bad that I missed your graduation from college.

The residents are somewhat <u>angrily</u> that teenagers speed through their neighborhood.

The modifier after the verb *are* describes the noun *residents,* so it should be an adjective, not an adverb. Replace *angrily* with *angry* to make the sentence grammatically correct.

The residents are somewhat <u>angry</u> that teenagers speed through their neighborhood.

Appropriate Comparative and Superlative Degree Forms

When you compare two things, you either add *–er* to the modifier or precede the modifier with the word *more* or *less.* The resulting grammatical construction is called the *comparative* form of the adjective or adverb. When you compare more than two things, you either add *–est* to the modifier or precede the modifier with the word *most* or *least.* The resulting grammatical construction is called the *superlative* form of the adjective or adverb.

Use *–er* to form the comparative and *–est* to form the superlative of most one-syllable adjective and adverbs. For most two-syllable adjectives and adverbs, you can use either *–er* and *–est,* or *more* and *most,* or *less* and *least.* With all adjectives and adverbs of three or more syllables, use *more* and *most* or *less* and *least.* Look at these examples.

The boy on the left is taller than the boy on the right, but the boy in the middle is the tallest of all three.

The lab assistant poured the liquid more (or less) carefully the second time than he did the first time.

Tip: You'll often find the word *than* used with an adjective or adverb to form the comparative. *The cheetah ran faster than the antelope. Peggy's bookbag is larger than Alicia's.*

If an adverb ends in *–ly,* change the *-y* to *-i* when using the *–er* or *–est* ending. Look at this example.

Sam is lucky, but Kendra is luckier than he.

Some common adjectives and adverbs have irregular forms (*good/well, better, the best*; *bad/badly, worse, the worst*). Look at these examples.

Kim submitted a good essay, but Juan's was better because it was more interesting. When your essay is due, you should try to write the best one of all.

My favorite driver drove badly in the race last week. This week he drove worse than before. Frankly, I think he drove the worst of all the drivers in the race.

You should avoid redundant constructions like *more better, most easiest*, and so on.

The room temperature is better (not *more better*) after you lowered the thermostat.

That was the easiest (not *most easiest*) exam I have ever taken.

Tip: For some adjectives and adverbs, such as *unique, universal, perfect*, and so on, it is illogical to form comparative and superlative forms. These words are absolute in their meaning, so constructions like *more unique* or *most unique*, for example, should be avoided.

What Do You Need to Know About Spelling, Punctuation, and Capitalization?

Standard English has many rules for spelling, punctuation, and capitalization. This CliffsTestPrep describes the basic rules that should prove most helpful on the FTCE GK test.

Spelling

Memorize the following rules:

- When you know a word contains *ie* or *ei*, recall the following rhyme:

  I before *e*, except after *c*,

  Or when sounding like "*ay*" as in *neighbor* and *weigh*.

  Look at these examples.

i before *e*	comes after *c*	Sounds like "*ay*"
Believe	Receive	Eight

- When a word ends in silent *–e*, drop the *–e* before adding an ending that begins with a vowel. Keep the final *–e* if the ending begins with a consonant or to prevent mispronunciation. Look at these examples.

ending begins with a vowel	ending begins with a consonant	mispronunciation may occur
care + -ing = caring	care + -ful = careful	notice + -able = noticeable

- When a word ends in *–y* preceded by a consonant, change *–y* to *–i* before adding an ending. Keep the *–y* if it is preceded by a vowel, the ending is *–ing*, or the word is a proper name. Look at these examples.

-y preceded by a consonant	-y preceded by a vowel	ending is *–ing*	proper noun
happy + -ly = happily	day + -s = days	study + -ing = studying	Murphy + -s = Murphys

- When adding a prefix (*mis-, dis-*), do not add to or drop a letter from the original word. For instance, *mis-* + *spell* = *misspell*.
- Check how the word is used in the sentence when it has a *homonym*, a word that sounds like it, but is spelled differently. Look at this example of a spelling error caused by homonym confusion.

  The students displayed there projects at the science fair.

In this sentence the word preceding the noun *project* should be a possessive pronoun referring back to the antecedent *students*. Change *there* to *their* to make the sentence grammatically correct.

The students displayed their projects at the science fair.

- Avoid faulty pronunciation that can lead to misspelling. For instance, mathematics has an *e* that you might omit in the spelling if you say *math mat ics* instead of *math e mat ics*.

Punctuation

You use end punctuation to show when a sentence ends. Depending on the type of sentence, end punctuation might be a period, a question mark, or an exclamation point.

- Use a period at the end of a statement. Example: *I love to read.*
- Use a question mark at the end of a question. Example: *Is this your book?*
- Use an exclamation point after an emphatic statement. Example: *That is an exciting idea!*

You use commas to indicate pauses and to prevent confusion.

- Use commas to separate three or more words or phrases in a series. Example: *I will need scissors, paper, and glue.*
- Use a comma to separate a date from its year. Example: *He was born on August 7, 1976.*
- Use a comma to separate a date and year from the rest of the sentence. Example: *Our family reunion on July 4, 2005, was a memorable one.*
- Use a comma to separate a city and its state from the rest of the sentence. Example: We were living in Austin, Texas, before we moved to Florida.
- Use a comma to set off most introductory elements. Example: *Fortunately, I was allowed to use a calculator when I took the mathematics portion of the test.*
- Use a comma to separate two main clauses joined by a connector word (*and, or, but, so, for, nor, yet*). Example: *I broke my watch, so I couldn't tell what time it was.*
- Use a comma to set off an introductory subordinate clause: Example: *When I'm working on a project, I find it hard to stop to eat.*
- Use a comma to set off an introductory participial phrase. Example: *Driving through the park, I saw several squirrels gathering nuts.*
- Use commas to separate nonrestrictive elements from the rest of the sentence. Nonrestrictive elements are elements that are not essential to the meaning of the sentence. Example: *My neighbor, who is a mathematics professor, often chats with me in the front yard.*
- Use a comma to set off a direct quotation. Example: *"I wish you wouldn't do that," she pleaded.*

Semicolons are used in two main ways.

- Use a semicolon between two independent clauses when no connector word is used. Example: *I broke my watch; I couldn't tell what time it was.*
- Use semicolons to separate three or more items in a series that already contains commas. Example: *We have lived in Chicago, Illinois; Austin, Texas; and Tampa, Florida.*

Colons are used in three main ways.

- Use a colon to alert the reader to pay attention to something that follows. Example: *The number 13 has only two factors: 1 and 13.*
- Use a colon to punctuate time. Example: *We will leave at 12:15 p.m.*
- Use a colon in the salutation of a business letter. Example: *Dear Committee Members:*

Apostrophes are used in three main ways.

- Use an apostrophe to stand in for a missing letter or letters in a contraction: Example: *You shouldn't worry.*
- Use an apostrophe to show possession. Add *–'s* to singular nouns or indefinite pronouns and to plural nouns that do not end in *–s*. Add *–'s* to singular nouns ending in *–s*. Add only an apostrophe to plural nouns ending in *–s*. Look at these examples.

Singular noun or indefinite pronoun	Plural noun not ending in –s	Plural noun ending in –s
the car's motor, everyone's name, James's father	*the children's mother*	*the dogs' collars*

- Use *–'s* to form the plural of words, letters, and numbers used as words. Example: *How many s's are in that word?*

Quotation marks are used to show the exact words of a speaker and to set off certain titles (e.g., song titles). Place commas and periods within quotation marks. Place other punctuation within the quotation marks only when the punctuation is part of the quotation. Look at these examples.

Commas and periods go inside	Other punctuation not part of the quotation goes outside	Punctuation that's part of the quotation goes inside
"I dislike washing my car," she complained.	*I am excited about singing "The Star-Spangled Banner"!*	*"Stop that!" the teacher demanded.*

Capitalization

Capitalization tells the reader when a sentence begins and when specific persons, places, or things are being named.

- Capitalize the first word of a sentence. Example: *This sentence begins with a capital letter.*
- Capitalize proper nouns. Example: *I live in Florida.*
- Capitalize adjectives derived from proper nouns. Example: *My English teacher has a good sense of humor.*
- Capitalize titles only when they precede a proper name. Look at these examples.

Title precedes proper name	Title does not precede proper name
The memo came from Dean Jacobson.	*The memo came from Dr. Jacobson, the dean of the college.*

Test Yourself

Directions: For questions 1–3, select the answer choice that corrects an error in the underlined portion. If there is no error, choose **D** indicating "No change is necessary."

1. The <u>Dean</u> of the College of Education
   [A]
   <u>occasionally</u> likes to visit the <u>professors'</u> classes.
   [B]   [C]

   A. dean
   B. ocassionally
   C. professor's
   D. No change is necessary.

2. When the guest of honor <u>arrived, everyone</u> in the
   [A]
   room <u>cheered</u> <u>loud</u> and with gusto.
   [B]   [C]

   A. arrived everyone
   B. cheared
   C. loudly
   D. No change is necessary.

3. As the curtain <u>closes</u>, the audience rose and gave
   the performance a standing ovation.

   A. is closing
   B. closed
   C. is closed
   D. No change is necessary.

4. Choose the option that is punctuated correctly.

   A. The bridesmaids' dresses for the bride's three sisters were the boldest blue color that I have ever seen.
   B. The bridesmaid's dresses for the bride's three sisters were the boldest blue color that I have ever seen.
   C. The bridesmaids' dresses, for the brides three sisters' were the boldest blue color that I have ever seen.
   D. The bridesmaids dresses for the brides three sisters were the boldest blue color, that I have ever seen.

Answer Explanations for Test Yourself

1. **A.** The title *dean* at **A** should not be capitalized. Titles are capitalized when they precede proper names, but as a rule are not capitalized when used alone. The word *occasionally* at **B** is spelled correctly. The possessive word *professors'* is punctuated correctly. Add only an apostrophe to plural nouns ending in –s.

2. **C.** The word at **C** tells how everyone cheered, so it is an adverb. Change *loud* at **C** to *loudly* to make the sentence grammatically correct. A comma is needed at **A** to separate the introductory subordinate clause from the rest of the sentence. The word *cheered* at **B** is spelled correctly.

3. **B.** The tense of the verb in Choice **B** relates logically to the verb in the main clause. The verb tenses in choices **A** and **C** do not. These choices result in a faulty tense shift in the sentence.

4. **A.** All punctuation in Choice **A** is correct. In Choice **B**, the word *bridesmaid's* needs to be *bridesmaids'*. To form the possessive of a plural noun ending in -s, add an apostrophe after the -s. In Choice **C** the word *sisters'* should not have an apostrophe because no ownership is indicated for this word in the sentence. Also, in Choice **C** no comma is needed after the word *dresses*. In Choice **D**, the word *brides* needs to be *bride's* because ownership is indicated for this word in the sentence. Also, in Choice **D**, no comma is needed after the word *color*.

Review for the GK Mathematics Subtest

The mathematics subtest of the FTCE GK consists of 45 multiple-choice questions, which you must complete in 80 minutes. Each test question requires that you choose among four answer choices labeled **A, B, C,** or **D.** You must fill in the space corresponding to your answer choice in a separate answer booklet. The test center provides a 4-function calculator and a mathematics reference sheet for you to use during the test. The only other materials that you are permitted to use when taking the test are pens, pencils, and erasers. You cannot bring written notes or scratch paper into the testing center. You will have to write in your test booklet when working out problems.

The Math Review in This Study Guide

The mathematics review in this CliffsTestPrep Book is organized around the five mathematics areas tested on the FTCE GK Test:

1. Operations and Numeration
2. Measurement
3. Geometry
4. Algebraic Reasoning
5. Probability and Data Analysis

Each area has a general review and sample questions. The review sections present math concepts with examples and explanations for each area. "Test Yourself" exercises are found throughout the review sections. These exercises give you an opportunity to practice what you just learned. The answers to the "Test Yourself" exercises are found immediately following the set of exercises. When doing the "Test Yourself" exercises, you should cover up the answers. Then check your answers when you've finished the exercises. The sample questions are multiple-choice questions that are similar to what you might expect to see on the FTCE GK Test. The answer explanations for the sample questions are provided immediately after the questions. A mathematics reference sheet is included on pages 89–90.

Mathematics Reference Sheet

Area

Triangle 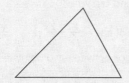 $A = \frac{1}{2} bh$

Rectangle  $A = lw$

Trapezoid  $A = \frac{1}{2} h (b_1 + b_2)$

Key	
b = base	d = diameter
h = height	r = radius
l = length	A = area
w = width	C = circumference
$S.A.$ = surface area	V = volume
	B = area of base
Use π = 3.14 or $\frac{22}{7}$	

Parallelogram  $A = bh$

Circle  $A = \pi r^2$
$C = \pi d = 2\pi r$

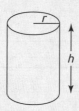

Surface Area

1. Surface area of a prism or pyramid = the sum of the areas of all faces of the figure.

2. Surface area of a cylinder = the sum of the two bases + its rectangular wrap.

$$S.\,A. = 2(\pi r^2) + 2(\pi r)h$$

3. Surface area of a sphere: $S.A. = 4\pi r^2$

Volume

1. Volume of a prism or cylinder equals (Area of the Base) times (height): $V = Bh$

2. Volume of a pyramid or cone equals $\frac{1}{3}$ times (Area of the Base) times (height): $V = \frac{1}{3} Bh$

3. Volume of a sphere: $V = \frac{4}{3} \pi r^3$

Mathematics Reference Sheet, continued

Pythagorean Theorem: $a^2 + b^2 = c^2$

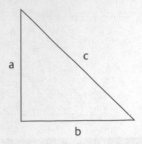

Simple Interest Formula: $I = prt$

I = simple interest, p = principal

r = rate, t = time

Distance Formula: $d = rt$

d = distance, r = rate, t = time

Given a line containing points

(x_1, y_1) and (x_2, y_2)

- Slope of line $= \dfrac{y_2 - y_1}{x_2 - x_1}$

- Distance between two points =

$$\sqrt{\left(x_2 - x_1\right)^2 + \left(y_2 - y_1\right)^2}$$

- Midpoint between two points =

$$\left(\dfrac{x_1 + x_2}{2}, \dfrac{y_1 + y_2}{2}\right)$$

Conversions	
1 yard = 3 feet = 36 inches	1 cup = 8 fluid ounces
1 mile = 1,760 yards = 5,280 feet	1 pint = 2 cups
1 acre = 43,560 square feet	1 quart = 2 pints
1 hour = 60 minutes	1 gallon = 4 quarts
1 minute = 60 seconds	1 pound = 16 ounces
	1 ton = 2,000 pounds
1 liter = 1000 milliliters = 1000 cubic centimeters	
1 meter = 100 centimeters = 1000 millimeters	
1 kilometer = 1000 meters	
1 gram = 1000 milligrams	
1 kilogram = 1000 grams	

Note: Metric numbers with four digits are written without a comma (e.g., 2543 grams).

For metric numbers with more than four digits, a space is used instead of a comma (e.g., 24 300 liters).

CUT HERE

Numeration and Operations

As listed in the *Competencies and Skills Required for Teacher Certification in Florida, Ninth Edition* (available at www.firn.edu/doe/sas/ftce/ftcecomp.htm), the competencies/skills you should be able to do for this area of mathematics are the following:

- Compare and order real numbers (that is, fractions, decimals, integers, percents, irrational numbers, and numbers expressed in exponential or scientific notation).

- Select and use appropriate operations to solve real-world problems involving rational numbers (that is, whole numbers, integers, fractions, decimals, and percents).

- Solve problems involving number theory concepts including primes, composites, factors, and multiples.

- Simplify expressions using the order of operations.

What Are Operations?

Addition, subtraction, multiplication, and **division** are the four basic arithmetic operations. Each of the operations has special symbolism and terminology associated with it. Make it a point to learn this symbolism and terminology, so that you can better understand mathematical "talk." Table 4.1 shows the terminology and symbolism you need to know.

Table 4.1: Terminology and Symbolism for the Four Basic Arithmetic Operations

Operation	Symbols(s) Used	Name of Parts	Example
Addition	+ (plus sign)	addend + addend = sum	$4 + 9 = 13$
Subtraction	– (minus sign)	sum – addend = difference	$13 - 4 = 9$
Multiplication	× (times sign) · (raised dot) ( )( ) parentheses	factor × factor = product factor · factor = product (factor)(factor) = product	$10 \times 5 = 50$ $10 \cdot 5 = 50$ $(10)(5) = 50$
Division	÷ (division sign) $\overline{)}$ (long division symbol) / (slash or fraction bar)	dividend ÷ divisor = quotient $\dfrac{\text{quotient}}{\text{divisor} \,\overline{)\,\text{dividend}}}$ dividend/divisor = quotient $\dfrac{\text{dividend}}{\text{divisor}}$ = quotient	$50 \div 10 = 5$ $10\overline{)\underset{}{50}}^{\,5}$ $50/10 = 5$ $\dfrac{50}{10} = 5$

As you can see from the examples in Table 4.1, addition and subtraction "undo" each other. Mathematicians express this relationship by saying that addition and subtraction are **inverses** of each other. Similarly, multiplication and division are **inverses** of each other; they "undo" each other, *as long as division by 0 is not involved*.

You must be *very* careful when division involves zero. Zero can be a dividend; that is, you can divide a nonzero number into zero. However, 0 *cannot* be a divisor, which means that you *cannot* divide by 0. The quotient of any number divided by zero has no meaning; that is, **division by zero is undefined—you can't do it!** Table 4.2 provides a summary of division involving zero.

Table 4.2: Division Involving Zero		
Rule	**Meaning**	**Example**
You <u>cannot</u> divide by zero.	any number ÷ 0 = can't do it!	6 ÷ 0 = can't do it!
	$\frac{\text{any number}}{0}$ = can't do it!	$\frac{25}{0}$ = can't do it!
	$0\overline{)\text{any number}}$ = can't do it!	$0\overline{)14}$ = can't do it!
	0 ÷ 0 = can't do it!	0 ÷ 0 = can't do it!
	$\frac{0}{0}$ = can't do it!	$\frac{0}{0}$ = can't do it!
	$0\overline{)0}$ = can't do it!	$0\overline{)0}$ = can't do it!
You <u>can</u> divide zero by a nonzero number.	0 ÷ any nonzero number = 0	0 ÷ 8 = 0
	$\frac{0}{\text{any nonzero number}}$ = 0	$\frac{0}{15}$ = 0
	$\text{any nonzero number}\overline{)0}$	$3\overline{)0}$

Test Yourself

1. The parts of an addition problem are _____ + _____ = _____ .

2. The answer to a subtraction problem is called the _____ .

3. The numbers that are multiplied together in a multiplication problem are called _____ .

4. The answer to a multiplication problem is called the _____ .

5. Zero _____ (can, cannot) be a divisor in a division problem.

6. 30 ÷ 0 = _____ .

7. 0 ÷ 30 = _____ .

8. $\frac{0}{17}$ = _____ .

9. $\frac{17}{0}$ = _____ .

10. $\frac{0}{0}$ = _____ .

Answers

1. addend + addend = sum

2. difference

3. factors

4. product

5. cannot

6. can't do it!

7. 0

8. 0

9. can't do it!

10. can't do it!

What Are Rational Numbers?

The **rational numbers** are the numbers that you are familiar with from school and from your everyday experiences with numbers. The rational numbers include the whole numbers, integers, positive and negative fractions, decimals, and percents.

The **whole numbers** are the counting numbers and zero:

$$0, 1, 2, 3, ...$$

The three dots to the right of the number 3 mean that you are to keep going in the same manner. Whole numbers that are greater than 1 are either *prime* or *composite*. A **prime number** is a whole number greater than 1 that has exactly two distinct factors: itself and 1. Thus, the primes are

$$2, 3, 5, 7, 11, 13, 17, 19, ...$$

The whole numbers greater than 1 that are *not* prime are called the **composite numbers.** They are

$$4, 6, 8, 9, 10, 12, 14, 15, ...$$

The whole numbers 0 and 1 are neither prime nor composite.

To find the prime factors of a number you can use a factor tree. Here is an example of using a factor tree to find the prime factors of the number 28.

The numbers at the bottom of the "tree" are the prime factors of 28—you cannot factor them any further. So the prime factors of 28 are 2 and 7. You can write 28 as the product of its prime factors like this: $28 = 2 \times 2 \times 7$.

The **integers** are the positive and negative whole numbers and zero:

$$...,-3, -2, -1, 0, 1, 2, 3, ...$$

Negative numbers have a small horizontal line (–) on the left of the number. Notice you do not have to write the + sign on positive numbers (although it's not wrong to do so). If no sign is written with a number, then you know that it is a positive number. The number zero is neither positive nor negative.

Besides classifying the integers as positive (1, 2, 3, ...), negative (..., –3, –2, –1), or zero, the integers can be classified as either *even* or *odd*. Integers that are divisible by 2 are called **even integers.** The **even integers** are

$$...,-8, -6, -4, -2, 0, 2, 4, 6, 8, ...$$

Notice that zero is an even integer because 0 divided by 2 is 0 (no remainder). Integers that are *not* divisible by 2 are called **odd integers.** The **odd integers** are

$$..., -9, -7, -5, -3, -1, 1, 3, 5, 7, 9, ...$$

The **rational numbers** are all the numbers that can be written as a ratio of two integers, where zero is *not* the denominator of the ratio. In other words, the rational numbers include all the numbers that can be written as positive or negative fractions. Here are some examples:

The fraction $\frac{3}{4}$ is a rational number: It is the ratio of two integers.

The fraction $\frac{-2}{5}$ is a rational number: It is the ratio of two integers. This rational number can also be written as $-\frac{2}{5}$.

The fraction $\frac{9}{2}$ is a rational number: It is the ratio of two integers.

All the counting numbers, whole numbers, and integers are rational numbers because you can write them as ratios whose denominator is 1. For instance,

$$-3 = \frac{-3}{1}, -2 = \frac{-2}{1}, -1 = \frac{-1}{1}, 0 = \frac{0}{1}, 1 = \frac{1}{1}, 2 = \frac{2}{1}, 3 = \frac{3}{1}$$

Rational numbers can be expressed as **fractions, decimals,** or **percents.**

Test Yourself

1. Which of the numbers in the following set are prime numbers? 1, 4, 5, 7, 10

2. What are the prime factors of 24?

3. Write 36 as a product of its prime factors.

4. Which of the numbers in the following set are even numbers? –4, 0, 3, 6, 22

5. A rational number is the ratio of two _____, where zero is *not* the _____ of the ratio.

6. Which of the numbers in the following set are rational numbers? $\frac{3}{4}, 0, \frac{-1}{1}, 100, -\frac{2}{5}$

7. Is $\frac{0}{4}$ a rational number?

8. Is $\frac{12}{0}$ a rational number?

9. Is $\frac{0}{0}$ a rational number?

10. Which of the following sets of numbers are rational numbers? whole numbers, integers, positive and negative fractions, decimals, and percents.

Answers

1. 5 and 7

2. 2 and 3

3. $36 = 2 \times 2 \times 3 \times 3$

4. –4, 0, 6, and 22

5. integers, denominator

6. all of them

7. Yes, $\frac{0}{4} = 0$, which is a rational number.

8. No, $\frac{12}{0}$ has no meaning because you can't divide by zero.

9. No, $\frac{0}{0}$ has no meaning because you can't divide by zero.

10. all of them

Fractions

Fractions are used to express parts of a whole, for example, $\frac{3}{4}$. The number below the division line (**fraction bar**), called the **denominator,** tells you the number of equal parts into which the whole has been divided. The number above the division line, called the **numerator,** tells how many equal parts you have.

The whole can be a single quantity or entity or the whole can be a set of objects or quantities. Here is an example when the whole is a single entity, a circle.

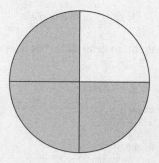

3/4 of a Circle

Here is an example when the whole is a set of 8 smiley faces.

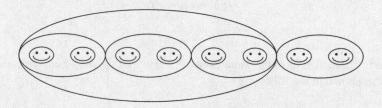

3/4 of a Set of 8

When you work with a fraction, you need to make sure you know what the whole for the fraction is. This isn't always easy because in some problems the whole shifts from one quantity to another quantity. Here is an example:

What is $\frac{3}{4}$ of $\frac{1}{2}$?

To illustrate this problem, you must first show $\frac{1}{2}$ of a whole. Let's use Rectangle A for the whole.

Rectangle A

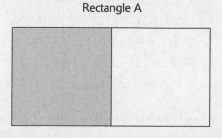

1/2 of Rectangle A

Next, you must find $\frac{3}{4}$ of the $\frac{1}{2}$. This means you must treat the $\frac{1}{2}$ of Rectangle A as a whole and divide it into 4 equal parts. Three of these 4 equal parts is $\frac{3}{4}$ of the $\frac{1}{2}$.

Rectangle A

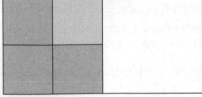

³/4 of ¹/2 of Rectangle A

Finally, you shift back to Rectangle A as the whole, to determine that the part shaded is $\frac{3}{8}$ of Rectangle A.

Rectangle A

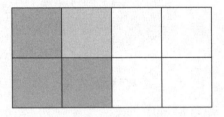

³/8 of Rectangle A

Thus, $\frac{3}{4}$ of $\frac{1}{2} = \frac{3}{8}$.

Equivalent fractions are fractions that have the same value. For example, $\frac{4}{8}$ and $\frac{1}{2}$ are equivalent fractions. You can illustrate the equivalency as shown in the following.

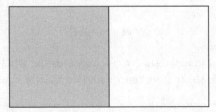

¹/2 of a Whole

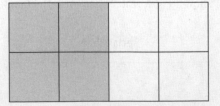

⁴/8 of a Whole

The shaded portion is the same size in the two figures, which shows that $\frac{4}{8} = \frac{1}{2}$.

If the numerator and denominator of a fraction can be divided by the same number, you can **reduce** the fraction to an equivalent fraction in **lowest terms** by doing the division, as in $\frac{4}{8} = \frac{4 \div 4}{8 \div 4} = \frac{1}{2}$. The number you divide by is called the greatest common factor (GCF) of the numerator and denominator. In this case, GCF(4,8) = 4. It is the largest number that will divide into both the numerator and denominator.

Other times when you are working with fractions, you may need to write a fraction as an equivalent fraction with a larger denominator. You can accomplish this by multiplying the numerator and denominator by the same whole number (greater than 1). For example, $\frac{3}{4} = \frac{3 \times 2}{4 \times 2} = \frac{6}{8}$.

Fractions like $\frac{1}{2}, \frac{3}{4}$ and $\frac{7}{10}$, in which the numerator is smaller than the denominator, are called **proper fractions.**

Fractions like $\frac{7}{2}, \frac{9}{8}$ and $\frac{6}{6}$, in which the numerator is greater than or equal to the denominator, are called **improper fractions.** Any improper fraction has a value greater than or equal to one. A **mixed number** is the sum of a whole number and a fraction, written together like this: $2\frac{1}{3}$, $1\frac{3}{4}$ and $3\frac{7}{10}$. Although a mixed number is a sum, you don't put a plus sign in it, but you do say the word "and" in between the whole number and the fraction when you read it. For instance, $2\frac{1}{3}$ is read as "Two and one-third."

An improper fraction can be changed to a mixed number or a whole number by dividing the numerator by the denominator and writing the remainder like this: $\frac{\text{remainder}}{\text{denominator}}$. For example, $\frac{7}{2} = 2\overset{3R1}{\overline{)7}} = 3\frac{1}{2}$.

Decimals

Decimals are rational numbers that are written using a base-10 place-value system. The value of a number is based on the placement of the decimal point in the number as shown below.

PLACE VALUE									
Millions	Hundred Thousands	Ten Thousands	Thousands	Hundreds	Tens	Ones	Tenths	Hundredths	Thousandths
2	5	7	5	4	0	3			

2,575,403 ⟶

To interpret the value of a decimal number, look at each digit and determine the value it represents according to its place in the number. For example, the value of the number 2,575,401 is

2 millions + 5 hundred thousands + 7 ten thousands + 5 thousands + 4 hundreds + 0 tens + 3 ones

or

2,000,000 + 500,000 + 70,000 + 5000 + 400 + 0 + 3.

Each digit has a face value and a place value. For example, in the number 2,575,403, starting at the decimal point (which is understood to be at the far right of a whole number) and counting left, the 4th digit and the 6th digit both have the same face value, namely 5. However, they represent different amounts because their place values are different. The 5 that is the 4th digit from the decimal point represents 5000, while the 5 that is the 6th digit from the decimal point represents 500,000. Place value makes a big difference!

To write numbers that are less than 1, you must recognize that numbers to the right of the decimal point represent fractions whose denominators are powers of 10: 10, 100, 1000, and so on. Here are some examples.

PLACE VALUE										
Millions	Hundred Thousands	Ten Thousands	Thousands	Hundreds	Tens	Ones	.	Tenths	Hundredths	Thousandths
						0		7		
						0		0	7	
						0		0	0	7

0.7 ⟶

0.07 ⟶

0.007 ⟶

The value of 0.7 is 7 tenths or $\frac{7}{10}$.

The value of 0.07 is 7 hundredths or $\frac{7}{100}$.

The value of 0.007 is 7 thousandths or $\frac{7}{1000}$.

In a decimal number, the number of digits to the right of the decimal point up to and including the final digit is the number of decimal places in the number. In the number 35.62 there are two digits after the decimal point, and the number is said to have two decimal places. In the number 4.250, there are three digits after the decimal point, and the number is said to have three decimal places.

You can obtain the decimal representation of a fractional number by dividing the numerator by the denominator. Here is an example.

$$\frac{3}{5} = 0.6 \text{ because } 5\overline{)3.0} \quad \genfrac{}{}{0pt}{}{0.6}{}$$

In this case, the decimal **terminates** (eventually has a zero remainder). For some rational numbers, the decimal keeps going, but in a block of one or more digits that repeats over and over again. These decimals are **repeating.**

Here is an example of a repeating decimal.

$$\frac{2}{3} = \overline{)2.000....} \quad \genfrac{}{}{0pt}{}{0.666....}{}$$

No matter how long you continue to add zeroes and divide, the 6's in the quotient continue without end. Put a bar over the repeating digit (or digits when more than one digit repeats) to indicate the repetition. Thus, $\frac{2}{3} = 0.\overline{6}$. When decimals repeat, they are usually rounded to a specified degree of accuracy; for example, 0.6666... is 0.67 when rounded to two decimal places. All terminating and repeating decimals are rational numbers.

Percents

You can also write rational numbers as **percents.** Percent means "per hundred." The percent sign is a short way of writing $\frac{1}{100}$ or 0.01. When you see a percent sign, you can substitute $\frac{1}{100}$ or 0.01 for the percent sign.

A percent is a way of writing a fraction as an equivalent fraction in which the denominator is 100. Thus, $25\% = 25 \cdot \frac{1}{100} = \frac{25}{100} = 0.25$. You can think of percents as special ways to write ordinary decimals or fractions. For instance, 100% is just a special way to write the number 1, because $100\% = 100 \cdot \frac{1}{100} = \frac{100}{100} = 1$. If you have 100% of something, you have all of it. Here are some examples.

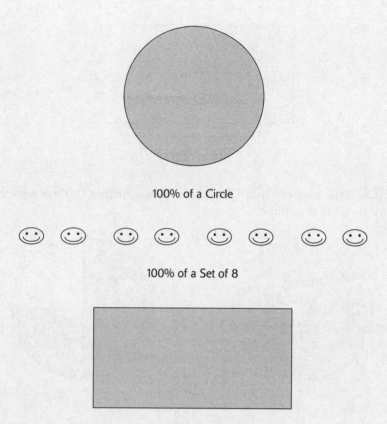

100% of a Circle

100% of a Set of 8

100% of a Rectangle

A percent that is less than 100% is less than 1. When you have less than 100% of something, you have less than the whole thing. Here are some examples.

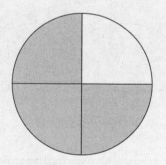

75% of a Circle

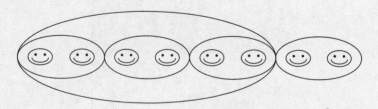

75% of a Set of 8

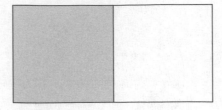

50% of a Rectangle

A percent that is greater than 100% is greater than 1. When you have more than 100% of something, you have more than the whole thing. Here are some examples.

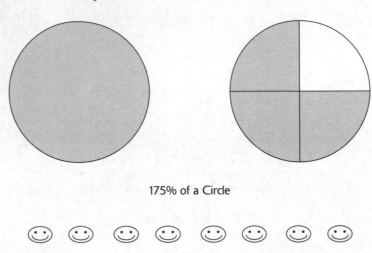

175% of a Circle

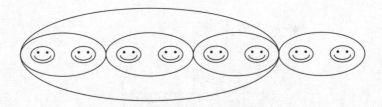

175% of a Set of 8

150% of a Rectangle

Any percent can be written as an equivalent fraction by writing the number in front of the percent sign as the numerator of a fraction in which the denominator is 100. The resulting fraction may then be reduced to lowest terms. Here are some examples.

$$50\% = \frac{50}{100} = \frac{50 \div 50}{100 \div 50} = \frac{1}{2}$$

$$75\% = \frac{75}{100} = \frac{75 \div 25}{100 \div 25} = \frac{3}{4}$$

$$25\% = \frac{25}{100} = \frac{25 \div 25}{100 \div 25} = \frac{1}{4}$$

$$1\% = \frac{1}{100}$$

$$125\% = \frac{125}{100} = \frac{125 \div 25}{100 \div 25} = \frac{5}{4} = 1\frac{1}{4}$$

When percents contain decimal fractions, multiply the numerator and denominator by 10, 100, or 1000, and so on, to remove the decimal in the numerator and then reduce the resulting fraction, if possible. Here are some examples.

$$12.5\% = \frac{12.5}{100} = \frac{12.5 \times 10}{100 \times 10} = \frac{125}{1000} = \frac{125 \div 125}{1000 \div 125} = \frac{1}{8}$$

$$0.2\% = \frac{.2}{100} = \frac{.2 \times 10}{100 \times 10} = \frac{2}{1000} = \frac{2 \div 2}{1000 \div 2} = \frac{1}{500}$$

If a percent contains a simple common fraction, multiply the fraction by $\frac{1}{100}$ and then reduce, if possible. Here is an example.

$$\frac{1}{2}\% = \frac{1}{2} \times \frac{1}{100} = \frac{1}{200}$$

When percents contain mixed fractions, change the mixed fraction to an improper fraction, use $\frac{1}{100}$ for the percent sign, and then multiply and reduce, if possible. Here are some examples.

$$12\frac{1}{2}\% = \frac{25}{2} \times \frac{1}{100} = \frac{25}{200} = \frac{25 \div 25}{200 \div 25} = \frac{1}{8}$$

$$33\frac{1}{3}\% = \frac{100}{3} \times \frac{1}{100} = \frac{100}{300} = \frac{100 \div 100}{300 \div 100} = \frac{1}{3}$$

A percent can be written as an equivalent decimal by changing it to an equivalent fraction in which the denominator is 100, and then dividing by 100. For example, $75\% = \frac{75}{100} = 100\overline{)75}^{\,0.75}$. A shortcut for this process is to move the decimal point two places to the left (which is the same as dividing by 100) and drop the percent sign. Here are some examples.

$$25\% = 0.25$$

$$32\% = 0.32$$

$$45.5\% = 0.455$$

$$8\% = 0.08$$

$$200\% = 2.00 = 2$$

To write a decimal in percent form, move the decimal point two places to the right and attach the percent sign (%) at the end. Why does this make sense? Recall that the percent sign is a short way to write $\frac{1}{100}$, which means 1 divided by 100. When you move the decimal place in your number two places to the right, you are multiplying by 100. Since the percent sign has division by 100 built into it, when you put the percent sign at the end of the number, you undo the multiplication by 100 that you did earlier. Thus, the value of the number does not change. Here are some examples.

$$0.45 = 45\%$$
$$0.01 = 1\%$$
$$0.125 = 12.5\%$$
$$2 = 2.00 = 200\%$$
$$0.0025 = 0.25\%$$

To write a fraction in percent form, first convert the fraction to a decimal by performing the indicated division and then change the resulting decimal to a percent. When the quotient is a repeating decimal, carry the decimal to two places, and then write the remainder as a fraction like this: $\frac{remainder}{denominator}$.

$$\frac{1}{4} = 4\overline{)1.00}^{0.25} = 25\%$$

$$\frac{3}{5} = 5\overline{)3.00}^{0.60} = 60\%$$

$$\frac{1}{3} = 3\overline{)1.00}^{0.33R1} = 0.33\frac{1}{3} = 33\frac{1}{3}\%$$

Before you take the FTCE GK test, you should memorize the following list of common percents with their fraction and decimal equivalents. Make a set of flashcards to drill with when you have spare time.

$$100\% = 1.00 = 1, \ 75\% = 0.75 = \frac{3}{4}, \ 50\% = 0.5 = \frac{1}{2}, \ 25\% = 0.25 = \frac{1}{4},$$

$$0.33\frac{1}{3} = 33\frac{1}{3}\% = \frac{1}{3}, \ 0.66\frac{2}{3} = 66\frac{2}{3}\% = \frac{2}{3},$$

$$20\% = 0.20 = 0.2 = \frac{1}{5}, \ 40\% = 0.40 = 0.4 = \frac{2}{5}, \ 60\% = 0.60 = 0.6 = \frac{3}{5}, \ 80\% = 0.80 = 0.8 = \frac{4}{5},$$

$$10\% = 0.10 = 0.1 = \frac{1}{10}, \ 30\% = 0.30 = 0.3 = \frac{3}{10}, \ 5\% = 0.05 = \frac{1}{20}.$$

Test Yourself

1. In the fraction $\frac{3}{10}$, the whole is divided into _____ equal parts. How many equal parts do you have?

2. Which of the following fractions are equivalent to $\frac{3}{5}$? $\frac{30}{100}, \frac{6}{10}, \frac{12}{20}$

3. What is the greatest common factor of 16 and 24? Write the fraction $\frac{16}{24}$ in lowest terms by dividing the numerator and denominator by the GCF (16,24).

4. Which of the following fractions are improper fractions? $\frac{20}{17}, 1\frac{3}{5}, \frac{12}{24}, \frac{4}{4}$

5. Change $\frac{8}{5}$ to a mixed fraction.

6. In the number 564.27, the 6 represents what value?

7. Write the fraction $\frac{4}{5}$ as a percent and as a decimal.

8. Write 0.34 as a percent.

9. Write 73.5% as a decimal.

10. Which of the following are rational numbers?

    $\frac{3}{8}, 0, \frac{-5}{1}, 100, -\frac{6}{10}, 23\%, \frac{9}{0}, 0.85, 19.2, -2.5, \frac{25}{24}, 100\%, 225\%, \frac{7}{0}, 0.\overline{3}, \frac{20}{17}$

Answers

1. 10, 3

2. $\frac{6}{10}$, because $\frac{3}{5} = \frac{3 \times 2}{5 \times 2} = \frac{6}{10}$; and $\frac{12}{20}$, because $\frac{3}{5} = \frac{3 \times 4}{5 \times 4} = \frac{12}{20}$.

3. The greatest common factor of 16 and 24 is the largest number that will divide into both 16 and 24 evenly. The numbers that will divide evenly into 16 are 1, 2, 4, 8, and 16. The numbers that will divide evenly into 24 are 1, 2, 3, 4, 6, 8, 12, and 24. Looking at the two sets of divisors, you can see that 8 is the largest number that will divide into both 16 and 24 evenly. Thus, GCF(16,24) = 8. $\frac{16}{24} = \frac{16 \div 8}{24 \div 8} = \frac{2}{3}$.

4. $\frac{20}{17}$ and $\frac{4}{4}$

5. $\frac{8}{5} = 5\overline{)8}^{\,1R3} = 1\frac{3}{5}$

6. 6 tens or 60

7. $\frac{4}{5} = 5\overline{)4.0}^{\,0.8} = 0.80 = 80\%$

8. $0.34 = 34\%$

9. $73.5\% = 0.735$

10. all of them, except $\frac{7}{0}$ and $\frac{9}{0}$ (which have no meaning because you can't divide by zero)

What Are Irrational Numbers?

Irrational numbers are numbers that cannot be written as the ratio of two integers. They have nonterminating, nonrepeating decimal representations. An example of an irrational number is the number that multiplies by itself to give 2. We call this number the square root of 2. Usually, the square root symbol ($\sqrt{}$) is used to show a square root. Thus, the square root of 2 is written like this: $\sqrt{2}$. You cannot express $\sqrt{2}$ as the ratio of two integers, nor can you express it precisely in decimal form. No matter how many decimal places you use, you can only approximate $\sqrt{2}$. If you put the number 2 in your calculator and take the square root, the display will show a decimal approximation of $\sqrt{2}$. An approximation of $\sqrt{2}$ to nine decimal places is 1.414213562. You can check to see whether this is the $\sqrt{2}$ by multiplying it by itself to see whether you get 2.

$$1.414213562 \cdot 1.414213562 = 1.999999999$$

The number 1.999999999 is very close to 2, but it is not equal to 2. For most purposes, you can use 1.41 as an approximation for $\sqrt{2}$.

Even though an exact value for $\sqrt{2}$ cannot be determined, $\sqrt{2}$ is a number that occurs frequently in the real world. For instance, architects, carpenters, and other builders encounter $\sqrt{2}$ when they measure the length of the diagonal of a square that has sides with length of one unit as shown here,

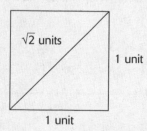

The diagonal of such a square measures $\sqrt{2}$ units.

There are other square roots that are irrational. Here are some examples.

$\sqrt{3}$ is irrational.

$\sqrt{24}$ is irrational.

$\sqrt{10}$ is irrational.

$\sqrt{41}$ is irrational.

On the FTCE GK test, you may have to estimate the value of an irrational square root by finding a pair of consecutive whole numbers that the square root lies between. Here is an example.

Estimate $\sqrt{41}$.

To do this problem, you need to find two consecutive integers such that the square of the first integer is less than 41 and the square of the second integer is greater than 41. Since $6 \times 6 = 36$, which is less than 41, and $7 \times 7 = 49$, which is greater than 41, the approximate value of $\sqrt{41}$ is between 6 and 7.

Another important irrational number is the number represented by the symbol π (pi). The number π also occurs frequently in the real world. For instance, π is the number you get when you divide the circumference of a circle by its diameter. The number π cannot be expressed as the ratio of two integers, nor can it be written as a terminating or repeating decimal. Here is an approximation of π to nine decimal places: 3.141592654.

> **Tip: There is no pattern to the digits of π. For the FTCE GK test, you are told to use the rational number 3.14 as an approximation for the irrational number π in the problems involving π.**

Are All Square Roots Irrational?

Not all square roots are irrational. For example, $\sqrt{25}$ is *not* irrational because $\sqrt{25} = 5$, which is a rational number. When you want to find the square root of a number, try to find a factor that multiplies by itself to give the number. Since you will not be allowed to use a calculator with a square root key on the FTCE GK test, you should memorize the following 18 square roots. Make yourself a set of flashcards or make matching cards for a game of "Memory." For the Memory game, turn all the cards face down. Turn up two cards at a time. If they match, remove the two cards; otherwise, turn them face down again. Repeat until you have matched all the cards.

$$\sqrt{1} = 1, \sqrt{4} = 2, \sqrt{9} = 3, \sqrt{16} = 4, \sqrt{25} = 5, \sqrt{36} = 6,$$
$$\sqrt{49} = 7, \sqrt{64} = 8, \sqrt{81} = 9, \sqrt{100} = 10, \sqrt{121} = 11, \sqrt{144} = 12,$$
$$\sqrt{169} = 13, \sqrt{196} = 14, \sqrt{225} = 15, \sqrt{256} = 16, \sqrt{400} = 20, \sqrt{625} = 25.$$

What Are the Real Numbers?

The real numbers are the numbers that describe the world in which we live. They are made up of all the rational numbers plus all the irrational numbers. You can show the real numbers on a number line. Every point on the number line corresponds to a real number.

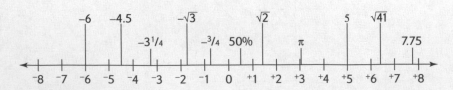

Test Yourself

1. A real number is any _____ or _____ number.

2. Which of the following numbers are rational? -15, 0, $\sqrt{36}$, -3.45, 130%, $\sqrt{12}$, $\frac{6}{10}$, $-\frac{1}{20}$, 0.0005, π, 3.14

3. Which of the following numbers are irrational?, -25, 0, $\sqrt{36}$, -125.4, 50%, $\sqrt{6}$, $-\frac{1}{200}$, 0.0005, π, 3.14, $0.\overline{3}$

4. Which of the following numbers are real numbers? -16, 0, $\sqrt{37}$, -13.25, 30%, $\sqrt{49}$, $\frac{3}{5}$, $-\frac{12}{24}$, 0.03, π

5. A decimal number that terminates is a _____ (rational, irrational) number.

6. A decimal number that repeats is a _____ (rational, irrational) number.

7. Nonterminating and nonrepeating decimal numbers are _____ (rational, irrational).

8. Estimate the value of $\sqrt{37}$.

9. The number $\sqrt{400}$ is _____ (rational, irrational).

10. Is $\frac{1}{0}$ a real number?

Answers

1. rational, irrational

2. all except $\sqrt{12}$ and π

3. $\sqrt{6}$ and π

4. all of them

5. rational

6. rational

7. irrational

8. between 6 and 7

9. rational, because $\sqrt{400} = 20$.

10. No, $\frac{1}{0}$ has no meaning because you can't divide by zero.

What Is Exponential Notation?

You can use **exponential notation** to write a compact version of a product in which the same number is repeated as a factor. The compact version for a product such as $10 \times 10 \times 10$ is 10^3. The ^{3}, which is written as a small number to the upper right, is called the **exponent.** If the exponent is a whole number, it tells how many times the 10, called the **base,** is used as a factor. The resulting **exponential expression** is called a **power** of the base. For instance, 10^3 is the third power of 10. Here are other examples of exponential notation using whole number exponents.

$$3 \times 3 \times 3 \times 3 = 3^4$$
$$(2)(2)(2)(2)(2) = 2^5$$
$$10 \cdot 10 = 10^2$$
$$2 \cdot 2 \cdot 2 \cdot 10 \cdot 10 = 2^3 \cdot 10^2$$

You **evaluate** numbers written in exponential notation using whole number exponents by performing the indicated multiplication. Here are some examples.

$$3^4 = 3 \times 3 \times 3 \times 3 = 81$$
$$2^5 = (2)(2)(2)(2)(2) = 32$$
$$2^3 \cdot 10^2 = 2 \cdot 2 \cdot 2 \cdot 10 \cdot 10 = 8 \cdot 100 = 800$$

Negative exponents are used to show reciprocals. Here are some examples.

$$2^{-3} = \frac{1}{2^3}$$
$$10^{-4} = \frac{1}{10^4}$$

You **evaluate** numbers written in exponential notation using negative (integer) exponents by writing the reciprocal, performing the indicated multiplication, and converting to a decimal (if desired). Here are some examples.

$$2^{-3} = \frac{1}{2^3} = \frac{1}{8} = 0.125$$
$$10^{-4} = \frac{1}{10^4} = \frac{1}{10000} = 0.0001$$

> **Here's a caution: Do *not* make the mistake of putting a negative sign in front of your answer. The negative part of the exponent means for you to write a reciprocal; it does not mean that you should make your answer negative.**

You can also use zero as an exponent. When zero is the exponent on a nonzero number, the value of the exponential expression is 1. Here are some examples.

$$3^0 = 1$$
$$2^0 = 1$$
$$10^0 = 1$$

What Is Scientific Notation?

Scientific notation is a way to write real numbers in a shortened form. When the numbers are very large or very small, scientific notation helps keep track of the decimal places and makes performing computations with these numbers easier.

A number written in scientific notation is written as a product of two factors. The first factor is a number that is greater than or equal to 1, but less than 10. The second factor is a power of 10. The idea is to make a product that will equal the given number. Any decimal number can be written in scientific notation. Here are some examples of numbers written in scientific notation.

- Written in scientific notation, 34,000 is 3.4×10^4
- Written in scientific notation, 6.5 is 6.5×10^0
- Written in scientific notation, 1,235,000 is 1.235×10^6
- Written in scientific notation, 0.00047 is 4.7×10^{-4}
- Written in scientific notation, 0.00000001662 is 1.662×10^{-8}

Follow these steps to write a number in scientific notation:

1. Move the decimal point to the immediate right of the first *nonzero* digit of the number.
2. Indicate multiplication by the proper power of 10. The exponent for the power of 10 is the number of places you moved the decimal point in Step 1.

If you moved the decimal point to the *left*, make the exponent positive. For example,

$$34{,}000 = 3.\underset{4}{\underbrace{0}}\underset{3}{\underbrace{0}}\underset{2}{\underbrace{0}}\underset{1}{\underbrace{0}} \times 10^4 = 3.4 \times 10^4$$

If you moved the decimal point to the *right,* make the exponent negative. For example,

$$0.00047 = \underset{1}{\underbrace{0}}\underset{2}{\underbrace{0}}\underset{3}{\underbrace{0}}\underset{4}{\underbrace{0}}4.7 \times 10^{-4} = 4.7 \times 10^{-4}$$

As long as you make sure your first factor is greater than or equal to 1 and less than 10, you can always check to see whether you did it right by multiplying out your answer to see whether you get your original number back. Look at these examples.

$$3.4 \times 10^4 = 3.4 \times 10 \times 10 \times 10 \times 10 = 3.4 \times 10{,}000 = 34{,}000 \checkmark$$

$$4.7 \times 10^{-4} = 4.7 \times \frac{1}{10^4} = 4.7 \times \frac{1}{10000} = 0.00047 \checkmark$$

Test Yourself

1. In the exponential expression 4^3 _____ is the base, and _____ is the exponent.

2. Write 36 as a product of its prime factors using exponential notation.

3. Evaluate 4^3.

4. Evaluate 5^{-3}.

5. Evaluate 10^0.

6. Write 456,000,000 in scientific notation.

7. Write 0.000000975 in scientific notation.

8. Write 2.68×10^9 in standard form.

9. Write 1.572×10^{-3} in standard form.

10. Exponential expressions such as 10^{-2}, 10^{-8}, 10^3, and 10^7 are called _____ of 10.

Answers

1. 4, 3
2. $36 = 2^2 \cdot 3^2$
3. $4^3 = 4 \times 4 \times 4 = 64$
4. $5^{-3} = \frac{1}{5^3} = \frac{1}{125} = 0.008$
5. 1
6. 4.56×10^8
7. 9.75×10^{-7}
8. 2,680,000,000
9. 0.001572
10. powers

How Do You Compare and Order Real Numbers?

For the FTCE GK test you will need to know how to compare two or more real numbers to determine which is greater and which is less. For these questions, you will need to understand inequality symbols. Table 4.3 summarizes commonly used inequality symbols.

Table 4.3: Common Inequality Symbols		
Inequality Symbol	*Read As*	*Example*
<	"is less than"	$0.5 < 1$
>	"is greater than"	$7.2 > 3.1$
≤	"is less than or equal to"	$9 \leq 9$
≥	"is greater than or equal to"	$3\frac{4}{5} \geq 2$
≠	"is not equal to"	$0 \neq -10$

A number line is helpful when you want to compare real numbers. On a number line, positive numbers are located to the right of zero and negative numbers are to the left of zero.

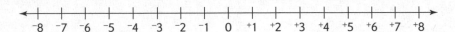

When comparing two real numbers, think of their relative location on the number line. The number that is farthest to the right is the greater number. For example, $-7 < -2$ because as you can see on the number line below, -2 lies to the right of -7 on the number line.

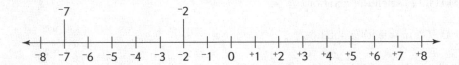

When you compare decimals, compare the digits in each place value from left to right. If the decimals do not have the same number of decimal places, annex or delete zeros after the last digit to the right of the decimal point to make the number of decimal places the same. Remember, annexing or deleting zeros after the last digit to the right of the decimal point does not change the value of a decimal.

For example, $2.5 = 2.50 = 2.500 = 2.5000$ and so on. Thus, $2.28 < 2.5$ because $2.28 < 2.50$.

When comparing fractions that have the same denominator, compare the numerators.

For example, $\frac{7}{8} > \frac{5}{8}$ because $7 > 5$.

If the denominators of the fractions are not the same, write the fractions as equivalent fractions using a common denominator. For example, $\frac{3}{4} < \frac{7}{8}$ because $\frac{6}{8} < \frac{7}{8}$.

To compare a mixture of decimals and fractions, use your calculator to change the fractions to decimals. Round them off if they repeat. When you are instructed to **order** a list of numbers, you put them in order from **least to greatest** or from **greatest to least,** depending on how the question is stated. Here is an example.

Order the numbers $\frac{7}{8}$, 0.35, 4.8, $\frac{2}{3}$ from smallest to largest.

Before proceeding, write $\frac{7}{8}$ as a decimal by performing the division on your calculator like this: $7 \div 8 = 0.875$. Similarly, write $\frac{2}{3}$ as 0.667 (rounding to 3 places).Write 0.35 as 0.350 and 4.8 as 4.800. Next, compare the transformed numbers and put them in order as follows: 0.350, 0.667, 0.875, 4.800. Lastly, substitute the original numbers for their stand-ins to obtain the final answer: 0.35, $\frac{2}{3}$, $\frac{7}{8}$, 4.8.

Here are some tips on handling other situations that may occur in problems that involve comparing and ordering real numbers.

- If negative numbers are involved, they will be less than all the positive numbers and 0.
- If percents are involved, change the percents to decimals.
- If the problem contains exponential expressions, evaluate them before making comparisons.
- If you have square roots that are rational numbers, find the square roots before making comparisons.
- If you have irrational square roots, estimate the square roots before comparing them to other numbers.

For example, order the following series of numbers from smallest to largest.

$\sqrt{37}$, 3^2, 4.39, -4, $\frac{9}{2}$

You do not have to proceed in the order the numbers are listed. Clearly, -4 is less than all the other numbers. Evaluate 3^2 to obtain 9. Write $\frac{9}{2}$ as 4.50. In order from least to greatest, these four numbers are -4, 4.39, 4.50, 9. Estimate $\sqrt{37}$ to be between 6 and 7, which puts it between 4.5 and 9 in the list. Thus, your final answer is -4, 4.39, $\frac{9}{2}$, $\sqrt{37}$, 3^2.

Test Yourself

For questions, 1–8 put < or > in the blank.

1. -100 _____ -2

2. -25 _____ 0

3. -3.25 _____ -3.5

4. 3^2 _____ 0

5. $\frac{7}{15}$ _____ $\frac{4}{15}$

6. $\frac{1}{3}$ _____ 0.35

7. $\sqrt{36}$ _____ 5.4

8. 3.98 _____ $\sqrt{20}$

9. Order the following series of numbers from smallest to largest.

   -25, 0, $\sqrt{36}$, 50%, $\sqrt{6}$

10. Order the following series of numbers from smallest to largest.

    3.256, $\frac{3}{5}$, $-\frac{6}{7}$, 3.9, 2^2

Answers

1. <
2. <
3. >
4. >
5. >
6. <
7. >
8. <
9. $-25, 0, 50\%, \sqrt{6}, \sqrt{36}$
10. $\frac{-6}{7}, \frac{3}{5}, 3.256, 3.9, 2^2$

How Do You Add and Subtract Fractions and Decimals?

Even though you are allowed to use a calculator on the FTCE GK test, you still need to know and understand how to add and subtract fractions and decimals. Understanding the process will make it less likely that you will make an error when performing a calculation and will also help you evaluate the reasonableness of the result of your computation.

Adding and Subtracting Fractions

Table 4.4 summarizes the rules for addition and subtraction with fractions.

Table 4.4: Rules for Addition and Subtraction of Fractions		
Operation	**Rule**	**Example**
Addition	1. To add two fractions that have the same denominator:	$\frac{5}{8} + \frac{1}{8} =$
	Add the numerators of the fractions to find the numerator of the answer, which is placed over the common denominator.	$\frac{5+1}{8} = \frac{6}{8}$
	Reduce to lowest terms, if needed.	$= \frac{6 \div 2}{8 \div 2} = \frac{3}{4}$
	2. To add two fractions that have different denominators:	$\frac{1}{4} + \frac{2}{3} =$
	Find a common denominator. The common denominator is the least common multiple (LCM) of the denominators.	LCM(3,4) = 12
	Write each fraction as an equivalent fraction having the common denominator as a denominator.	$\frac{1}{4} = \frac{1 \times 3}{4 \times 3} = \frac{3}{12}$ $\frac{2}{3} = \frac{2 \times 4}{3 \times 4} = \frac{8}{12}$
	Add the numerators of the fractions to find the numerator of the answer, which is placed over the common denominator.	$\frac{1}{4} + \frac{2}{3} = \frac{3}{12} + \frac{8}{12} =$ $\frac{3+8}{12} = \frac{11}{12}$
	Reduce to lowest terms, if needed.	Not needed in this problem.

Operation	Rule	Example
Subtraction	1. To subtract two fractions that have the same denominator:	$\frac{5}{8} - \frac{1}{8} =$
	Subtract the numerators of the fractions to find the numerator of the answer, which is placed over the common denominator.	$\frac{5-1}{8} = \frac{4}{8}$
	Reduce to lowest terms, if needed.	$= \frac{4 \div 4}{8 \div 4} = \frac{1}{2}$
	2. To subtract two fractions that have different denominators:	$\frac{3}{4} - \frac{2}{3} =$
	Find a common denominator.	LCM(4,3) = 12
	Write each fraction as an equivalent fraction having the common denominator as a denominator.	$\frac{3}{4} = \frac{3 \times 3}{4 \times 3} = \frac{9}{12}$ $\frac{2}{3} = \frac{2 \times 4}{3 \times 4} = \frac{8}{12}$ $\frac{3}{4} - \frac{2}{3} = \frac{9}{12} - \frac{8}{12} =$
	Subtract the numerators of the fractions to find the numerator of the answer, which is placed over the common denominator.	$\frac{9-8}{12} = \frac{1}{12}$
	Reduce to lowest terms, if needed.	Not needed in this problem.

Adding and Subtracting Decimals

Since you are allowed to use a calculator on the FTCE GK test, you should do your decimal computations with your calculator when you take the test. Just to refresh your memory, Table 4.5 summarizes rules for addition and subtraction with decimals.

Table 4.5: Rules for Addition and Subtraction of Decimals		
Operation	**Rule**	**Example**
Addition	To add decimals:	65.3 + 0.34 + 7.008 =
	Line up the decimal points vertically.	65.300
	Hint: Fill in empty decimal places with zeros to avoid adding incorrectly.	0.340
		+ 7.008
	Add as you would with whole numbers. Place the decimal point in the answer directly under the decimal points in the problem.	72.648
Subtraction	To subtract decimals:	9.4 − 3.65 =
	Line up the decimal points vertically, filling in empty decimal places with zeros when needed.	9.40
		− 3.65
	Subtract as you would with whole numbers. Place the decimal point in the answer directly under the decimal points in the problem.	5.75

Test Yourself

1. Find the greatest common factor of 16 and 20.

2. Find the sum: $\frac{3}{10} + \frac{1}{2} =$

3. Find the difference: $\frac{1}{2} - \frac{3}{10} =$

4. Find the sum: $0.125 + 7.2 + 320 + 4.23 =$

5. Find the difference: $75.2 - 35.046 =$

Answers

1. The largest number that will divide evenly into both 16 and 20 is 4, so GCF (16, 20) = 4.

2. $\frac{3}{10} + \frac{1}{2} = \frac{3}{10} + \frac{5}{10} = \frac{8}{10} = \frac{8 \div 2}{10 \div 2} = \frac{4}{5}$

3. $\frac{1}{2} - \frac{3}{10} = \frac{5}{10} - \frac{3}{10} = \frac{2}{10} = \frac{2 \div 2}{10 \div 2} = \frac{1}{5}$

4. 331.555

5. 40.154

How Do You Multiply and Divide Fractions and Decimals?

As with adding and subtracting, if you know and understand how to multiply and divide fractions and decimals, you will be less likely to make an error when doing these calculations, and you will be better able to evaluate the reasonableness of the results of your computations.

Multiplying and Dividing Fractions

Table 4.6 summarizes the rules for multiplication and division with fractions.

Table 4.6: Rules for Multiplication and Division of Fractions		
Operation	*Rule*	*Example*
Multiplication	1. To multiply two proper fractions, two improper fractions, or a proper fraction and an improper fraction:	$\frac{1}{3} \times \frac{3}{4} =$
	Multiply the numerators to obtain the numerator of the product and multiply the denominators to find the denominator of the product.	$\frac{1 \times 3}{3 \times 4} = \frac{3}{12}$
	Reduce to lowest terms, if needed.	$= \frac{3 \div 3}{12 \div 3} = \frac{1}{4}$

Operation	Rule	Example
	2. To multiply a fraction times a whole number:	$\frac{33}{4} \times 12 =$
	Write the whole number as an equivalent fraction with denominator 1, and then follow multiplication rule 1.	$\frac{3}{4} \times \frac{12}{1} = \frac{3 \times 12}{4 \times 1} = \frac{36}{4}$ $= \frac{36 \div 4}{4 \div 4} = \frac{9}{1} = 9$
	3. To multiply fractions when mixed numbers are involved:	$2\frac{3}{4} \times 1\frac{1}{3} =$
	Change the mixed numbers to improper fractions and then follow multiplication rule 1.	$\frac{11}{4} \times \frac{4}{3} = \frac{11 \times 4}{4 \times 3} = \frac{44}{12}$ $= \frac{44}{12} = \frac{44 \div 4}{12 \div 4} = \frac{11}{3}$ or $3\frac{2}{3}$
Division	1. To divide two proper fractions, two improper fractions, or a proper fraction and an improper fraction:	$\frac{4}{3} \div \frac{1}{2} =$
	Multiply the first fraction by the reciprocal of the second fraction using multiplication rule 1.	$\frac{4}{3} \times \frac{2}{1} =$ $\frac{4 \times 2}{3 \times 1} = \frac{8}{3}$ or $2\frac{2}{3}$
	2. To divide a fraction by a whole number:	$\frac{4}{5} \div 3 =$
	Write the whole number as an equivalent fraction with denominator 1, and then follow division rule 1.	$\frac{4}{5} \div \frac{3}{1} =$ $\frac{4}{5} \times \frac{1}{3} =$ $\frac{4 \times 1}{5 \times 3} = \frac{4}{15}$
	3. To divide fractions when mixed numbers are involved:	$2\frac{1}{3} \div 1\frac{1}{2} =$
	Change the mixed numbers to improper fractions, and then follow division rule 1.	$\frac{7}{3} \div \frac{3}{2} =$ $\frac{7}{3} \times \frac{2}{3} =$ $\frac{7 \times 2}{3 \times 3} = \frac{14}{9}$ or $1\frac{5}{9}$

The process of multiplying or dividing fractions can be simplified by dividing out common factors, if any, before any multiplication is performed. For example, $\frac{1}{3} \times \frac{3}{4} = \frac{1}{4}$. Also, remember you do *not* have to find a common denominator when multiplying or dividing fractions.

Multiplying and Dividing Decimals

As mentioned before, you should do your decimal computations with your calculator when you take the FTCE GK test. Just for review, Table 4.7 summarizes the rules for multiplication and division with decimals.

Table 4.7: Rules for Multiplication and Division of Decimals

Operation	Rule	Example
Multiplication	To multiply decimals:	$55.7 \times 0.25 =$
	Multiply the numbers as whole numbers.	55.7 (1 place)
	Place the decimal point in the proper place in the product. The number of decimal places in the product is the sum of the number of decimal places in the numbers being multiplied. If there are not enough places, insert one or more zeros at the *left* end of the number.	$\times \underline{0.25}$ (+ 2 places) 13.925 (3 places)
Division	To divide two decimals:	$2.04 \div 0.002 =$
	Rewrite the problem as an equivalent problem with a whole number divisor. Do this by counting the number of decimal places in the divisor and then moving the decimal point that many places in both the divisor and the dividend. Annex additional zeroes after the dividend, if needed.	$0.002\overline{)2.040}$ $00\,02.\overline{)20\,4\,0.}$
	Divide as with whole numbers. Place the decimal point in the quotient directly above the decimal point in the dividend.	$\begin{array}{r} 1020. \\ 0002\overline{)2040.} \end{array}$

Don't be concerned about having to do computations on the FTCE GK test. Since you are allowed to use a calculator, you should be able to do the calculations with little or no difficulty. Most of the required computations on the test will be simple calculations, some of which you could probably do mentally.

Test Yourself

1. Find the product: $\frac{3}{10} \times \frac{1}{2} =$

2. Find the product: $1\frac{1}{2} \times \frac{2}{5} =$

3. Find the quotient: $\frac{3}{10} \div \frac{1}{2} =$

4. Find the product: $(0.0125)(7.2) =$

5. Find the quotient: $345.75 \div 0.0005 =$

Answers

1. $\frac{3}{10} \times \frac{1}{2} = \frac{3 \times 1}{10 \times 2} = \frac{3}{20}$

2. $1\frac{1}{2} \times \frac{2}{5} = \frac{3}{2_1} \times \frac{\cancel{2}^1}{5} = \frac{3}{5}$

3. $\frac{3}{10} \div \frac{1}{2} = \frac{3}{\cancel{10}_5} \times \frac{\cancel{2}^1}{1} = \frac{3}{5}$

4. 0.09

5. 691,500

How Do You Add and Subtract Signed Numbers?

The real numbers are often called **signed numbers** because they may be positive (+), negative (–), or zero (no sign). On the FTCE GK Test you will need to know how to perform addition, subtraction, multiplication, and division with signed numbers.

Addition of Signed Numbers

When you add two signed numbers, you must note whether the two numbers have the same sign (both positive or both negative) or have different signs (one positive and one negative). How you do the addition depends on which of these situations is the case. This type of addition is called **algebraic addition.** Table 4.8 summarizes the rules for algebraic addition of two signed numbers.

Table 4.8: Rules for Algebraic Addition of Two Signed Numbers		
If the signs are:	*The rule is:*	*Examples*
1. the same—both positive or both negative	Ignore the signs, add the two numbers like you would nonsigned numbers, and use the common sign as the sign for the answer.	4 + 6 = 10 –4 + –6 = –10
2. different—one positive and one negative	Ignore the signs, subtract the two numbers like you would nonsigned numbers, and use the sign of the greater nonsigned number as the sign for the answer.	–4 + 6 = 2 4 + –6 = –2

As you can see, algebraic addition is different from arithmetic addition; particularly, since you don't always "add" to get the sum. In fact, if the signs are different, you subtract to find the sum. How does this make sense? What you must keep in mind is that the numbers you worked with in arithmetic were amounts only—they had no signs. Real numbers have an amount *and* a sign. The sign adds a direction to the number. Every real number has an amount and a direction. The number +5 is 5 units in the positive direction. The number –5 is 5 units in the negative direction. When you add signed numbers, you have to take into account both the amount and the direction of the number.

You can model addition on the number line to help you understand the process. Here are examples.

2 + 5 = ?

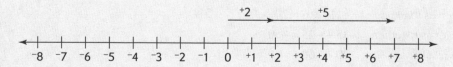

Start at 0 and go 2 units in the positive direction. Then from that point go 5 additional units in the positive direction. You end up at +7. The model shows that 2 + 5 = 7.

$$-2 + -5 = ?$$

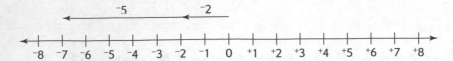

Start at 0 and go 2 units in the negative direction. Then from that point go 5 additional units in the negative direction. You end up at –7. The model shows that –2 + –5 = –7.

$$2 + -5 = ?$$

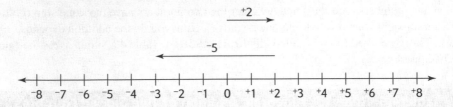

Start at 0 and go 2 units in the positive direction. Then from that point go 5 units in the negative direction. You end up at –3. The model shows that 2 + –5 = –3.

$$-2 + 5 = ?$$

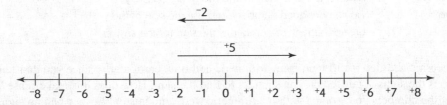

Start at 0 and go 2 units in the negative direction. Then from that point go 5 units in the positive direction. You end up at +3. The model shows that –2 + 5 = 3.

If you have three or more signed numbers to add together, you may find it convenient to, first, add up all the positive numbers; second, add up all the negative numbers; and then add the resulting two answers. Here is an example.

$$14 + -35 + 6 + -25 =$$

Add the positives together: 14 + 6 = 20

Add the negatives together: –35 + –25 = –60

Add the two results: 20 + –60 = –40

Subtraction of Signed Numbers

You may be happily surprised to learn that you do not have to memorize a set of new rules for subtraction of signed numbers! The reason is that subtraction of signed numbers is accomplished by changing the subtraction problem in a special way to an algebraic addition problem, so that the rules in Table 4.8 will apply. Here's how you do it (see Table 4.9).

Table 4.9: Algebraic Subtraction of Signed Numbers		
Operation	**Rule**	**Example**
Subtraction	To subtract two signed numbers:	$-10 - 4 =$
	Change the sign of the number that immediately follows the minus sign (–).	Change 4 to –4.
	Change the minus (–) sign to a plus sign (+).	$-10 + -4 =$
	Perform algebraic addition according to the rules of Table 4.8.	$-10 + -4 = -14$

Think of the minus sign as "+ opposite of." Incorrectly interpreting subtraction is a common mistake. Here are examples of correctly rewriting subtraction problems.

$$9 - 16 = 9 + \text{opposite of } 16 = 9 + -16$$
$$24 - 15 = 24 + \text{opposite of } 15 = 24 + -15$$
$$-8 - 20 = -8 + \text{opposite of } 20 = -8 + -20$$
$$3 - -6 = 3 + \text{opposite of } -6 = 3 + 6$$
$$-18 - -4 = -18 + \text{opposite of } -4 = -18 + 4$$

Here are examples of algebraic subtraction.

$$9 - 16 = 9 + -16 = -7$$
$$24 - 15 = 24 + -15 = 9$$
$$-8 - 20 = -8 + -20 = -28$$
$$3 - -6 = 3 + 6 = 9$$
$$-18 - -4 = -18 + 4 = -14$$

Multiplication and Division of Signed Numbers

Algebraic multiplication and division of signed numbers share the same pattern. Table 4.10 summarizes the rules for multiplication or division of two signed numbers.

Table 4.10: Rules for Algebraic Multiplication or Division of Two Signed Numbers		
If the signs are:	**The rule is:**	**Examples**
1. the same—both positive or both negative	Ignore the signs, multiply or divide the two numbers like you would nonsigned numbers, and use a positive sign as the sign for the answer.	$2 \times 5 = 10$ $-2 \times -5 = 10$ $12 \div 4 = 3$ $-12 \div -4 = 3$
2. different—one positive and one negative	Ignore the signs, multiply or divide the two numbers like you would nonsigned numbers, and use a negative sign as the sign for the answer.	$-2 \times 5 = -10$ $2 \times -5 = -10$ $-12 \div 4 = -3$ $12 \div -4 = -3$

Notice that, unlike algebraic addition, for algebraic multiplication/division when the signs are the same, it doesn't matter what the common sign is, the product/quotient is positive no matter what.

Similarly, unlike algebraic addition, for algebraic multiplication/division when the signs are different, it doesn't matter which number is the greater unsigned number—the product/quotient is negative no matter what.

The rules for algebraic addition, subtraction, multiplication, and division apply to all real numbers. Here are examples.

$$-\frac{5}{8} + -\frac{1}{8} = -\frac{6}{8} = -\frac{3}{4}$$

$$\frac{2}{3} - \frac{3}{4} = \frac{8}{12} - \frac{9}{12} = -\frac{1}{12}$$

$$24.5 + 134.28 = 158.78$$

$$-18.5 + 7.25 = -11.25$$

$$\frac{3}{4} \times -12 = \frac{3}{\cancel{4}_1} \times \frac{-\cancel{12}^3}{1} = \frac{-9}{1} = -9$$

$$-2\frac{3}{4} \times -1\frac{1}{3} = -\frac{11}{\cancel{4}_1} \times -\frac{\cancel{4}^1}{3} = \frac{11}{3} \text{ or } 3\frac{2}{3}$$

$$(-0.75)(400) = -300$$

$$(-125.43)(-0.005) = 0.62715$$

Test Yourself

1. The sum of two positive numbers is always _____ (positive, negative).

2. The sum of two negative numbers is always _____ (positive, negative).

3. The sum of a positive number and a negative number can be either positive or negative, depending on which of the two numbers has the _____(lesser, greater) unsigned value.

4. The product of two positive numbers is always _____ (positive, negative).

5. The product of two negative numbers is always _____ (positive, negative).

6. The product of a positive number and a negative number is always _____ (positive, negative).

7. $-5 + 20 =$ _____ .

8. $2.45 + -8 =$ _____ .

9. $-\frac{2}{5} + -\frac{4}{5} =$ _____ .

10. $45 - -15 = 45 +$ _____ $=$ _____ .

11. $-\frac{1}{2} - -\frac{1}{2} = -\frac{1}{2} +$ _____ $=$ _____ .

12. $-304.75 - 20.015 = -304.75 +$ _____ $=$ _____ .

13. $\frac{1}{2} \times -\frac{2}{5} =$ _____ .

14. $-\frac{3}{10} \div 2 =$ _____ .

15. $(-0.0125)(-7.2) =$ _____ .

Answers

1. positive

2. negative

3. greater

4. positive

5. positive

6. negative

7. 15

8. –5.55

9. $-\frac{6}{5}$ or $-1\frac{1}{5}$

10. 15, 60

11. $\frac{1}{2}$, 0

12. –20.015, –324.765

13. $\frac{1}{2} \times -\frac{2}{5} = \frac{1}{\cancel{2}_1} \times \frac{\cancel{2}^1}{5} = -\frac{1}{5}$

14. $-\frac{3}{10} \div 2 = -\frac{3}{10} \times \frac{1}{2} = -\frac{3}{20}$

15. 0.09

In What Order Do You Do the Operations?

When more than one operation is involved in a numerical expression, you must follow the **order of operations** to **simply** the expression:

1. Do computations inside **Parentheses.** If there is more than one operation inside the parentheses, follow the order of operations given here as you do the computations inside the parentheses.

2. Evaluate any terms with **Exponents.**

3. **Multiply** and **Divide** in the order in which they occur from left to right.

4. **Add** and **Subtract** in the order in which they occur from left to right.

Here is a sentence to help you remember the order of operations: **Please Excuse My Dear Aunt Sally**—abbreviated as **PE(MD)(AS).** The first letter of each word gives the order of operations:

1. **P**arentheses

2. **E**xponents

3. **M**ultiply and **D**ivide from left to right, whichever comes first.

4. **A**dd and **S**ubtract from left to right, whichever comes first.

Note that multiplication does not have to be done before division, or addition before subtraction. You multiply and divide in the order they occur in the problem. Similarly, you add and subtract in the order they occur in the problem. That's why there are parentheses around **MD** and **AS** in **PE(MD)(AS).**

Here are examples of using the order of operations to simplify numerical expressions.

Simplify: $90 - 5 \cdot 3^2 + 42 \div (5 + 2)$

$90 - 5 \cdot 3^2 + 42 \div (5 + 2) = 90 - 5 \cdot 3^2 + 42 \div (7)$	First, do computations inside parentheses.
$= 90 - 5 \cdot 9 + 42 \div (7)$	Next, evaluate exponents.
$= 90 - 45 + 6$	Then, multiply and divide from left to right.
$= 51$	Finally, add and subtract from left to right.

When simplified, the numerical expression $90 - 5 \cdot 3^2 + 42 \div (5 + 2) = 51$.

Simplify: $-50 + 40 \div 2^3 - 5(4 + 6)$

$-50 + 40 \div 2^3 - 5(4 + 6) = -50 + 40 \div 2^3 - 5(10)$	First, do computations inside parentheses.
$= -50 + 40 \div 8 - 5(10)$	Next, evaluate exponents.
$= -50 + 5 - 50$	Then, multiply and divide from left to right.
$= -95$	Finally, add and subtract from left to right.

When simplified, the numerical expression $-50 + 40 \div 2^3 - 5(4 + 6) = -95$.

Simplify: $8 - 4 \div (7 - 5) - (7 + 3) \div 2$

$8 - 4 \div (7 - 5) - (7 + 3) \div 2 = 8 - 4 \div 2 - 10 \div 2$	First, do computations inside parentheses.
$= 8 - 4 \div 2 - 10 \div 2$	Next, evaluate exponents—none, so skip this step.
$= 8 - 2 - 5$	Then, divide from left to right.
$= 1$	Finally, subtract from left to right.

When simplified, the numerical expression : $8 - 4 \div (7 - 5) - (7 + 3) \div 2 = 1$.

An important caution: Don't count on the calculator from the testing center to follow the order of operations. Most 4-function calculators do *not* follow the order of operations. They usually perform operations in the order they are keyed into the calculator. If you start at the left and key in the problem from left to right and then press the equal sign, most likely the answer displayed will *not* be the correct answer. Instead, key in the computations according to the order of operations, starting with the computations inside parentheses and ending with addition and subtraction from left to right. As shown in the examples, rewrite the problem as you work through the computations to avoid making careless errors.

Test Yourself

1. When simplifying numerical expressions, follow the _____ .

2. Simplify: $(3+2)(14 + 4) \div 9 - 2^4 \cdot 10 + 148$

3. Simplify: $24 \div 6 - 2 \cdot 10 + 34$

4. Simplify: $-2(3 - 8) + 9^2 \div 3$

5. Simplify: $20 + 5 \times 7 - 4$

Answers

1. order of operations

2. $(3+2)(14 + 4) \div 9 - 2^4 \cdot 10 + 148$

$= (5)(18) \div 9 - 2^4 \cdot 10 + 148$

$= (5)(18) \div 9 - 16 \cdot 10 + 148$

$= 90 \div 9 - 160 + 148$

$= 10 - 160 + 148$

$= -2$

3. $24 \div 6 - 2 \cdot 10 + 34$

$= 4 - 20 + 34$

$= 18$

4. $-2(3 - 8) + 9^2 \div 3$

$= -2(-5) + 9^2 \div 3$

$= -2(-5) + 81 \div 3$

$= 10 + 27$

$= 37$

5. $20 + 5 \times 7 - 4$

$= 20 + 35 - 4$

$= 51$

How Do You Solve Real-World Problems Involving Rational Numbers?

On the FTCE GK test, you will have real world problems in the form of word problems involving rational numbers to solve. Use the following steps when solving word problems.

1. **Understand the problem.**

   Read the problem and identify what you need to find. Look for a sentence that has words like *find, determine, what is, how many, how far,* and *how much.* Often (but not always) this is the last sentence in the problem. Draw a line under this sentence in your test booklet.

   Organize the information you are given. Ask yourself, "What information is given in the problem that will help me answer the question? Is there a formula I need that is not provided? Are any facts missing? Is there information given that I don't need? Are measurement units involved and, if so, what units should my answer have? Can I draw a picture to help me better understand the problem? Would it help to make a chart or table?

2. **Make a plan.**

   Decide how you can use the information you are given to solve the problem. Ask yourself, "What math concepts apply to this situation?" Decide which operation or operations to use. Table 4.11 has some guidelines to help you decide.

Table 4.11 Guidelines for Selecting Operations

When You Need to:	Use:
Find a sum. Find a total. Combine quantities. Increase a quantity.	Addition
Find a difference. Take away. Find how many or how much is left. Find out how many more or how many less. Decrease a quantity.	Subtraction
Find a product. Put equal quantities together to find a total. Determine how much or how many is a portion of a whole. Find the cost of a given number of units when you know the unit price. Find a percent of a quantity. Determine how many different ways something can occur. Determine how many different combinations are possible.	Multiplication
Find a quotient. Find a ratio or fractional part. Determine how many equal parts are in a whole. Determine the size of equal parts of a whole. Separate an amount into groups of equal size. Find the probability of a simple event.	Division

After you have decided on what operation or operations to use, roughly outline how you will proceed. If measurement units are involved, make sure they work out to give the proper units. This is a powerful tool that is used extensively in the sciences.

3. **Carry out your plan.**

   Solve the problem, using the information and the operation or operations you decided upon.

   Double-check to make sure you copied all information accurately. Check the order of the numbers if subtraction or division is involved. Check the signs if you are using positive and negative numbers.

   Key the numbers into your calculator carefully. Look at the display after every entry to make sure you entered what you intended to enter. Be especially careful when decimals or fractions are involved.

4. **Look back.**

   Check whether you've answered the question.

   Ask yourself, "Does my answer make sense? Is my answer consistent with my knowledge of the real world? Is it stated in the correct units?"

Here is an example of using the problem-solving steps.

Problem: A motor home rents for $250 per week plus $0.20 per mile. Find the rental cost for a 3-week trip of 600 miles for a family of 4.

1. **Understand the problem.**

    What do you need to find?

    > The rental cost for a 3-week trip of 600 miles

    What information are you given?

    > cost per week: $250

    > cost per mile: $0.20

    > number of weeks: 3

    > number of miles: 600

    Is there information given that you don't need?

    > number of family members: 4

2. **Make a plan.**

    You want the total rental cost for the motor home, which includes the cost for 3 weeks of rental and the cost for mileage. Solving the problem will involve three steps: find the cost for the 3 weeks of rental, find the cost for mileage, and then find the total rental cost.

3. **Carry out the plan.**

    Step 1. Find the cost for 3 weeks of rental. You know the cost per week is $250. Multiply to get the cost for 3 weeks.

    $$3 \text{ wk} \times \frac{\$250}{\text{wk}} = \frac{3 \text{ wk}}{1} \times \frac{\$250}{\text{wk}} = \$750 \qquad \text{Notice that weeks "cancel out," leaving \$ as the units.}$$

    Step 2. Find the cost for mileage. You know the cost per mile is $0.20. Multiply to get the cost for 600 miles.

    $$600 \text{ mi} \times \frac{\$0.20}{\text{mi}} = \frac{600 \text{ mi}}{1} \times \frac{\$0.20}{\text{mi}} = \$120 \quad \text{Notice that miles "cancel out," leaving \$ as the units.}$$

    Step 3. Find the total rental cost for the motor home. Add the results from steps 1 and 2 to find the total.

    cost for 3 weeks of rental + cost for mileage = $750 + $120 = $870.

4. **Look back.**

    Did I answer the question? Yes, I found the total rental cost for the motor home. ✓

    Does my answer make sense? Is it consistent with my knowledge of the real world? Yes, the answer seems like a reasonable cost. ✓

    Is the answer stated in the correct units? Yes, the units are dollars, which is correct. ✓

Ratios and Proportions

A ratio is the comparison of two quantities. In a paint mixture that uses 2 parts white paint to 5 parts blue paint, the ratio of white paint to blue paint is two to five. You can express this ratio in three different forms: 2 to 5, 2:5, or $\frac{2}{5}$. The numbers 2 and 5 are called the **terms** of the ratio. A ratio is a pure number—it does not have any units. When you find the ratio of two quantities, you must make sure they have the same units so that when you write the ratio, the units will "cancel out." For example, the ratio of 2 pints to 5 quarts is *not* $\frac{2}{5}$ because these quantities are not expressed in the same units. Since 2 pints = 1 quart, the ratio is 1 quart to 5 quarts $= \frac{1 \text{ qt}}{5 \text{ qt}} = \frac{1}{5}$. If the two quantities cannot be converted to like units, then you must keep the units and write the quotient as a **rate**. For instance, $\frac{140 \text{ mi}}{2 \text{ h}} = 70$ mph is a rate of speed.

A **proportion** is a mathematical statement that two ratios are equal. The **terms** of the proportion are the four numbers that make up the two ratios. For example, take the proportion $\frac{3}{4} = \frac{9}{12}$. This proportion has terms 3, 4, 9, and 12. In a proportion, cross products are equal. **Cross products** are the product of the numerator of the first ratio times the denominator of the second ratio and the product of the denominator of the first ratio times the numerator of the second ratio.

$$\frac{3}{4} \bowtie \frac{9}{12}$$

Here is an example showing the equal cross products for the proportion $\frac{3}{4} = \frac{9}{12}$.

$$3 \times 12 = 4 \times 9$$
$$36 = 36$$

When you are given a proportion that has a missing term, you can use cross products to find the missing term. Look at this example.

Find the value of x that makes the following proportion true.

$$\frac{x}{40} = \frac{3}{4}$$

$x \times 4 = 40 \times 3$ Find the cross products.

$x \times 4 = 120$

You can see from the cross products that x is the number that multiplies times 4 to give 120. Logical reasoning should tell you that

$$x = \frac{120}{4}$$

$$x = 30$$

Note: In the "Algebraic Reasoning" section of this chapter, you will learn to solve the equation $x \times 4 = 120$ by dividing both sides of the equation by 4, which also gives $x = 30$.

You can shorten the preceding process for solving a proportion by doing the following: find a cross product that you can calculate and then divide by the numerical term in the proportion that you did not use. Since you are allowed to use a calculator on the FTCE GK test, this is the quickest and most reliable way to solve a proportion on the test. Here's how it would work for the previous example.

Find the value of x that makes the following proportion true.

$$\frac{x}{40} = \frac{3}{4}$$

40×3 Find a cross product you can calculate. You don't know the value of x, so the only cross product you can calculate is 40 times 3.

$x = \frac{40 \times 3}{4}$ Divide by 4, the numerical term you didn't use.

$x = \frac{120}{4}$

$x = 30$

Here's how you key the computations into your calculator: $40 \times 3 \div 4 =$. The display will show 30, the correct answer.

Word problems involving proportional relationships are one type of word problem you will encounter on the FTCE GK test. These are problems that deal with ratios, map scales, and scale factors. Here is an example.

Problem: On a map, the distance between two cities is 10.5 inches. If 0.5 inch represents 20 miles, how far, in miles, is it between the two cities (to the nearest mile)?

1. **Understand the problem.**

   What do you need to find?

   the actual distance in miles between the two cities

   What information are you given?

   distance between the cities on the map is 10.5 inches

   scale for map: 0.5 inch represents 20 miles

   Is there information given that you don't need?

   No

2. **Make a plan.**

   This problem is a proportion problem involving a map scale. To solve the problem, determine the ratios being compared, being sure to compare corresponding quantities in the same order; write a proportion using the two ratios; and then use cross products to solve the proportion.

3. **Carry out the plan.**

   Step 1. Determine the ratios being compared.

   Let *d* be the actual distance in miles between the two cities. The first sentence gives the first ratio: $\frac{d\,(\text{in miles})}{10.5\text{ in.}}$. The second sentence gives the second ratio: $\frac{20\text{ miles}}{0.5\text{ in.}}$. (Notice, you put miles in the numerator in the second ratio because you have miles in the numerator in the first ratio.)

   Step 2. Write a proportion using the two ratios.

   $$\frac{d\,(\text{in miles})}{10.5\text{ in.}} = \frac{20\text{ miles}}{0.5\text{ in.}}$$

   Step 3. Use cross products to solve the proportion (omitting the units for convenience).

   $$\frac{d}{10.5} = \frac{20}{0.5}$$

   10.5×20 Find a cross product you can calculate. You don't know the value *d*, so the only cross product you can calculate is 10.5 times 20.

   $d = \frac{10.5 \times 20}{0.5}$ Divide by 0.5, the numerical term you didn't use.

   $d = \frac{210}{0.5}$

   $d = 420$ miles

   Here's how you key the computations into your calculator: $10.5 \times 20 \div 0.5 =$. The display will show 420, the correct answer.

4. **Look back.**

   Did I answer the question? Yes, I found the actual distance in miles between the two cities. ✓

   Does my answer make sense? Is it consistent with my knowledge of the real world? Yes, if 0.5 inches corresponds to 20 miles, then 1 inch corresponds to 40 miles, so 10.5 inches should represent at least 400 miles. ✓

   Is the answer stated in the correct units? Yes, the units are miles, which is correct. ✓

Percent Problems

Percent problems can be solved in several ways. Most of the percent problems on the FTCE GK test can be solved using a "percent" proportion that has the following form:

$$\frac{r}{100} = \frac{\text{part}}{\text{whole}}$$

   r = the number in front of the % sign

   part = the number that is near the word "is"

   whole = the number that follows the word "of"

The relationship between the three elements *r*, **part**, and **whole** can be explained in a percent statement like this:

The part is *r*% of the whole.

The secret to solving percent problems is being able to identify the three elements correctly. Start with *r* and the whole because they are usually easier to find. The part will be the other amount in the problem. The value of two of the elements will be given in the problem, and you will be solving for the third element. After you identify the three elements, plug the two you know into the proportion and solve for the one that you don't know.

Here is an example of what to do when the part is missing.

What is 20% of 560?

Identify the elements.

$$r = 20$$
$$\text{part} = ?$$
$$\text{whole} = 560$$

Plug into the percent proportion.

$$\frac{r}{100} = \frac{\text{part}}{\text{whole}}$$
$$\frac{20}{100} = \frac{x}{560}$$

Solve the proportion.

20×560 Find a cross product you can calculate. You don't know the value of *x*, so the only cross product you can calculate is 20 times 560.

$$x = \frac{20 \times 560}{100}$$ Divide by 100, the numerical term you didn't use.
$$x = 112$$

Here's how you key the computations into your calculator: $20 \times 560 \div 100 =$. The display will show 112, the correct answer.

Here is an example of what to do when the whole is missing.

30 is 25% of what amount?

Identify the elements.

$$r = 25$$
$$\text{part} = 30$$
$$\text{whole} = ?$$

Plug into the percent proportion.

$$\frac{r}{100} = \frac{\text{part}}{\text{whole}}$$

$$\frac{25}{100} = \frac{30}{x}$$

Solve the proportion.

100×30 Find a cross product you can calculate. You don't know the value of x, so the only cross product you can calculate is 100 times 30.

$x = \dfrac{100 \times 30}{25}$ Divide by 25, the numerical term you didn't use.

$x = 120$

Here's how you key the computations into your calculator: $100 \times 30 \div 25 =$. The display will show 120, the correct answer.

Here is an example when r is missing.

---

400 is what percent of 500?

Identify the elements.

$r = ?$

part $= 400$

whole $= 500$

Plug into the percent proportion.

$\dfrac{r}{100} = \dfrac{\text{part}}{\text{whole}}$

$\dfrac{r}{100} = \dfrac{400}{500}$

Solve the proportion.

100×400 Find a cross product you can calculate. You don't know the value of r, so the only cross product you can calculate is 100 times 400.

$r = \dfrac{100 \times 400}{500}$ Divide by 500, the numerical term you didn't use.

$r = 80$

$\dfrac{r}{100} = 80\%$

Notice that since r is the number in front of the percent sign in the percent statement, you have to put a % sign after your calculated value of r to answer the question.

Just so you know, there are other ways to work percent problems. For instance, to answer "What is 20% of 560?", change 20% to a fraction or a decimal fraction and then multiply 560 by the converted number.

$$20\% \text{ of } 560 = 0.20 \times 560 = 112 \qquad \text{or} \qquad 20\% \text{ of } 560 = \dfrac{1}{\cancel{5}_1} \times \dfrac{\overset{112}{\cancel{560}}}{1} = 112$$

You get the same answer as was obtained earlier. The proportion method is emphasized in this study guide because when you are allowed to use a calculator, it is a reliable and efficient way to solve percent problems.

Word Problems Involving Percents

You can expect to encounter word problems involving percents on the FTCE GK test. These are problems that deal with finding percentages, percents, and wholes in various every day situations. Here is an example.

Problem: A stereo system that regularly sells for $650 is marked 20% off for a one-day sale. What is the amount saved if the stereo is purchased at the sale price?

---

1. **Understand the problem.**

   What do you need to find?

   the amount saved at the sale price

   What information are you given?

   regular price: $650

   amount saved: 20% off regular price

   Is there information given that you don't need?

   that it's a one-day sale

2. **Make a plan.**

   To find the amount saved, you will need to answer the question: What is 20% of $650? To solve the problem: Identify the elements of the percent problem, plug the values into the percent proportion, and then solve the proportion.

3. **Carry out the plan.**

   Step 1. Identify the elements.

   $$r = 20$$

   $$\text{part} = ?$$

   $$\text{whole} = \$650$$

   Step 2. Plug into the percent proportion (omitting the units for convenience).

   $$\frac{r}{100} = \frac{\text{part}}{\text{whole}}$$

   $$\frac{20}{100} = \frac{x}{650}$$

   Step 3. Solve the proportion.

   20×650 Find a cross product you can calculate. You don't know the value of x, so the only cross product you can calculate is 20 times 650.

   $x = \frac{20 \times 650}{100}$ Divide by 100, the numerical term you didn't use.

   $x = \$130$

Here's how you key the computations into your calculator: $20 \times 650 \div 100 =$. The display will show 130, the correct answer.

4. **Look back.**

   Did I answer the question? Yes, I found the amount saved. ✓

   Does my answer make sense? Is it consistent with my knowledge of the real world? Yes, 20% is $\frac{1}{5}$. For a $500 item, the savings would be $100. For a $650 item, the savings would be a little over $100. ✓

   Is the answer stated in the correct units? Yes, the units are dollars, which is correct. ✓

Test Yourself

1. The four problem-solving steps are _____ , _____ , _____ , and _____ ,

2. A _____ is the comparison of two quantities. It is a pure number. It does not have any _____ .

3. A _____ is a statement that two _____ are equal.

4. If 12 ounces of salt are mixed with 5 ounces of ground pepper, what is the ratio of salt to pepper?

5. What are the terms of the proportion $\frac{x}{50} = \frac{7}{25}$?

6. In a proportion, the _____ are equal.

7. Solve the proportion $\frac{x}{50} = \frac{7}{25}$ for x.

8. What is 40% of $1200?

9. In a paint mixture that uses 2 parts white paint to 5 parts blue paint, how many quarts of white paint are needed to mix with 20 quarts of blue paint?

10. At an art exhibit at a local gallery, 15 of the 25 paintings displayed were purchased by a well-known art connoisseur. What percent of the paintings were purchased by the art connoisseur?

Answers

1. Understand the problem, make a plan, carry out the plan, look back.

2. ratio, units

3. proportion, ratios

4. 12 to 5

5. x, 50, 7, 25

6. cross products

7. $\frac{x}{50} = \frac{7}{25}$

    50×7 Find a cross product you can calculate. You don't know the value of x, so the only cross product you can calculate is 50 times 7.

    $x = \frac{50 \times 7}{25}$ Divide by 25, the numerical term you didn't use.

    $x = 14$

8. What is 40% of $1200?

Identify the elements.

    $r = 40$

   part = ?

  whole = $1200

Plug into the percent proportion.

    $\frac{r}{100} = \frac{\text{part}}{\text{whole}}$

    $\frac{40}{100} = \frac{x}{\$1200}$

Solve the proportion (omitting the units for convenience).

    40×1200 Find a cross product you can calculate. You don't know the value of x, so the only cross product you can calculate is 40 times 1200.

    $x = \frac{40 \times 1200}{100}$ Divide by 100, the numerical term you didn't use.

    $x = \$480$

9. This problem is a proportion problem involving ratios in a mixture. To solve the problem, determine the ratios being compared, being sure to compare corresponding quantities in the same order; write a proportion using the two ratios; and then use cross products to solve the proportion.

   Step 1. Determine the ratios being compared.

   The first sentence gives the first ratio: $\dfrac{2 \text{ parts white paint}}{5 \text{ parts blue paint}}$. The second sentence gives the second ratio: $\dfrac{x\,(\text{quarts}) \text{ white paint}}{20 \text{ quarts blue paint}}$.

   Step 2. Write a proportion using the two ratios.

   $$\frac{2 \text{ parts white paint}}{5 \text{ parts blue paint}} = \frac{x\,(\text{quarts}) \text{ white paint}}{20 \text{ quarts blue paint}}$$

   Step 3. Use cross products to solve the proportion (omitting the units for convenience).

   $$\frac{2}{5} = \frac{x}{20}$$

   2×20 — Find a cross product you can calculate. You don't know the value of x, so the only cross product you can calculate is 2 times 20.

   $x = \dfrac{2 \times 20}{5}$ — Divide by 5, the numerical term you didn't use.

   $x = 8$ quarts of white paint

   Did I answer the question? Yes, I found the number of quarts of white paint needed. ✓

   Does my answer make sense? Is it consistent with my knowledge of the real world? Yes. ✓

   Is the answer stated in the correct units? Yes, the units are quarts, which is correct. ✓

10. To find the percent purchased, you will need to answer the question: 15 is $r\%$ of 25? To solve the problem: identify the elements of the percent problem, plug the values into the percent proportion, and solve the proportion.

    Step 1. Identify the elements.

    $r = ?$

    part = 15

    whole = 25

    Step 2. Plug into the percent proportion (omitting the units for convenience).

    $$\frac{r}{100} = \frac{\text{part}}{\text{whole}}$$
    $$\frac{r}{100} = \frac{15}{25}$$

    Step 3. Solve the proportion.

    100×15 — Find a cross product you can calculate. You don't know the value of r, so the only cross product you can calculate is 100 times 15.

    $r = \dfrac{100 \times 15}{25}$ — Divide by 25, the numerical term you didn't use.

    $r = 60$

    $\dfrac{60}{100} = 60\%$

    Did I answer the question? Yes, I found the percent of the paintings purchased by the art connoisseur. ✓

    Does my answer make sense? Is it consistent with my knowledge of the real world? Yes. ✓

    Is the answer stated in the correct units? The answer is a percent, so it should not have any units. ✓

Sample Questions

1. Find the greatest common factor of 18 and 30.

    A. 2
    B. 3
    C. 6
    D. 90

2. How is the product $5 \times 5 \times 7 \times 7 \times 7$ expressed in exponential notation?

    A. $2^5 \times 3^7$
    B. 57^5
    C. $5^2 \times 7^3$
    D. $5^3 \times 7^2$

3. Which of the following should be performed first to simplify this expression?

$-8 + 45 \cdot 18 \div 3^2$

    A. $-8 + 45$
    B. $45 \cdot 18$
    C. $18 \div 3$
    D. 3^2

4. If 25% of a monthly salary of $2800 is budgeted for food, how much money is budgeted for food?

    A. $70
    B. $210
    C. $700
    D. $2100

Answer Explanations for Sample Questions

1. C. The greatest common factor of 18 and 30 is the largest number that will divide into both 18 and 30 evenly. The numbers that will divide evenly into 18 are 1, 2, 3, 6, 9, and 18. The numbers that will divide evenly into 30 are 1, 2, 3, 5, 6, 10, 15, and 30. Looking at the two sets of divisors, you can see that 6 is the largest number that will divide into both 18 and 30 evenly. Thus, GCF (18,30) = 6.

2. C. Expressed in exponential notation, the product $5 \times 5 \times 7 \times 7 \times 7$ is $5^2 \times 7^3$, which indicates 2 factors of 5 and 3 factors of 7. The other answer choices do not indicate 2 factors of 5 and 3 factors of 7.

3. D. To simplify the expression $-8 + 45 \cdot 18 \div 3^2$, follow "Please Excuse My Dear Aunt Sally." The order of operations requires that any operations in parentheses be performed first. There are no parentheses in this expression, so the next step is to simplify any exponents. Since 3^2 is in exponential form, it should be performed first. It would be incorrect to perform $-8 + 45$ first (Choice **A**) because addition and subtraction, from left to right, are performed last when there are no parentheses indicating to do otherwise. It would be incorrect to perform $45 \cdot 18$ (Choice **B**) or $18 \div 3$ (Choice **C**) *first* because multiplication and division, from left to right, are performed after exponentiation, unless there are parentheses indicating to do otherwise.

4. C. To find the amount budgeted for food, you will need to answer the question: what is 25% of 2800?

Method 1: To solve the problem, identify the elements of the percent problem, plug the values into the percent proportion, and solve the proportion.

Step 1. Identify the elements.

$$r = 25$$

$$\text{part} = ?$$

$$\text{whole} = \$2800$$

Step 2. Plug into the percent proportion (omitting the units for convenience).

$$\frac{r}{100} = \frac{\text{part}}{\text{whole}}$$

$$\frac{25}{100} = \frac{x}{\$2800}$$

Step 3. Solve the proportion (omitting the units for convenience).

25×2800 Find a cross product you can calculate. You don't know the value of *x*, so the only cross product you can calculate is 25 times 2800.

$x = \dfrac{25 \times 2800}{100}$ Divide by 100, the numerical term you didn't use.

$x = \$700$

The amount budgeted for food is $700, Choice **C**.

Did I answer the question? Yes, I found the amount budgeted for food. ✓

Does my answer make sense? Is it consistent with my knowledge of the real world? Yes. ✓

Is the answer stated in the correct units? Yes, the units are dollars, which is correct. ✓

Method 2: Change 25% to a decimal fraction or common fraction and multiply:

$$25\% \text{ of } \$2800 = 0.25 \times \$2800 = \$700.00$$

$$25\% \text{ of } \$2800 = \frac{1}{4} \times \$2800 = \frac{\$2800}{4} = \$700$$

Choice **A** results if you make a decimal point error. Choice **B** results if you solve the problem incorrectly by finding 75% of $2800 and you make a decimal point error. Choice **D** results if you solve the problem incorrectly by finding 75% of $2800.

Measurement

As listed in the *Competencies and Skills Required for Teacher Certification in Florida, Ninth Edition* (see the first section of this chapter for the Web address), the competencies/skills you should be able to do for this area of mathematics are the following:

- Convert units of measure of length, weight, mass, volume, and time.
- Estimate measurements.
- Solve real-world problems involving unit rate.
- Read a measuring instrument (for example, ruler, graduated cylinder, thermometer, gauge) to a specified degree of accuracy.
- Solve real-world problems involving scaled drawings such as maps and models.
- Solve real-world problems involving perimeter, area, and volume.

How Do You Convert from One Measurement Unit to Another?

On the FTCE GK test, you will have to demonstrate your knowledge of measurement using the U.S. customary system and the metric system. Your Mathematics Reference Sheet contains the conversion facts, as reproduced here, that you will need to know for the test.

Conversions	
1 yard = 3 feet = 36 inches	1 cup = 8 fluid ounces
1 mile = 1,760 yards = 5,280 feet	1 pint = 2 cups
1 acre = 43,560 square feet	1 quart = 2 pints
1 hour = 60 minutes	1 gallon = 4 quarts
1 minute = 60 seconds	1 pound = 16 ounces
	1 ton = 2,000 pounds
1 liter = 1,000 milliliters = 1,000 cubic centimeters	
1 meter = 100 centimeters = 1,000 millimeters	
1 kilometer = 1,000 meters	
1 gram = 1,000 milligrams	
1 kilogram = 1,000 grams	

You can convert from one measurement unit to another by using an appropriate "conversion fraction." You make conversion fractions by using the conversion facts given in the Mathematics Reference Sheet. For each conversion fact in the table, you can write *two* conversion fractions. For example, for the conversion fact 1 yard = 3 feet, you have $\frac{1 \text{ yd}}{3 \text{ ft}}$ and $\frac{3 \text{ ft}}{1 \text{ yd}}$ as your two conversion fractions. Each of these conversion fractions is equivalent to the number 1 because the numerator and denominator are different names for the same length. Therefore, if you multiply a quantity by either of these fractions, you will not change the value of the quantity. When you need to change one measurement unit to another unit, multiply by the conversion fraction whose *denominator is the same as the units of the quantity to be converted*. This strategy is called **unit analysis.** When you do the multiplication, the units you started out with will divide ("cancel") out, and you will be left with the new units. If this doesn't happen, then you used the wrong conversion fraction, so do it over again with the other conversion fraction. It is a good idea to assess your final answer to see whether it makes sense. When you are converting from a larger unit to a smaller unit, you should expect that it will take more of the smaller units to equal the same amount. When you are converting from a smaller unit to a larger unit, you should expect that it will take less of the larger units to equal the same amount.

Here is an example of converting from a larger unit to a smaller unit:

> Convert 5 yards to feet.

The conversion fractions are $\frac{1 \text{ yd}}{3 \text{ ft}}$ and $\frac{3 \text{ ft}}{1 \text{ yd}}$. Multiply 5 yards by $\frac{3 \text{ ft}}{1 \text{ yd}}$ because the denominator has the same units as the quantity to be converted:

$$5 \text{ yd} \times \frac{3 \text{ ft}}{1 \text{ yd}} = \frac{5 \text{ yd}}{1} \times \frac{3 \text{ ft}}{1 \text{ yd}} = 15 \text{ ft}$$ The yards (yd) units cancel out, leaving feet (ft) as the units for the answer.

Does this answer make sense? Feet are smaller than yards, so it should take more of them to equal the same length as 5 yards.

Here is an example of converting from a smaller unit to a larger unit:

> Convert 250 centimeters to meters.

The conversion fractions are $\frac{1 \text{ m}}{100 \text{ cm}}$ and $\frac{100 \text{ cm}}{1 \text{ m}}$. Multiply 250 centimeters by $\frac{1 \text{ m}}{100 \text{ cm}}$ because the denominator has the same units as the quantity to be converted:

$$250 \text{ cm} \times \frac{1 \text{ m}}{100 \text{ cm}} = \frac{250 \text{ cm}}{1} \times \frac{1 \text{ m}}{100 \text{ cm}} = 2.5 \text{ m}$$

The centimeters (cm) units cancel out, leaving meters (m) as the units for the answer. Notice that since 100 is in the denominator, you divide 250 by 100 to obtain the 2.5 in the answer.

Does this answer make sense? Meters are larger than centimeters, so it should take fewer of them to equal the same distance as 250 centimeters.

For some conversions, you may need to make a "chain" of conversion fractions to obtain your desired units. Here is an example:

Convert 3 gallons to cups.

The conversion table does not have a fact that shows the equivalency between gallons and cups. You have 1 pint = 2 cups, 1 quart = 2 pints, and 1 gallon = 4 quarts. These facts yield 6 conversion fractions, respectively: $\frac{1 \text{ pt}}{2 \text{ c}}, \frac{2 \text{ c}}{1 \text{ pt}}, \frac{1 \text{ qt}}{2 \text{ pt}}, \frac{2 \text{ pt}}{1 \text{ qt}}, \frac{1 \text{ gal}}{4 \text{ qt}}$, and $\frac{4 \text{ qt}}{1 \text{ gal}}$. Start with your quantity to be converted and keep multiplying by conversion fractions until you obtain your desired units.

$$3 \text{ gal} \times \frac{4 \text{ qt}}{1 \text{ gal}} \times \frac{2 \text{ pt}}{1 \text{ qt}} \times \frac{2 \text{ c}}{1 \text{ pt}} = 48 \text{ c}$$

Does this answer make sense? Cups are smaller than gallons, so it should take more of them to equal the same amount as 3 gallons.

For the FTCE GK test, you will not have to convert between the customary system and the metric system. You will convert only within a given system. If you are not very familiar with the metric system, here are some "rough" equivalencies of the more common units for your general knowledge.

Equivalencies Chart	
Meter	about 3 inches longer than a yard
Centimeter	about the width of a large paper clip
Millimeter	about the thickness of a dime
Kilometer	about 5 city blocks or a little farther than half a mile
Liter	a little more than a quart
Milliliter	takes about five of them to make a teaspoon
Gram	about the weight of a small paper clip
Milligram	about the weight of a grain of salt
Kilogram	the weight of a liter of water or a little more than 2 pounds

How Do You Solve Problems Involving Unit Rates?

A **unit rate** is an amount per unit. It is a rated measure such as miles per hour, cost per item, cost per unit, words per page, and so on. Unit rates are used in many real-life situations.

Here is an example of using unit rates for comparison shopping.

Which is a better buy? 3 cans of soup for $2.00 or 4 cans for $3.50?

The unit price for 3 cans for $2.00 = $\frac{\$2.00}{3 \text{ cans}}$ = $0.67 per can (rounded to the nearest cent).

The unit price for 4 cans for $3.50 = $\frac{\$3.50}{4 \text{ cans}}$ = $0.88 per can (rounded to the nearest cent).

Assuming there's no difference in quality, the better buy is 3 cans for $2.00.

Here is an example of using unit rates to compare the speeds of two vehicles.

Car A traveled 156 miles in 2.4 hours. Car B traveled 245 miles in 3.5 hours. Which car averaged the faster speed?

The average speed (unit rate) for car A is $\frac{156 \text{ mi}}{2.4 \text{ h}}$ = 65 miles per hour (mph).

The average speed (unit rate) for car B is $\frac{245 \text{ mi}}{3.5 \text{ h}}$ = 70 miles per hour (mph).

Car B had a faster average speed.

You can use unit rates to find the total miles, total cost, total words, and so on by multiplying by the unit rate.

Here are examples.

A train travels 3 hours at a rate of 55 miles per hour. How many miles did the train travel?

To find the total miles traveled, multiply 3 hours by 55 mph (the unit rate):

$3 \text{ h} \times \frac{55 \text{ mi}}{1 \text{ h}} = 165 \text{ miles}$ The hours (h) units cancel out, leaving miles (mi) as the units for the answer.

If it costs $220 to rent a motor home for one week, how much will it cost to rent the motor home for 2 weeks?

To find the total cost, multiply 2 weeks by $220 per week (the unit rate).

$2 \text{ wk} \times \frac{\$220}{1 \text{ wk}} = \$440$ The weeks (wk) units cancel out, leaving dollars ($) as the units for the answer.

How Do You Read Measurement Instruments?

On the FTCE GK test, you will have to read a measurement instrument to the nearest specified unit. The gauge or scale of the measuring instrument will have markings that divide the gauge or scale into equal intervals. Usually, not every mark is labeled with a number. For example, on a standard customary ruler, inches will be labeled, but not the markings in between, as shown in the following.

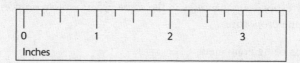

To read a measuring instrument, it is most important that you determine what each mark on the measuring instrument represents. To do this, find the two consecutive labeled points immediately below and above the reading on the scale. Find the difference between the two points. Count the number of markings it takes to get from the lower point to the higher point. Divide the difference between the two points by the number of marks you counted. After you determine what each mark represents, take the reading.

Here is an example.

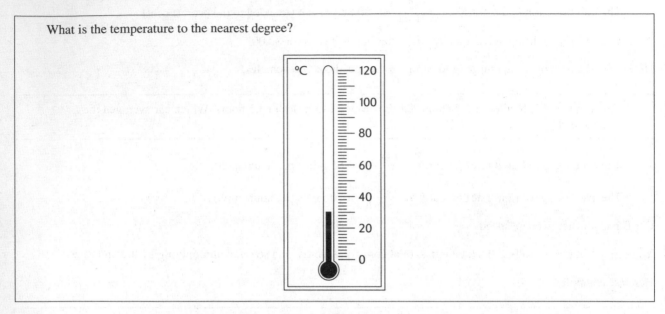

What is the temperature to the nearest degree?

The thermometer is reading between 20° and 40°. The difference between these two points is 40° − 20° = 20°. It takes ten marks to go from 20° up to 40°. Divide the difference between the two points by 10: 20° ÷ 10 = 2°. Therefore, each mark on the thermometer represents 2°. The thermometer is reading five marks above 20°. Since each mark represents 2°, the thermometer is reading 10° above 20°, which is 30°C.

How Do You Solve Problems Involving Scaled Drawings or Models?

The scale for a drawing or model is a ratio that compares the measurement on the drawing (or model) to the actual measurement in real life. For example, if a drawing has a scale of 1 cm = 10 meters, for every centimeter measured on the drawing, the actual length is 10 meters. To solve problems involving scaled drawings or models, set up a proportion and solve the problem.

Here is an example.

Problem: On a map, the distance between two cities is 18 inches. If 0.75 inch represents 20 miles, how far, in miles, is it between the two cities (to the nearest mile)?

This problem is a proportion problem involving a map scale. To solve the problem, determine the ratios being compared, being sure to compare corresponding quantities in the same order; write a proportion using the two ratios; and then use cross products to solve the proportion.

Step 1. Determine the ratios being compared.

Let d be the actual distance in miles between the two cities. The first sentence gives the first ratio: $\frac{d \text{ (in miles)}}{18 \text{ in.}}$. The second sentence gives the second ratio: $\frac{20 \text{ miles}}{0.75 \text{ in.}}$. (Notice, you put miles in the numerator in the second ratio because you have miles in the numerator in the first ratio.)

Step 2. Write a proportion using the two ratios.

$$\frac{d \text{ (in miles)}}{18 \text{ in.}} = \frac{20 \text{ miles}}{0.75 \text{ in.}}$$

Step 3. Use cross products to solve the proportion (omitting the units for convenience).

$\dfrac{d}{18} = \dfrac{20}{0.75}$

18×20 Find a cross product you can calculate. You don't know the value of *d*, so the only cross product you can calculate is 18 times 20.

$d = \dfrac{18 \times 20}{0.75}$ Divide by 0.75, the numerical term you didn't use.

$d = 480$ miles

Did I answer the question? Yes, I found the actual distance in miles between the two cities. ✓

Does my answer make sense? Is it consistent with my knowledge of the real world? Yes. ✓

Is the answer stated in the correct units? Yes, the units are miles, which is correct. ✓

Test Yourself

1. The conversion fractions for the conversion fact 1 yard = 36 inches are _____ and _____ .

2. To change 2.5 yards to inches multiply by _____ .

3. To change 720 inches to yards multiply by _____ .

4. 720 inches = _____ yards.

5. 4.35 kilometers = _____ meters.

6. 2 hours = _____ seconds.

7. Which is a better buy for an item? 5 for $4.25 or 6 for $5.00?

8. A motor home rents for a weekly rate plus $0.25 per mile. What is the total cost for mileage for a trip of 500 miles?

9. The scale for a model airplane is 1:10. If the actual airplane has a wingspan of 42 feet, what is the wingspan of the model airplane?

10. What is the temperature to the nearest degree?

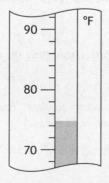

Answers

1. $\dfrac{1 \text{ yd}}{36 \text{ in.}}$ and $\dfrac{36 \text{ in.}}{1 \text{ yd}}$

2. $\dfrac{36 \text{ in.}}{1 \text{ yd}}$

3. $\dfrac{1 \text{ yd}}{36 \text{ in.}}$

4. $720 \text{ in.} \times \dfrac{1 \text{ yd}}{36 \text{ in.}} = 20$ yards

5. $4.35 \text{ km} \times \dfrac{1000 \text{ m}}{1 \text{ km}} = 4350$ meters

6. $2 \text{ h} \times \dfrac{60 \text{ min}}{1 \text{ h}} \times \dfrac{60 \text{ s}}{1 \text{ min}} = 7200$ seconds

7. The unit price for 5 items for $4.25 = $\dfrac{\$4.25}{5 \text{ items}}$= $0.85 per item.

   The unit price for 6 items for $5.00 = $\dfrac{\$5.00}{6 \text{ items}}$ = $0.83 per item (rounded to the nearest cent).

   The better buy is 6 items for $5.00.

   Did I answer the question? Yes, I found the better buy. ✓

   Does my answer make sense? Is it consistent with my knowledge of the real world? Yes. ✓

   Is the answer stated in the correct units? No units are required. ✓

8. To find the total cost for mileage, multiply 500 miles by $0.25 per mile (the unit rate).

   $500 \text{ mi} \times \dfrac{\$0.25}{1 \text{ mi}} = \$125$ The miles (mi) units cancel out, leaving dollars ($) as the units for the answer.

   Did I answer the question? Yes, I found the total cost for the mileage. ✓

   Does my answer make sense? Is it consistent with my knowledge of the real world? Yes. ✓

   Is the answer stated in the correct units? Yes, the units are dollars, which is correct. ✓

9. This problem is a proportion problem involving a scale model. To solve the problem, determine the ratios being compared, being sure to compare corresponding quantities in the same order; write a proportion using the two ratios; and then use cross products to solve the proportion.

   Step 1. Determine the ratios being compared.

   The scale of the model as 1:10.This means: $\dfrac{\text{wingspan of model}}{\text{wingspan of actual airplane}} = \dfrac{1}{10}$

   Step 2. Let w = the wingspan of the model. Write a proportion using the two ratios.

   $\dfrac{w \text{ (in feet)}}{42 \text{ ft}} = \dfrac{1}{10}$

   Step 3. Use cross products to solve the proportion (omitting the units for convenience).

   $\dfrac{w}{42} = \dfrac{1}{10}$

   42×1 Find a cross product you can calculate. You don't know the value of w, so the only cross product you can calculate is 42 times 1.

   $w = \dfrac{42 \times 1}{10}$ Divide by 10, the numerical term you didn't use.

   $w = 4.2$ feet

Did I answer the question? Yes, I found the wingspan of the model. ✓

Does my answer make sense? Is it consistent with my knowledge of the real world? Yes. ✓

Is the answer stated in the correct units? Yes, the units are feet, which is correct. ✓

10.

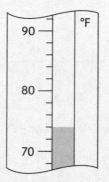

The thermometer is reading between 70° and 80°. The difference between these two points is 80° − 70° = 10°. It takes five marks to go from 70° up to 80°. Divide the difference between the two points by 5: 10° ÷ 5 = 2°. Therefore, each mark on the thermometer represents 2°. The thermometer is reading two marks above 70°. Since each mark represents 2°, the thermometer is reading 4° above 70°, which is 74°F.

How Do You Find Perimeter and Circumference?

The **perimeter** of a figure is the distance around it. You measure perimeter in units of length, such as inches, feet, yards, miles, kilometers, meters, centimeters, and millimeters. To find the perimeter of a closed figure that is made up of line segments, add up the lengths of the line segments.

Here is an example.

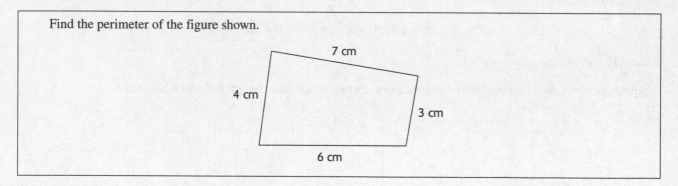

To find the perimeter, add the lengths of the four sides:

Perimeter = 6 cm + 3 cm + 7 cm + 4 cm = 20 cm

Sometimes, the lengths for every side are not labeled. This occurs when the figure is a special geometric shape. On the FTCE GK, the four figures that you most likely will encounter when this happens are a rectangle, square, or an equilateral or an isosceles triangle. The Mathematics Reference Sheet does not give formulas for the perimeters of these figures. If you are finding the perimeter of such a figure, you can simply add up the length of the sides—so you really don't need a formula as such. In the discussion that follows, formulas are given because they often simplify the process of finding the perimeter, but more important, the formulas are very useful when you are given a perimeter and asked to determine one or more dimensions of these special geometric shapes.

Tip: **When you work problems involving geometric figures, sketch a diagram if no diagram is given.**

A **rectangle** is a closed, four-sided plane figure that has four right angles. It has two dimensions: **length** and **width.** Both pairs of opposite sides are congruent (the same size).

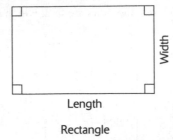

Length

Rectangle

The formula for the perimeter of a rectangle is $P = 2l + 2w$, where l is the length and w is the width.

Here is an example of finding the perimeter of a rectangle.

How many feet of fencing are needed to enclose a rectangular garden that is 25 feet by 35 feet?

Sketch a diagram and label it.

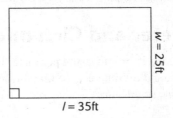

$l = 35$ft

Plug into the formula:

$$P = 2l + 2w = 2(35 \text{ ft}) + 2(25 \text{ ft}) = 70 \text{ ft} + 50 \text{ ft} = 120 \text{ ft}$$

Thus, 120 feet of fencing are needed.

A **square** is a rectangle that has four congruent **sides**. Its two dimensions, length and width, are equal.

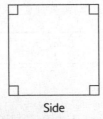

Side

The formula for the perimeter of a square is $P = 4s$, where s is the length of one of its congruent sides.

Here is an example of finding the perimeter of a square.

What is the perimeter of a square that is 3.5 meters on a side?

Sketch a diagram and label it:

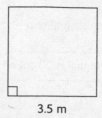

3.5 m

Plug into the formula:

$$P = 4s = 4(3.5 \text{ m}) = 14 \text{ m}$$

A **triangle** is a closed, three-sided plane figure.

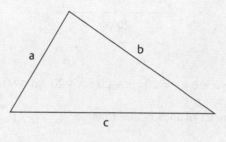

Triangle

An **equilateral triangle** has three congruent sides.

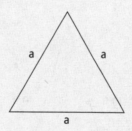

Equilateral Triangle

An **isosceles triangle** has at least two congruent sides.

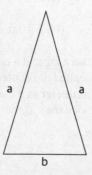

Isosceles Triangle

The formula for the perimeter of a triangle is $P = a + b + c$, where a, b, and c are the lengths of the sides of the triangle.

Here is an example of finding the perimeter of an equilateral triangle.

What is the perimeter of an equilateral triangle that is 20 cm on a side?

Sketch a diagram and label it:

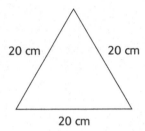

Plug into the formula:

$$P = a + b + c = 20 \text{ cm} + 20 \text{ cm} + 20 \text{ cm} = 60 \text{ cm}$$

Here is an example of finding the perimeter of an isosceles triangle.

Find the perimeter of an isosceles triangle with congruent sides of 10 feet and a third side of 6 feet.

Sketch a diagram and label it:

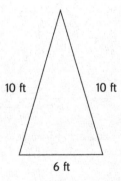

Plug into the formula:

$$P = a + b + c = 10 \text{ ft} + 10 \text{ ft} + 6 \text{ ft} = 26 \text{ ft}$$

On the FTCE GK test, you may have to find the distance around a circle. A **circle** is a closed plane figure for which all points are the same distance from a point within, called the **center.** A **radius** of a circle is a line segment joining the center of the circle to any point on the circle. A **diameter** is a line segment through the center of the circle with endpoints on the circle. The diameter of a circle is twice the radius. Conversely, the radius of a circle is half the diameter.

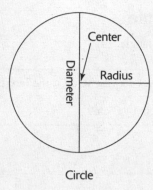

Circle

The **circumference** of a circle is the distance around the circle. In other words, the circumference of a circle is its perimeter. The formula for the circumference of a circle is given on the Mathematics Reference Sheet as $C = \pi d = 2\pi r$, where d and r are the diameter and radius of the circle, respectively. The Mathematics Reference Sheet states that you are to use 3.14 or $\frac{22}{7}$ for the number π. Since you are allowed to use a calculator, you should use 3.14 for π for ease of calculation.

Here is an example of finding the circumference of a circle.

> Find the circumference of the circle in the diagram.

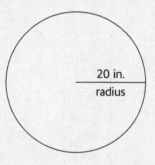

20 in.
radius

From the diagram, you can see that the radius of the circle is 20 in. Plug into the formula:

$$C = 2\pi r = 2\pi(20\text{in.}) = 2 \cdot 3.14 \cdot 20 \text{ in.} = 125.6 \text{ in.}$$

How Do You Find Area?

The **area** of a plane figure is the amount of surface enclosed by the boundary of the figure. You measure area in square units, such as square inches (in.^{2}), square feet (ft^2), square miles (mi^2), square meters (m^2), square kilometers (km^2), square centimeters (cm^2), and square millimeters (mm^2). The area is always described in terms of square units, regardless of the shape of the figure.

The boundary measurements of a figure are measured in two dimensions (that is, length and width, base and height). The units for the boundary measurements are linear units (for example, inches, feet, miles, meters, and so on). You obtain the square units needed to describe area when you multiply the unit by itself. For example, 1 in. × 1 in. = 1 in.^{2} = 1 square inch.

143

Finding the Area of a Rectangle

Here is an example of finding the area of a rectangle.

The formula for the area of a rectangle is $A = lw$, where l is the **length** and w is the **width.**

What is the area of a rectangle that is 4 cm by 3 cm?

Sketch a diagram and label it.

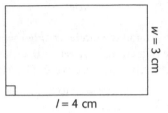

Plug into the formula:

$$A = lw = (4 \text{ cm})(3 \text{ cm}) = 12 \text{ cm}^2$$

You can verify that the formula works by dividing the rectangle into 1-cm squares and counting how many square centimeters are inside the boundary.

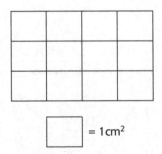

Multiplying 4 cm by 3 cm gives you the same number of square centimeters as counting the squares inside the rectangle. The rectangle has an area of 12 cm^2.

Finding the Area of a Square

The formula for the area of a square is:

$$A = s^2, \text{ where } s \text{ is the length of a } \textbf{side.}$$

This formula is not given on the Mathematics Reference Sheet. To find the area of a square, you can use the formula for the area of a rectangle, $A = lw$. You will get the same answer either way.

Here is an example of finding the area of a square.

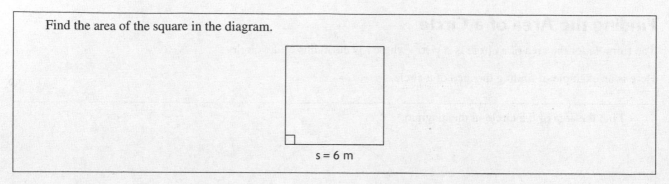

Find the area of the square in the diagram.

s = 6 m

From the diagram, you can see that s, the length of a side of the square, is 6 m. Since all sides are congruent, the width is also 6 m. Plug into either formula:

$$A = lw = (6m)(6m) = 36 \text{ m}^2 \quad \text{or} \quad A = s^2 = (6 \text{ m})^2 = 36 \text{ m}^2$$

Finding the Area of a Triangle

To find the area of a triangle, you must know the measure of the triangle's **base** and **height.** The base can be any of the three sides of the triangle. The height for the base is a line drawn from the opposite vertex that meets that base at a right angle. A **vertex** of a triangle is the point where two sides meet.

The formula for the area of a triangle is $A = \frac{1}{2}bh$, where b is the length of a base of the triangle, and h is the height for that base. When you are finding the area of a triangle, you can pick any convenient side of the triangle to serve as the base in the formula.

Here is an example of finding the area of a triangle.

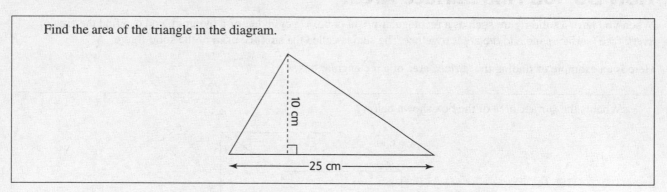

Find the area of the triangle in the diagram.

10 cm

25 cm

From the diagram, you can see that b = 25 cm and h = 10 cm. Plug into the formula:

$$A = \frac{1}{2} bh = A = \frac{1}{2}(25 \text{ cm})(10 \text{ cm}) = \frac{(25 \text{ cm})(10 \text{ cm})}{2} = 125 \text{ cm}^2$$

Here is how to key in the calculation: 25 × 10 ÷ 2 = . The display will show 125, the correct value.

Finding the Area of a Circle

The formula for the area of a circle is $A = \pi r^2$, where r is the radius of the circle.

Here is an example of finding the area of a circle.

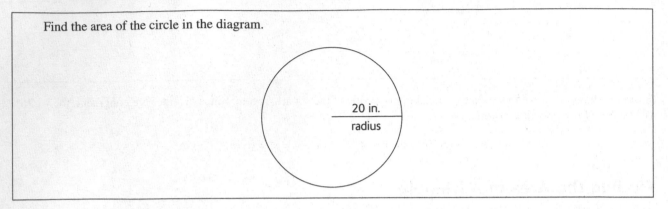

Find the area of the circle in the diagram.

20 in.
radius

From the diagram, you can see that the radius is 20 in. Plug into the formula:

$$A = \pi r^2 = \pi(20\text{in.})^2 = 3.14 \cdot 400 \text{ in.}^2 = 1256 \text{ in.}^2.$$

Notice, that you must perform the exponentiation before multiplying by 3.14. Don't forget to follow **PE(MD)(AS)** when performing calculations. You cannot rely on the calculator to do the operations in the correct order.

How Do You Find Surface Area?

When you have a solid figure such as a rectangular prism (a box), a cylinder, or a pyramid, you can find the area of every face (surface) and add the areas together. The sum is called the **surface area** of the solid figure.

Here is an example of finding the surface area of a rectangular box.

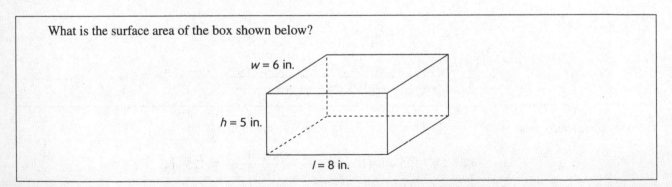

What is the surface area of the box shown below?

$w = 6$ in.

$h = 5$ in.

$l = 8$ in.

The box is composed of six **faces,** all of which are rectangles. Use the length and height to find the areas of the front and back faces. Use the length and width to find the areas of the top and bottom faces. Use the width and height to find the areas of the two side faces.

$$\text{Surface Area} = 2(8 \text{ in.})(5 \text{ in.}) + 2(8 \text{ in.})(6 \text{ in.}) + 2(6 \text{ in.})(5 \text{ in.}) = 80 \text{ in.}^2 + 96 \text{ in.}^2 + 60 \text{ in.}^2 = 236 \text{ in.}^2$$

How Do You Find Volume?

The **volume** of a solid figure is the amount of space inside the solid. Solid figures have three dimensions (for example, length, width, and height of a box). When you use the dimensions of a solid to find its volume, the units for the volume are cubic units, such as cubic inches (in.³), cubic feet (ft³), cubic miles (mi³), cubic meters (m³), cubic kilometers (km³), cubic centimeters (cm³), and cubic millimeters (mm³).

The Mathematics Reference Sheet gives the formula for the volume of a prism as $V = Bh$, where B = the Area of the Base of the solid. For a rectangular prism, $B = lw$. Thus, the formula for the volume of a rectangular prism is $V = lwh$, where l is the **length,** w is the **width,** and h is the **height.**

Here is an example of finding the volume of a rectangular prism.

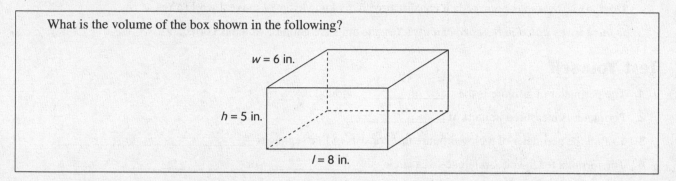

What is the volume of the box shown in the following?

$w = 6$ in.

$h = 5$ in.

$l = 8$ in.

Plug into the formula:

$$V = lwh = (8 \text{ in.})(6 \text{ in.})(5 \text{ in.}) = 240 \text{ in.}^3.$$

Notice that the units for the volume of the box are in.³ = cubic inches. Cubic units are obtained when a unit is used as a factor in a product three times, as in the following: in. × in. × in. = in.³.

How Do You Solve Real-World Problems Involving Perimeter, Area, and Volume?

When you have real-world problems in the form of word problems involving perimeter, area, or volume on the FTCE GK test, you should always make a sketch to help you understand the problem. Otherwise, you solve these problems the same way you solve other word problems on the test.

Here is an example.

Brady wants to paint the walls in a large playroom that is 20 feet by 14 feet with an 8-foot-high ceiling. One gallon of paint will cover 350 square feet. The paint is sold in gallon containers only. How many gallons of paint will he need to buy?

Make a sketch to illustrate the problem.

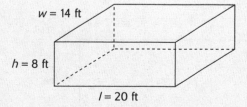

$w = 14$ ft

$h = 8$ ft

$l = 20$ ft

Two steps are needed to solve the problem. First, find the surface area of the walls to be painted. Second, find the number of gallons needed to cover the walls by using the unit rate: 350 square feet per gallon.

Step 1. Find the surface area of the walls to be painted. Use the length and the height to find the areas of the two longer walls. Use the width and the height to find the area of the other two walls.

Surface area to painted = 2(20 ft)(8 ft) + 2(14 ft)(8 ft) = 320 ft² + 224 ft² = 544 ft²

Step 2. Find the number of gallons of paint needed.

one gallon of paint per 350 square feet $= \dfrac{350 \text{ ft}^2}{1 \text{ gal}}$

number of gallons needed $= 544 \text{ ft} \div \dfrac{350 \text{ ft}^2}{1 \text{ gal}} = 544 \text{ ft} \times \dfrac{1 \text{ gal}}{350 \text{ ft}^2} = 1.55 \text{ gal}$

Brady will need to buy 2 gallons of paint to have enough paint to paint the walls.

Did I answer the question? Yes, I found the number of gallons of paint needed. ✓

Does my answer make sense? Is it consistent with my knowledge of the real world? Yes. ✓

Is the answer stated in the correct units? Yes, the units are gallons, which is correct. ✓

Test Yourself

1. The perimeter of a figure is the _____ around it.

2. Perimeter is measured in units of _____.

3. To find the perimeter of a closed figure that consists of line segments _____ .

4. The formula for the circumference of a circle is _____ or _____ .

5. The area of a plane figure is the amount of _____ enclosed by the boundary of the figure.

6. Area is measured in _____ units.

7. The formula for the area of a rectangle is _____ .

8. The formula for the area of a circle is _____ .

9. The formula for the volume of a rectangular prism is _____ .

10. How many square yards of carpet are needed to carpet a room that measures 15 feet by 18 feet?

Answers

1. distance

2. length

3. add up the lengths of the sides

4. πd, $2\pi r$

5. surface

6. square

7. $A = lw$

8. $A = \pi r^2$

9. $V = Bh$ or $V = lwh$

10. Sketch a diagram.

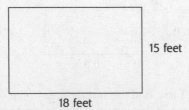

15 feet

18 feet

Square yards are units of area, so you will need to find the area of the carpet in square yards. To find how many square yards of carpet are needed, two steps are needed. First, convert the dimensions of the room from feet to yards. Next, find the area of the rectangular room in square yards.

Step 1. Convert the dimensions of the floor to yards.

The Mathematics Reference Sheet shows 1 yard = 3 feet. You can write this fact as $\frac{3 \text{ ft}}{1 \text{ yd}}$ or as $\frac{1 \text{ yd}}{3 \text{ ft}}$.

Write your measurement as a fraction with denominator 1 and let unit analysis tell you whether to multiply by $\frac{3 \text{ ft}}{1 \text{ yd}}$ or $\frac{1 \text{ yd}}{3 \text{ ft}}$. Since you want the feet to divide out, multiply by $\frac{1 \text{ yd}}{3 \text{ ft}}$.

$$\frac{18 \text{ ft}}{1} \times \frac{1 \text{ yd}}{3 \text{ ft}} = 6 \text{ yd}$$

$$\frac{15 \text{ ft}}{1} \times \frac{1 \text{ yd}}{3 \text{ ft}} = 5 \text{ yd}$$

Step 2. Find the area of the carpet:

The Mathematics Reference Sheet shows the formula for the area of a rectangle is $A = lw$.

$A = lw = 6 \text{ yd} \cdot 5 \text{ yd} = 30 \text{ yd}^2$

At least 30 yd^2 of carpet are needed to carpet the room.

Did I answer the question? Yes, I found how many square yards of carpet are needed. ✓

Does my answer make sense? Is it consistent with my knowledge of the real world? Yes. ✓

Is the answer stated in the correct units? Yes, the units are square yards, which is correct. ✓

Sample Questions

1. A runner ran a cross country race of 14 500 meters. How many kilometers did the runner run in the race?

   A. 1.45 kilometers
   B. 14.5 kilometers
   C. 145 kilometers
   D. 14 500 000 kilometers

2. What is the temperature to the nearest degree?

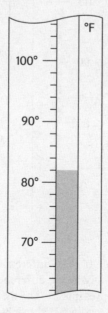

   A. 80°
   B. 81°
   C. 82°
   D. 85°

3. What is the perimeter of a rectangle that measures 6 yards by 5 yards?

   A. 11 yd
   B. 22 yd
   C. 30 yd
   D. 60 yd

4. How many cubic feet of cement are in a rectangular cement slab that is 0.25 feet thick and measures 10 feet long and 5 feet wide?

   A. 12.5 ft.^{3}
   B. 15.25 ft.^{3}
   C. 40 ft.^{3}
   D. 125 ft.^{3}

Answer Explanations for Sample Questions

1. B. Use the conversion fact, 1 kilometer = 1000 meters, from the Mathematics Reference Sheet to obtain two conversion fractions: $\frac{1 \text{ km}}{1000 \text{ m}}$ and $\frac{1000 \text{ m}}{1 \text{ km}}$.

Write your measurement as a fraction with denominator 1 and let unit analysis tell you whether to multiply by $\frac{1 \text{ km}}{1000 \text{ m}}$ or $\frac{1000 \text{ m}}{1 \text{ km}}$. Since you want the meters to divide out, multiply by $\frac{1 \text{ km}}{1000 \text{ m}}$.

$$\frac{14500 \text{ m}}{1} \times \frac{1 \text{ km}}{1000 \text{ m}} = \frac{14500 \text{ km}}{1000} = 14.5 \text{ km}$$

The runner ran 14.5 kilometers in the race, Choice **B.**

The other choices occur if you make a mistake in placing the decimal point in your answer.

2. C.

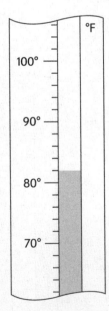

The thermometer is reading between 80° and 90°. The difference between these two points is 90° − 80° = 10°. It takes five marks to go from 80° up to 90°. Divide the difference between the two points by 5: 10° ÷ 5 = 2°. Therefore, each mark on the thermometer represents 2°. The thermometer is reading one mark above 80°. Since each mark represents 2°, the thermometer is reading 2° above 80°, which is 82°F (Choice **C**). Choice **A** results if you incorrectly determine that the reading is at 80°. Choice **B** results if you determine incorrectly that each mark represents 1°, Choice **D** results if you determine incorrectly that each mark represents 5°.

3. B. First, sketch a diagram to illustrate the problem:

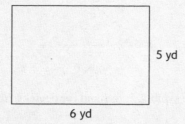

5 yd

6 yd

Plug into the formula.

$P = 2l + 2w = 2(6 \text{ yd}) + 2(5 \text{ yd}) = 12 \text{ yd} + 10 \text{ yd} = 22 \text{ yd}$, Choice **B.**

Choice **A** results if you fail to multiply each dimension by 2. Choice **C** results if you incorrectly confuse perimeter with area. Choice **D** results if you use an incorrect formula.

4. A. First, sketch a diagram to illustrate the problem:

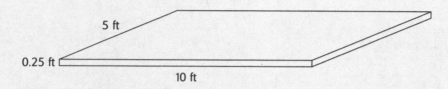

5 ft

0.25 ft

10 ft

Cubic feet are units of volume. The amount of cement in the slab is equal to the volume of the slab, which is a rectangular prism. The volume of the cement is

$V = lwh = 10 \text{ ft} \cdot 5 \text{ ft} \cdot 0.25 \text{ ft} = 12.5 \text{ ft}^3$

There are 12.5 ft^3 of cement in the slab, Choice **A.**

Did I answer the question? Yes, I found how many cubic feet of cement are in the slab. ✓

Does my answer make sense? Is it consistent with my knowledge of the real world? Yes. ✓

Is the answer stated in the correct units? Yes, the units are cubic feet, which is correct. ✓

Choices **B** and **C** result if you use an incorrect formula for the volume of a rectangular prism. Choice **D** results if you place the decimal point incorrectly when computing the volume.

Geometry

As listed in the *Competencies and Skills Required for Teacher Certification in Florida, Ninth Edition* (see the first section of this chapter for the Web address), the competencies/skills you should be able to do for this area of mathematics are the following:

- Identify and classify geometric shapes and solids according to their properties.
- Identify examples of geometric concepts including perpendicularity, parallelism, tangency, symmetry, and transformations.
- Solve real-world problems involving similar and congruent figures and the Pythagorean theorem.
- Locate and name points on a coordinate graph and use the concepts of slope and distance to solve problems.

How Do You Classify Angles?

A **ray** is a line extending from a point. When two rays meet at a common point, they form an **angle.** The point where the rays meet is called the **vertex** of the angle.

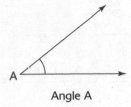

Angle A

You measure angles in degrees. You use the symbol, °, to stand for degrees. You can classify angles by the number of degrees in their measurement.

An **acute angle** measures between 0° and 90°.

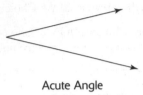

Acute Angle

A **right angle** measures exactly 90°.

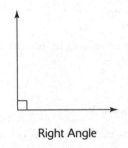

Right Angle

An **obtuse angle** measures between 90° and 180°.

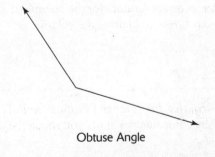

Obtuse Angle

A **straight angle** measures exactly 180°.

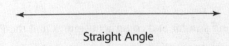

Straight Angle

Two angles whose sum is 90° are **complementary angles.**

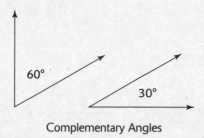

Complementary Angles

Two angles whose sum is 180° are **supplementary angles.**

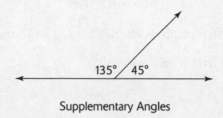

Supplementary Angles

How Do You Classify Lines?

A **plane** is a set of points that form a flat surface. Lines in a plane can be parallel or intersecting.

Intersecting lines cross at a point in the plane.

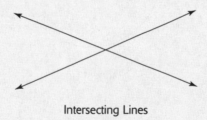

Intersecting Lines

Parallel lines (in a plane) never meet. The distance between them is always the same.

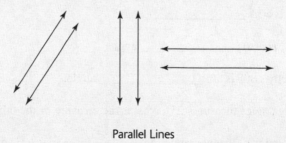

Parallel Lines

A shorthand way to indicate that a line *AB* is parallel to a line *CD* is to write *AB*//*CD*.

Perpendicular lines intersect at right angles.

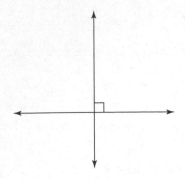

Perpendicular Lines

A shorthand way to indicate that a line *AB* is perpendicular to a line *CD* is to write $AB \perp CD$.

A **tangent line** to a circle intersects the circle in only one point.

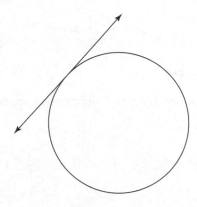

Tangent Line

Test Yourself

1. A right angle measures exactly _____ .

2. An angle that measures 40° is a(n) _____ angle.

3. An angle that measures 165° is a(n) _____ angle.

4. An angle that measures exactly 180° is a(n) _____ angle.

5. If one of two complementary angles measures 25°, what is the measure of the other angle?

6. If two angles measure 120° and 60°, the two angles are _____ angles.

7. Two lines that cross at a point in the plane are _____ lines.

8. Two lines in a plane that never meet are _____ lines.

9. Two lines that intersect at right angles are _____ lines.

10. A line that meets a circle in exactly one point is called a _____ line to the circle.

Answers

1. 90°

2. acute

3. obtuse

4. straight

5. 90° − 25° = 65°

6. supplementary

7. intersecting

8. parallel

9. perpendicular

10. tangent

What Are Two-Dimensional Figures?

Two-dimensional (plane) figures are flat shapes that lie in a plane. The plane figures that are most important for you to know for the FTCE GK test are polygons including triangles, quadrilaterals, pentagons, hexagons, and octagons and the circle (which was discussed in the Measurement section, earlier in this chapter).

How Do You Classify Polygons?

A **polygon** is a closed plane figure, whose **sides** are line segments. The point at which the two sides of a polygon intersect is called a **vertex.** A **regular polygon** has all sides congruent. Polygons are classified by the number of sides they have. Following are examples of regular polygons.

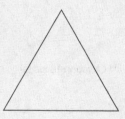

Triangle (3 sides)

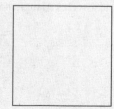

Quadrilateral (4 sides)

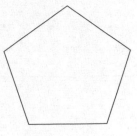

Pentagon (5 sides)

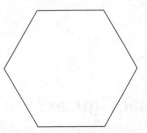

Hexagon (6 sides)

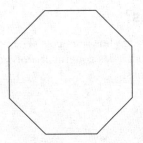

Octagon (8 sides)

How Do You Classify Triangles?

A **triangle** is a three-sided polygon. The sum of the interior angles of a triangle is 180°. Triangles can be classified in two different ways. You can classify triangles according to their sides as equilateral, isosceles, or scalene.

An **equilateral** triangle has three congruent sides. An **isosceles** triangle has at least two congruent sides. A **scalene** triangle has no congruent sides.

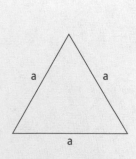

Equilateral Triangle

Isosceles Triangle

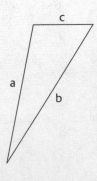

Scalene Triangle

Another way to classify triangles is according to their interior angles. An **acute** triangle has three acute angles. A **right** triangle has exactly one right angle. An **obtuse** triangle has exactly one obtuse angle.

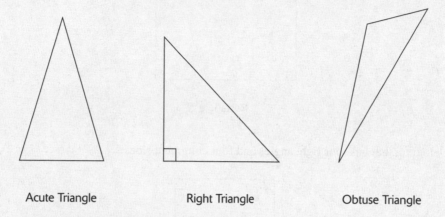

Acute Triangle   Right Triangle   Obtuse Triangle

How Do You Classify Quadrilaterals?

Quadrilaterals can be classified as either trapezoids or parallelograms. A **trapezoid** has exactly one pair of parallel sides.

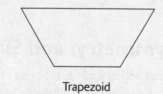

Trapezoid

In a **parallelogram** opposite sides are parallel and congruent.

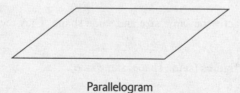

Parallelogram

Some parallelograms have special names because of their special properties.

A **rhombus** is a parallelogram that has four congruent sides.

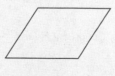

Rhombus

A **rectangle** is a parallelogram that has four right angles.

Rectangle

A **square** is a parallelogram that has four right angles and four congruent sides.

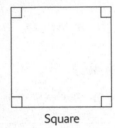

Square

What Are Congruence, Symmetry, and Similarity?

For the FTCE GK test you will need to know and understand the meaning of the terms congruence, symmetry, and similarity. The test assesses your skills in identifying examples of symmetry and your ability to solve real world problems involving congruence and similarity.

Congruence

Congruent geometric figures have exactly the same size and same shape. They are superimposable, meaning that they will fit exactly on top of each other.

Here are three examples of congruent figures (same shape, same size).

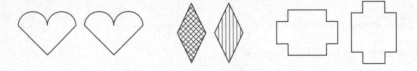

Congruent Figures

These figures are not congruent. They have the same shape, but not the same size.

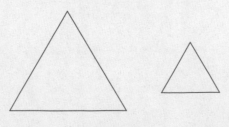

Not Congruent

These figures are not congruent. They are about the same size, but they do not have the same shape. One is a right triangle, and the other one is an equilateral triangle.

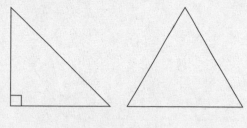

Not Congruent

Symmetry

Symmetry describes the shape of a figure or object. A figure or object is **symmetric** if it can be folded exactly in half and the two parts are congruent. The line along the fold is the **line of symmetry.**

Here are three examples of symmetric shapes. A line of symmetry is shown in each figure.

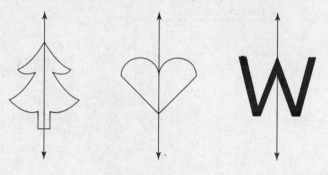

Symmetric Figures

Some shapes have more than one line of symmetry. For the figures that follow, you can fold along any of the lines of symmetry and the two halves will be congruent.

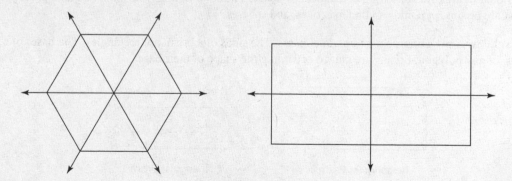

Symmetric Figures

Similarity

Similar geometric figures have the same shape, but not necessarily the same size.

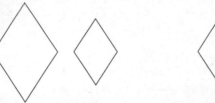 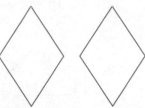

Similar, but <u>not</u> congruent   **Similar** <u>and</u> congruent

Corresponding sides of similar shapes are proportional. That is, the ratios of the lengths of corresponding sides are equal. Here is an example.

In the figure shown, rectangle A is similar to rectangle B. What is the ratio of the lengths of the sides of rectangle A compared to the corresponding sides of rectangle B?

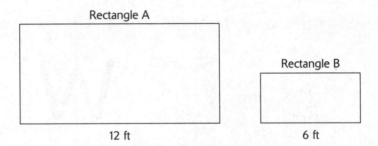

Rectangle A

Rectangle B

12 ft   6 ft

The ratio of corresponding sides is $\frac{12 \text{ ft}}{6 \text{ ft}} = \frac{12}{6} = \frac{2}{1}$.

What Are Three-Dimensional Figures?

Three-dimensional figures are solid figures that occupy space. The solid figures you should be able to recognize for the FTCE GK test are prisms, pyramids, cylinders, cones, and spheres.

A **prism** is a solid with two congruent and parallel bases. The sides of a prism are rectangles. The bases of a prism can have the shape of any polygon. Prisms are named according the shape of their bases.

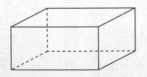   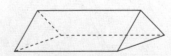

Rectangular Prism   Triangular Prism

A **cube** is a special rectangular prism that has six congruent faces, all of which are squares.

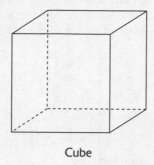

Cube

A **pyramid** is a solid with exactly one base. The sides of a pyramid are triangles. The base can have the shape of any polygon. Pyramids are named according to the shape of their bases.

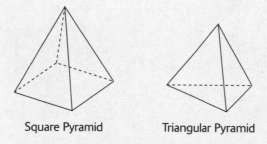

Square Pyramid   Triangular Pyramid

A **cylinder** has two parallel congruent bases, which are circles. It has one rectangular side that wraps around.

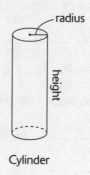

Cylinder

A **cone** is a three-dimensional solid that has one circular base. It has a curved side that wraps around.

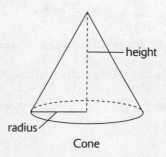

Cone

A **sphere** is a three-dimensional solid that is shaped like a ball. Every point on the sphere is the same distance from a point within, called the **center** of the sphere. The **radius** of the sphere is a line segment from the center of the sphere to any point on the sphere. The **diameter** of the sphere is a line segment joining two points of the sphere and passing through its center. The radius of the sphere is half the diameter. Conversely, the diameter is twice the radius.

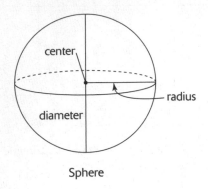

Sphere

Test Yourself

1. A four-sided polygon is called a _____ .

2. A pentagon has exactly _____ sides.

3. A hexagon has exactly _____ sides.

4. An octagon has exactly _____ sides.

5. A scalene triangle has _____ congruent sides.

6. The sum of the interior angles of a triangle is _____.

7. An acute triangle has _____ acute angles.

8. A _____ is a quadrilateral that has exactly one pair of parallel sides.

9. In a parallelogram, opposite sides are _____ and _____.

10. Rhombuses, rectangles, and squares are _____.

11. Rectangles and squares have four _____ angles.

12. Rhombuses and squares have four _____ sides.

13. Congruent geometric figures have exactly the same _____ and same _____.

14. A figure is _____ if it can be folded exactly into congruent halves.

15. Similar geometric figures have the same _____, but not necessarily the same _____.

16. In the figure shown, hexagon A is similar to hexagon B. What is the ratio of the lengths of the sides of hexagon A compared to the corresponding sides of hexagon B?

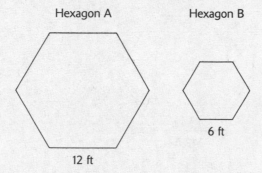

Hexagon A   Hexagon B

12 ft   6 ft

17. Prisms and cylinders have _____ congruent and parallel bases.

18. _____ and _____ have exactly one base.

19. A _____ is a rectangular prism that has six congruent faces.

20. The points on the three-dimensional solid that is called a _____ are the same distance from a point within, called its center.

Answers

1. quadrilateral
2. five
3. six
4. eight
5. no
6. 180°
7. three
8. trapezoid
9. congruent, parallel
10. parallelograms
11. right
12. congruent
13. size, shape
14. symmetric
15. shape, size

16.

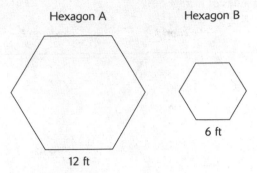

Hexagon A   Hexagon B

12 ft   6 ft

The ratio of corresponding sides is $\frac{12 \text{ ft}}{6 \text{ ft}} = \frac{12}{6} = \frac{2}{1}$.

17. two

18. pyramids, cones

19. cube

20. sphere

How Do You Solve Problems Involving the Pythagorean Relationship?

A **right triangle** is a triangle that has exactly one right angle. The side opposite the right angle is called the **hypotenuse** of the triangle. The hypotenuse is *always* the longest side of the right triangle. The other two sides are called the **legs** of the triangle. Commonly, the letter c is used to represent the hypotenuse of a right triangle, and the letters a and b to represent the legs.

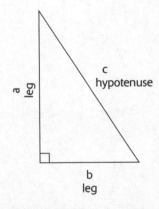

a leg

c hypotenuse

b leg

A special relationship, named after the famous Greek mathematician Pythagoras, exists between the sides of a right triangle. This special relationship is the **Pythagorean Theorem,** which states that $c^2 = a^2 + b^2$.

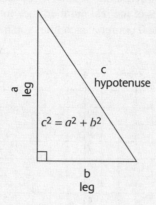

The Pythagorean relationship applies only to right triangles. If you know any two sides of a right triangle, you can find the third side by using the formula $c^2 = a^2 + b^2$.

Here is an example.

Using the diagram, find the length of the diagonal of a rectangular flower garden that has dimensions of 16 feet by 12 feet.

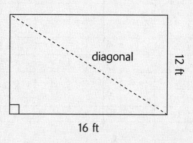

From the diagram, you can see that the diagonal is the hypotenuse of a right triangle that has legs of 12 ft and 16 ft. Plug into the formula:

c = hypotenuse = ?, $a = 12$ ft, and $b = 16$ ft

$c^2 = a^2 + b^2 = (12 \text{ ft})^2 + (16 \text{ ft})^2 = 144 \text{ ft}^2 + 256 \text{ ft}^2 = 400 \text{ ft}^2$

To solve this equation, you must think of a number that multiplies by itself to give 400. From the list of square roots given on page xx, you know that $\sqrt{400} = 20$, so $c = 20$ ft.

Did I answer the question? Yes, I found the length of the diagonal of the flower garden. ✓

Does my answer make sense? Is it consistent with my knowledge of the real world? Yes. ✓

Is the answer stated in the correct units? Yes, the units are feet, which is correct. ✓

How Do You Locate and Name Points in a Coordinate System?

In the Numerations and Operations section (earlier in this chapter), you learned that the real numbers can be represented on a number line. If you take two copies of the real number line, one horizontal and one vertical, and position them at right angles so that they intersect at the 0 point on each line, you have a **coordinate system (graph).**

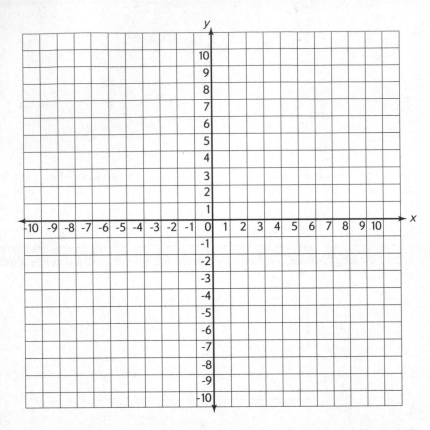

The horizontal number line with positive direction to the right is usually called the **x-axis,** and the vertical number line with positive direction upward is called the **y-axis.** The intersection of the two lines is called the **origin.** The two intersecting x- and y-axes divide the coordinate grid into four sections, called **quadrants.** The quadrants are numbered *counterclockwise* using Roman numerals as shown in the following.

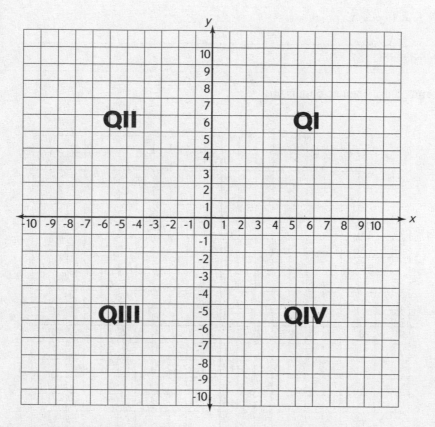

With this coordinate system you can match points with an **ordered pair** of numbers, called **coordinates.** An ordered pair of numbers is written in a definite order so that one number is first, and the other is second. The first number is called the **x-coordinate,** and the second number is called the **y-coordinate.** You write ordered pairs in parentheses with the two numbers separated by commas. The ordered pair (0, 0) designates the origin.

Look at these examples.

(3, 5) is the ordered pair with x-coordinate = 3, and y-coordinate = 5

(–2, 3) is the ordered pair with x-coordinate = –2, and y-coordinate = 3

An ordered pair gives you directions on how to graph a point on the coordinate grid, starting from the origin (0, 0). The x-coordinate tells you how far to go right (for positive numbers) or left (for negative numbers). From that spot, the y-coordinate tells you how far you need to go up (for positive numbers) or down (for negative numbers) to mark the location of the point.

Here are examples of how to graph a point.

Graph the ordered pair (3, 5).

Start at (0, 0). Go 3 units right. Then go 5 units up.

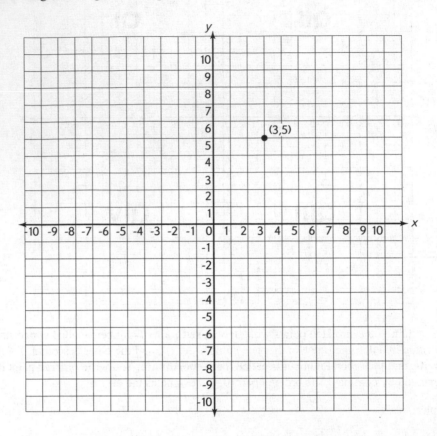

Graph the ordered pair (–2, 3).

Start at (0, 0). Go 2 units left. Then go 3 units up.

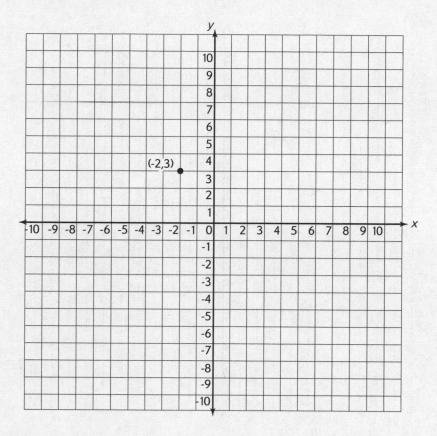

Graph the ordered pair (−4, −5).

Start at (0, 0). Go 4 units left. Then go 5 units down.

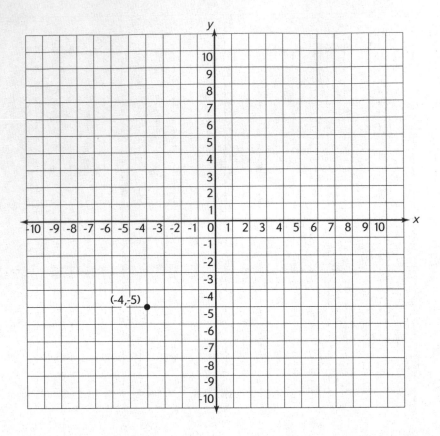

Graph the ordered pair (1, –6).

Start at (0, 0). Go 1 unit right. Then go 6 units down.

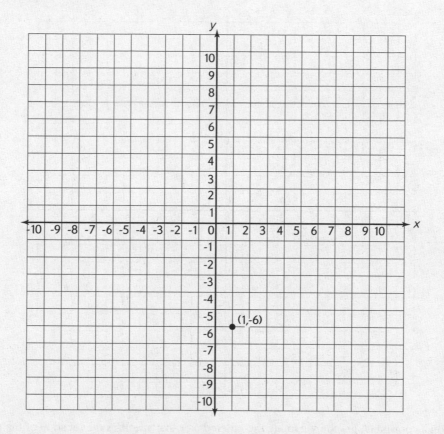

Tip: Note that in Quadrant 1, both the *x*-coordinate and the *y*-coordinate are positive; in Quadrant II, the *x*-coordinate is negative, and the *y*-coordinate is positive; in Quadrant III, both the *x*-coordinate and the *y*-coordinate are negative; and in Quadrant IV, the *x*-coordinate is positive, and the *y*-coordinate is negative.

Points that have zero as one or both of the coordinates lie on the axes. If the *x*-coordinate is zero, the point lies on the *y*-axis. If the *y*-coordinate is zero, the point lies on the *x*-axis. If both coordinates of a point are zero, the point is at the origin. For example, as shown in the following, the point (0, 4) lies on the *y*-axis, and the point (–5, 0) lies on the *x*-axis.

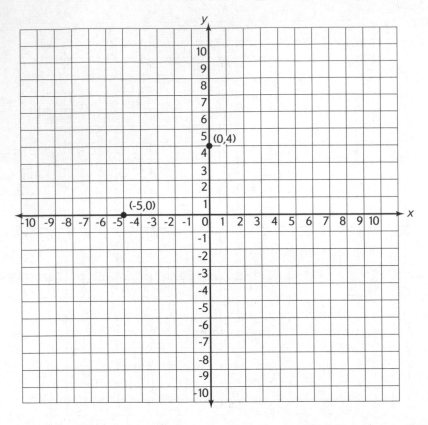

You name a point on a coordinate graph by naming the ordered pair that specifies the location of the point.

Here is an example.

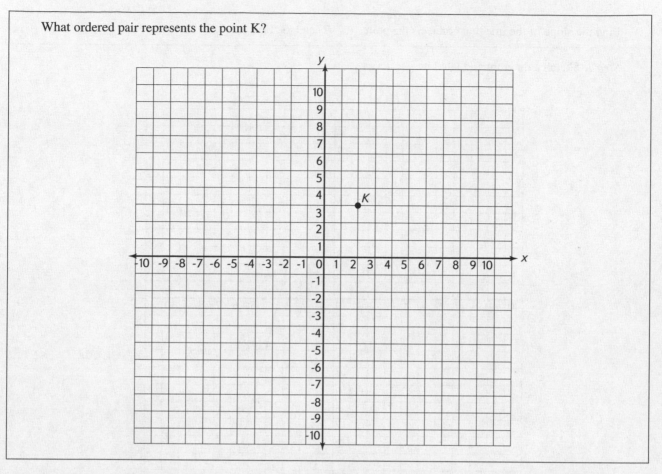

What ordered pair represents the point K?

The point K is 2 units to the right and 3 units up from the origin. The ordered pair (2, 3) represents the point K.

How Do You Find the Slope of the Line Between Two Points?

To find the slope of the line that connects the points (x_1, y_1) and (x_2, y_2) on a coordinate graph, do these steps:

Step 1. Sketch a diagram and label it.

Step 2. Specify (x_1, y_1) and (x_2, y_2). This step is *very* important, so don't skip it. Notice the subscript written to the lower right of each variable. The subscripts are used to emphasize that the coordinates x_1 and y_1 go together and the coordinates x_2 and y_2 go together. Keep this in mind when you do step 2.

Step 3. Plug into the formula given on the Mathematics Reference Sheet:

$$\text{Slope of line} = \frac{y_2 - y_1}{x_2 - x_1}$$

Tip: Enclose in parentheses any substituted value that is negative to avoid making a sign error.

Here are examples.

Find the slope of the line that connects the points (5, –7) and (3, 1).

Step 1. Sketch a diagram and label it.

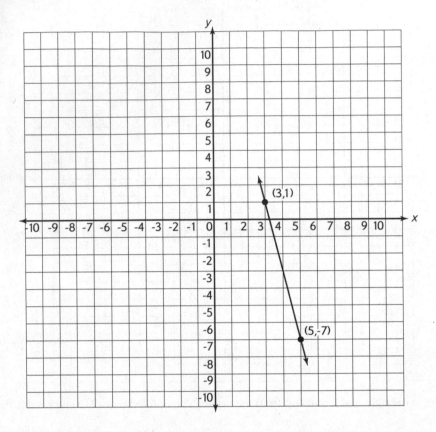

Step 2. Specify (x_1, y_1) and (x_2, y_2).

Let $(x_1, y_1) = (5, -7)$ and $(x_2, y_2) = (3, 1)$. Then $x_1 = 5$, $y_1 = -7$, $x_2 = 3$, and $y_2 = 1$.

Step 3: Plug into the formula.

$$\text{Slope of line} = \frac{y_2 - y_1}{x_2 - x_1} = \frac{1 - (-7)}{3 - 5} = \frac{1 + 7}{3 - 5} = \frac{8}{-2} = -4$$

The line through the points (5, –7) and (3, 1) has slope –4.

Find the slope of the line that connects the points (–4, –5) and (2, 3).

Step 1. Sketch a diagram and label it.

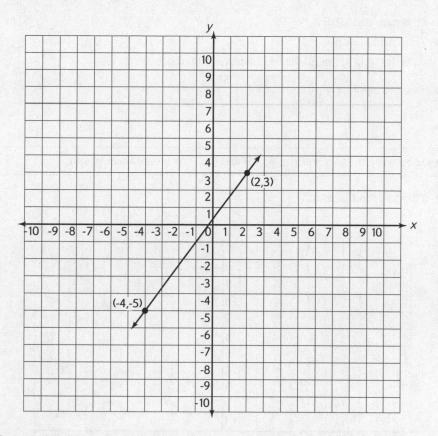

Step 2. Specify (x_1, y_1) and (x_2, y_2).

Let $(x_1, y_1) = (-4, -5)$ and $(x_2, y_2) = (2, 3)$. Then $x_1 = -4$, $y_1 = -5$, $x_2 = 2$, and $y_2 = 3$.

Step 3: Plug into the formula.

$$\text{Slope of line} = \frac{y_2 - y_1}{x_2 - x_1} = \frac{3 - (-5)}{2 - (-4)} = \frac{3 + 5}{2 + 4} = \frac{8}{6} = \frac{4}{3}$$

The line through the points (–4, –5) and (2, 3) has slope $\frac{4}{3}$.

Tip: Lines that slant to the right (that is, go up from left to right) have positive slope. Lines that slant to the left (that is, go down from left to right) have negative slope. The slope of a horizontal line is zero. A vertical line has no slope. When you calculate the slope between two points, be sure to note the slant, if any. If your answer has a sign that disagrees with the slant, you made an error.

How Do You Find the Distance between Two Points?

The steps to find the distance between two points on a coordinate graph are basically the same as the steps for finding the slope of the line between the points:

Step 1. Sketch a diagram and label it.

Step 2. Specify (x_1, y_1) and (x_2, y_2).

Step 3. Plug into the formula given on the Mathematics Reference Sheet:

Distance between two points = $\sqrt{(x_2 - x_1)^2 + (y_2 - y_1)^2}$

Here is an example.

Find the distance between the two points (−4, −5) and (2, 3) on a coordinate graph.

Step 1. Sketch a diagram and label it.

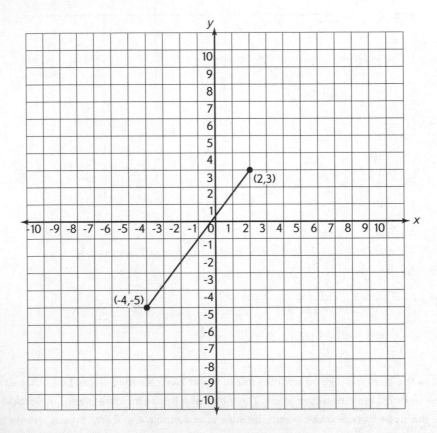

Step 2. Specify (x_1, y_1) and (x_2, y_2).

Let $(x_1, y_1) = (-4, -5)$ and $(x_2, y_2) = (2, 3)$. Then $x_1 = -4$, $y_1 = -5$, $x_2 = 2$, and $y_2 = 3$.

Step 3: Plug into the formula.

Distance between two points = $\sqrt{(x_2 - x_1)^2 + (y_2 - y_1)^2} = \sqrt{(2 - (-4))^2 + (3 - (-5))^2} =$
$$\sqrt{(2 + 4)^2 + (3 + 5)^2} = \sqrt{(6)^2 + (8)^2} = \sqrt{36 + 64} = \sqrt{100} = 10$$

The distance between the two points (−4, −5) and (2, 3) is 10 units.

How Do You Find the Midpoint between Two Points?

The steps to find the midpoint between two points on a coordinate graph are basically the same as the steps for finding the slope of the line and the distance between the points:

Step 1. Sketch a diagram and label it.

Step 2. Specify (x_1, y_1) and (x_2, y_2).

Step 3. Plug into the formula given on the Mathematics Reference Sheet:

Midpoint between two points $= \left(\dfrac{x_1 + x_2}{2}, \dfrac{y_1 + y_2}{2} \right)$

Tip: Notice that you add, not subtract, the coordinates in the numerator.

Here is an example.

What is the midpoint of the line segment that connects the points (5, −7) and (3, 1) on a coordinate graph?

Step 1. Sketch a diagram and label it.

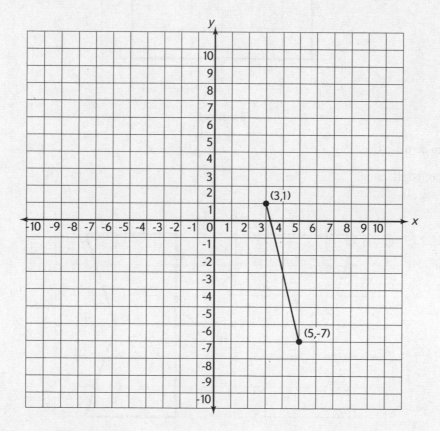

Step 2. Specify (x_1, y_1) and (x_2, y_2).

Let $(x_1, y_1) = (5, -7)$ and $(x_2, y_2) = (3, 1)$. Then $x_1 = 5$, $y_1 = -7$, $x_2 = 3$, and $y_2 = 1$.

Step 3: Plug into the formula.

Midpoint between two points $= \left(\dfrac{x_1 + x_2}{2}, \dfrac{y_1 + y_2}{2} \right) = \left(\dfrac{5 + 3}{2}, \dfrac{-7 + 1}{2} \right) = \left(\dfrac{8}{2}, \dfrac{-6}{2} \right) = (4, -3)$

The midpoint of the line segment that connects the points (5, −7) and (3, 1) is the point (4, −3).

What Are Geometric Transformations?

Geometric transformations are ways to change geometric figures without changing their basic properties. The four geometric transformations are translations, reflections, rotations, and dilations.

A **translation** is a sliding movement, horizontally, vertically, or both.

Here is an example of a translation consisting of four units down.

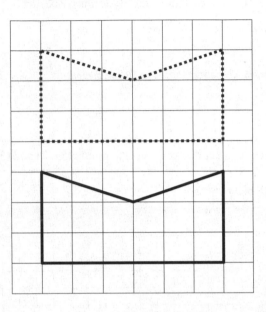

Translation

A **reflection** is a flip across a line.

Here is an example of a reflection.

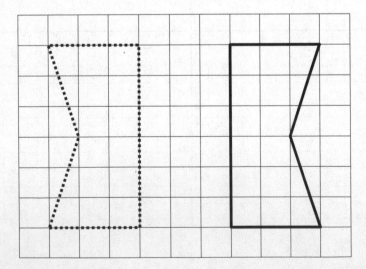

Reflection

A **rotation** is a turn around a point.

Here is an example of a rotation.

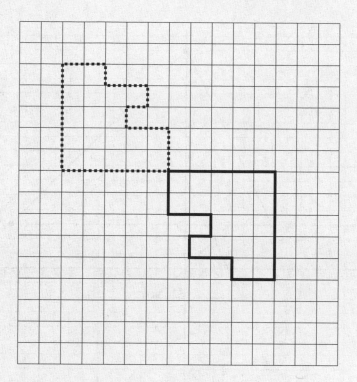

Rotation

A **dilation** is an expanding or shrinking of a geometric shape.

Here is an example of a dilation. Triangle X'Y'Z' is a dilation of triangle XYZ.

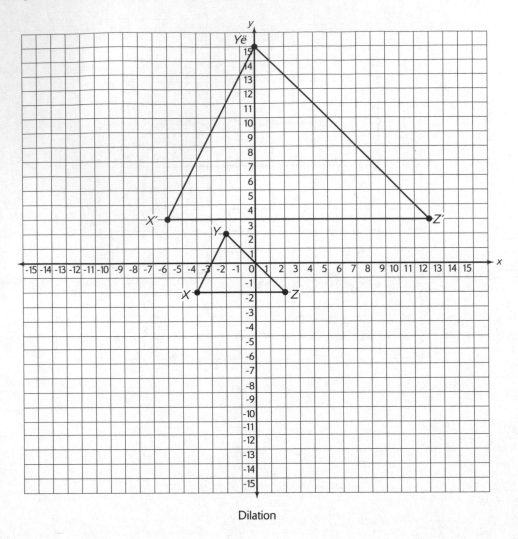

Dilation

Test Yourself

1. In a right triangle, the _____ is the side opposite the right angle.

2. What is the length of the hypotenuse of a right triangle that has legs $a = 3$ units and $b = 4$ units?

3. The point (0, 0) is the _____ of a coordinate graph.

4. The quadrants of a coordinate system are numbered _____ (clockwise, counterclockwise) using Roman numerals.

5. In the ordered pair (−5, 8), −5 is the _____, and 8 is the _____.

6. In Quadrant _____, both coordinates are positive.

7. In Quadrant II, the x-coordinate is _____ (positive, negative), and the y-coordinate is _____ (positive negative).

8. In Quadrant IV, the *x*-coordinate is _____ (positive, negative), and the *y*-coordinate is _____ (positive, negative).

9. In Quadrant _____, both coordinates are negative.

10. What ordered pair represents the point *P*?

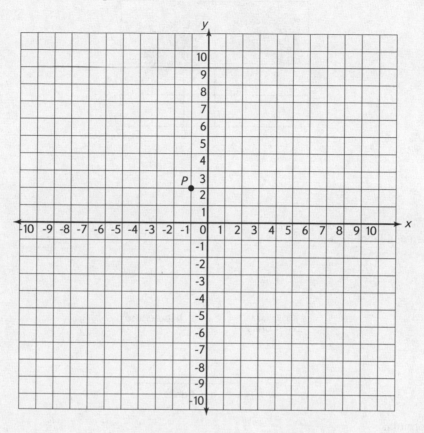

11. What is the slope of the line that passes through the points (–4, 1) and (0, 5)?

12. If a line slants to the left, its slope is _____ (positive, negative).

13. The *x*-coordinate of the midpoint of the line segment between two points is the _____ of the *x*-coordinates of the two points divided by 2, and the *y*-coordinate is the _____ of the *y*-coordinates of the two points divided by 2.

14. The following diagram shows an example of a _____.

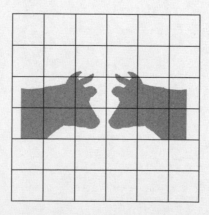

15. The following diagram shows an example of a _____.

Answers

1. hypotenuse

2. $c = 5$ units

   Sketch a diagram and label it.

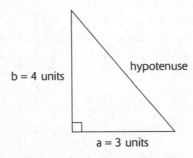

   Plug into the formula:

   c = hypotenuse = ?, $a = 3$ units, and $b = 4$ units

   $c^2 = a^2 + b^2 = (3 \text{ units})^2 + (4 \text{ units})^2 = 9 \text{ unit}^2 + 16 \text{ unit}^2 = 25 \text{ unit}^2$

   To solve this equation, you must think of a number that multiplies by itself to give 25. From the list of square roots given on page 104, you know that $\sqrt{25} = 5$, so $c = 5$ units.

3. origin

4. counterclockwise

5. x-coordinate, y-coordinate

6. I

7. negative, positive

8. positive, negative

9. III

10. The point P is 1 unit to the left and 2 units up from the origin. The ordered pair $(-1,2)$ represents the point P.

11. slope = 1.

Solution:

Step 1. Sketch a diagram and label it.

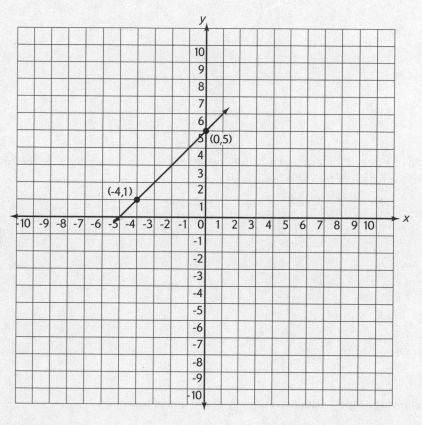

Step 2. Specify (x_1, y_1) and (x_2, y_2).

Let $(x_1, y_1) = (-4, 1)$ and $(x_2, y_2) = (0, 5)$. Then $x_1 = -4$, $y_1 = 1$, $x_2 = 0$, and $y_2 = 5$.

Step 3: Plug into the formula.

$$\text{Slope of line} = \frac{y_2 - y_1}{x_2 - x_1} = \frac{5 - 1}{0 - (-4)} = \frac{5 - 1}{0 + 4} = \frac{4}{4} = 1$$

The line through the points $(-4, 1)$ and $(0, 5)$ has slope 1.

12. negative

13. sum, sum

14. reflection

15. rotation

Sample Questions

1. Which of the following is the most specific name for the figure below, given that *AB//DC*?

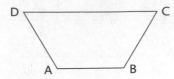

    A. parallelogram
    B. rectangle
    C. rhombus
    D. trapezoid

2. A length of cable is attached to the top of a 12-foot building. The cable is anchored 5 feet from the base of the building. What is the length of the cable?

    A. 7 feet
    B. 13 feet
    C. 17 feet
    D. 169 feet

3. A square is also a:

    A. trapezoid.
    B. pentagon.
    C. parallelogram.
    D. cube.

4. Which of the following shapes contains a correctly drawn line of symmetry?

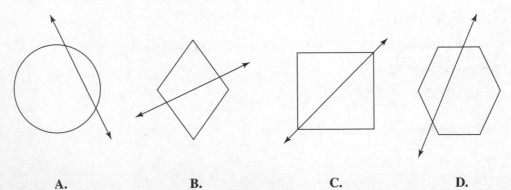

    A.   **B.**   **C.**   **D.**

Answer Explanations for Sample Questions

1. **D.** Examine the diagram. The figure has four sides, so it is a quadrilateral. Note that *AB//DC* means *AB* is parallel to *DC*.

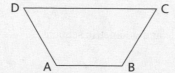

A trapezoid is a quadrilateral that has exactly one pair of opposite sides parallel. The figure shown is a trapezoid. Choices **A, B,** and **C** are incorrect because these figures are parallelograms, which have both pairs of opposite sides parallel.

2. **B.** First, sketch a diagram to illustrate the problem:

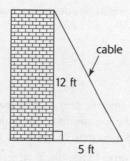

The building and the cable form a right triangle. From the diagram, you can see that the length of the cable is the hypotenuse of the right triangle that has legs of 12 feet and 5 feet. Plug into the formula:

c = hypotenuse = ?, a = 12 ft, and b = 5 ft

$c^2 = a^2 + b^2 = (12 \text{ ft})^2 + (5 \text{ ft})^2 = 144 \text{ ft}^2 + 25 \text{ ft}^2 = 169 \text{ ft}^2$

To solve this equation, you must think of a number that multiplies by itself to give 169. From the list of square roots given on page 104, you know that $\sqrt{169} = 13$, so c = 13 ft. The length of the cable is 13 feet, Choice **B.**

Did I answer the question? Yes, I found the length of the cable. ✓

Does my answer make sense? Is it consistent with my knowledge of the real world? Yes. ✓

Is the answer stated in the correct units? Yes, the units are feet, which is correct. ✓

Choice **A** results if you mistakenly decide to solve the problem by finding the difference between the lengths of the two legs to find the length of the hypotenuse. Choice **C** results if you mistakenly decide to solve the problem by adding the lengths of the two legs to find the length of the hypotenuse. Choice **D** results if you fail to find the square root of 169.

3. **C.** A square is a parallelogram that has four congruent sides. Choice **A** is incorrect because a trapezoid has exactly one pair of opposite sides parallel, but a square has two pairs of opposite sides parallel. Choice **B** is incorrect because a pentagon has exactly five sides, but a square has exactly four sides. Choice **D** is incorrect because a cube is a three-dimensional figure, but a square is a two-dimensional figure.

4. **C.** Only the figure for Choice **C** has a correctly drawn line of symmetry that cuts the figure into two congruent halves. The lines in the figures for choices **A, B,** and **D** do not cut the figures into two congruent halves.

Algebraic Reasoning

As listed in the *Competencies and Skills Required for Teacher Certification in Florida, Ninth Edition* (see first section of this chapter for Web address), the competencies/skills you should be able to do for this area of mathematics are the following:

- Recognize patterns including arithmetic and geometric sequences.
- Interpret algebraic expressions.
- Solve equations and inequalities.
- Determine whether a number or ordered pair satisfies a system of equations or inequalities.

What Is a Sequence?

A sequence is a list of numbers, called **terms** of the sequence, written in a particular order. On the FTCE GK test, you will have to identify patterns in sequences. Here are some common sequences you may encounter.

Arithmetic Sequences

An **arithmetic sequence** has one of two patterns:

1. The same number is *added* to each term to find the next term in the list. For example, in the list 4, 9, 14, 19, 24, …, the ellipsis is used to indicate that the list continues on in the same manner. The number 5 is added to a term to get the term that follows it, so the next term in the list is $24 + 5 = 29$.

2. The same number is *subtracted* from each term to find the next term in the list. For example, in the list 10, 6, 2, –2, –6, …, 4 is subtracted from a term to get the term that follows it, so the next term in the list is $-6 - 4 = -10$.

Geometric Sequences

A **geometric sequence** has one of two patterns:

1. Each term in the list is *multiplied* by the same number to find the next term in the list. For example, in the list 4, 8, 16, 32, 64, …, each term is multiplied by 2 to get the term that follows it, so the next term in the list is $64 \times 2 = 128$.

2. Each term in the list is *divided* by the same number to find the next term in the list. For example, in the list 125, 25, 5, 1, $\frac{1}{5}$, …, each term is divided by 5 to get the term that follows it, so the next term in the list is $\frac{1}{5} \div 5 = \frac{1}{5} \times \frac{1}{5} = \frac{1}{25}$.

Fibonacci Sequences

A **Fibonacci sequence** begins with two repeating terms, and thereafter, each term is the sum of the two preceding terms. Here is an example.

$$1, 1, 2, 3, 5, 8, \dots .$$

Additional Patterns

Sequences may also have **repeating patterns.**

Here is an example of a repeating pattern in which the block of numbers 3, 2, 1 repeats.

$$3, 2, 1, 3, 2, 1, 3, 2, 1, \dots .$$

A common pattern for sequences involves using the position number of the term to produce the term. For example, if you write the sequence 1, 4, 9, 16, 25, … in a table like the following:

Position Number	Term
1	1
2	4
3	9
4	16
5	25
⋮	⋮

You can see that each term is the square of its position number. Symbolically, the nth term is n^2.

How Do You Find Patterns in Sequences?

When a problem requires that you find a pattern in a sequence, you should use a systematic plan of attack. First, look for an easily recognizable pattern. For example, the sequence

$$5, 10, 20, 5, 10, 20, \ldots$$

has an easily recognizable repeating pattern of the block of numbers 5, 10, 20.

If you do not see a pattern right away, check for an arithmetic sequence. Do this by subtracting each term from the term that follows it. If the differences are the same, the sequence is arithmetic and you should add the common difference to a term to get the term that follows.

Here is an example.

> Find the missing term in the following sequence: 10, 12, _____, 16, 18, …

Subtract consecutive terms listed from the terms that follow them.

$$12 - 10 = 2$$
$$18 - 16 = 2$$

You get 2 as the difference both times, so the sequence is arithmetic with a common difference of 2. Add 2 (the common difference) to 12 to obtain the missing term: $2 + 12 = 14$.

If the sequence is not arithmetic, check for a geometric sequence. Do this by dividing each term by the term that follows it. If the quotients are the same, the sequence is geometric and you should multiply a term by the common quotient to get the term that follows.

Here is an example.

> Find the missing term in the following sequence: 2, __, 18, 54, 162, …

Divide consecutive terms listed by the terms that follow them.

$$54 \div 18 = 3$$
$$162 \div 54 = 3$$

You get 3 as the quotient both times, so the sequence is geometric with a common quotient of 3. Multiply 2 by 3 (the common quotient) to obtain the missing term: $2 \times 3 = 6$.

If the sequence is not arithmetic or geometric, then make a table listing the position numbers and corresponding terms side by side. Look for a relationship between the term and its position number.

Here is an example.

Find the missing term in the following sequence: $1, \frac{1}{2}, \frac{1}{3}, \underline{\hspace{1cm}}, \frac{1}{5} \cdots$

Make a table.

Position Number	Term
1	1
2	$\frac{1}{2}$
3	$\frac{1}{3}$
4	?
5	$\frac{1}{5}$

From the table you can see that the nth term is $\frac{1}{n}$, so the 4th term is $\frac{1}{4}$.

If no pattern has been found, then check for a Fibonacci sequence. With persistence, you should be able to find a pattern that can help you find a missing term of a sequence.

Test Yourself

1. The terms of an arithmetic sequence have a common _____ .

2. The terms of a geometric sequence have a common _____ .

3. A _____ sequence begins with two repeating terms, and thereafter, each term is the sum of the two preceding terms.

4. Find the missing term in the following sequence: 13, 18, ___, 28, 33, ...

5. Find the missing term in the following sequence: 5, ___, 20, –40, 80, ...

Answers

1. difference

2. quotient

3. Fibonacci

4. Check for an arithmetic sequence by subtracting consecutive terms listed from the terms that follow them.

    $18 - 13 = 5$

    $33 - 28 = 5$

    You get 5 as the difference both times, so the sequence is arithmetic with a common difference of 5. Add 5 (the common difference) to 18 to obtain the missing term: $18 + 5 = 23$.

5. Check for an arithmetic sequence by subtracting consecutive terms listed from the terms that follow them.

$$-40 - 20 = -60$$

$$80 - (-40) = 80 + 40 = 120$$

No common difference is found. Next, check for a geometric sequence by dividing consecutive terms listed by the terms that follow them.

$$-40 \div 20 = -2$$

$$80 \div -40 = -2$$

You get -2 as the quotient both times, so the sequence is geometric with a common quotient of -2. Multiply 5 by -2 (the common quotient) to obtain the missing term: $5 \times -2 = -10$.

How Do You Interpret Algebraic Expressions?

For the FTCE GK test you will need to know how to translate algebraic expressions into words. The language of algebra is symbolic. A **variable** is a symbol used in algebra to represent some unknown quantity that can take the value of a specific number or, in some cases, a set of numbers. On the FTCE GK test, letters are used as variables. If there is a number in front of the letter, that number is called the **numerical coefficient** of the variable. For instance, in the expression $2x$, 2 is the numerical coefficient of x. If no number is written in front of the variable, it is understood that the numerical coefficient is 1. Writing a variable with a coefficient or writing two or more variables in juxtaposition (side by side) is a way to show multiplication. In other words, $2x$ means 2 times x and abc means a times b times c. No multiplication symbol is necessary.

An **algebraic expression** is any combination of symbols that represents a number. Algebraic expressions consist of one or more variables joined by one or more operational symbols, with or without numerical quantities included.

Look at these examples of algebraic expressions.

$2x$	$3(x + 4)$	$\dfrac{3x^4 y^6}{5x^3}$
$5(a + b)$	$\dfrac{1}{2}mv^2$	$\dfrac{1}{2}h(b_1 + b_2)$
$p^2 n$	$x + 2y$	$2(\pi r^2) + 2(\pi r)h$
$9x^2 - 6x + 1$	abc	$\dfrac{4}{3}\pi r^3$

You likely recognized the last three expressions in the third column as formulas from the Mathematics Reference Sheet. Formulas are examples of algebraic expressions.

The first step in learning to interpret the language of algebra is to understand how addition, subtraction, multiplication, and division are expressed algebraically. Table 4.12 summarizes the most commonly used algebraic symbolism for the operations. The letter x is used in the table to represent an unknown number.

Table 4.12: Algebraic Symbolism for the Operations

Operation	Symbol(s) Used	Example	Sample Word Phrases
Addition	+	$x + 10$	x plus 10, the sum of x and 10, x increased by 10, 10 added to x
Subtraction	−	$x - 2$	x minus 2, 2 subtracted from x, the difference between x and 2, 2 less than x, x decreased by 2
Multiplication	juxtaposition or ( )	$2x$ $2(x)$	2 times x, x multiplied by 2, the product of 2 and x, twice x, 2 of x
Division	fraction bar	$\dfrac{x}{5}$	x divided by 5, the quotient of x and 5, the ratio of x to 5

Besides indicating multiplication, parentheses are used as grouping symbols. Similarly, a fraction bar can be a grouping symbol as well as indicating division. When interpreting an algebraic expression, it is common to use the word "quantity" to indicate that terms are enclosed in a grouping symbol and to avoid ambiguity.

Here are examples.

$3(x + 10)$ is "3 times the quantity $x + 10$."

$\frac{x-2}{5}$ is "the quantity $x - 2$ divided by 5."

$(ab)^2$ is "the quantity ab squared."

When you have more than one operation involved in an algebraic expression, keep in mind that the variables are standing in for numbers, so the indicated calculations must follow the order of operations.

Also, as mentioned earlier, it is important to avoid ambiguity. That is, you want your translation to have only one meaning.

Here is an example of an ambiguous translation.

"the product of 3 and x squared"   Does this mean $(3x)^2$ or $3x^2$?

Here are examples of translating algebraic expressions into words.

Translate the formula $\frac{4}{3}\pi r^3$ into words.

This expression is a product of three terms: $\frac{4}{3}$, π, and r^3. Notice that the exponent ^{3} on r applies only to r. A correct translation of the expression is "$\frac{4}{3}$ times π times r to the third power." Another correct translation is "the product of $\frac{4}{3}$ times π times r times r times r."

Translate the expression $\frac{1}{2}h(b_1 + b_2)$ into words.

This expression is the product of three terms: $\frac{1}{2}$, h, and the quantity $(b_1 + b_2)$. A correct translation of the expression is "half the product of h times the quantity $b_1 + b_2$." Another correct translation is "$\frac{1}{2}$ times h times the quantity $b_1 + b_2$."

How Do You Simplify Algebraic Expressions?

You simplify algebraic expressions by using the commutative, associative, and distributive properties of the real numbers. These properties are summarized in Table 4.13.

Table 4.13 Properties of the Real Numbers Used in Simplifying		
Property	*Explanation*	*Example*
Commutative Property of Addition	When you add two real numbers, you can change the order of the numbers being added and still obtain the correct sum.	$10 + 25 = 25 + 10$ $35\checkmark = 35\checkmark$
Commutative Property of Multiplication	When you multiply two real numbers, you can change the order of the numbers being multiplied and still obtain the correct product.	$(10)(25) = (25)(10)$ $250\checkmark = 250\checkmark$
Associative Property of Addition	When you add more than two real numbers, you can group the way you add the numbers in different ways and still obtain the correct sum.	$(4 + 6) + 5 = 4 + (6 + 5)$ $10 + 5 = 4 + 11$ $15\checkmark = 15\checkmark$

Property	Explanation	Example
Associative Property of Multiplication	When you multiply more than two real numbers, you can group the way you multiply the numbers in different ways and still obtain the correct product.	$(4)(6) \cdot 5 = 4 \cdot (6)(5)$ $24 \cdot 5 = 4 \cdot 30$ $120\checkmark = 120\checkmark$
Distributive Property	When a sum of two real numbers is multiplied by a real number, you can add first and then multiply, or you can multiply first and then add the products. Either way, you still obtain the correct result.	$5(10 + 8) = 5 \cdot 10 + 5 \cdot 8$ $5 \cdot 18 = 50 + 40$ $90\checkmark = 90\checkmark$

You may use one or a combination of these properties to simplify algebraic expressions. Here is an example.

Simplify $5(2x + 3)$.

$5(2x + 3) = 5(2x) + 5 \cdot 3 =$ Using the distributive property, multiply each term in the parentheses by 5.

$(5 \cdot 2)x + 5 \cdot 3 = 10x + 15$ Using the associative property, regroup $5(2x)$ as $(5 \cdot 2)x$, then multiply.

Of course, in practice you can do the intermediate steps mentally as shown in this example.

Simplify $3(x + 4)$

$3(x + 4) = 3x + 12$ Using the distributive property, multiply each term in the parentheses by 3.

Notice that the distributive property means that if you have the sum of two products that have a common factor, you can rewrite the expression as the common factor times the sum of the other two factors.

Here is an example.

$6 \cdot 30 + 6 \cdot 70 =$ 6 is a common factor in the two products.

$6(30 + 70) =$ Use the distributive property to rewrite the expression as 6 times the sum of the other two factors.

$6 \cdot 100 = 600$

This use of the distributive property allows you to combine variable expressions that are the same except for their numerical coefficients into a single term. Variable expressions that are the same except for their numerical coefficients are called **like terms.** Here are examples of simplifying like terms.

Simplify $2x + 3x$.

$2x + 3x =$ The variable x is a common factor in the two products.

$x(2 + 3) =$ Use the distributive property to rewrite the expression as x times the sum of the other two factors.

$x \cdot 5 = 5x$ Apply the commutative property of multiplication.

Simplify $15y - 8y$.

$15y - 8y = 15y + -8y$ Apply the definition for algebraic subtraction. The variable y is a common factor in the two products.

$y(15 + -8) =$ Use the distributive property to rewrite the expression as y times the sum of the other two factors.

$y \cdot 7 = 7y$ Apply the commutative property of multiplication.

When you understand the mathematical basis for combining like terms, you can abbreviate the process to the following rule:

To add like terms, you add (algebraically) their numerical coefficients and use the result as the numerical coefficient for the common variable.

Here are examples.

$20x + 30x = 50x$

$15z - 40z = -25z$ *Hint:* Using the rules for combining signed numbers (see the "Numerations and Operations" section, earlier in this chapter), $15 - 40 = 15 + -40 = -25$.

The addition or subtraction of terms that are *not* like terms can only be indicated. You cannot put them together into a single term. For instance, you would have to leave $2a + 3b$ as it is—you can't make it into a single term.

One further note: When you simplify expressions containing subtraction, as a practical matter, you might find it more convenient not to rewrite subtraction in terms of algebraic addition. You can think of the minus sign as "+ the opposite." For the remainder of this study guide, we will adopt the practice of not rewriting subtraction unless it is necessary to do so to avoid making a sign error in the problem.

Test Yourself

1. An algebraic expression is a combination of symbols that represents a _____ .

2. The numerical coefficient of x is _____ .

3. Translate $2x$ into words.

4. Translate $\frac{m}{3}$ into words.

5. Translate mv^2 into words.

6. Express 10 less than y in symbols.

7. Translate the expression $\frac{1}{2}(x + 10)$ into words.

8. Simplify $3(x + 4) + 2x$.

9. Simplify $5 + 2(x - 4)$.

10. Simplify $x + 2$.

Answers

1. number

2. 1

3. "2 times x"

4. "m divided by 3"

5. "the product of m times v times v" or "m times the quantity v squared"

6. $y - 10$

7. "half the quantity $x + 10$" or "$\frac{1}{2}$ times the quantity $x + 10$"

8. $3(x + 4) + 2x = 3x + 12 + 2x = 3x + 2x + 12 = 5x + 12$

9. $5 + 2(x - 4) = 5 + 2(x + -4) = 5 + 2x + -8 = 2x + 5 + -8 = 2x + -3 = 2x - 3$

10. Leave $x + 2$ as it is. This expression cannot be simplified further.

How Do You Solve Equations?

An **equation** is a statement that two mathematical expressions are equal. An equation may be true or false. For instance, the equation $8 + 5 = 13$ is true, but the equation $0 = 2$ is false. An equation has two sides. Whatever is on the left side of the equal sign is the *left side* of the equation, and whatever is on the right side of the equal sign is the *right side* of the equation.

A variable or variables might hold the place for numbers in an equation. For example, the equation

$$5x + 8 = 2x - 1$$

is an equation that has one variable. To **solve an equation** that has one variable means to find a numerical replacement for the variable that makes the equation true. An equation is true when the left side has the same value as the right side.

To solve an equation, you work backward to find the value of the variable. You "undo" what has been done to the variable until you get an expression like this: variable = number. In other words, the equation is solved when you succeed in getting the variable by itself on one side of the equation only and the coefficient of the variable is an understood 1.

An equation is like balance scales. To keep the equation in balance, whatever you do to one side of the equation you must do to the other side of the equation. The main tools you use in solving equations are:

- Adding the same number to both sides.
- Subtracting the same number from both sides.
- Multiplying both sides by the same *nonzero* number.
- Dividing both sides by the same *nonzero* number.

What has been done to the variable determines the operation you choose to do. You do it to both sides to keep the equation balanced. You "undo" an operation by using the inverse of the operation. Addition and subtraction undo each other as do multiplication and division.

With that said, how do you proceed? To solve an equation, follow these five steps.

Step 1. If parentheses are involved, use the distributive property to remove parentheses.

Step 2. Combine like terms, if any, on each side of the equation.

Step 3. If the variable appears on both sides of the equation, add a variable expression to both sides of the equation so that the variable appears on only one side of the equation, and then simplify.

Step 4. Undo addition or subtraction and then simplify. If a number is added to the variable term, subtract that number from both sides of the equation. If a number is subtracted from the variable term, add that number to both sides of the equation.

Step 5. Divide both sides of the equation by the coefficient of the variable.

Here are examples of solving an equation.

> Solve $5x + 8 = 2x - 1$

No parentheses are involved, and there are no like terms to combine, so skip Steps 1–2.

$5x + 8 - 2x = 2x - 1 - 2x$ $5x - 2x + 8 = 2x - 2x - 1$	The variable appears on both sides of the equation, so subtract $2x$ from the right side to remove it from that side. To keep the equation balanced, subtract $2x$ from the left side, too. Then simplify.
$3x + 8 = -1$ $3x + 8 - 8 = -1 - 8$ $3x = -9$	8 is added to the variable term, so subtract 8 from both sides of the equation. Then simplify.
$\dfrac{3x}{3} = \dfrac{-9}{3}$ $x = -3$	You want the coefficient of x to be 1, so divide both sides by 3.

You can check your solution by plugging it back into the original equation.

Put in -3 for x on the left side of the equation: $5(-3) + 8 = -15 + 8 = -7$. Put in -3 for x on the right side of the equation: $2(-3) - 1 = -6 + -1 = -7$. Both sides equal -7, so -3 is the correct solution.

> Solve $5(x + 7) = 15$

$5x + 35 = 15$	Use the distributive property to remove parentheses.
$5x + 35 - 35 = 15 - 35$ $5x = -20$	35 is added to the variable term, so subtract 35 from both sides of the equation. Then simplify.
$\dfrac{5x}{5} = \dfrac{-20}{5}$ $x = -4$	You want the coefficient of x to be 1, so divide both sides by 5.

Check:

Put in -4 for x on the left side of the equation: $5(-4 + 7) = 5(3) = 15$. The right side of the equation is also 15. Both sides equal 15, so -4 is the correct solution.

Sometimes you can find a replacement for the variable that makes the equation true simply by "guessing and checking." This is a good test-taking strategy for multiple-choice math tests.

Here is an example of using "guessing and checking" to solve an equation.

> Solve $5x + 8 = 2x - 1$
>
> A. -1
> B. -3
> C. 1
> D. 3

Check the answer choices by plugging the values into the equation, being careful to enclose in parentheses the values that you put in and to follow the order of operations PE(MD)(AS) when you do your calculations.

Check Choice **A**: Put in -1 for x on the left side of the equation: $5(-1) + 8 = -5 + 8 = 3$. Put in -1 for x on the right side of the equation: $2(-1) - 1 = -2 + -1 = -3$. Choice **A** is incorrect because $3 \neq -3$.

Check Choice **B**: Put in –3 for *x* on the left side of the equation: 5(–3) + 8 = –15 + 8 = –7. Put in –3 for *x* on the right side of the equation: 2(–3) – 1 = –6 + –1 = –7. Choice **B** is the correct response because *x* = –3 made the equation true—both sides equal –7.

When you're taking the FTCE GK test, you would not have to check the other answer choices because the correct answer is **B**. Since the test is timed, it would be best to move on to the next question.

How Do You Solve Inequalities?

An **inequality** is a mathematical statement that contains one of the following four inequality symbols: $<$, $>$, $\leq$, or $\geq$. Like equations, inequalities may be true or false. For instance, the inequality $7 + 5 < 20$ is true, but the inequality $0 \geq 5$ is false.

Inequalities may contain variables. For example, the inequality $x \leq 6$ is *true* if *x* is 2 and is *false* if *x* is 10. In fact, this inequality is true if *x* is any number that is less than or equal to 6 and is false if *x* is any number greater than 6. You can show the set of numbers that make the inequality true on a number line. You shade the numbers to the left of 6, and to indicate that the number 6 also belongs in the solution set, you shade in a small circle at the point 6.

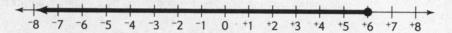

For the inequality $x < 6$, you would indicate that the number 6 does *not* belong in the solution set, by drawing an open circle at the point 6.

You solve inequalities the same way you solve equations. However, there is one main difference. When you multiply or divide the inequality by a *negative* number, you must *reverse* the direction of the inequality. To understand why you must do this, consider the following.

You know that $8 > 2$ is a true inequality because 8 is to the right of 2 on the number line as shown in the following figure.

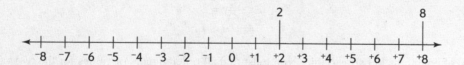

If both sides of the inequality $8 > 2$ are multiplied by a negative number, say –1, the direction of the inequality must be reversed, yielding the inequality $-8 < -2$. This is a true inequality because –2 is to the right of –8 on the number line as shown in the following figure.

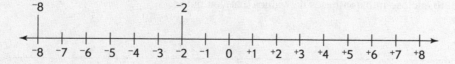

If you do not reverse the inequality symbol after multiplying both sides of $8 > 2$ by –1, you obtain $-8 > -2$, which is clearly false.

Here are examples of solving an inequality.

195

Solve $6x - 5 < 37$

$6x - 5 + 5 < 37 + 5$ 5 is subtracted from the variable term, so add 5 to both sides of the inequality.

$6x < 42$ Then simplify.

$\dfrac{\cancel{6}x}{\cancel{6}} < \dfrac{42}{6}$ You want the coefficient of x to be 1, so divide both sides by 6.

$x < 7$

Solve $-5(x - 2) \geq 15$

$-5x + 10 \geq 15$ Use the Distributive Property to remove parentheses.

$-5x + 10 - 10 \geq 15 - 10$ 10 is added to the variable term, so subtract 10 from both sides of the inequality.

$-5x \geq 5$ Then simplify.

$\dfrac{\cancel{-5}x}{\cancel{-5}} \leq \dfrac{5}{-5}$ You want the coefficient of x to be 1, so divide both sides by -5 and reverse the inequality because you divided both sides by a negative number.

$x \leq -1$

Here is a word of caution. You reverse the direction of the inequality only when you are *multiplying* or *dividing* both sides by a *negative* number. It does *not* apply if the number is positive or if the operation is addition or subtraction.

How Do You Decide Whether an Ordered Pair Satisfies a System of Equations?

A set of two equations, each with the same two variables, is called a **system** when the two equations are considered simultaneously.

Here is an example of a system of two equations with variables x and y.

$$3x + 4y = 2$$
$$4x - y = 9$$

To solve a system of equations in two variables, you must find all ordered pairs of values for the two variables that make *both* equations true simultaneously. An ordered pair that makes an equation true is said to **satisfy** the equation. When an ordered pair makes both equations in a system true, the order pair **satisfies** the system.

To determine whether an ordered pair satisfies a system of two equations, you will need to check whether the ordered pair satisfies both equations in the system. Do this by plugging the x and y values of the ordered pair into the two equations, being careful to enclose in parentheses the values that you put in.

Here is an example.

Determine whether the ordered pair $(1, -2)$ satisfies the following system.

$$3x + 4y = 2$$
$$4x - y = 9$$

First, check whether $(1, -2)$ satisfies $3x + 4y = 2$.

On the left side of the equation put in 1 for x and –2 for y and simplify: $3(1) + 4(-2) = 3 - 8 = -5$. The right side of the equation is 2, since $-5 \neq 2$, $(1, -2)$ does not satisfy $3x + 4y = 2$. Therefore, $(1, -2)$ does *not* satisfy the given system because it fails to satisfy one of the equations in the system.

Determine whether the ordered pair $(2, -1)$ satisfies the following system.

$$3x + 4y = 2$$
$$4x - y = 9$$

First, check whether $(2, -1)$ satisfies $3x + 4y = 2$.

On the left side of the equation, put in 2 for x and –1 for y and simplify: $3(2) + 4(-1) = 6 - 4 = 2$. The right side of the equation is also 2, so $(2, -1)$ satisfies $3x + 4y = 2$.

Next, check whether $(2, -1)$ satisfies $4x - y = 9$.

On the left side of the equation put in 2 for x and –1 for y and simplify: $4(2) - (-1) = 8 + 1 = 9$. The right side of the equation is also 9, so $(2, -1)$ satisfies $4x - y = 9$.

Therefore, $(2, -1)$ satisfies the given system because it satisfies both equations in the system.

Test Yourself

1. An equation is true when the left side has the _____ value as the right side.

2. When solving an equation, should you "undo" addition or multiplication first?

3. Solve $3x + 50 = 35$.

4. Solve $25 - 3y = 3y + 1$.

5. Solve $6x - 36 = 6(2 - 3x)$

6. Does $x = -5$ make the inequality $x \geq -9$ true?

7. When you _____ or _____ an inequality by a _____ number, you must reverse the direction of the inequality.

8. Solve $2x + 5 > 21$.

9. Solve $3x - 4(x + 2) \leq -6$.

10. Determine whether the ordered pair $(1, 2)$ satisfies the following system.

    $x + 2y = 5$
    $4x - y = 2$

Answers

1. same

2. addition

3. $x = -5$

Solution:

Solve $3x + 50 = 35$.

$3x + 50 - 50 = 35 - 50$ 50 is added to the variable term, so subtract 50 from both sides of the equation. Then simplify.

$3x = -15$

$\dfrac{\cancel{3}x}{\cancel{3}} = \dfrac{-15}{3}$ You want the coefficient of x to be 1, so divide both sides by 3.

$x = -5$

4. $y = 4$

Solution:

Solve $25 - 3y = 3y + 1$.

$25 - 3y - 3y = 3y + 1 - 3y$ The variable appears on both sides of the equation, so subtract $3y$ from the right side to remove it from that side. To keep the equation balanced, subtract $3y$ from the left side, too. Then simplify.

$25 - 3y - 3y = 3y - 3y + 1$

$25 - 6y = 1$

$25 - 6y - 25 = 1 - 25$ 25 is added to the variable term, so subtract 25 from both sides of the equation. Then simplify.

$-6y = -24$

$\dfrac{\cancel{-6}y}{\cancel{-6}} = \dfrac{-24}{-6}$ You want the coefficient of x to be 1, so divide both sides by -6.

$y = 4$

5. $x = 2$

Solution:

Solve $6x - 36 = 6(2 - 3x)$.

$6x - 36 = 12 - 18x$ Use the distributive property to remove parentheses.

$6x - 36 + 18x = 12 - 18x + 18x$ The variable appears on both sides of the equation, so add $18x$ to the right side to remove it from that side. To keep the equation balanced, add $18x$ to the left side, too. Then simplify.

$6x + 18x - 36 = 12 - 18x + 18x$

$24x - 36 = 12$

$24x - 36 + 36 = 12 + 36$ 36 is subtracted from the variable term, so add 36 to both sides of the equation. Then simplify.

$24x = 48$

$\dfrac{\cancel{24}x}{\cancel{24}} = \dfrac{48}{24}$ You want the coefficient of x to be 1, so divide both sides by 24.

$x = 2$

6. Yes, -5 is located to the right of -9 on the number line, so $-5 \geq -9$ is true.

7. multiply, divide, negative

8. $x > 8$

Solution:

Solve $2x + 5 > 21$.

$$2x + 5 - 5 > 21 - 5$$

5 is added to the variable term, so subtract 5 from both sides of the inequality. Then simplify.

$$2x > 16$$

$$\frac{\cancel{2}x}{\cancel{2}} > \frac{16}{2}$$

You want the coefficient of x to be 1, so divide both sides by 2.

$$x > 8$$

9. $x \geq -2$

Solve $3x - 4(x + 2) \leq -6$.

$$3x - 4x - 8 \leq -6$$

Use the distributive property to remove parentheses.

$$-x - 8 \leq -6$$

$$-x - 8 + 8 \leq -6 + 8$$

8 is subtracted from the variable term, so add 8 to both sides of the inequality. Then simplify.

$$-x \leq 2$$

$$\frac{-x}{-1} \geq \frac{2}{-1}$$

You want the coefficient of x to be 1, so divide both sides by -1 and reverse the inequality because you divided both sides by a negative number.

$$x \geq -2$$

10. **Yes,** (1, 2) satisfies the given system.

Solution:

First, check whether (1, 2) satisfies $x + 2y = 5$.

On the left side of the equation, put in 1 for x and 2 for y and simplify: $(1) + 2(2) = 1 + 4 = 5$. The right side of the equation is also 5, so (1, 2) satisfies $x + 2y = 5$.

Next, check whether (1, 2) satisfies $4x - y = 2$.

On the left side of the equation, put in 1 for x and 2 for y and simplify: $4(1) - (2) = 4 - 2 = 2$. The right side of the equation is also 2, so (1, 2) satisfies $4x - y = 2$.

Therefore, (1, 2) satisfies the given system because it satisfies both equations in the system.

Sample Questions

1. Find the missing number in the following sequence: 3, _____, 12, –24, 48

    A. –5
    B. 5
    C. –6
    D. 6

2. The volume of a cone is $V = \frac{1}{3} h\pi r^2$ where h is the height of the cone and r is the radius of the base of the cone. Translate the expression $\frac{1}{3} h\pi r^2$ into words.

    A. one-third the product of h times π times r times r
    B. the quantity of one-third the height times π times the radius, all squared
    C. one-third the height times one-third π times r squared
    D. one-third the square of the quantity of h times π times r

3. Solve for x in $2(x + 6) = 50$

    A. 19
    B. 22
    C. 31
    D. 38

4. Determine which of the following ordered pairs satisfies the given system.

$$x - 2y = -7$$
$$2x + y = -4$$

    A. $(2, -3)$
    B. $(-2, 3)$
    C. $(-3, 2)$
    D. $(3, -2)$

Answer Explanations for Sample Questions

1. C. Check for an arithmetic sequence by subtracting consecutive terms listed from the terms that follow them.

$$-24 - 12 = -36$$

$$48 - (-24) = 48 + 24 = 72$$

No common difference is found. Next, check for a geometric sequence by dividing consecutive terms listed by the terms that follow them.

$$-24 \div 12 = -2$$

$$48 \div -24 = -2$$

You get -2 as the quotient both times, so the sequence is geometric with a common quotient of -2. Multiply 3 by -2 (the common quotient) to obtain the missing term: $3 \times -2 = -6$, Choice **C**.

The other choices result if you multiply 3×-2 incorrectly.

2. A. This expression is a product of four terms: $\frac{1}{3}$, h, π, and r^2. Notice that the exponent ^{2} on r applies only to r. A correct translation of the expression is "one-third the product of h times π times r times r." Choices **B** and **D** are incorrect because only r, the radius, is squared in the expression. Choice **C** is incorrect because $\frac{1}{3}$ is a factor only once, not twice, in the expression.

3. A.

    Solve $2(x + 6) = 50$

$2x + 12 = 50$	Use the distributive property to remove parentheses.
$2x + 12 - 12 = 50 - 12$	12 is added to the variable term, so subtract 12 from both sides of the equation. Then simplify.
$2x = 38$	
$\dfrac{2x}{2} = \dfrac{38}{2}$	You want the coefficient of x to be 1, so divide both sides by 2.
$x = 19$	

Choice **B** results if you fail to use the distributive property correctly. Choice **C** results if you add 12 to both sides instead of subtracting it. Choice **D** results if you fail to divide by 2.

4. C. To determine which ordered pair satisfies the system, you will need to find the ordered pair that satisfies *both* equations. Check each ordered pair by plugging the x and y values into the two equations, being careful to enclose in parentheses the values you put in.

Checking **A:** $x - 2y = (2) - 2(-3) = 2 + 6 = 8 \neq -7$. Choice **A** is incorrect because $(2, -3)$ does not satisfy $x - 2y = -7$.

Checking **B:** $x - 2y = (-2) - 2(3) = -2 - 6 = -8 \neq -7$. Choice **B** is incorrect because $(-2, 3)$ does not satisfy $x - 2y = -7$.

Checking **C:** $x - 2y = (-3) - 2(2) = -3 - 4 = -7$✓. Since $(-3, 2)$ works in the first equation, try it in the second equation. $2x + y = 2(-3) + (2) = -6 + 2 = -4$ ✓. Choice **C** is the correct response because the ordered pair $(-3, 2)$ satisfies both equations in the system.

You would not have to continue since Choice **C** is the correct response. However, in case you're interested, Choice **D** is incorrect because $x - 2y = (3) - 2(-2) = 3 + 4 = 7 \neq -7$.

Data Analysis and Probability

As listed in the *Competencies and Skills Required for Teacher Certification in Florida, Ninth Edition* (see the first section in this chapter for the Web address), the competencies/skills you should be able to do for this area of mathematics are the following:

- Analyze and interpret graphical representation of data.
- Recognize how graphical representation of data can lead to inappropriate interpretations.
- Calculate and interpret measures of central tendency and measures of dispersion.
- Calculate probabilities.
- Solve real-world problems involving probability using counting procedures.

How Can You Organize and Present Data?

There are several ways to record, organize, and present data. On the FTCE GK test, you will be expected to perform data analysis by reading and interpreting information from **charts** and **tables, pictographs, bar graphs, histograms, circle graphs,** and **line graphs.**

Charts and tables are used to put related information into an organized form. Pictographs, bar graphs, and circle graphs display information that is organized into categories. Histograms summarize data by using totals within intervals. Line graphs show trends, usually, over time.

Charts and Tables

Charts and **tables** organize information in columns and rows. Each column or row is labeled to explain the entries.

Look at this example.

The table that follows shows the number of snow cone sales for each month during the summer. According to the chart shown, in which month was snow cone sales the highest?

SUMMER SNOW CONE SALES

Month	Number of Snow Cones Sold
June	650
July	800
August	950

Examination of the chart shows that the highest number of sales was 950 snow cones, which occurred in the month of August.

Pictographs

In a **pictograph,** pictures or symbols are used to represent numbers. Each symbol represents a given number of a particular item. The symbol, its meaning, and the quantity it represents should be stated on the graph. To read a pictograph, count the number of symbols in a row and multiply this number by the scale indicated on the graph. Sometimes, a fraction of a symbol is shown. In that case, approximate the fraction and use it accordingly.

Look at this example.

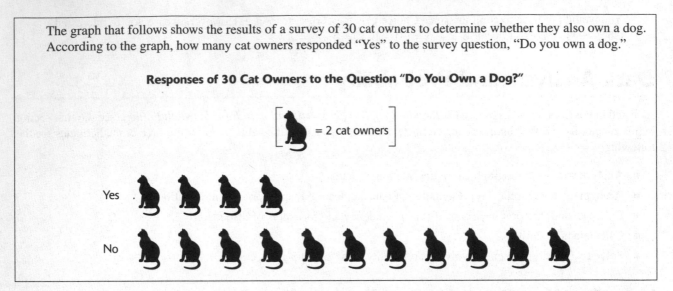

According to the graph, each symbol stands for 2 cat owners. The 4 symbols shown in the graph for "Yes" show that of the 30 cat owners surveyed, the number who also own a dog is $4 \times 2 = 8$ cat owners.

Bar Graphs

A **bar graph** uses bars to represent frequencies, percents, or amounts. The bars correspond to different categories that are labeled at the base of the bars. The bars in a bar graph may be arranged vertically or horizontally. The widths of the bars are equal. The length or height of the bar indicates the number, percent, or amount for the category for that particular bar. A scale (usually beginning with 0) marked with equally spaced values will be shown on the graph. To read a bar graph, examine the scale to determine the units and the amount between the marked values. Then determine where the endpoints of the bars fall in relation to the scale.

Look at these examples.

The table that follows shows the number of snow cone sales for each month during the summer. According to the chart shown, how many snow cones were sold in July?

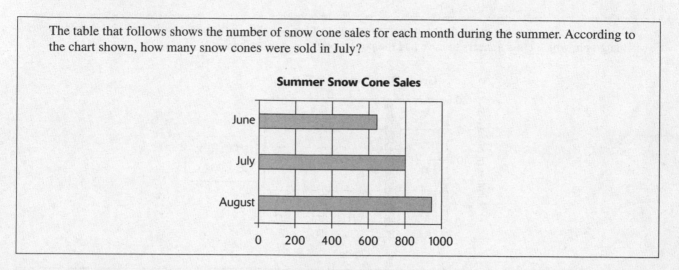

The scale on the horizontal axis shows the number of snow cones sold. The scale is marked in multiples of 200. The bar for July ends at 800, indicating 800 snow cones were sold in July.

The bar graph that follows shows the grade distribution for the first test in a social studies class. According to the graph, how many students made an A on the first test?

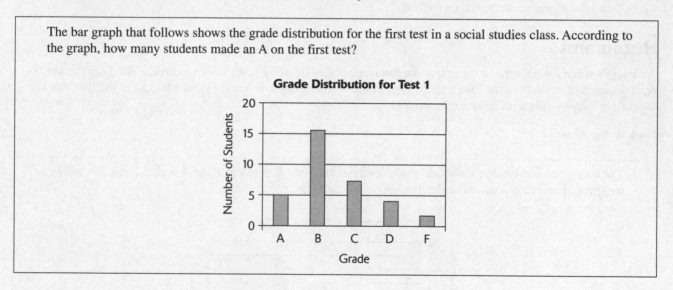

The scale on the vertical axis shows the number of students who achieved the grade. The scale is marked in multiples of 5. The top of the bar for the A category is at 5, indicating 5 students made an A on Test 1.

Bar graphs can show two or more sets of data on the same graph. This allows you to compare how the data sets measure up to each other.

Look at this example.

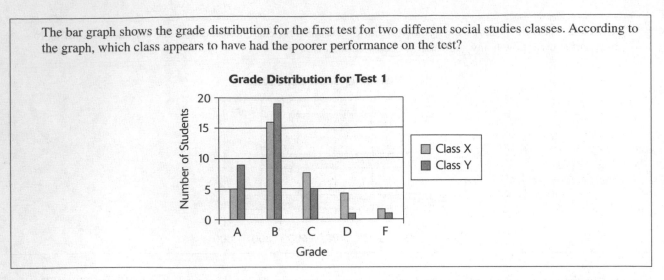

The bar graph shows the grade distribution for the first test for two different social studies classes. According to the graph, which class appears to have had the poorer performance on the test?

The graph shows that Class X had fewer A's and B's and more C's, D's, and F's than Class Y. Therefore, it appears that Class X had the poorer performance on the test.

Histograms

A **histogram** is a special type of bar graph that summarizes data by using totals within intervals. The intervals are of equal length and cover from the lowest to the highest data value. Unlike the bars in other bar graphs, the bars in a histogram are side-by-side with no space in between.

Look at this example.

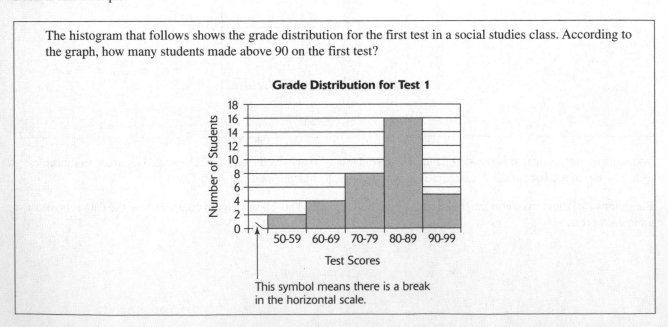

The histogram that follows shows the grade distribution for the first test in a social studies class. According to the graph, how many students made above 90 on the first test?

The scale on the vertical axis shows the number of students who achieved the grade. The scale is marked in multiples of 2. The top of the bar for the interval 90-99 is halfway between 4 and 6, indicating that 5 students made above 90 on Test 1.

Circle Graphs and Pie Charts

A **circle graph,** or **pie chart,** is a graph in the shape of a circle. Circle graphs are used to display the relationship of each type or class of data within a whole set of data in a visual form. It is also called a "pie" chart because it looks like a pie cut into wedge-shaped slices. The wedges are labeled to show the categories for the graph. Each sector angle represents a specific part of the whole. Usually percents are used to show the amount of the graph that corresponds to each category. The total amount in percentage shown on the graph is 100%. The graph is made by dividing the 360 degrees of the circle into portions that correspond to the percentages for each category. Reading a circle graph is a simple matter of reading the percents displayed on the graph for the different categories.

Look at this example.

The following circle graph shows how a student plans to budget $2000 each month. According to the graph, how much money is budgeted for food?

Monthly Budget of $2000

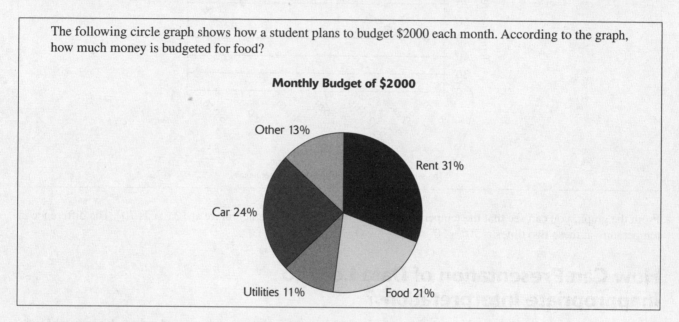

The graph shows that 21% of the budget is designated for food. To find how much money is designated for food, find 21% of $2000 = $420.

Line Graphs

A **line graph** uses lines or broken lines for representing data. It has both a horizontal and a vertical scale. The data points for the graph are plotted as ordered pairs of numbers, according to the two scales. Line segments are used to connect consecutive points. Sometimes, two or more sets of data are plotted on the same graph. The slant of the line between the points shows whether the data values are increasing, decreasing, or remaining at a constant value. If the line slants upward, the data values are increasing; if the line slants downward, the data values are decreasing; and a horizontal line (no slant) means that the data values remain constant. Line graphs are useful for showing change over time.

Look at this example.

The following line graph shows the temperature at different times during the day. According to the graph, how much higher is the temperature at 12 P.M. than it is at 8 A.M.?

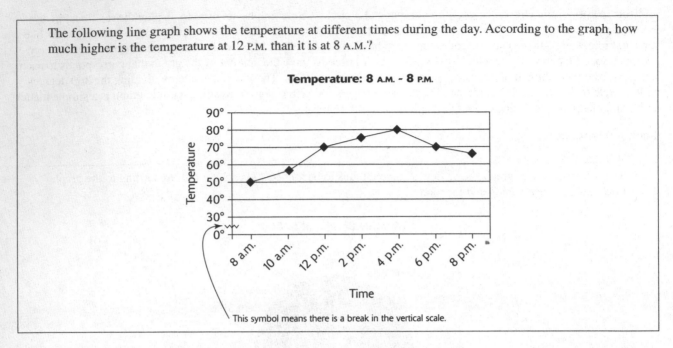

From the graph, you can see that the temperature at 8 A.M. is 50° and the temperature at 12 P.M. is 70°. The difference in temperature at these two times is 70° − 50° = 20°.

How Can Presentation of Data Lead to Inappropriate Interpretations?

Drawing valid conclusions from graphical representations of data requires that you have read the graph accurately and analyzed the graphical information correctly. Sometimes a graphical representation will distort the data in some way, leading you to draw an invalid conclusion.

Look at these examples.

Responses of 30 Owners of One Pet to the Question "Do You Own a Cat or a Dog?"

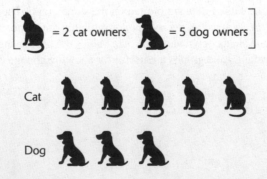

This graph has two major problems. The first problem is that the data are distorted. Visually, it appears that the number of cat owners is greater than the number of dog owners. However, each cat picture represents 2 cats, and each dog picture represents 5 dogs. Thus, the number of dog owners is 15 compared to 10 cat owners, making the number of dog owners greater. The other problem is that the number of pet owners represented in the table is 25, but the number surveyed is 30. The graph should have an additional category for those pet owners surveyed who own neither a cat nor a dog.

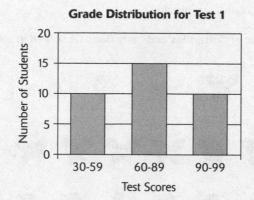

Grade Distribution for Test 1

At first glance, the data for this graph look evenly distributed. Upon closer examination, you can see that each of the first two intervals cover a 29-point spread, but the last interval covers only a 19-point spread, making it difficult to draw conclusions from the graph.

When you have to interpret graphical information on the FTCE GK test, follow these suggestions:

- Make sure that you understand the title of the graph.
- Read the labels on the parts of the graph to understand what is being represented.
- Examine carefully the scale of bar graphs, line graphs, and histograms.
- Make sure you know what each picture in a pictograph represents.
- Look for trends such as increases (rising values), decreases (falling values), and periods of inactivity (constant values, horizontal lines) in line graphs.
- Make sure the numbers add up correctly.
- Be prepared to do some simple arithmetic calculations.
- Use only the information in the graph. Do not answer based on your personal knowledge or opinion.
- Mark and draw on the graphs in the test booklet.

Test Yourself

1. Pictographs, bar graphs, and circle graphs show information that is organized into _____.

2. In a _____ pictures or symbols are used to represent numbers.

3. The _____ or _____ of a bar graph indicates the number, percent, or amount for its corresponding category.

4. When reading a bar graph, line graph, or histogram, be sure to examine carefully the _____ to determine the amount between the marked values.

5. A histogram summarizes information using _____ labels for the bars. The bars are _____ with no space in between.

6. The total percentage in a circle graph is _____...

7. _____ graphs are useful for showing change over time.

8. When interpreting information from a graph, do not draw _____ beyond those represented in the graph.

9. What is a problem with the following pictograph?

Number of Butterflies and Lady Bugs Observed in a Month

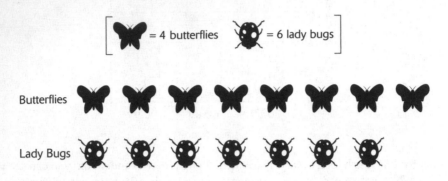

10. According to the bar graph shown here, in which quarter is the number of points scored by each of the two teams closest?

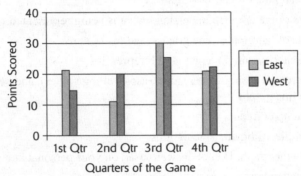

Answers

1. categories

2. pictograph

3. height, length

4. scale

5. interval, side-by-side

6. 100%

7. line

8. conclusions

9.

Number of Butterflies and Lady Bugs Observed in a Month

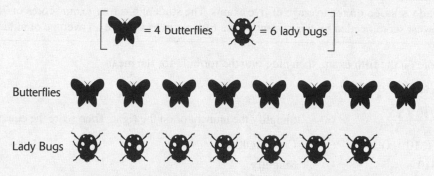

The graph is misleading, giving the visual impression that the number of butterflies and lady bugs are roughly the same. However, the butterfly picture represents 4 butterflies, but the lady bug picture represents 6 lady bugs. Thus, more lady bugs than butterflies were observed.

10.

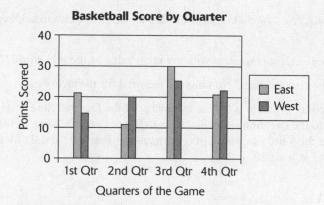

The heights of the two bars are closest in the 4th quarter, indicating that the number of points scored by each of the two teams is closest is in that quarter.

What Are Measures of Central Tendency?

A **measure of central tendency** is a numerical value that describes a data set by providing a "central" or "typical" value of the data set. The three most common measures of central tendency are the **mean, median,** and **mode.** Each of these measures represents a different way of describing a typical value of a set of data. Measures of central tendency should have the same units as those of the data values. If no units are specified, as in test scores, then the measure of central tendency will not specify units.

Finding the Mean

The **mean** of a set of numbers is another name for the arithmetic average of the numbers. To calculate the mean: first, sum the numbers; then, divide by how many numbers are in the set. Thus, you have the following formula:

$$\text{mean} = \frac{\text{the sum of the numbers}}{\text{how many numbers in the set}}$$

For example, to find the mean for the set of scores 50, 87, 50, 95, 78, you would proceed as follows:

$$\text{mean} = \frac{50 + 87 + 50 + 95 + 78}{5} = \frac{360}{5} = 72$$

On the FTCE GK test, you may be given a set of numbers and asked to find the missing number that gives the set a certain average (mean).

Here is an example.

> A student's grade is based on the average of five exams. The student has four exam scores of 78, 62, 91, and 79. What is the lowest score needed by the student on the fifth exam to achieve an average of at least 80?

Let x = the score on the fifth exam, then plug into the formula for the mean.

$$80 = \frac{78 + 62 + 91 + 79 + x}{5}$$

$$\frac{80}{1} = \frac{310 + x}{5} \qquad \text{Simplify the numerator on the right. Then write the equation as a proportion.}$$

$$(80)(5) = 1(310 + x) \qquad \text{Cross multiply.}$$

$$400 = 310 + x \qquad \text{Simplify.}$$

$$400 - 310 = 310 + x - 310 \qquad \text{Subtract 310 from both sides of the equation.}$$

$$90 = x \qquad \text{Simplify.}$$

The lowest score needed on the fifth exam to achieve an average of 80 for the five exams is 90.

Did I answer the question? Yes, I found the score needed on the fifth exam to achieve an average of 80 for the five exams is 90. ✓

Does my answer make sense? Is it consistent with my knowledge of the real world? Yes. ✓

Is the answer stated in the correct units? No units are required for the answer. ✓

Another way to work the preceding problem is to take advantage of the fact that the FTCE GK test is a multiple-choice test. You are given the answer to the question—you just have to figure out which one of the four answer choices is the correct one. For a problem like this one, you would plug each answer into the formula for the mean until you found the one that gives you an average of at least 80.

Finding the Median

The **median** is the middle number or the average of the two middle numbers in an *ordered* set of numbers. Determining the median of a set of numbers is a two-step process.

Step 1: Put the numbers in order from least to greatest (or greatest to least).

Step 2: Find the middle number. If there is no single middle number, average the two middle numbers.

Look at these examples.

> Find the median for the set of scores 50, 87, 50, 95, 78.

Step 1: Put the numbers in order from least to greatest.

50, 50, 78, 87, 95

Step 2: Find the middle number, which is the median. In this example, which contains an odd number of values, there is a middle number. The median = 78.

Here is a note of caution: When you are asked to find a median, don't make the common mistake of neglecting to put the numbers in order first. In the preceding example, the middle number before the numbers are put in order is 50 (wrong answer).

> Find the median for the set of numbers 100, 10, 10, 36, 30, 36.

Step 1: Put the numbers in order from least to greatest.

    10, 10, 30, 36, 36, 100

Step 2: Find the middle number. This example contains an even number of values and there is no single middle number. In this case, the median is the average of the two middle numbers, 30 and 36. The median = $\frac{30 + 36}{2} = 33$.

Finding the Mode

The **mode** is the number or numbers that occur most frequently in a set of numbers; there can be one mode, more than one mode, or no mode. If two or more numbers occur most frequently, then each will be a mode. When each number in the data set appears the same number of times, there is no mode.

Look at these examples.

- There is one mode in the data set consisting of the numbers 50, 87, 50, 95, 78. The number 50 occurs most often. Therefore, the mode is 50.

- There are two modes in the data set consisting of the numbers 10, 10, 30, 36, 36, 100. The numbers 10 and 36 both occur most often. Therefore, the modes are 10 and 36.

- There is no mode for the data set consisting of the numbers 40, 52, 145, 96, 60. Each number in the data set appears the same number of times.

What Are Important Characteristics of the Measures of Central Tendency?

The mean, median, and mode are ways to describe a central or typical value of a data set. To know which of these measures of central tendency you should use to describe a data set, consider their characteristics.

The **mean** has several important characteristics.

- Although the mean represents a central or typical value of a data set, the mean does not have to be one of the numbers in the set. For instance, the mean of 50, 50, 87, 78, and 95 is 72, yet none of the five numbers in this data set equals 72.

- The actual data values are used in the computation of the mean. If any number is changed, the value of the mean will change. For example, the mean of the data set consisting of 50, 50, 87, 78, and 95 is 72. If the 95 in this set is changed to 100, the mean of the new data set would be 73.

- A disadvantage of the mean is that it is influenced by outliers, especially in a small data set. An **outlier** is a data value that is extremely high or extremely low in comparison to most of the other data values. If a data set contains extremely high values that are not balanced by corresponding low values, the mean will be misleadingly high. For example, the mean of the data set consisting of 15, 15, 20, 25, and 25 is 20. If the 20 in this set is changed to 100, the mean of the new data set would be 36. The value 36 does not represent the data set consisting of 15, 15, 100, 25, and 25 very well, since four of the data values are less than 30. Similarly, if a data set contains extremely low values that are not balanced by corresponding high values, the mean will be misleadingly low. For example, the mean of the data set consisting of 100, 100, 130, and 150 is 120. If the 150 in this set is changed to 10, the mean of the new data set would be 60. The value 60 does not represent the data set consisting of 100, 100, 130, and 10 very well, since three of the data values are greater than or equal to 100.

The **median** is the most useful alternative to the mean as a measure of central tendency.

- Like the mean, the median does not have to be one of the numbers in the set. If the data set contains an odd number of data values, the median will be the middle number; however, for an even number of data values, the median is the arithmetic average of the two middle numbers.

- The median is not influenced by outliers. For instance, the median of the data set consisting of 10, 15, 20, 25, and 30 is 20. If the 30 in this set is changed to 100, the median of the new data set remains 20.
- A disadvantage of the median as an indicator of a central value is that it is based on relative size rather than on the actual numbers in the set. For instance, a student who has test scores of 44, 47, and 98 shows improved performance that would not be reflected if the median of 47, rather than the mean of 63, was reported as the representative grade.

The **mode** is the least commonly used measure of central tendency.

- The mode is the simplest measure of central tendency to calculate.
- If a data set has a mode, the mode (or modes) is one of the data values.
- The mode is the only appropriate measure of central tendency for data that are strictly nonnumeric like data on ice cream flavor preferences (vanilla, chocolate, strawberry, and so on). Although it makes no sense to determine a mean or median ice cream flavor for the data, the ice cream flavor that was named most frequently would be the modal flavor.
- A disadvantage of the mode as an indicator of a central value is that it is based on relative frequency than on all the values in the set. For instance, a student who has test scores of 45, 45, and 99 shows improved performance that would not be reflected if the mode of 45, rather than the mean of 63, was reported as the representative grade.

What Are Measures of Dispersion?

A **measure of dispersion** is a value that describes the spread of the data about the central value. Although measures of central tendency are important for describing data sets, their interpretation is enhanced when the spread or dispersion about the central value is known. Two groups of 10 students, both with means of 70 on a 100-point test, may have very different sets of scores. One set of scores may be extremely consistent, with scores like 60, 62, 65, 68, 70, 70, 72, 75, 78, and 80; while the other set of scores may be very erratic, with scores like 40, 40, 50, 55, 60, 80, 85, 90, 100, and 100. The scores in the first set cluster more closely about the mean of 70 than do the scores in the second set. The scores in the second set are more spread out than are the scores in the first set.

For the FTCE GK test, the two measures of dispersion you will need to know are the **range** and the **standard deviation.** Measures of dispersion should have the same units as those of the data values. If no units are specified, then the measure of dispersion will not specify units.

The **range** for a data set is the difference between the greatest value and the least value in the data set:

range = greatest value – least value

Here are examples of finding the range of a data set.

What is the range for this set of data?   50, 50, 60, 70, 70

range = greatest value – least value = 70 – 50 = 20

What is the range for this data set?   10, 10, 60, 110, 110

range = greatest value – least value = 110 – 10 = 100

The range gives some indication of the spread of the values in a data set, but its value is determined by only two of the data values. The extent of spread of the other numbers is not considered. A measure of dispersion that takes into account all the data values is the **standard deviation.** The **standard deviation** is a measure of the dispersion of a set of data values about the mean of the data set. If there is no dispersion in a data set, each data value would equal the mean, giving a standard deviation of zero. The more the data values vary from the mean, the greater the standard deviation. You will not have to calculate a standard deviation on the FTCE GK test. Questions about standard deviation will require you to examine two or more data sets and decide which data set has the greatest (or least) standard deviation.

Here is an example.

> The means of the following two data sets are equal to 50.
>
> Set 1: 30, 40, 50, 60, 70
>
> Set 2: 10, 10, 50, 90, 90
>
> Which data set has the greater standard deviation?

The data values in Set 1 cluster more closely around the mean of 50 than do the data values in Set 2. Therefore, Set 2 has the greater standard deviation.

Test Yourself

1. The mean, median, and mode are measures of _____ (two words).

2. The _____ of a set of numbers is another name for the arithmetic average of the numbers.

3. The median is the middle number or the average of the two middle numbers in an _____ set of numbers.

4. The _____ is the data value that occurs most frequently.

5. A disadvantage of the mean is that it is influenced by _____.

6. The median _____ (is, is not) influenced by outliers.

7. The _____ is the only appropriate measure of central tendency for data that are strictly nonnumeric.

8. A measure of dispersion is a value that describes the _____ of the data about the central value.

9. Find the mean, median, mode, and range for the following data set.

    10, 60, 30, 90, 10, 30, 40, 50

10. The standard deviation of a data set is a measure of the spread of the data values about the _____ of the data set.

Answers

1. central tendency
2. mean
3. ordered
4. mode
5. outliers
6. is not
7. mode
8. spread

9. To find the mean, sum the data values and then divide by 8.

$$mean = \frac{10 + 60 + 30 + 90 + 10 + 30 + 40 + 50}{8} = \frac{320}{8} = 40$$

To find the median, do the following:

Step 1: Put the numbers in order from least to greatest.

10, 10, 30, 30, 40, 50, 60, 90

Step 2: Find the middle number. The median is the average of the two middle numbers, 30 and 40.
The median = $\frac{30 + 40}{2} = 35$.

To find the mode, find the value that occurs most often in the data set. The numbers 10 and 30 both occur most often. Therefore, the modes are 10 and 30.

To find the range, find the difference between the greatest value and the least value in the data set.

range = greatest value – least value = 90 – 10 = 80.

10. mean

What Is Probability?

Probability is a measure of the chance that an event will happen. If all outcomes are equally likely, the probability that an event X will occur is determined this way:

$$\text{Probability of event } X = P(X) = \frac{\text{number of outcomes favorable to event } X}{\text{number of total outcomes possible}}$$

On the FTCE GK test, you will be asked to find simple probabilities. Here is an example.

> Given a bag of 5 tiles, numbered 1, 2, 3, 4, and 5, if a person picks out a single tile from the bag without looking, what is the probability that the number on the tile will be even?

The possible outcomes are a 1, 2, 3, 4, or 5 on the tile. There are two favorable outcomes for this event: drawing a 2 or a 4. These are the "favorable" outcomes because these are the outcomes you are looking for.

The probability of drawing an even-numbered tile is

$$P(\text{even-numbered tile}) = \frac{\text{number of favorable outcomes}}{\text{number of total outcomes possible}} =$$

$$\frac{\text{number of even numbers } (2 \text{ or } 4)}{\text{number of total outcomes possible } (1, 2, 3, 4, \text{ or } 5)} = \frac{2}{5}$$

Probabilities can be expressed as fractions, decimals, or percents. In the preceding example, the probability of drawing an even-numbered tile can be expressed as $\frac{2}{5}$, 0.4, or 40%.

The probability that an event is certain to happen is 1, 1.00, or 100%. The probability of drawing a whole-numbered tile from a bag containing tiles numbered 1, 2, 3, 4, and 5 is 1, since the numbers 1, 2, 3, 4, and 5 are all whole numbers.

If an event cannot occur, then it has a probability of 0. For instance, the probability of drawing a tile with the number 6 on it from a bag containing tiles numbered 1, 2, 3, 4, and 5 is 0, since none of the tiles has a 6 on it.

Thus, the lowest probability you can have is 0, and the highest probability you can have is 1. All other probabilities fall between 0 and 1. You can express this relationship symbolically this way: $0 \leq P(X) \leq 1$, for any event X. Therefore, if you work a probability problem, and your answer is greater than 1 or your answer is negative, you've made a mistake! Go back and check your work.

How Do You Count the Number of Ways to Arrange or Combine Things?

There are different methods to find the number of ways to arrange or combine things. Two ways that are commonly used are to list every possibility in an organized table or in a tree diagram. Another way is use multiplication to count the total number of possibilities.

Here is an example of using an organized table to count the number of possibilities.

A woman has a choice of a blue, red, orange, or yellow blouse. She also may select either a brown, white, or black skirt. How many different outfits can she make of 1 blouse and 1 skirt?

You should proceed systematically. In the table that follows, first list a blue blouse color with each of the skirt colors that can be chosen. Next, list a red blouse color with each of the skirt colors that can be chosen. Then, list an orange blouse color with each of the skirt colors that can be chosen. Finally, list a yellow blouse color with each of the skirt colors that can be chosen.

Blouse Color	Skirt Color
blue	brown
blue	white
blue	black
red	brown
red	white
red	black
orange	brown
orange	white
orange	black
yellow	brown
yellow	white
yellow	black

The table shows that the woman can choose 12 possible outfits of 1 blouse and 1 skirt.

You can also use a tree diagram to find the total number of possible outfits.

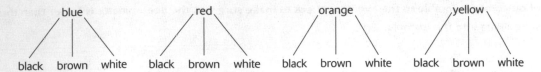

There are 12 branches in the tree diagram. This shows that the woman can choose a total of 12 possible outfits of 1 blouse and 1 skirt.

You can also use multiplication to find the total number of possible outfits.

Number of blouse colors $\times$ Number of skirt colors = Total number of possible outfits

4   3   12

When the order in which you make a selection determines different outcomes, the arrangement is called a **permutation.** For instance, if a club is selecting a president, vice-president, and secretary from three possible candidates (A, B, and C), the order in which the selections are made makes a difference in the possible outcomes as shown in the following table.

President	Vice-President	Secretary
Candidate A	Candidate B	Candidate C
Candidate A	Candidate C	Candidate B
Candidate B	Candidate A	Candidate C
Candidate B	Candidate C	Candidate A
Candidate C	Candidate A	Candidate B
Candidate C	Candidate B	Candidate A

If the order does not determine different outcomes, the arrangement is called a **combination.** For instance, if a club is selecting a committee of three people from 5 members (A, B, C, D, or E), the order in which the selections are made does not determine different outcomes, as shown below.

1st Committee Member	2nd Committee Member	3rd Committee Member
Member A	Member B	Member C
Member A	Member B	Member D
Member A	Member B	Member E
Member A	Member C	Member D
Member A	Member C	Member E
Member A	Member D	Member E
Member B	Member C	Member D
Member B	Member C	Member E
Member B	Member D	Member E
Member C	Member D	Member E

The table shows there are a total of 10 different possible committees.

How Do You Solve Real-World Problems Involving Counting and Probability?

To solve real-world word problems involving counting and probability, use the problem-solving process that you learned in the "Numerations and Operations" section (earlier in this chapter).

Here is an example of solving a probability problem.

> Given a bag of 15 marbles containing 7 green, 5 red, and 3 yellow marbles, if a person picks out a single marble from the bag without looking, what is the probability that it will be a red marble?

This problem is a probability problem. To solve the problem, find the number of total outcomes possible, find the number of favorable outcomes, and then plug into the probability formula.

There are 15 total possible outcomes. There are 5 favorable outcomes. The probability of drawing a red marble is

$$P(red) = \frac{\text{number of favorable outcomes}}{\text{number of total outcomes possible}} = \frac{\text{number of red marbles}}{\text{total number of marbles}} = \frac{5}{15} = \frac{1}{3}.$$

Did I answer the question? Yes, I found the probability of drawing a red marble from the bag. ✓

Does my answer make sense? Is it consistent with my knowledge of the real world? Yes. ✓

Is the answer stated in the correct units? No units are required for the answer. ✓

Here is an example of solving a counting problem.

> A man has a choice of a white shirt or a blue shirt. He also may select a striped blue tie, a paisley blue tie, or a solid red tie. How many different outfits can he make of 1 shirt and 1 tie?

This problem is a counting problem. To solve the problem, multiply the number of ways the man can select a shirt by the number of ways the man can select a tie.

number of ways to select a shirt		number of ways to select a tie	total number of possible outfits
2	×	3	6

Did I answer the question? Yes, I found the number of possible outfits. ✓

Does my answer make sense? Is it consistent with my knowledge of the real world? Yes. ✓

Is the answer stated in the correct units? No units are required for the answer. ✓

Test Yourself

1. _____ is a measure of the chance that an event will happen.

2. The probability that an event is certain to happen is _____.

3. The probability that an event cannot occur is _____.

4. Given a bag of 10 colored tiles containing 5 blue, 3 red, and 2 yellow tiles, if a person picks out a single tile from the bag without looking, what is the probability that it will be a red tile?

5. Sammy is wrapping a gift. She can choose from three different kinds of wrapping paper, and she can select from four different colors of ribbon. How many different ways can Sammy wrap the gift?

Answers

1. Probability

2. 1

3. 0

4. This problem is a probability problem. To solve the problem, find the number of total outcomes possible, find the number of favorable outcomes, and then plug into the probability formula.

   There are 10 total possible outcomes. There are 3 favorable outcomes. The probability of drawing a red tile is

   $$P(red) = \frac{number\ of\ favorable\ outcomes}{number\ of\ total\ outcomes\ possible} = \frac{number\ of\ red\ tiles}{total\ number\ of\ tiles} = \frac{3}{10}$$

   Did I answer the question? Yes, I found the probability of drawing a red tile from the bag. ✓

   Does my answer make sense? Is it consistent with my knowledge of the real world? Yes. ✓

   Is the answer stated in the correct units? No units are required for the answer. ✓

5. This problem is a counting problem. To solve the problem, multiply the number of ways Sammy can select a wrapping paper by the number of ways she can select a ribbon color.

number of ways to select wrapping paper		number of ways to select ribbon color		total number of possible ways
3	×	4		12

   Did I answer the question? Yes, I found the number of possible ways Sammy can wrap the gift. ✓

   Does my answer make sense? Is it consistent with my knowledge of the real world? Yes. ✓

   Is the answer stated in the correct units? No units are required for the answer. ✓

Sample Questions

1. The graph that follows represents the monthly average temperature in the city of Townville for 6 months of the year. How much higher is the average temperature in May than in January?

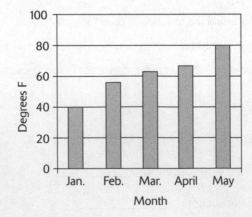

Average Monthly Temperatures

   A. 2°
   B. 20°
   C. 40°
   D. 80°

2. Given here are students' scores on a social studies test. What is the median of the set of scores?

Student	Score
A	95
B	42
C	55
D	87
E	68
F	72
G	66
H	87

A. 70
B. 71
C. 77.5
D. 87

3. You are given a bag of 25 colored tiles containing 10 blue, 7 red, 5 green, and 3 yellow tiles. If a person picks out a single tile from the bag without looking, what is the probability that it will be a green tile?

A. $\frac{2}{5}$

B. $\frac{7}{25}$

C. $\frac{1}{5}$

D. $\frac{3}{25}$

4. A boy is making a sandwich for lunch. He has a choice of two kinds of bread (white and whole wheat) and three sandwich fillings (peanut butter, tuna salad, and pimiento cheese). How many different sandwiches can he make if he chooses one type of bread and one kind of sandwich filling?

A. 5
B. 6
C. 8
D. 9

Answer Explanations for Sample Questions

1. C.

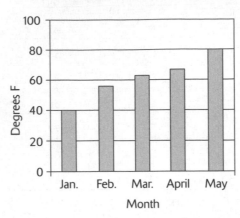

Average Monthly Temperatures

The bar for January goes up to 40°, and the bar for May goes up to 80°. The difference is 80° – 40° = 40°. Choice **A** results if you mistakenly decide that there is 1° between marks on the graph. Choice **B** results if you mistakenly decide that there are 10° between marks on the graph. Choice **D** results if you fail to subtract, and use the temperature in May as your answer.

2. **A.** To find the median, do the following:

Step 1: Put the numbers in order from least to greatest   42, 55, 66, 68, 72, 87, 87, 95

Step 2: Find the middle number. The median is the average of the two middle numbers, 68 and 72.

The median = $\dfrac{68 + 72}{2} = 70$

Choice **B** results if you fail to order the scores and mistakenly decide to average 55 and 87 to find the median. Choice **C** results if you fail to order the scores and mistakenly decide to average 68 and 87 to find the median. Choice **D** is the mode, not the median.

3. **C.** This problem is a probability problem. To solve the problem, find the number of total outcomes possible, find the number of favorable outcomes, and then plug into the probability formula.

There are 25 total possible outcomes. There are 5 favorable outcomes. The probability of drawing a green tile is

$$P\left(\text{green}\right) = \frac{\text{number of favorable outcomes}}{\text{number of total outcomes possible}} = \frac{\text{number of green tiles}}{\text{total number of tiles}} = \frac{5}{25} = \frac{1}{5}$$

Did I answer the question? Yes, I found the probability of drawing a green tile from the bag. ✓

Does my answer make sense? Is it consistent with my knowledge of the real world? Yes. ✓

Is the answer stated in the correct units? No units are required for the answer. ✓

Choice **A** is the probability of drawing a blue tile. Choice **B** is the probability of drawing a red tile. Choice **D** is the probability of drawing a yellow tile.

4. B. This problem is a counting problem. To solve the problem, multiply the number of ways the boy can select a bread by the number of ways he can select a sandwich filling.

number of ways to select a bread		number of ways to select a sandwich filling	total number of possible sandwiches
2	×	3	6

Did I answer the question? Yes, I found the number of possible sandwiches. ✓

Does my answer make sense? Is it consistent with my knowledge of the real world? Yes. ✓

Is the answer stated in the correct units? No units are required for the answer. ✓

Choice **A** results if you add, instead of multiply, in the problem. Choices **C** and **D** result if you count or compute incorrectly.

Review for the GK Reading Subtest

The Reading subtest of the FTCE GK Test consists of 40 multiple-choice questions, which you must complete in 40 minutes. Each test question consists of a reading comprehension passage followed by multiple-choice questions. Each question requires that you choose among four answer choices labeled **A, B, C,** or **D.** You must darken your answer choice in a separate answer booklet. The only other materials that you are permitted to use when taking the test are pens, pencils, and erasers. You cannot bring written notes or scratch paper into the testing center. You will have to write in your test booklet when analyzing the reading passages.

The Reading Review in This Study Guide

The Reading review in this CliffsTestPrep is organized around the two reading areas tested on the FTCE GK Test:

1. Literal Comprehension Skills
2. Inferential Comprehension Skills

The review sections present reading concepts with examples and explanations for each area. Each area, furthermore, contains a general review and sample questions. The sample questions are multiple-choice questions similar to what you might expect to see on the FTCE General Knowledge Test. The answer explanations for the sample questions are provided immediately after the questions. At the conclusion of this chapter is a "Test Yourself" exercise, which gives you an opportunity to practice what you just learned. When doing the "Test Yourself" exercises, you should cover up the answers. Then check your answers when you've finished the exercises.

Literal Comprehension Skills

As listed in the *Competencies and Skills Required for Teacher Certification in Florida, Ninth Edition* (available at www.firn.edu/doe/sas/ftce/ftcecomp.htm), there are three main Reading Literal Comprehension competencies/skills in which you should be proficient. They are as follows:

- Recognizing main ideas
- Identifying supporting details
- Determining the meaning of words or phrases in context

Recognize Main Ideas

Recognizing the main idea(s) in a reading passage is essential to mastering reading comprehension questions. The key to recognizing main ideas is to identify the *topic sentence* of a reading passage. In the topic sentence, the author states the main idea of the paragraph, and it is the sentence upon which all other sentences in the paragraph are dependent. You can identify the topic sentence as the one sentence that explains the paragraph without any further explanation. Look at this example reading passage and see whether you can identify the main idea.

> Staring at my plate, I realized I was now fully awake and ready to face the day. I was shaved, groomed, and dressed, sitting at my kitchen table, contemplating my next move. I realized, however, that I could not do anything without eating a good breakfast. By midday, my stomach would be growling, and I would be in a lousy mood if I did not have my daily regimen of orange juice and toast—and hot cereal. I definitely preferred hot cereal. For without hot cereal, I would certainly feel grumpy. Yes, for me, breakfast is the most important meal of my day.

The main idea of this passage is clearly stated in the last sentence (*Yes, for me, breakfast is the most important meal of my day*). All of the accompanying sentences support this main idea.

Generally, the topic sentence of a paragraph is its first or last sentence. Sometimes, its location may be embedded inside the paragraph, but in every instance, the topic sentence of a well-written paragraph can be recognized as the essential or main idea of the passage.

Identify Supporting Details

Identifying the supporting details in a reading passage is important in learning to master reading comprehension questions. The supporting details are the examples that support and clarify the topic sentence or main idea of a written passage. When you analyze a paragraph, the supporting details underscore the writer's main idea by providing vivid examples of its meaning. Look at this example of a written passage and identify the supporting details.

> Beyond reason, I did everything I could to help my ailing mother. Since I was her only child and my father had long passed, I was my mother's chief caregiver, in charge of both her immediate and long-range needs. She had been sick for months with everything you could possibly imagine. She was 86 and her frail, but still vibrant self, was gradually weakening. Her mind was sharp, and her mouth was quick, yet everything else was deteriorating rapidly. Soon, she could not feed herself. This was accompanied by a failure of her eyesight, followed by an inability to hear well. Her rapid descent into a weak and agonizing state was, to be sure, depressing to watch. Still, she was my mother, and I was determined to do everything I could to make her final days comfortable. I fed her, bathed her, read to her, took her to doctors' appointments, cooked her favorite meals, washed her clothes and linens, cleaned her house inside and out, paid her bills, and made all the arrangements for her eventual funeral. Finally, after about six months of deteriorating health, my mother passed away and I sobbed myself to sleep.

The supporting details of this passage describe the things the author did to help his mother in her dying days. These explicit sentences demonstrate how essential supporting details are to the development of a main idea. They provide substance to your writing by making vivid the thesis or main point of your paper.

All writing—whether serious or humorous, objective or personal—depends on support to be effective. The type of support you use in your writing depends on your answers to the following three questions:

- What is your writing goal?
- Who is your intended audience?
- What is the nature of the piece that you are writing?

Knowing the answers to these questions will improve your writing considerably as both you and your reader will have a better understanding of what it is you want to say and how you want to say it.

Moreover, it is also wise to know that writers rely on more than one kind of supportive detail to influence their readers. There are

- **Personal observations:** descriptive remarks and observations about a person, place, or thing
- **Facts:** objective information collected by research or analysis
- **Testimony:** statements, quotations, accounts, observations, and assertions from experts or eyewitnesses
- **Statistics:** hard evidence or facts expressed numerically
- **Examples:** specific pieces of evidence that vividly portray your thesis statement

Finally, when writing supporting details, always adhere to the following guidelines:

- Select details that reinforce your thesis statement or main idea.
- Use sources that are reliable, credible, and verifiable.
- Organize supporting details logically and coherently.
- Avoid introducing extraneous or irrelevant information.

Determine the Meaning of Words or Phrases in Context

Determining the meaning of words or phrases in context is essential to mastering skills in reading comprehension. When you know how to interpret the meaning of a word or phrase in context, then you possess the ability to discern logical arguments and conclusions in your reading. Often, readers misinterpret or skip over key words or phrases in their reading and thus fail to comprehend the meaning of a passage. This can be corrected by learning to read with a sharp and discerning eye any given reading passage.

Look at the examples of these written passages and identify the key words or key phrases.

Example 1:

The study of intellectual growth cannot be separated from that of physical growth. During the same years that a child is developing physically, his mental concepts and skills are taking form. Studies have indicated a positive correlation between physical maturity and intellectual ability, although, of course, caution should be exercised in making sweeping generalizations from these findings. Studies of Stanford-Binet scales correlated with indices of physical maturity have borne out this statement.

Please note that the key phrase in this paragraph is "caution should be exercised." This phrase means that before any assumptions are made between physical maturity and intellectual ability, the reader should realize that this study is, at best, tentative and only a suggestive predictor of intellectual growth, not an actual assessment.

Example 2:

The importance of effective motivation is of primary concern in curricular planning. Motivation involves a two-pronged responsibility, which rests both with the teacher and the child. The child must want to learn and the teacher must provide motivating experiences. Elementary school teachers must be constantly sensitive to the various facets of motivation as they face the study, planning, and revision of their curricular offerings. They must be concerned with short-term and long-term motivation, intrinsic and extrinsic motivation, natural and contrived motivation, a child's level of aspiration, and the ultimate goal of self-motivation.

Again, please note that the key phrase in this paragraph is "Elementary school teachers must be constantly sensitive to the various facets of motivation . . ." This phrase means that motivation is not determined by one absolute cause, but by a series of causes that directly relate to the developmental needs of the children who are being motivated.

Example 3:

Teachers must be emotionally prepared for children who dislike them and for whom they dislike. Teachers, like all other human beings, will naturally react negatively to anyone who makes life more difficult for them. It would require a kind of super human to react with loving kindness towards a sixteen-year-old who continually makes irritating remarks in class. Teachers might easily develop a healthy dislike for such a youngster. But the teaching situation is not an ordinary circumstance, and the teacher is not justified in reacting as she would in a normal social situation. The teacher is one of several special adults who has the special responsibility of helping young people grow up in a pattern best suited to their own growth needs. Dislike is a strong impediment to providing such help. Yet, the students who need the most help are almost always those who are the most trying.

The key phrase is "a healthy dislike for such a youngster." This ironic phrase is the key to understanding this passage and its implications for what it means to be a professional educator. To the best of her ability, the teacher should not consider the student as one who makes trouble for the teacher, but one who, by his misbehavior, makes trouble for himself.

Inferential Comprehension Skills

Determining the meaning from information that is either explicit or implied is an essential reading comprehension skill. Careful and perceptive readers must be able to find coherent meaning and be able to draw conclusions about the text they are reading. Simply getting the facts in reading is not enough; you must think about what those facts mean to you.

To accomplish this goal, readers must be able to use two sets of skills. They are:

- Literal reading comprehension skills
- Inferential reading comprehension skills

Literal comprehension skills refer to the reader's ability to identify and/or recall information that is explicitly stated in a text. Specifically, the reader should be able to determine and define:

- Sequence of events
- Main ideas
- Directly-stated facts
- Supporting details, including words, phrases, or sentences
- Directly stated opinions

The word literal means "the truth," or "the most obvious meaning of a word." When writers refer to the literal meaning of a word or a passage, they are referring to the unabashed truth without embellishment or exaggeration.

Inferential comprehension skills refer to the reader's ability to use information explicitly stated in a passage to determine what is not stated. Using these skills, the reader should be able to make predictions and draw conclusions about:

- Relationships in a reading passage, like cause and effect, sequence and time, comparisons and contrasts, and classifications and generalizations
- Events and sequences that could follow logically
- Symbols, patterns, and images that would give heightened meaning to the text
- Implicit themes or main ideas embedded in the text
- Unstated reasons for actions and beliefs as implied in the text

Inferring is the process of creating a *personal meaning* from the reading passage. Inferring is the blending of the reader's prior knowledge with what he or she is reading in the text. When readers infer, they create meaning that is not necessarily stated implicitly in the passage that they are reading.

Look at these examples and identify possible meanings of the words in this context.

Sue blew out the candles and got presents.

Is it Sue's birthday? Anniversary? Graduation? Birthday seems most likely, as one does not usually blow out candles for one's graduation. If it were a wedding anniversary, it would likely be Sue and Mike blowing out the candles, not Sue by herself.

Mary practices her clarinet for three hours a day.

Is Mary a great clarinetist? Does she practice because she "must" or she "wants to?" We don't know the answer to these questions. All we know is that Mary is faithfully committed to practicing.

When I woke up, there were branches and leaves all over the yard.

Is it the result of a storm? Yard work? Vandalism? A storm seems most likely; yard work, even done in one's sleep, shouldn't result in a chaotic mess. Vandalism is a possibility, but ranks second to a storm.

These examples show that the meaning of words or phrases can only be determined when the reader understands the greater context in which the words and phrases appear. Without context, words can mean almost anything.

These two sets of reading comprehension skills—literal and inferential—are used in all reading activities and play a considerable role in helping to determine the meaning of a reading passage. To become proficient in reading comprehension, readers should familiarize themselves with these two distinct skills.

As listed in the *Competencies and Skills Required for Teacher Certification in Florida, Ninth Edition* (mentioned earlier in the chapter), there are eight Reading Inferential Comprehension competencies/skills in which you should be proficient. They are as follows:

- Determining the purpose
- Identifying overall organizational pattern
- Distinguishing between fact and opinion
- Recognizing bias
- Recognizing tone
- Determining relationships between sentences
- Analyzing the validity of arguments
- Drawing logical inferences and conclusions

More specifically, skilled inferential readers are able to:

- Recognize the meaning of pronouns in a given reading passage
- Determine the definition of unknown words from the given context
- Discern intonation of a character's or narrator's words
- Understand relationships among characters in given text
- Recognize author's bias in a given passage
- Offer conclusions from facts presented in a specific passage

Determine the Purpose

Determining the purpose of a reading passage is essential to understanding the meaning in context. Authors write for many reasons and knowing their reasons for writing can help you considerably in determining meaning and purpose in their writing. Some passages explicitly state their purposes. Other passages leave you to guess or interpret their purposes. As a good reader, you should always try to determine the purpose of a passage because doing so enables you to evaluate the passage in terms of whether the author got his or her point across effectively.

Essentially, there are four common purposes for writing. They are

- Self-expression
- Exposition
- Entertainment
- Persuasion

Often these purposes overlap. For instance, you might want to persuade someone to take an action and decide that the best way to accomplish this goal is to write an essay that is persuasive yet entertaining.

In any event, each writing purpose has its own style. **Self-expressive writing** is more free flowing in its choice of words and ideas and is often the province of journals and diaries. **Expository writing** is designed to inform or convey beliefs and opinions to an outside audience. Generally, this writing is more structured and stylized in content and tone. **Entertaining writing** is meant to amuse or arouse interest in the reader so that they find enjoyment in the writer's words. Communicating the writer's interest and enthusiasm for his or her subject is one such method to generate such interest. Finally, **persuasive writing** is meant to convince the reader to adopt the writer's point of view. The effectiveness of persuasive writing is dependent on the clarity of the author's argument, the strength of the author's supporting detail, and the attitude of the audience that the author is trying to convince.

When readers know the meaning of a passage in context, they are more equipped to discern the details of the passage. Knowledge of purpose implies an understanding of the overall design of a reading passage and an implicit comprehension of what the passage means in a larger context. Thus, knowing the purpose in a given reading passage is key to mastering reading comprehension skills. Look at this example of a reading passage and try to determine the purpose of the passage.

All day long, wind howled at unheard of speeds. Houses shook, cars swayed, and water overflowed. The storm, directly off the Atlantic Ocean, was raging with all that a violent wind and rain could possibly bring. Still, the tiny hamlet, nestled between large cliffs and set off behind a protective tanker, had seen worse in its long and torturous history of enduring violent hurricanes. The angry gods of thunder and wind would not disturb the town's sturdy inhabitants. They had seen much before and were confident they would see more in the future.

1. The purpose of this passage is

    A. to describe a violent storm.
    B. to explain small town life.
    C. to demonstrate resilience.
    D. to illustrate ocean currents.

The correct answer is Choice **C,** *to demonstrate resilience*. Clearly, the author's purpose or intent is to describe the strength and courage with which the citizens of this small ocean town resist its violent storms. By drawing a vivid picture of the storm, the author is showing us how even such raging weather cannot destroy this town's historical precedent for enduring even the most treacherous weather. Choice **A** is not the correct choice because although the passage does describe a violent storm, the author's purpose is to use the storm as an example or illustration of the reading passage's larger purpose. Choice **B** is not the correct choice because although the passage does refer to this town as being small in size, the author's purpose is not to explain life in a small town. Finally, Choice **D** is not the correct choice because the passage makes no mention of ocean currents.

Identify Overall Organizational Patterns

When reading a given passage, it is always best to recognize or identify its overall organizational pattern. Knowledge of the organizational pattern of a reading passage increases comprehension and enhances fluency skills. Readers who can discern the general structure of a passage tend to have a better grasp of the passage's meaning and the purpose for the choices made in the selection. Seeing a larger pattern clearly helps in improving inferential reading comprehension skills and permits a larger understanding of the author's intent and design in structuring the reading passage.

The organizational pattern of a reading passage may be arranged in a number of ways—but most notably, it will be either direct or indirect. A passage written in a **direct organizational pattern** is written in a literal, "straightforward" style. The author writes about a person, an object, or an event by simply listing the important facts that the reader needs to know about the subject in question. **A passage written in an indirect organizational pattern** is written in a figurative "creative" style. The two styles distinguish themselves by the author's intent and the technique employed to illustrate the intention.

The most common **direct organizational** patterns are

- **Time-ordered sequence of events:** In this pattern, the events are presented in the order in which they occurred or in a specifically planned order in which they must develop. In either arrangement, the order is important and changing it would change the meaning of the passage. Signal words or phrases often used to indicate chronological sequence are:

    first, second, third

    before, after

    when

    later

    until

    at last

    next

- **Simple listing of events, ideas, and activities:** In this pattern, the items or topics are listed in a series of supporting facts or details. These supporting elements are of equal value, and the order in which they occur in the passage is of no significant importance. Also, changing the order of the topics presented does not alter the meaning of the paragraph. Signal words often used for simple listing are:

  in addition

  another

  for example

  also

  several

  a number of

- **Definition followed by examples of the definition:** In this pattern, the concept is initially defined and then followed by an explanation with examples or simple restatements of the original concept. This pattern is a familiar organizational technique of most textbook passages. Signal words often used for defining by example are:

  is defined as

  is described as

  is called

  term or concept

  refers to

  means

- **Division or classification of ideas from general to specific:** In this pattern, the organization of ideas is presented from a general concept to a specific detail. The passage discusses a concept or idea and then divides the discussion into its component parts.

- **Cause-and-effect relationships:** In this pattern, one topic or idea is shown as having produced another topic or idea. An event or effect has occurred because of a particular situation or cause. Simply, the cause stimulates the effect or the outcome of the event. Signal words often used for cause and effect are

  hence

  because

  made

  for this reason

  consequently

  on that account

- **Comparison and contrast relationships:** In this pattern, topics or ideas are described by their relationship to similar topics or ideas. The author's purpose is to show similarities (comparisons) or differences (contrasts) between or among contrasting elements. Signal words often used for comparing and contrasting relationships are

  similar

  different

  but

  however

  bigger than

  smaller than

  on the other hand

  in the same way

  parallels

- **Description of place, person, or event:** In this pattern, the topics or ideas that comprise a description are no more than a simple listing of details. In a description, you are writing about what a person, place, or thing is like. No specific order is required. Signal words often used for describing a place, person or event are:

is

like

resembles

in

above

below

beside

near

north, east, south, west

- **Sequence or process of an event:** In this pattern, the listing of processes or events follows a similar arrangement as the time sequence of events or chronological order. The only difference is that the passage is describing a complex sequence of events, and not single isolated incidents. In sequence of events, each event is rich in detail and complexity. Signal words often used for describing a sequence or process of an event are:

    first, second, third

    in the beginning

    before

    then

    after

    finally

    at last

    subsequently

    recently

    previously

    afterwards

    when

    after

- **Description of spatial or place order:** In this pattern, the topics or ideas are described as they appear in space or place order. Attention is paid to classification or grouping things or ideas into specific categories. Signal words often used in description of spatial or place order are:

    is a kind of

    can be divided into

    is a type of

    falls under

    belongs to

    is a part of

    fits into

    is grouped with

    is related to

    is associated with

- **Stating and defining a choice or opinion:** In this pattern, a preference is indicated for a specific idea, object, or action. Attention is paid to stating an opinion or a choice on an action, idea, or event. Signal words often used in the stating and defining of choice or opinion are:

    in my opinion

    belief

    idea

understanding

I think that

I consider

I believe

it seems to me

I prefer

hope

feel

The most common **indirect organizational** patterns are

- **Allegorical:** In an allegorical passage, the objects, persons, and actions in a narrative are compared in meanings that lie outside the narrative itself. The true meaning of an allegory lies in its moral, social, religious, or political significance. In an allegory, the characters are often personifications of abstract ideas—like charity, hope, faith, goodness, evil—and thus represent concepts far greater than themselves. An allegory is a story with two meanings; its literal or everyday meaning ("This is the story of two people who. . . .") and its symbolic meaning ("This story is really about the true meaning of the word. . . .")

- **Narrative:** In a narrative passage, an event or incident is recreated for the central purpose of revealing an insight into the actions of the people or events involved. A narrative has a central focus, is highly descriptive in its presentation, is action-oriented, and is usually based on a personal experience.

- **Inferential:** In an inferential passage, a conclusion is drawn based upon available information. For an inference to be considered valid, sufficient evidence supporting the claim and/or supposition must be presented. The result is a thorough examination of the topic in discussion that captures the essence of the text and results in a whole new presentation of the topic.

- **Spontaneous:** In a spontaneous passage, the spoken and uncensored free-flowing of ideas and feelings takes precedence in one's writing. No particular organizational pattern is employed besides the general whimsical nature of the writer's preferences and predilections.

- **Conversational:** In a conversational passage, the narration is written in the vernacular of everyday language, making the passage highly accessible and user-friendly for the reader. Not as free-flowing as spontaneous, the writing is more tightly controlled and constructed, allowing the reader to learn only what the writer intends, and not what the writer deliberately censors. The object of conversational writing is accessibility, not objectivity.

Look at these examples for identifying overall organizational patterns.

The day was long. The workers arrived at the factory by 7:30 A.M. Upon arrival, they changed into their work clothes and headed directly to the factory's main floor, where they all went to their respective positions and got to work. Each person had an assigned task, and with few interruptions, they proceeded to do their jobs until noon. Then, at 12 and 1 P.M., in two previously assigned shifts, they broke and went to lunch, the second group waiting for all the members of the first group to return before they would go to lunch themselves. After lunch, the factory would again be humming with the sound of workers diligently doing their jobs until around 5 P.M. Then, the whistle would blow throughout the factory, and the workers would immediately quit their tasks, gather their belongings, and head home to rest and prepare for another day.

1. The overall organizational pattern of this passage is:

- **A.** Chronological
- **B.** Inferential
- **C.** Allegorical
- **D.** Descriptive

The correct answer is **A,** *chronological.* Clearly, the author is providing a timeline description of the exact events in a typical day at this factory. The author chronicles the sequence of events experienced by the workers and no more.

Choice **B** is not correct because the author is not making inferences about the worker's day nor is inferential an organizational pattern for presenting reading material. Choice **C** is not correct because this author has not written an allegory about life in the factory. Choice **D** is not correct because although the passage is descriptive, the word *chronological* more aptly describes the passage's organizational pattern.

Look at another example for identifying the overall organizational pattern.

Thermodynamics is a field of interest studied by a wide array of scientists. They include, among many, physicists, chemists, and engineers. For physicists and chemists, thermodynamics is of interest because they are primarily concerned with basic physical laws, properties of chemical substances, and changes in physical and chemical properties that are caused by the interaction of different kinds of energy. Engineers, however, are interested in these elements as well as in the application of thermodynamic principles to the design and construction of machines. For example, they would most apply these principles to mechanisms that convert energy from one form or substance into another. And in the field of engineering, specific thermodynamic conversions are the domain of particular engineers. Electrical engineers are primarily interested in the conversion of mechanical energy into electrical energy, whereas, mechanical engineers devote their time to the design of systems that will most efficiently convert thermal or heat energy into mechanical energy.

2. The overall organizational pattern of this passage is

    A. Chronological
    B. Definitional
    C. Inspirational
    D. Allegorical

The correct answer is **B,** definitional. The author constructs this passage by defining terms and distinctions as they appear. Choice **A,** chronological, is not the correct choice because the author does not provide a timeline of events. Choice **C,** inspirational, is not the correct choice because the author's intent is not to evoke a mood, but simply to define information. Choice **D,** allegorical, is not the correct choice because the author is not telling a story that is representative of a larger meaning.

After I arrived at my college, I realized there were many similarities between my high school and my new school. First, both schools—my high school and my college—were small in size and number. I attended a small high school with less than 1,100 total students, and my college has only about 1,600 students. Second, both were situated in primarily rural communities. My high school was surrounded by farmland which was devoted to growing corn and wheat. My college was situated in a rural homestead that was devoted to raising cattle and hogs. Third, my high school and my college were filled with generations of students whose parents attended the very same institutions. Thus, both student bodies felt a deep and intimate connection to their school, their teachers, and to each other.

3. The overall organizational pattern of this passage is

    A. Allegorical
    B. Narrative
    C. Comparsion
    D. Cause and effect

The correct answer is **C,** comparison. The author constructs this passage by comparing two distinct entities, their high school and college. Choice **A,** allegorical, is not the correct choice because the author is not telling a story that is representative of a larger meaning. Choice **B,** narrative, is not the correct choice because the author is not retelling an incident or an event that has occurred. Choice **D,** cause and effect, is not correct because the author does not demonstrate that one incident causes another to occur.

In recent years, modern cities and their surrounding suburbs have grown exponentially in size. There are many reasons for this sudden and significant growth. First, as cities become ever more the place for commerce and business, they simply attract more people. People from both rural and urban areas find themselves attracted to urban life because this is where the jobs and opportunities are. Second, as individuals settle into the cities and surrounding suburbs, they, in turn, attract other individuals who are seeking the advantages of urban living. Thus, old and young alike gravitate to urban dwellings seeking affordable housing, strong schools, sophisticated health care, and convenient shopping. Third, as cities and suburbs grow, places of leisure, entertainment and culture began to grow as well. Sport stadiums, theatres, and museums soon dot the landscape of these newly defined urban dwellings. For many people, these facilities and conveniences make life in the city and its surrounding communities much more appealing than life on the farm, and thus, they draw people away from rural communities.

4. The overall organizational pattern of this passage is

    A. Narrative

    B. Cause and effect

    C. Compare and contrast

    D. Allegorical

The correct answer is **B,** cause and effect. The author constructs this passage by showing how a series of events, relating to commerce in cities and their surrounding suburbs, resulted in other events occurring. Choice **A,** narrative, is not the correct choice as the author is not retelling an incident or an event that has occurred. Choice **B,** compare and contrast, is not the correct choice as the author is not primarily showing the differences between living in an urban and rural setting; they are simply telling why urban areas have seen a significant increase in population. Choice **D,** allegorical, is not the correct choice because the author is not telling a story that is representative of a larger meaning.

My hometown is noted for several man-made features. First, it has the largest ice-cream store in America. Serving every flavor imaginable, my hometown ice-cream store occupies an old high school gymnasium. In this large and roomy building, all that is served is ice cream and assorted desserts. People come from miles around just to sample this delicious treat and to watch how ice cream is actually made. Also, parties and functions are regularly held in this wonderful old building, making it a very special place for all who enjoy its old-fashioned decorations and traditional furnishings. Second, my town boasts the largest windmill ever. Built originally to celebrate the Dutch who live in my hometown, this windmill now serves as a tourist attraction throughout the year. Especially during the summer, visitors come to my town just to marvel at its size, nearly six stories, and to walk the winding stairs leading to the top. Finally, my hometown has a genuine castle. Built in the late 1800s when a wealthy landowner came to my town to settle and live, this castle resembles something from King Arthur's court. Complete with moat, turret and drawbridge, this fully-staffed and furnished castle serves as both a meeting place and tourist attraction for conventioneers and visitors from far and wide. To be sure, these three man-made landmarks make my hometown a very special place.

5. The overall organizational pattern of this passage is

    A. Descriptive

    B. Conversational

    C. Comparison

    D. Cause and effect

The correct answer is **A,** descriptive. The author constructs this passage by simply listing the characteristics that make his hometown special. Choice **B,** conversational, is not the correct choice as the author does not present a dialogue or discussion as the heart of the narrative. Choice **C,** comparison, is not the correct choice as the author is not comparing and/or contrasting two different sides or issues. Choice **D,** cause and effect, is not the correct choice as the author is not showing how a series of events has resulted in another series of events.

Distinguish between Fact and Opinion

In any given passage, the reader must be able **to distinguish between fact and opinion.** A **fact** is verifiable. Its truth can be determined by researching the evidence. An **opinion** is a judgment based on facts. It is an honest attempt to draw a reasonable conclusion from factual evidence. Look at these examples and determine whether the sentences express a fact or an opinion.

    A. World War II ended in 1945.
    B. The Vietnam War was an unjust war.
    C. Horror movies are the best entertainment.
    D. Lauren served baked Alaska for dessert.
    E. The wind was moving at 20 miles per hour.
    F. Cold weather is enjoyable.

The answers are

    A. Fact. World War II did end in 1945. This is a verifiable fact.

    B. Opinion. This sentence is a statement of opinion. As in any war, there are those who believe the war is a just cause, and there are others who believe the cause, and therefore the war, is unjust. If someone were to say, "The Vietnam War was an unjust war," that person would be stating an opinion, as the justification for the Vietnam War is highly debatable. Please note that if the sentence read, "Some say the Vietnam War was an unjust war," this would be a statement of fact because, in the opinion of some, it *was* an unjust war and thus this is a true statement of their beliefs.

    C. Opinion. This sentence is a statement of opinion. When someone says what their favorite "anything" is, they are stating their preference or opinion. In this example, "Horror movies are the best entertainment," the writer is announcing his or her predilection for a particular movie genre. Like any other statement of preference, this is a pronouncement of bias and not fact. Again, if the sentence read, "Some say that horror movies are the best entertainment," this would be a statement of fact, as it is true that for some people, horror movies are their favorite movie genre.

    D. Fact. This sentence is a statement of fact. Lauren did serve baked Alaska for dessert. This is a true and observable incident.

    E. Fact. This sentence is a statement of fact. The wind was moving at 20 miles per hour. The evidence for this event can be documented.

    F. Opinion. This sentence is a statement of opinion. A description of one's feelings about the weather is an example of a personal predilection. Some enjoy hot weather, others cold, and still others enjoy whatever the weather brings them. Again, if the sentence read, "Many say cold weather is enjoyable," this would be a statement of fact because in the opinion of some, cold weather is considered enjoyable.

Recognize Bias

Recognizing bias in a given reading passage is a critical task in reading comprehension. Bias is a slanted or prejudiced attitude that presents opinion as factual information. The conclusions drawn are based on preconceived beliefs or prejudices and not on the evidence discovered. Recognizing bias protects the reader from accepting the personal opinions of others as truths. Look at these examples and determine whether they are biased or not biased.

    A. The Civil War was a war invented by Northerners to make quick money.
    B. The Apollo space mission broke new ground in space travel.
    C. Our ballet followed the choral presentation.
    D. After lunch, the President spoke about his new proposal.
    E. Music videos are designed to corrupt today's youth.

The answers are

A. Biased. This statement, though presented as fact, is expressing the author's point of view.

B. Not biased. This statement is a self-evident truth. The Apollo space mission did break new ground in space travel.

C. Not biased. This is a statement of literal fact.

D. Not biased. This is a statement of literal fact.

E. Biased. This statement is presented as fact when it is clearly the author's opinion.

Recognize Tone

In any given passage, the author's **tone** is the "voice" or attitude that the author adopts toward the subject of the passage. **Recognizing tone** is directly related to understanding the author's purpose for writing the passage.

A helpful technique for determining an author's tone is to imagine the sound of the author's voice as if they were reading the passage aloud. Often, helpful adjectives—optimistic, pessimistic, cheerful, cynical, instructive, ominous, and informative—are apt descriptions used to determine the tone of a given passage.

Which of the preceding adjectives can be used to describe the tone of each statement that follows?

A. Attention ladies and gentlemen! Global warming is destroying our planet—and we are doomed!

B. The beginning of the Civil Rights movement was sparked by the refusal of Rosa Parks to move to the back of a city bus. She quietly told the bus driver that she was not going to move to the rear of the bus where African-Americans, or Negroes as they were called then, were designated to sit.

C. I like lollipops! In fact, lollipops make me smile as soon as I plop one in my mouth.

D. When the skies turn gray, I caution you to be on the alert for an impending thunderstorm.

E. Although Jack was disappointed in his math score, he felt better about his overall understanding of algebra.

The correct answers are

A. Pessimistic. The author is clearly presenting a strong and dire point of view.

B. Informative. The author is describing the results of a factual event.

C. Cheerful. The author is communicating feelings.

D. Ominous. The author is sounding a warning.

E. Optimistic. The author presents the positive outlook of a central figure.

Determine Relationships between Sentences

Recognizing relationships between words, phrases, and sentences is a vital reading comprehension skill. This skill requires the reader to go beyond the ideas expressed in a passage and make certain inferences and conclusions about them. Knowing whether sentences are related in context and tone is critical to understanding a reading passage.

Relationships among words, phrases, and sentences can either be **implicit** or **explicit**. **Implicit** implies that the reader understands the *intuitive* meaning of the given passage. The meaning of the passage is implied and not directly stated. **Explicit** implies that the meaning of the passage is stated directly.

Transitional words and phrases serve to identify the relationship between one sentence and the next, and as links between paragraphs. Understanding the selection of the transitional word that links the two sentences or paragraphs is critical to perceiving the author's meaning of the text.

For example, take the statements "John is incredibly smart. He does not do well in school."

The explicit meaning of those statements can be simply stated: John *is* incredibly smart and he *does not* do well in school.

The implicit relationship is that smart people should do well in school and, unfortunately, John does not.

Yet, notice that the use of transitional words directly affects the meaning of these two sentences.

> John is incredibly smart, *but* he does not do well in school.

This implies that John is very smart, but as a matter of fact, he does not do well in school.

> John is incredibly smart *and* he does not do well in school.

This implies that John is very smart and, unfortunately, he does not do well in school.

> John is incredibly smart, *yet* he does not do well in school.

This implies that although John is very smart, he surprisingly does not do well in school.

In each instance, the distinction is subtle but significant, and of course open to interpretation by the reader.

Here is a list of transitional words that are extremely effective in indicating the relationships of meanings between parts of sentences, between sentences, and between paragraphs.

- To repeat an idea just started: *in other words, to repeat, that is, again*
- To illustrate an idea: *for example, for instance, in particular, in this manner*
- To announce a contrast or change in direction: *yet, however, still, nevertheless, in contrast, instead of*
- To restate an idea: *to be exact, to be specific, to be precise*
- To mark a new idea: *also, too, besides, furthermore*
- To connect two or more ideas: *and, but, or, nor, because*
- To show cause and effect: *as a result, for this reason, consequently, accordingly*
- To bring to a conclusion: *in short, in brief, to conclude, on the whole*

A related concept is the understanding of the causality and logical sequence of sentence ideas. Causality implies an understanding of the relationship between or among sentence ideas and that each idea is generated from the idea that preceded it. A logical sequence of sentence ideas is when the concepts expressed in the sentence flow together in a coherent fashion.

Here is an example that demonstrates logical causality.

> Professor Wilson is a man. All men are mortal. Therefore, Professor Wilson is mortal.

Or

> Julia is a trained athlete. Athletes enjoy being physically fit. Therefore, Julia is a trained athlete who enjoys being physically fit.

In this example, determine if logical causality exists in the relationships between the sentences.

> Alonzo and Julia loved the roller coaster. The day began with high excitement. Alonzo and Julia had planned the perfect outing. On their coaster ride, however, Julia fell ill. She got a headache and threw up. Sadly, she spent the rest of the day relaxing and nursing a bad stomach. Undaunted, they headed to the roller coaster and waited patiently on a very long line for their ride to begin. They decided to take a trip to the local amusement park. When they arrived, they noticed lots of people heading toward the roller coaster.

Clearly, the sentences in this paragraph are not presented in correct order. The logical order is as follows:

> The day began with high excitement. Alonzo and Julia had planned the perfect outing. They decided to take a trip to the local amusement park. Alonzo and Julia loved the roller coaster. When they arrived, they noticed lots of people heading toward the roller coaster. Undaunted, they headed to the roller coaster and waited patiently on a very long line for their ride to begin. On their coaster ride, however, Julia fell ill. She got a headache and threw up. Sadly, she spent the rest of the day relaxing and nursing a bad stomach.

The new order makes logical sense and shows the direct relationship between sentences.

Analyzing the Validity of Arguments

Persuasive writing involves the use of argument to motivate the reader to adopt a certain viewpoint, opinion, or attitude. It is up to the reader to decide whether the arguments are valid or invalid. Thus, analyzing the validity of arguments presented in a reading comprehension passage is essential to understanding the passage's meaning. And all writers must inform their readers by writing passages in a logical, coherent progression of ideas in order to be recognized as a valid source of information.

Generally speaking, there are two basic kind of arguments or reasoning—**inductive** and **deductive.**

Inductive arguments move from the specific points to general ideas, whereas **deductive** arguments are considered to be the reverse; they begin with general ideas and move to specific points. Inductive arguments are usually based on experience and observation, and deductive arguments are based on widely accepted principles or known truths.

Here are examples of each.

> **Inductive reasoning:** A math student notices that every time she measures the interior angles of a triangle, the sum of the measures of the angles is either 180 degrees or very close to 180 degrees. She concludes that the measures of the interior angles of any triangle sum to 180 degrees.

> **Deductive reasoning:** The measure of the interior angles of any triangle sum to 180 degrees. This figure is a triangle. Therefore, the sum of the measures of its interior angles is 180 degrees.

As you can see, the difference between inductive and deductive reasoning lies mostly in the way the arguments are presented. As logic tells you, any inductive argument can be presented deductively, and any deductive argument can be presented inductively.

Knowing the difference between these two types of reasoning—inductive and deductive—is essential to analyzing the validity of arguments. When you use inductive reasoning, your previous observations support the argument in question. When you use deductive reasoning you apply known truths or generalizations to an issue to arrive at a logical conclusion, which, of course, is the focus of the argument in question.

Because inductive arguments are based on observations and examples, you can never be absolutely certain of the validity of their conclusions. You should, therefore, evaluate an inductive argument in terms of its reasonableness: Does the conclusion make sense, and is it supported by sound assertions?

Deductive arguments use known assertions or premises to logically arrive at their conclusions. You evaluate a deductive argument based on the reasonableness of its assertions and the soundness of the logic used. If the assertions are true and the logic is sound, the conclusion of the argument is valid.

Directions: For the following examples, ask yourself which is used: inductive or deductive reasoning? Then, more importantly, ask yourself "Does the argument make sense? Are the assertions reasonable? Do they support the conclusions?"

1. All high school marching bands play exceptionally well. Angela plays exceptionally well. Angela is in a high school marching band.

2. My friend, Angelo, will win his tennis match because he has won all the county and state tournaments in his division.

3. No sane person would jump off a cliff. Stephano is a sane person. Stephano will not jump off the cliff.

4. Michael is very wealthy. Since Michael is very wealthy, we know that he must be the child of someone famous, as you have to be the child of someone famous to be wealthy.

5. Most animals nurture their young. All dogs are animals. Most dogs nurture their young.

Answers

1. *Deductive.* The correct choice is *deductive reasoning* because the statement begins with a general statement and then proceeds to a specific point. Still, the argument makes no sense. Just because Angela plays well does not mean she is in a high school marching band.

2. *Inductive.* The correct choice is *inductive reasoning* because the statement relies on specific details to arrive at a general statement. Still, the conclusion is debatable because even though Angelo is a championship player, there is no guarantee that he will win his next tennis match. Please note, though, that the inclusion of the word *probably* would change the meaning of the text and make the argument more acceptable.

3. *Deductive.* The correct choice is *deductive reasoning* because the statement begins with a general statement and then proceeds to a specific point. The argument makes sense because the assertions are reasonable and the logic is sound.

4. *Inductive.* The correct choice is *inductive reasoning* because the statement relies on a specific detail or case to arrive at a general conclusion. The argument, however, is faulty because the statement is drawn from just one piece of evidence; obviously, a person can be or become wealthy without being the child of someone famous.

5. *Deductive.* The correct choice is *deductive reasoning* because the statement begins with a general statement and then proceeds to a specific point. The argument is reasonable because of the use of the qualifying word "most." The use of the word "most" allows for exceptions to the rule.

Below are examples of persuasive writing that try to convince the reader to adopt the author's point of view. See if you can discern how the writers are presenting their arguments and the validity of their work.

Example 1:

Today in the United States we face considerable unfinished business in public education, for the complexities of modern society have left their impact on current educational issues. Populations are increasing rapidly. The world is shrinking steadily as a result of the rapid progress made in transportation and communication. Many differing ethnic groups—some unable to speak English, some bilingual, or even multilingual are appearing in our elementary school classrooms. Children are moving frequently, many of them changing schools five or six times in fewer than four years. They lack the security of firmly established roots. Space travel, rockets, jets, movies, radio, television, and the Internet vie for the interests of each child, creating for them images of an exciting world, but also a confusing one. Broken homes and juvenile delinquency are not uncommon, and the child of today, the same as the adult of today, can scarcely be expected to remain unaware of the tensions and upheavals in the modern world. Already, they both sense that if the promise of the future is immense, so is the danger.

In this passage, the author lists example after example to prove the point that today's world is filled with inherent contradictions—great pleasures and great pains—that can make life both pleasurable and confusing for young people. The author is using **inductive reasoning** to make his argument.

Example 2:

For the colonists who arrived in New England, a singleness of religious purpose was a determining influence in the development of their early educational programs. They believed in a close unity between the church and state. To them it was the responsibility of the government to "govern," to support their Calvinistic theology, and to foster the intellectual growth of their children. This was made clear as early as 1642 when the governmental leaders in Massachusetts were empowered to require parents to educate their children. While this law did not require the establishment of schools, it did require compulsory instruction for youth. It even set up minimum essentials: the reading of English, knowledge of capital laws, the catechism, and apprenticeship in a trade. Thus, the early educational developments in New England clearly reflected the values and beliefs of its early colonists and were instrumental in the design and creation of today's public school system.

In this passage, the author cites known assertions to arrive at a logical conclusion. The author is using **deductive reasoning** to make his argument.

Both deductive and inductive reasoning are central to understanding persuasive writing and essential to analyzing the validity of arguments as they appear in reading passages.

Drawing Logical Inferences and Conclusions

An essential skill for understanding a reading passage is the ability to draw logical inferences and conclusions.

Techniques to help the reader draw inferences and conclusions regarding a reading passage are

- Focus on the passage's purpose—Is it well-stated? Clearly implied? Justifiable?
- Focus on the passage's key questions—Are they answered? Are the answers objectively stated?
- Focus on the passage's evidence—Is it relevant? Unbiased? Informative?
- Focus on the passage's concepts—Are they clear? Relevant? Justifiable?
- Focus on the passage's assumptions—Are they valid? Reasonable?
- Focus on the passage's conclusions—Are they sound? Logical? Justifiable?
- Focus on the passage's point of view—Is it direct? Indirect? Does it consider alternatives?
- Focus on the passage's implications—Do you understand the consequences?

Look at the following example, drawing logical inferences and conclusions in a reading passage.

The leaders of the progressive education movement emphasize the importance of individualized education, the need for a child-centered school, the necessity for a direct relation of learning experiences to the interests and current needs of each child, and the relationship of the child to his cultural and social environment. Leading educational thinkers—from the early twentieth-century works of John Dewey to the contemporary writings of Nel Noddings—have all advocated passionately for educational reform that involves understanding the developmental needs of the whole child. Unfortunately, in recent years, this movement has become popularly identified with the concept that teaching and learning require a "laissez-faire" approach and should be dependent on the interests and desires of solely the students.

1. In analyzing this passage, the reader is most likely to draw the conclusion that

   A. the progressive education movement has been highly successful.
   B. the progressive education movement has been marginalized.
   C. the progressive education movement is a recent phenomena.
   D. the progressive education movement is universally accepted.

The correct answer is **B**. Although the thought is not finished, the reader can infer from the concluding sentence that the Progressive education movement has come under attack by those who advocate a more standardized approach to public education. One can infer that the paragraphs to follow will elaborate on why the progressive education movement has been marginalized. Choice **A** is incorrect because the passage does not state or infer that the progressive education movement has been highly successful; it has simply been advocated by leading educational thinkers. Choice **C** is incorrect because the passage indicates that John Dewey, a leading educational thinker of the early twentieth century, advocated for progressive education. Choice **D** is incorrect because as the last sentence of the passage states, progressive education has its detractors.

Test Yourself

Read the following passage and answer questions 1 through 6.

(1)   Predicting weather patterns is a difficult job, at best. Meteorology is a demanding science, and it requires patience, fortitude, and know-how to make careful and accurate forecasts. Most of the time, weather forecasters can be trusted, and their predictions allow others to plan their lives accordingly. Modern forecasting involves technology, science, and advanced math to accurately predict the weather. Relying on time-tested instruments and mathematical models, meteorologists are able to predict weather patterns reasonably rapidly and accurately.

(2)   The first step in weather forecasting is to get information about the weather. Weather data is collected from the atmosphere by launching balloons twice a day all around the world. These weather balloons gather basic information about the climate conditions around the globe; they record data such as temperature, pressure, humidity, and wind speed. Another successful tool for weather forecasters is satellite technology. Satellites permit meteorologists to see what the earth and its clouds appear like from space. With such knowledge, scientists can see how the Earth's atmosphere is behaving. Finally, using sophisticated computers, weather forecasters are able to discern what ordinary people might logically miss. They can predict oncoming storms, ominous weather patterns, and unpredictable hurricanes. They know enough—both intuitively and mathematically—to discern when there is a movement afoot that might predict danger ahead. Thus, their scientific knowledge has implications far beyond simply just predicting the weather.

(3)   Meteorologists are also instrumental in helping local and state communities prepare for future weather patterns. In fact, the biggest employer of meteorologists is government agencies. They help predict weather patterns, climatic changes, and environmental problems. Furthermore, sure knowledge of impending storms—in the near future or years to come—helps responsible government agencies and organizations prepare their citizens for possible dangerous and threatening conditions. Such notification is imperative as emergency and contingency procedures must often be set in place long before a real danger might eventually occur.

(4)   Finally, meteorologists help people live their lives. So much of our daily existence depends upon what we do in the outside world. Our work and play is contingent upon our knowledge of what our day

"weatherwise" will be like. That is why clear, easy-to-understand, and accurate weather forecasts are so much appreciated by the general public. Accuracy and promptness are the hallmarks of good meteorologists and, fortunately, many meteorologists now have sophisticated tools to make predicting the weather easier. Using satellite data, climate theory, and computer models of the world's atmosphere, meteorologists can more effectively interpret the results of these models to make national, regional, and local area forecasts. Their good work informs not only the general public, but also those public, private, and governmental agencies that who need accurate weather information for both economic and safety reasons. Indeed, our entire world economy is dependent upon such accuracy.

1. Which sentence best states the main idea of this passage?

   A.   Weather forecasting is a fairly routine and mundane task.

   B.   Weather forecasting is limited in scope and design.

   C.   Weather forecasting has far-reaching significance.

   D.   Weather forecasting is primitive in design and content.

2. According to the passage, what is one way that weather forecasting has importance beyond predicting the daily weather?

   A.   It informs community leaders about weather conditions.

   B.   It entertains people watching television news.

   C.   It increases understanding of foreign countries.

   D.   It demonstrates the limitations of meteorology.

3. As used in the third paragraph, the word *instrumental* most nearly means

   A.   *limited.*

   B.   *assisting.*

   C.   *cautious.*

   D.   *skeptical.*

4. The tone of this passage can best be described as

    A. anxious.

    B. skeptical.

    C. curious.

    D. informative.

5. Identify the relationship between the following two sentences in the fourth paragraph:

"Our work and play is contingent upon our knowledge of what our day "weatherwise" will be like. That is why clear, easy-to-understand, and accurate weather forecasts are so much appreciated by the general public at large."

The second sentence

    A. contradicts the first.

    B. restates the first.

    C. supports the first.

    D. distracts from the first.

6. Which word or phrase, when substituted for "discern" in the second paragraph, would maintain the same relationship between the two thoughts in the sentence?

    A. perceive

    B. deceive

    C. illustrate

    D. inform

Answers to Test Yourself

1. C. The sentence that best states the main idea of this passage is *"weather forecasting has far-reaching significance."*

2. A. The one way that weather forecasting has importance beyond informing people of the day's atmospheric conditions is to *"inform community leaders about weather conditions."*

3. B. As used in the third paragraph, the word *instrumental* most nearly means *assisting.*

4. D. The tone of this passage can best be described as *informative.*

5. C. The relationship between the two sentences lifted from the fourth paragraph is that the second sentence *supports the first.*

6. A. The word or phrase that best substitutes for the word *discern* in the second paragraph and maintains the same relationship between the two thoughts in the sentence is *perceive.*

PART III

TWO FULL-LENGTH PRACTICE TESTS

Answer Sheet for FTCE General Knowledge Practice Test 1

(Remove This Sheet and Use It To Mark Your Answers)

Diagnostic General Knowledge Test: Essay

Write your essay on lined paper.

General Knowledge Test: English Language Skills

1 Ⓐ Ⓑ Ⓒ Ⓓ	11 Ⓐ Ⓑ Ⓒ Ⓓ	21 Ⓐ Ⓑ Ⓒ Ⓓ	31 Ⓐ Ⓑ Ⓒ Ⓓ
2 Ⓐ Ⓑ Ⓒ Ⓓ	12 Ⓐ Ⓑ Ⓒ Ⓓ	22 Ⓐ Ⓑ Ⓒ Ⓓ	32 Ⓐ Ⓑ Ⓒ Ⓓ
3 Ⓐ Ⓑ Ⓒ Ⓓ	13 Ⓐ Ⓑ Ⓒ Ⓓ	23 Ⓐ Ⓑ Ⓒ Ⓓ	33 Ⓐ Ⓑ Ⓒ Ⓓ
4 Ⓐ Ⓑ Ⓒ Ⓓ	14 Ⓐ Ⓑ Ⓒ Ⓓ	24 Ⓐ Ⓑ Ⓒ Ⓓ	34 Ⓐ Ⓑ Ⓒ Ⓓ
5 Ⓐ Ⓑ Ⓒ Ⓓ	15 Ⓐ Ⓑ Ⓒ Ⓓ	25 Ⓐ Ⓑ Ⓒ Ⓓ	35 Ⓐ Ⓑ Ⓒ Ⓓ
6 Ⓐ Ⓑ Ⓒ Ⓓ	16 Ⓐ Ⓑ Ⓒ Ⓓ	26 Ⓐ Ⓑ Ⓒ Ⓓ	36 Ⓐ Ⓑ Ⓒ Ⓓ
7 Ⓐ Ⓑ Ⓒ Ⓓ	17 Ⓐ Ⓑ Ⓒ Ⓓ	27 Ⓐ Ⓑ Ⓒ Ⓓ	37 Ⓐ Ⓑ Ⓒ Ⓓ
8 Ⓐ Ⓑ Ⓒ Ⓓ	18 Ⓐ Ⓑ Ⓒ Ⓓ	28 Ⓐ Ⓑ Ⓒ Ⓓ	38 Ⓐ Ⓑ Ⓒ Ⓓ
9 Ⓐ Ⓑ Ⓒ Ⓓ	19 Ⓐ Ⓑ Ⓒ Ⓓ	29 Ⓐ Ⓑ Ⓒ Ⓓ	39 Ⓐ Ⓑ Ⓒ Ⓓ
10 Ⓐ Ⓑ Ⓒ Ⓓ	20 Ⓐ Ⓑ Ⓒ Ⓓ	30 Ⓐ Ⓑ Ⓒ Ⓓ	40 Ⓐ Ⓑ Ⓒ Ⓓ

General Knowledge Test: Mathematics

41 Ⓐ Ⓑ Ⓒ Ⓓ	51 Ⓐ Ⓑ Ⓒ Ⓓ	61 Ⓐ Ⓑ Ⓒ Ⓓ	71 Ⓐ Ⓑ Ⓒ Ⓓ	81 Ⓐ Ⓑ Ⓒ Ⓓ
42 Ⓐ Ⓑ Ⓒ Ⓓ	52 Ⓐ Ⓑ Ⓒ Ⓓ	62 Ⓐ Ⓑ Ⓒ Ⓓ	72 Ⓐ Ⓑ Ⓒ Ⓓ	82 Ⓐ Ⓑ Ⓒ Ⓓ
43 Ⓐ Ⓑ Ⓒ Ⓓ	53 Ⓐ Ⓑ Ⓒ Ⓓ	63 Ⓐ Ⓑ Ⓒ Ⓓ	73 Ⓐ Ⓑ Ⓒ Ⓓ	83 Ⓐ Ⓑ Ⓒ Ⓓ
44 Ⓐ Ⓑ Ⓒ Ⓓ	54 Ⓐ Ⓑ Ⓒ Ⓓ	64 Ⓐ Ⓑ Ⓒ Ⓓ	74 Ⓐ Ⓑ Ⓒ Ⓓ	84 Ⓐ Ⓑ Ⓒ Ⓓ
45 Ⓐ Ⓑ Ⓒ Ⓓ	55 Ⓐ Ⓑ Ⓒ Ⓓ	65 Ⓐ Ⓑ Ⓒ Ⓓ	75 Ⓐ Ⓑ Ⓒ Ⓓ	85 Ⓐ Ⓑ Ⓒ Ⓓ
46 Ⓐ Ⓑ Ⓒ Ⓓ	56 Ⓐ Ⓑ Ⓒ Ⓓ	66 Ⓐ Ⓑ Ⓒ Ⓓ	76 Ⓐ Ⓑ Ⓒ Ⓓ	
47 Ⓐ Ⓑ Ⓒ Ⓓ	57 Ⓐ Ⓑ Ⓒ Ⓓ	67 Ⓐ Ⓑ Ⓒ Ⓓ	77 Ⓐ Ⓑ Ⓒ Ⓓ	
48 Ⓐ Ⓑ Ⓒ Ⓓ	58 Ⓐ Ⓑ Ⓒ Ⓓ	68 Ⓐ Ⓑ Ⓒ Ⓓ	78 Ⓐ Ⓑ Ⓒ Ⓓ	
49 Ⓐ Ⓑ Ⓒ Ⓓ	59 Ⓐ Ⓑ Ⓒ Ⓓ	69 Ⓐ Ⓑ Ⓒ Ⓓ	79 Ⓐ Ⓑ Ⓒ Ⓓ	
50 Ⓐ Ⓑ Ⓒ Ⓓ	60 Ⓐ Ⓑ Ⓒ Ⓓ	70 Ⓐ Ⓑ Ⓒ Ⓓ	80 Ⓐ Ⓑ Ⓒ Ⓓ	

General Knowledge Test: Reading

86 Ⓐ Ⓑ Ⓒ Ⓓ	96 Ⓐ Ⓑ Ⓒ Ⓓ	106 Ⓐ Ⓑ Ⓒ Ⓓ	116 Ⓐ Ⓑ Ⓒ Ⓓ
87 Ⓐ Ⓑ Ⓒ Ⓓ	97 Ⓐ Ⓑ Ⓒ Ⓓ	107 Ⓐ Ⓑ Ⓒ Ⓓ	117 Ⓐ Ⓑ Ⓒ Ⓓ
88 Ⓐ Ⓑ Ⓒ Ⓓ	98 Ⓐ Ⓑ Ⓒ Ⓓ	108 Ⓐ Ⓑ Ⓒ Ⓓ	118 Ⓐ Ⓑ Ⓒ Ⓓ
89 Ⓐ Ⓑ Ⓒ Ⓓ	99 Ⓐ Ⓑ Ⓒ Ⓓ	109 Ⓐ Ⓑ Ⓒ Ⓓ	119 Ⓐ Ⓑ Ⓒ Ⓓ
90 Ⓐ Ⓑ Ⓒ Ⓓ	100 Ⓐ Ⓑ Ⓒ Ⓓ	110 Ⓐ Ⓑ Ⓒ Ⓓ	120 Ⓐ Ⓑ Ⓒ Ⓓ
91 Ⓐ Ⓑ Ⓒ Ⓓ	101 Ⓐ Ⓑ Ⓒ Ⓓ	111 Ⓐ Ⓑ Ⓒ Ⓓ	121 Ⓐ Ⓑ Ⓒ Ⓓ
92 Ⓐ Ⓑ Ⓒ Ⓓ	102 Ⓐ Ⓑ Ⓒ Ⓓ	112 Ⓐ Ⓑ Ⓒ Ⓓ	122 Ⓐ Ⓑ Ⓒ Ⓓ
93 Ⓐ Ⓑ Ⓒ Ⓓ	103 Ⓐ Ⓑ Ⓒ Ⓓ	113 Ⓐ Ⓑ Ⓒ Ⓓ	123 Ⓐ Ⓑ Ⓒ Ⓓ
94 Ⓐ Ⓑ Ⓒ Ⓓ	104 Ⓐ Ⓑ Ⓒ Ⓓ	114 Ⓐ Ⓑ Ⓒ Ⓓ	124 Ⓐ Ⓑ Ⓒ Ⓓ
95 Ⓐ Ⓑ Ⓒ Ⓓ	105 Ⓐ Ⓑ Ⓒ Ⓓ	115 Ⓐ Ⓑ Ⓒ Ⓓ	125 Ⓐ Ⓑ Ⓒ Ⓓ

CUT HERE

General Knowledge Practice Test 1: Essay

This section of the examination involves a written assignment. You are asked to prepare a written response for *one of the two topics* presented below. Select one of these two topics and prepare a 300- to 600-word response. Be sure to read both topics very carefully to make sure that you understand the topic for which you are preparing a written response. Use your allotted time to plan, write, review, and edit what you have written for the assignment.

Topic 1

    Why I want to become a teacher

Topic 2

    A person whom I admire

Be sure to read the two topics again before attempting to write your response. Remember, write your answer on the space provided in the examination booklet. Your answer also must be on only one of the topics presented, and it must answer the complete topic.

Your essay is graded holistically, meaning only one score is assigned for your writing—taking into consideration both mechanics and organization. *You are not scored on the nature of the content or opinions expressed in your work.* Instead, you are graded on your ability to write complete sentences, to express and support your opinions, and to organize your work.

At least two evaluators review your work and assign it a score. Special attention is paid to the following specific indicators of quality writing.

- Does your writing demonstrate a strong definitive purpose?
- Is there a clear thesis or statement of a main idea?
- Are your ideas organized?
- Do you support your thesis with clear details?
- Are effective transitions present?
- Do you demonstrate an effective use of language?
- Do you avoid inappropriate use of slang, jargon, and clichés?
- Are a variety of sentence patterns present?
- Is there a consistent point of view?
- Are the conventions of standard American English used?

Before you begin, be sure you plan what you want to say. Organize your thoughts and carefully construct your ideas. This should be your original work, written in your own hand, and in your own voice.

As you write your piece, you may cross out or add information as necessary. Although handwriting does not count, be sure to be legible in your response.

General Knowledge Practice Test 1: English Language Skills

Directions: For items 1 and 2, read the entire passage carefully and then answer the questions. Please note that intentional errors have been included in this passage. This passage is designed to measure both identification of logical order in a written passage and the presence of irrelevant sentences.

The passage reads as follows:

(1) Horses are one of the most useful animals in the world. (2) For centuries, they provided the fastest and most convenient way to travel on land. (3) Horses were used prominently by early settlers in America as they traveled the east coast, looking for land to call their home, and then by pioneers as they traversed the rugged plains and mountains of America's West in stagecoaches, covered wagons, and, of course, by the Pony Express. (4) Horses were used by hunters for securing food and by soldiers in battle. (5) Today, horses are used mostly for recreation. (6) Moreover, the automobile has become America's number one transportation problem. (7) Riding horses is one of America's favorite pastimes. (8) And, of course, horse racing remains a popular spectator sport. (9) Today, horses are seen mostly performing in circuses, parades, rodeos, and naturally, horse shows. (10) It is in horse shows, though, that the true worth of horses is determined as wealthy individuals purchase horses for both personal enjoyment and financial gain.

1. Select the arrangement of sentences 3, 4, and 5 that provides the most logical sequence of ideas and supporting details in the paragraph. If no change is needed, select Choice A.

   A. Horses were used prominently by early settlers in America as they traveled the east coast, looking for land to call their home, and then by pioneers as they traversed the rugged plains and mountains of America's West in stage coaches, covered wagons, and, of course, by the Pony Express. Horses were used by hunters for securing food and by soldiers in battle. Today, horses are used mostly for recreation.

   B. Horses were used by hunters for securing food and by soldiers in battle. Horses were used prominently by early settlers in America as they traveled the east coast, looking for land to call their home, and then by pioneers as they traversed the rugged plains and mountains of America's West in stage coaches, covered wagons, and, of course, by the Pony Express. Today, horses are used mostly for recreation.

   C. Today, horses are used mostly for recreation. Horses were used by hunters for securing food and by soldiers in battle. Horses were used prominently by early settlers in America as they traveled the east coast, looking for land to call their home, and then by pioneers as they traversed the rugged plains and mountains of America's West in stage coaches, covered wagons and, of course, by the Pony Express.

   D. Today, horses are used mostly for recreation. Horses were used prominently by early settlers in America as they traveled the east coast, looking for land to call their home, and then by pioneers as they traversed the rugged plains and mountains of America's West in stage coaches, covered wagons and, of course, by the Pony Express. Horses were used by hunters for securing food and by soldiers in battle. ⎯

2. Which numbered sentence is LEAST relevant to the passage?

    A.   Sentence 3

    B.   Sentence 4

    C.   Sentence 5

    D.   Sentence 6

The passage reads as follows:

(1) Diamonds are the hardest naturally occurring substance. (2) Diamonds are also one of the world's most valuable natural substances. (3) Since diamonds are the hardest substance, they are the most lasting of all gemstones. (4) Throughout the world, especially in Europe, America, and Japan, diamonds are widely used for engagement and wedding rings. (5) Some people prefer simple wedding bands without precious stones. (6) Diamonds are also widely used for industrial purposes, such as for cutting, grinding, and boring other materials. (7) About half the world's diamonds are used for such purposes, while an even smaller percentage is used for jewelry. (8) A true diamond can be cut by only another diamond. (9) Furthermore, diamonds cannot be destroyed in acid, although they can be damaged by intense heat. (10) Diamonds are precious stones, and only those with an expert knowledge of diamonds can truly judge the worth of individual stones.

3. Select the arrangement of sentences 2, 3, and 4 that provides the most logical sequence of ideas and supporting details in the paragraph. If no change is needed, select Choice D.

    A.   Since diamonds are the hardest substance, they are the most lasting of all gemstones. Throughout the world, especially in Europe, America, and Japan, diamonds are widely used for engagement and wedding rings. Diamonds are also one of the world's most valuable natural substances.

    B.   Throughout the world, especially in Europe, America, and Japan, diamonds are widely used for engagement and wedding rings. Since diamonds are the hardest substance, they are the most lasting of all gemstones. Diamonds are also one of the world's most valuable natural substances.

    C.   Throughout the world, especially in Europe, America, and Japan, diamonds are widely used for engagement and wedding rings. Diamonds are also one of the world's most valuable natural substances. Since diamonds are the hardest substance, they are the most lasting of all gemstones.

    D.   Diamonds are also one of the world's most valuable natural substances. Since diamonds are the hardest substance, they are the most lasting of all gemstones. Throughout the world, especially in Europe, America, and Japan, diamonds are widely used for engagement and wedding rings.

4. Which numbered sentence is LEAST relevant to the passage?

    A.   Sentence 3

    B.   Sentence 4

    C.   Sentence 5

    D.   Sentence 6

GO ON TO THE NEXT PAGE

Directions: For questions 5–37, select the answer choice that corrects an error in the underlined portion. If there is no error, choose Choice D, indicating "No change is necessary."

5. The passenger <u>who's</u> purse I found in the taxicab
   [A]

   <u>came</u> to the headquarters to <u>retrieve</u> his
   [B]   [C]

   belongings.

   A. whose
   B. is coming
   C. retreive
   D. No change is necessary.

6. All of the campers <u>at</u> the <u>summer</u> camp, <u>accept</u>
   [A]   [B]   [C]

   Jamie, will be required to take the swimming test.

   A. in
   B. Summer
   C. except
   D. No change is necessary.

7. I <u>respectively</u> submitted my <u>formal</u> letter of
   [A]   [B]

   resignation to the school's <u>principal</u>.
   [C]

   A. respectfully
   B. former
   C. principle
   D. No change is necessary.

8. The <u>fourth</u> box of supplies for the party was
   [A]

   <u>further</u> from my house <u>than</u> I thought.
   [B]   [C]

   A. forth
   B. farther
   C. then
   D. No change is necessary.

9. When my <u>aunt</u> came to visit, I <u>could of</u> baked
   [A]   [B]

   cookies for <u>dessert</u>.
   [C]

   A. Aunt
   B. could have
   C. desert
   D. No change is necessary.

10. Donald and Mary went to the state <u>capitol</u> to
    [A]

    <u>receive</u> an award for <u>their</u> outstanding
    [B]   [C]

    contributions to the local charity.

    A. capital
    B. recieve
    C. they're
    D. No change is necessary.

11. Despite the inclement <u>whether</u>, the musicians
    [A]

    performed <u>admirably</u> for the <u>congregants</u>.
    [B]   [C]

    A. weather
    B. admirable
    C. congregents
    D. No change is necessary.

12. After the team was declared <u>ineligible</u>, <u>everyone</u>
    [A]   [B]

    <u>preceded</u> to walk off the field.
    [C]

    A. ineligable
    B. every one
    C. proceeded
    D. No change is necessary.

13. We had <u>certainly</u> won more <u>board</u> games <u>then</u>
    [A]   [B]   [C]
    other players in the class.

    A. for certain
    B. bored
    C. than
    D. No change is necessary.

14. My son Juan's <u>exceptional</u> mechanical abilities
                   [A]
    <u>compliment</u> his wife's <u>considerable</u> analytical
    [B]   [C]
    skills.

    A. acceptional
    B. complement
    C. considerate
    D. No change is necessary.

15. Between you and <u>me</u>, I don't know <u>as to whether</u>
                    [A]   [B]
    you should be first or <u>I</u>.
                           [C]

    A. I
    B. whether
    C. me
    D. No change is necessary.

16. My brothers and sisters <u>may</u> leave after they find
                            [A]
    a <u>sight</u> to eat <u>beside</u> the river.
      [B]   [C]

    A. can
    B. site
    C. besides
    D. No change is necessary.

17. The archeologists <u>come</u> up with a list <u>that</u>
                      [A]   [B]
    included tombs, mummies, <u>pyramids, and</u> other
                             [C]
    Egyptian artifacts.

    A. came
    B. which
    C. pyramids and
    D. No change is necessary.

18. The <u>restaurants</u> location by the <u>beach</u> made it a
        [A]   [B]
    <u>really</u> romantic place for special dates.
    [C]

    A. restaurant's
    B. beech
    C. real
    D. No change is necessary.

19. When the <u>tourists</u> visited the <u>lighthouse they</u>
             [A]   [B]
    were amazed that it looked more like a

    skyscraper <u>than</u> a lighthouse.
               [C]

    A. tourists'
    B. lighthouse, they
    C. then
    D. No change is necessary.

20. The teacher felt <u>badly</u> about giving a failing
                     [A]
    grade on the <u>English</u> paper to the daughter of the
                 [B]
    school <u>superintendent</u>.
           [C]

    A. bad
    B. english
    C. Superintendent
    D. No change is necessary.

21. In 1492 <u>Columbus, the</u> <u>explorer</u>, landed on the
            [A]   [B]
    islands of the <u>west</u> Indies.
                   [C]

    A. Columbus the
    B. Explorer
    C. West
    D. No change is necessary.

22. <u>When</u> they got inside the <u>cabin, the</u> hunters
    [A]   [B]
    <u>builded</u> a huge fire in the fireplace.
    [C]

    A. Whenever
    B. cabin the
    C. built
    D. No change is necessary.

GO ON TO THE NEXT PAGE

251

23. I <u>am</u> convinced the reason there is animosity
    _[A]

    between <u>you and I</u> is <u>that</u> we are so much alike.
    _[B]   _[C]

    A. was
    B. you and me
    C. because
    D. No change is necessary.

24. My daughter, <u>who</u> is a track star, can run much
    _[A]

    <u>faster</u> than <u>them other athletes</u>.
    _[B]   _[C]

    A. whom
    B. more faster
    C. those other athletes
    D. No change is necessary.

25. It <u>don't</u> matter how smart you <u>are because</u> <u>you</u>
    _[A]   _[B]   _[C]

    still have to work hard to be a success in life.

    A. doesn't
    B. are, because
    C. one
    D. No change is necessary.

26. My <u>siblings</u> say they dislike <u>mathmatics</u>, but I
    _[A]   _[B]

    always have enjoyed <u>it myself</u>.
    _[C]

    A. siblings'
    B. mathematics
    C. it
    D. No change is necessary.

27. During the recent election, <u>there</u> <u>was</u> much
    _[A]   _[B]

    discussion as to whether the media <u>is</u> biased.
    _[C]

    A. their
    B. had been
    C. are
    D. No change is necessary.

28. Because the bus trip was going to take several

    hours, the students <u>should have ate</u> before they
    _{[A]   [B]   [C]}

    left.

    A. should of ate
    B. should have eaten
    C. should of eaten
    D. No change is necessary.

29. As the day <u>ends</u>, the planet Venus appeared in
    _{[A] [B] [C]}

    the sky.

    A. had ended
    B. has been ending
    C. ended
    D. No change is necessary.

30. Everyone in my family <u>have enjoyed</u> watching
    _[A]

    our five new <u>goldfish</u> scurry around the <u>castle</u> in
    _[B]   _[C]

    the fish tank.

    A. has enjoyed
    B. goldfishes
    C. castel
    D. No change is necessary.

31. Each of the boys thanked <u>their</u> parents for the
    _[A]

    support <u>provided prior</u> to the match <u>between</u> the
    _[B]   _[C]

    two teams.

    A. his
    B. provided, prior
    C. among
    D. No change is necessary.

32. My students collected <u>books that</u> were still in
    [A]

    good condition from various <u>organizations</u>
    [B]

    around town, so I gave <u>them</u> to our local library.
    [C]

    A. books, that
    B. organizations'
    C. the books
    D. No change is necessary.

33. Cory's favorite subject in <u>middle</u> school was
    [A]

    English because he enjoyed studying <u>grammar</u>,
    [B]

    reading books, and <u>to write</u> papers.
    [C]

    A. Middle
    B. grammer
    C. writing
    D. No change is necessary.

34. Barbara has become <u>quite</u> annoyed with <u>his</u>
    [A]   [B]

    meddling in her <u>personal</u> business.
    [C]

    A. quiet
    B. him
    C. personnel
    D. No change is necessary.

35. One of the forestry <u>professors</u> at the local
    [A]

    university <u>was</u> investigating the <u>affect</u> of a new
    [B]   [C]

    fertilizer on the growth of pine seedlings.

    A. professors'
    B. were
    C. effect
    D. No change is necessary.

36. Michael <u>measured</u> the length, width, and <u>heighth</u>
    [A]   [B]

    of the <u>box to</u> make sure it would fit in the trunk
    [C]

    of his car.

    A. measures
    B. height
    C. box, to
    D. No change is necessary.

37. <u>Rose's</u> <u>friends</u> tell her that she has the
    [A]   [B]

    <u>most unusual</u> hair style.
    [C]

    A. Roses'
    B. freinds
    C. unsualest
    D. No change is necessary.

38. Choose the option that is punctuated correctly.

    A. Within a year my new puppy should weigh
       about 18 pounds, I'm making sure that I feed
       him a nutritious diet.
    B. Within a year, my new puppy should weigh
       about 18 pounds I'm making sure that I feed
       him a nutritious diet.
    C. Within a year my new puppy should weigh
       about 18 pounds. I'm making sure that I feed
       him a nutritious diet.
    D. Within a year my new puppy should weigh
       about 18 pounds I'm making sure that I feed
       him a nutritious diet.

GO ON TO THE NEXT PAGE

39. Choose the option that is punctuated correctly.

    A. Preferring to be hand-fed canned tuna, our family's new Siamese cat refuses to eat dry cat food.

    B. Preferring to be hand-fed canned tuna, our familys' new Siamese cat refuses to eat dry cat food.

    C. Preferring to be hand-fed canned tuna. Our family's new Siamese cat refuses to eat dry cat food.

    D. Preferring to be hand-fed canned tuna our family's new Siamese cat refuses to eat dry cat food.

40. Choose the sentence in which the modifiers are placed correctly.

    A. Rushing to finish the surprise dinner on time, Melissa borrowed an egg from a neighbor that was rotten.

    B. Melissa borrowed an egg from a neighbor that was rotten, rushing to finish the surprise dinner on time.

    C. Rushing to finish the surprise dinner on time, Melissa borrowed an egg that was rotten from a neighbor.

    D. Melissa borrowed an egg that was rotten from a neighbor, rushing to finish the surprise dinner on time.

IF YOU FINISH BEFORE TIME IS CALLED, CHECK YOUR WORK ON THIS SECTION ONLY. DO NOT WORK ON ANY OTHER SECTION IN THE TEST.

General Knowledge Practice Test 1: Mathematics

Mathematics Reference Sheet

Area

Triangle 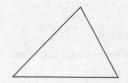 $A = \frac{1}{2} bh$

Rectangle  $A = lw$

Trapezoid  $A = \frac{1}{2} h (b_1 + b_2)$

Parallelogram 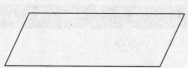 $A = bh$

Circle
$A = \pi r^2$
$C = \pi d = 2\pi r$

Key	
b = base	d = diameter
h = height	r = radius
l = length	A = area
w = width	C = circumference
$S.A.$ = surface area	V = volume
	B = area of base
Use $\pi = 3.14$ or $\frac{22}{7}$	

Surface Area

1. Surface area of a prism or pyramid = the sum of the areas of all faces of the figure.

2. Surface area of a cylinder = the sum of the two bases + its rectangular wrap.

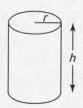 $S.\,A. = 2(\pi r^2) + 2(\pi r)h$

3. Surface area of a sphere: $S.A. = 4\pi r^2$

Volume

1. Volume of a prism or cylinder equals (Area of the Base) times (height): $V = Bh$

2. Volume of a pyramid or cone equals $\frac{1}{3}$ times (Area of the Base) times (height): $V = \frac{1}{3} Bh$

3. Volume of a sphere: $V = \frac{4}{3} \pi r^3$

255

CUT HERE

Mathematics Reference Sheet, continued

Pythagorean Theorem: $a^2 + b^2 = c^2$

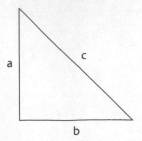

Given a line containing points

(x_1, y_1) and (x_2, y_2)

- Slope of line $= \dfrac{y_2 - y_1}{x_2 - x_1}$

- Distance between two points $=$

  $\sqrt{\left(x_2 - x_1\right)^2 + \left(y_2 - y_1\right)^2}$

- Midpoint between two points $=$

  $\left(\dfrac{x_1 + x_2}{2}, \dfrac{y_1 + y_2}{2}\right)$

Simple Interest Formula: $I = prt$

$I =$ simple interest, $p =$ principal

$r =$ rate, $t =$ time

Distance Formula: $d = rt$

$d =$ distance, $r =$ rate, $t =$ time

Conversions	
1 yard = 3 feet = 36 inches	1 cup = 8 fluid ounces
1 mile = 1,760 yards = 5,280 feet	1 pint = 2 cups
1 acre = 43,560 square feet	1 quart = 2 pints
1 hour = 60 minutes	1 gallon = 4 quarts
1 minute = 60 seconds	1 pound = 16 ounces
	1 ton = 2,000 pounds
1 liter = 1000 milliliters = 1000 cubic centimeters	
1 meter = 100 centimeters = 1000 millimeters	
1 kilometer = 1000 meters	
1 gram = 1000 milligrams	
1 kilogram = 1000 grams	

Note: Metric numbers with four digits are written without a comma (e.g., 2543 grams).

For metric numbers with more than four digits, a space is used instead of a comma (e.g., 24 300 liters).

CUT HERE

Directions: Read each question and select the best answer choice.

41. At an art exhibit at a local gallery, 15 of the 25 paintings displayed were purchased by a well-known art connoisseur. Which of the following numbers does <u>not</u> represent the part of the total number of paintings that were purchased by the art connoisseur?

   A. $\frac{10}{15}$

   B. 60%

   C. 0.6

   D. $\frac{3}{5}$

42. How many $\frac{3}{8}$ pound hamburger patties can be made from $4\frac{1}{2}$ pounds of ground beef?

   A. $1\frac{11}{16}$

   B. 12

   C. 8

   D. 6

43. Which of the following should be performed first to simplify this expression?

   $-9 + 36 \cdot 18 \div 3^2$

   A. $-9 + 36$

   B. $36 \cdot 18$

   C. $18 \div 3$

   D. 3^2

44. Three grandsons and two granddaughters inherit land from a grandparent's estate. The older granddaughter inherits $\frac{1}{3}$ of the land. The four other grandchildren equally share the remaining land. What fraction of the land does the younger granddaughter inherit?

   A. $\frac{1}{6}$

   B. $\frac{1}{4}$

   C. $\frac{1}{2}$

   D. $\frac{2}{3}$

GO ON TO THE NEXT PAGE

45. The low temperature recorded one morning was –6 °F. The high temperature recorded that afternoon was 35 °F. How many degrees did the temperature change from the morning low to the afternoon high?

A. 29 °F
B. 41 °F
C. –41 °F
D. –29 °F

46. The distance from Venus to the Sun is approximately 108 200 000 kilometers. Which of the following numbers shows the approximate distance from Venus to the Sun in scientific notation?

A. 108.2×10^6
B. 1.082×10^8
C. 108.2×10^{-6}
D. 1.082×10^{-8}

47. In right triangle ABC, the length of side *AB*, the hypotenuse of the right triangle, is $\sqrt{85}$. What is the approximate value of $\sqrt{85}$?

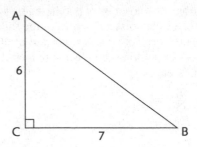

A. Between 6 and 7
B. Between 8 and 9
C. Between 9 and 10
D. Between 81 and 100

48. A cell phone company charges $29.99 per month for the first 500 minutes of calls and $0.30 a minute for any calls over the 500 minute limit. Last month Demetria made 615 minutes of calls on her cell phone. Excluding tax, what were the total charges for her cell phone calls last month?

A. $29.99
B. $34.50
C. $64.49
D. $184.50

49. A high school basketball player is 75 inches tall. The basketball hoop is 10 feet above the court. Find the distance in feet between the top of the player's head and the basketball hoop.

A. 2.5 feet
B. 3.25 feet
C. 3.75 feet
D. 6.25 feet

50. Carlos kept track of the exact time he spent playing video games last weekend. On Saturday, he played video games for 1 hour and 44 minutes, and on Sunday he played video games for 2 hours and 32 minutes. What is the total amount of time Carlos spent playing video games last weekend?

A. 3 hours 16 minutes
B. 4 hours 16 minutes
C. 4 hours 56 minutes
D. 4 hours

51. A couple want to replace their rectangular table that measures 3 feet by 4.5 feet with a circular table that has a diameter of 4 feet. About how much less will the area of the circular table be than the area of the rectangular table?

A. 0.94 ft^2
B. 12.56 ft^2
C. 26.06 ft^2
D. 36.74 ft^2

52. A rectangular garden has a perimeter of 50 feet. The width of the garden is 7 feet. What is the area of the garden?

A. 18 ft^2
B. 126 ft^2
C. 50 ft^2
D. 350 ft^2

GO ON TO THE NEXT PAGE

53. How many square yards of carpet are needed to cover a rectangular floor that measures 22 feet by 18 feet?

    A. 9 yd^2

    B. 44 yd^2

    C. 720 yd^2

    D. 3564 yd^2

54. If a crate is packed to capacity with 81 cubes measuring 4 inches on each edge, what is the volume of the crate in cubic inches?

    A. 64 in.^{3}

    B. 81 in.^{3}

    C. 1296 in.^{3}

    D. 5184 in.^{3}

55. What is the approximate volume of a cylinder that has a diameter of 8 feet and a height of 1.8 feet?

    A. 45 ft^3

    B. 90 ft^3

    C. 180 ft^3

    D. 362 ft^3

56. How many cubic feet of cement are in a rectangular cement slab that is 4 inches thick and measures 12.5 feet long and 9 feet wide?

    A. 37.5 ft^3

    B. 75 ft^3

    C. 450 ft^3

    D. 375 ft^3

57. Use the diagram below to answer the question that follows.

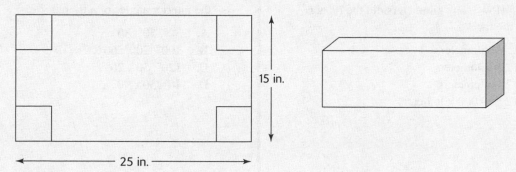

A small, open box is made by cutting out 5-in. squares on each corner from a rectangular piece of tag board, measuring 15 inches by 25 inches. The 5-in squares are discarded, and the box is formed by folding up the sides of the remaining tag board. What is the volume of the box in cubic inches?

A. 1125 in.^{3}
B. 1000 in.^{3}
C. 625 in.^{3}
D. 375 in.^{3}

58. A baseball diamond is a square that is 90 feet on a side. What is the approximate distance between bases in a scale model in which 9 feet = 1 inch?

A. 90 in.
B. 9 in.
C. 810 in.
D. 10 in.

59. How many cups of water does a 5-gallon container of water hold?

A. 20 cups
B. 40 cups
C. 60 cups
D. 80 cups

GO ON TO THE NEXT PAGE

60. A runner ran a cross-country race of 12 500 meters. How many kilometers did the runner run in the race?

    A. 1.25 kilometers
    B. 12.5 kilometers
    C. 125 kilometers
    D. 12 500 000 kilometers

61. What type of angle is angle B?

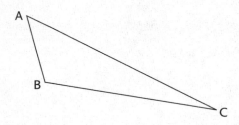

    A. acute
    B. obtuse
    C. right
    D. straight

62. Which of the following could be the measures of the interior angles of a triangle?

    A. 30°, 50°, 80°
    B. 100°, 200°, 60°
    C. 120°, 50°, 20°
    D. 40°, 50°, 90°

63. Which of the following expressions will yield the approximate diameter of a circle with a circumference of 48 inches?

    A. 48 in. × 3.14
    B. $\dfrac{3.14}{48 \text{ in.}}$
    C. 2 × 3.14 × 48 in.
    D. $\dfrac{48 \text{ in.}}{3.14}$

64. What are the coordinates of a point located 5 units to the right and 6 units down from point *P?*

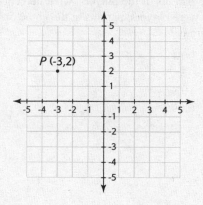

A. (2, 8)

B. (2, –4)

C. (–8, 8)

D. (–8, –4)

65. Which of the following is the most specific name for the figure below?

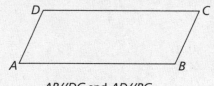

AB//DC and *AD//BC*

A. parallelogram

B. rectangle

C. square

D. trapezoid

66. Which of the following letters has both a horizontal and a vertical line of symmetry?

A. **H**

B. **A**

C. **W**

D. **N**

67. A 10-foot ladder is leaning against the side of a building. The bottom of the ladder is 6 feet from the base of the wall. How high up the side of the building does the ladder reach?

A. 4 feet

B. 8 feet

C. 10 feet

D. 16 feet

GO ON TO THE NEXT PAGE

68. Use the diagram below to answer the question that follows.

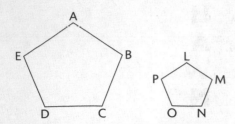

ABCDE and *LMNOP* are regular pentagons. If *AB* = 12 units and *LM* = 6 units, what is the ratio of the perimeter of *ABCDE* to the perimeter of *LMNOP*?

   A. 2:1

   B. 5:1

   C. 6:12

   D. 30:60

69. Television sets are described by the length of the diagonal across the rectangular screen. The rectangular screen of a television set measures 12 inches by 16 inches. What is the size of the television?

   A. 12-inch

   B. 16-inch

   C. 20-inch

   D. 28-inch

70. If 108 of the 120 fans who attended a Little League baseball game on a particular Saturday were parents of the players, what percent of the fans were players' parents at the game on that Saturday?

   A. 90%

   B. 9%

   C. 10%

   D. 0.09%

71. What is the midpoint of the line segment connecting points *T* and *U*?

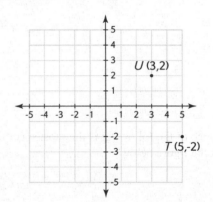

   A. (0, 4)

   B. (4, 0)

   C. (1, –2)

   D. (–2, 1)

72. If $x = -5$ and $y = -13$, then $x - y =$ what?

    A.   8

    B.   −8

    C.   18

    D.   −18

73. What is the distance between the two points R and S?

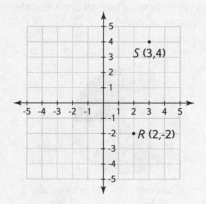

    A. $\sqrt{37}$ units

    B. $\sqrt{29}$ units

    C.   7 units

    D. $\sqrt{49}$ units

74. Four less than 5 times a number x is 6. Which of the following equations could be used to determine the number x?

    A. $4 - 5x = 6$

    B. $4x - 5 = 6$

    C. $-x = 6$

    D. $5x - 4 = 6$

75. Solve for x:

$$-2x - 5 = 3x + 15$$

    A. $x = -20$

    B. $x = -4$

    C. $x = 2$

    D. $x = 4$

76. Determine which of the following ordered pairs satisfies the given system.

$$x + 2y = -1$$
$$3x - 4y = 27$$

    A. $(5, -3)$

    B. $(-3, -5)$

    C. $(-5, 3)$

    D. $(3, 5)$

GO ON TO THE NEXT PAGE

77. What is the slope of the line that passes through the points T and U?

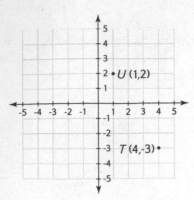

A. $-\dfrac{3}{5}$

B. $-\dfrac{5}{3}$

C. -1

D. $\dfrac{5}{3}$

78. What is the value of $3x^3 - x^2 + 5$ when $x = 2$?

A. 225

B. 217

C. 33

D. 25

79. Solve for x

$$4(x - 8) = 24$$

A. -2

B. 4

C. 8

D. 14

80. The graph shows a budget for a monthly salary after taxes.

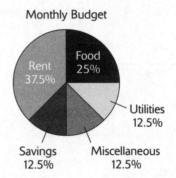

Monthly Budget

If the monthly salary is $2800, how much money is budgeted for food?

A. $105

B. $350

C. $700

D. $1050

81. A spinner for a board game has 4 red sections, 3 yellow sections, 2 blue sections, and 1 green section. The sections are all of equal size. What is the probability of spinning red on the first spin and green on the second spin?

A. $\frac{1}{4}$

B. $\frac{1}{2}$

C. 4

D. $\frac{1}{25}$

82. A student needs an average of at least 80 on four tests to earn a grade of B in algebra. The student has grades of 78, 91, and 75 on the first three tests. What is the *lowest* grade the student can make on the fourth test and still receive a B in the course?

A. 99

B. 82

C. 80

D. 76

83. Mario has participated in 8 track meets so far this season. His running times for the 440-meter race have been 73, 63, 68, 64, 69, 61, 66, and 64 seconds. What is Mario's median running time for the 8 meets?

A. 64 seconds

B. 65 seconds

C. 66 seconds

D. 66.6 seconds

84. For lunch at the end-of-school picnic, students can choose from four types of sandwiches: ham, turkey, tuna, or peanut butter. They can choose from two drinks: milk or juice. They can select from three types of chips: potato chips, corn chips, or cheese-flavored puffs. How many possible combinations of sandwiches, drinks, and chips can the students choose from for lunch?

A. 8

B. 9

C. 11

D. 24

85. Yuan has grades of 75, 89, 67, 56, and 92 in her English class and grades of 75, 78, 83, 84, 80, and 77 in her French class. Which of the following is a correct statement about Yuan's grades in the two classes?

A. The grades in the English class have greater variability.

B. The grades in the French class have greater variability.

C. The mean in the English class is higher than the mean in the French class.

D. The means in the two classes are equal.

IF YOU FINISH BEFORE TIME IS CALLED, CHECK YOUR WORK ON THIS SECTION ONLY. DO NOT WORK ON ANY OTHER SECTION IN THE TEST.

General Knowledge Practice Test 1: Reading

Directions: Please read the following passages carefully. Each passage in this section is followed by questions based on the passage's content. After reading each passage, answer the questions by choosing the best answer from among the four choices given. Be sure to base your answers on what is *implied* or *stated* in the passage.

Passage 1

(1) Young people, particularly teenagers, love escapist fare. They watch television, go to the movies, or even read books to get away to a world that is often, for many, foreign, or at least, unapproachable. They watch and read about others—maybe their own age, maybe not—fall in and out of love, have wild adventures, travel the globe, or just hang out with their friends. Each journey is marked by a rite of passage, a time-tested travail in which the hero or protagonist must struggle with some conflict—either external or internal—to become a fully realized human being. By challenging the system or overcoming a long-held fear, the hero of a tale embodies the best of what the watcher or reader hopes for in his own life and, thus, symbolizes the hopes and admiration of many.

(2) To entice young people to become avid readers, teachers and librarians often suggest works that, for some, are difficult to read. Well-intentioned as these informed advocates for young adult readers are, they often neglect a host of stories and novels that are aimed specifically at young adult readers. Too often, young people, particularly high school students, are handed material that is far beyond their knowledge or age range. Yes, Shakespeare, Dickens, and Hawthorne are representative of a class of time-honored, traditionally revered, classical authors, but they are, to be sure, not the only authors that young people should be encouraged to read. Indeed, there are many authors who young people often do not read, and should.

(3) The burgeoning field of young adult literature provides a rich panoply of good books from which young people can select to read and enjoy. Hours of escapist fare cloaked in realistic language and stories await eager young readers who find traditional literature too stuffy for their tastes. For younger readers (ages 9-12) there are works by Judy Blume (*Blubber; Are You There God? It's Me, Margaret*), Paula Danziger (*The Cat Ate My Gymsuit, There's a Bat in Bunk Five*), and E. L. Koningsburg (*From the Mixed up Files of Mrs. Basil E. Frankwiler*). For older readers (ages 13-17), there is S. E. Hinton (*The Outsiders, Rumblefish*), and Robert Cormier (*The Chocolate War, After the First Death*). These are but a few of the many books specifically written for young people that appeal to their needs and sensibilities and still provide the escape from their everyday lives that all human beings need when they long for entertainment.

(4) Thus, the task of lovers of good books—librarians, teachers, and parents, to name a few—is simple. They are duty bound to introduce young people to books that not only provide them a chance to explore new universes but edify them and engage their interest as well. Adults who make it their business to work with young people, to motivate them to become more than they ever could possibly imagine, should make it their business to familiarize themselves with the world of young adult fiction so that they can, in turn, recommend good books that speak to the interests and needs of the young people with whom they work. Otherwise, too often, these young people will never know the pure joy that reading can bring.

86. Which of the following best describes the focus of this passage?

    A. appropriate literature for young readers
    B. young people's choice of entertainment
    C. why young people should read the classics
    D. authors that young people should read

87. This passage states that teenagers:

    A. watch too much television.
    B. enjoy reading Shakespeare.
    C. need to escape from their everyday lives.
    D. prefer going to movies over reading books.

88. In the first paragraph, the word *travail* most nearly means:

    A. annoyance.
    B. parody.
    C. injustice.
    D. tribulation.

89. What is the main idea of the third paragraph?

   A. All human beings long to escape from their everyday lives.

   B. Many good books written for young readers are available.

   C. Traditional literature is too stuffy for young readers.

   D. There are only a few books written specifically for young readers.

90. According to this passage, Judy Blume is the author of:

   A. *The Cat Ate My Gymsuit.*

   B. *Are You There God?*

   C. *The Outsider.*

   D. *The Chocolate War.*

91. According to the passage, what is one way in which teenagers can be motivated to read?

   A. Introduce teenagers to classic works of literature.

   B. Substitute watching television for reading.

   C. Provide high-interest young adult novels.

   D. Increase attention to nonfiction works.

92. As used in the third paragraph, the phrase "escapist fare cloaked in realistic language" best describes

   A. fiction books.

   B. nonfiction books.

   C. textbooks.

   D. autobiographies.

93. The tone of this passage can best be described as

   A. caustic.

   B. optimistic.

   C. objective.

   D. subjective.

94. Which sentence best states the main idea of this passage?

   A. Young adults should be given literature that speaks to their developmental interests.

   B. Young adults should read literature that inspires good citizenship.

   C. Young adults must read books that underline traditional values.

   D. Young adults must be taught books with universal recognition.

95. Identify the relationship between the following two sentences in the second paragraph.

"To entice young people to become avid readers, teachers and librarians often suggest works that, for some, are difficult to read. Well-intentioned as these informed advocates for young adult readers are, they often neglect a host of stories and novels that are aimed specifically at young adult readers."

The second sentence

   A. expands the first.

   B. contradicts the first.

   C. illustrates the first.

   D. ignores the first.

Passage 2

(1)   Since the dawn of human history, individuals have longed to know the eternal mysteries of the universe. They have wanted to know why they are here, for what purpose do they serve, and what, if anything, is in the vast reaches beyond their world. For the first two questions, the reasons for humankind's existence and its noble purpose, people of all races and creeds have turned to religion. There, amidst ancient myths and modern realities, individuals have found great comfort and joy in the teachings and practices of many of the world's most ancient and revered religious traditions. For the other question, though, the mysteries of life beyond our imaginations, individuals have turned to exploration, and there, Americans, in particular, have found some of their greatest challenges.

(2)   We are fortunate to live in an age of intense exploration. Whether Americans are visiting the vast reaches of sea, land, or space, we seem to be always on the move, uncovering new riches and treasures in the vast outer reaches of our world. Indeed, our space program, marred as it is by tragic setbacks and fatal flaws, still beats a steady drumbeat toward unprecedented human progress and scientific growth.

(3)   Today, more than ever, we witness what only a few short years ago was considered unimaginable in even the most intimate and secure corners of scientific research and space exploration. Individuals now fly into space and stay for long periods of time with the regularity and accuracy of driving to the corner grocery story for a carton of milk. The efforts of our space program have led to the historic walk on the Moon by an American astronaut in July of 1969. This giant leap for humankind has spawned an age of travel and exploration into the far reaches of

GO ON TO THE NEXT PAGE

space that has yielded untold benefits and information for our modern industrial universe.

(4)   While ancient peoples saw a sky filled with mysterious lights and colors, we now know what we are seeing and why. We can recognize planets and stars with startling accuracy, and even more, send individuals hurtling into space with death-defying marksmanship; we can often use the targets that were once mysteries as guideposts for discovery. Astronauts hook up with the orbiting International Space Station almost as a matter of routine, as they guide their space vessels to lock and unlock with this floating home away from home above the Earth's gravitational pull. The speed and accuracy at which this regularly occurs still amazes the most experienced and learned scientists.

(5)   To be sure, Americans have seen their share of space tragedy. In January of 1986, the space shuttle Challenger—carrying seven astronauts, including America's first teacher to go into space—exploded immediately after takeoff. Then, space shuttle Columbia was lost on re-entry on February 1, 2003. These two space shuttle disasters dramatically curtailed America's exploration into space, but did not dampen the American spirit. Instead, with renewed vigor and intense self-examination, America's space program has set a course for exploration into the far reaches of the universe, to once again answer the eternal question of what lies in the vast reaches of the universe and how we can use the knowledge of what is there to help us know why we are here and to inspire who will we become.

96. Which of the following statements is implied in the first paragraph?

   A. Religion is an important part of many people's lives.

   B. Religion plays a limited role in most people's lives.

   C. Religion is the most important aspect of a person's life.

   D. Religion provides answers to all of life's questions.

97. Which of the following is an opinion expressed in this passage?

   A. Individuals now fly into space and stay for long periods of time.

   B. An American astronaut walked on the Moon.

   C. We are fortunate to live in an age of intense exploration.

   D. A teacher was on the space shuttle Challenger when it exploded.

98. In the second paragraph, the word *unprecedented* most nearly means:

   A. unparalleled.

   B. usual.

   C. unremarkable.

   D. unexceptional.

99. This passage states that the Challenger disaster occurred in:

   A. July of 1969.

   B. January of 1986.

   C. March of 1990.

   D. February of 2003.

100. According to information given in this passage:

   A. people seek answers to the reasons for humankind's existence.

   B. astronauts brought back rocks from the Moon.

   C. the Hubble space telescope provides images of planets and stars.

   D. the two shuttle disasters put an end to space exploration.

101. In this narrative, the author speaks of

   A. one shuttle disaster.

   B. two shuttle disasters.

   C. three shuttle disasters.

   D. no shuttle disasters.

102. Since the dawn of human history, individuals have been fascinated with exploration because of

   A. mankind's natural inquisitiveness about the universe.

   B. mankind's insatiable desire to rule the world.

   C. mankind's longing to live in isolation.

   D. mankind's fervent need to civilize the world.

103. The author would probably agree that

   A. scientific exploration is a risk-free strategy that is filled with unexpected pleasures.

   B. exploring unknown regions of the world is necessary for human development.

   C. only in desperate times do human beings feel the urge to explore.

   D. searching for the unknown is the province of rich entrepreneurs.

104. In the narrative, which of the following statements is NOT implied?

    A. Today, because of America's space program, the unimaginable has become reality.

    B. Our exploration of space has had a positive impact on America.

    C. America is a leader in scientific exploration.

    D. Tragedy has extinguished America's exploratory spirit.

105. Which word or phrase, when substituted for "Instead" in the fifth paragraph, would maintain the same relationship between the last two sentences?

    A. Therefore

    B. In addition

    C. Rather

    D. Obviously

Passage 3

(1)   Maria Montessori is considered a "woman who was ahead of her time." She is credited with founding a movement that placed children's needs and desires above all other considerations, which—at that time, in the early twentieth century—was considered radical and revolutionary thought, especially in Europe. Nevertheless, Maria, born of humble but progressive parents, learned to take what she had always intuitively felt about the value and dignity of all human beings—regardless of age, status, and ethnicity—and apply her understandings to the everyday world. In so doing, she changed the face of modern education as we know it.

(2)   Born in Chiaravalle, Italy in 1870, Maria moved five years later to Rome. There, under the tutelage of her parents, especially her liberal-minded mother, Maria reveled in her own curiosity. Her natural inclination to explore and learn was encouraged; more importantly, she recognized that she could do and become anything her heart desired. However in Italy, as elsewhere throughout Europe and the United States at that time, the role of women was primarily subservient to that of men. Asserting their independence—whether at home, at work, or at play—was not something that women in the early twentieth century did. Maria's own learning environment, which had no such restrictions, formed the foundation of her later independent, free-spirited, learning environment for children.

(3)   In 1896, Maria Montessori's strong academic record and natural drive to succeed led her to become the first female certified physician in Italy. Graduating at the top of her class, Maria continued her deep and abiding love of the study of psychology, philosophy, and education and gradually began to form the basis of her teaching method known as the "Montessori Method."

(4)   In 1904, she was appointed professor of anthropology at the University of Rome. Now, having authority and position, Maria was able to apply her theories of child development to work in practical settings. Two years later, in 1906, she wasted no time in founding and establishing the first house for children of the industrial working class in one of Rome's worst slum districts. There, in the house known as the Casa dei Bambini, or "Children's House," Maria, at the age of 36, instructed some 60 children in her care on how to do everyday chores. Her philosophy embraced the idea that by doing ordinary work, children would begin to develop a sense of self and pride that would spur their own growth and independence.

(5)   To her delight, the children in her charge prospered. Soon, they were demonstrating to their parents self-reliance and maturity. Left to assert their independence, these young people, who because of position and social class were thought to be useless and unacceptable beyond normal functions, began to demonstrate social usefulness by simply being encouraged. Taking heed to her observations, Maria Montessori began to codify her doctrine of respecting the rights and privileges of young people into a philosophical and practical treatise on how young people learn.

(6)   By treating young people with reverence and respect, Maria revolutionized the teaching profession. Young people were no longer regarded as passive, stoic learners, but active, involved, developing human beings who were quite capable of making sound and independent choices about their own learning. Advocating age-appropriate learning activities, Maria documented a teaching philosophy that garnered her worldwide attention and lasting influence in educational circles, most notably in the field of early childhood education.

(7)   Nominated three times for the Nobel Peace Prize (1949, 1950, 1951), Maria Montessori continued to work tirelessly, until her death in 1952, training adults in the United States, Europe, and India about her teaching methods for treating young children—indeed, all children—with the respect and dignity they deserve. She was truly ahead of her time.

GO ON TO THE NEXT PAGE

106. According to this passage Maria Montessori was born in:

    A. Germany.

    B. Spain.

    C. India

    D. Italy.

107. Which of the following statements is implied in the passage?

    A. Maria Montessori's parents were old-fashioned.

    B. In Maria Montessori's time, women were encouraged to pursue careers that traditionally were considered male careers.

    C. Maria Montessori believed that children should be passive learners.

    D. Maria Montessori was well-educated.

108. Which of the following is an opinion about Maria Montessori expressed in this passage?

    A. She revolutionized the teaching profession.

    B. She was the first female certified physician in Italy.

    C. She founded the Casa dei Bambini.

    D. She was nominated three times for the Nobel Peace Prize.

109. This passage states that Maria Montessori:

    A. advocated age-appropriate learning activities.

    B. believed that doing everyday chores was demeaning to children.

    C. had the greatest influence in the field of secondary education.

    D. won the Nobel Peace Prize in 1951.

110. According to this passage, Maria Montessori's teaching ideas:

    A. were rejected by most educators of her time.

    B. gained attention worldwide during her lifetime.

    C. retired from teaching to practice medicine in her later years.

    D. found practicing medicine to be a difficult and arduous career.

111. According to this passage, the best word to describe Maria Montessori is

    A. passive.

    B. progressive.

    C. cynical.

    D. active.

112. According to this passage, Maria Montessori revolutionized the education profession because

    A. she understood the importance of subject-matter instruction in the development of young people.

    B. she demonstrated the validity of standardized assessment in classroom instruction.

    C. she respected the emotional experiences that young people brought to their learning.

    D. she underscored the power of reading to reinforce rote memorization of material.

113. According to this passage, Maria Montessori's philosophy was

    A. learning by doing ordinary work.

    B. learning by memorization.

    C. learning by objectives.

    D. learning by competition.

114. According to the ideas in this passage, which of the following would best demonstrate active, involved learners who are capable of making independent choices?

    A. a five-year-old practicing geometry half-heartedly

    B. a four-year-old memorizing Shakespeare without choice

    C. a six-year-old taking a spelling test under extreme duress

    D. a seven-year-old playing dress-up enthusiastically

115. As used in the fifth paragraph, the word *self-reliance* most nearly means

    A. dependence.

    B. persistence.

    C. autonomy.

    D. caution.

Passage 4

(1)   Near the equator are woodlands so lush in vegetation and foliage that enrich our planet with beauty and resources to the extent that life on our planet would more than likely be unrecognizable without them. I am speaking of the world-renowned tropical rain forests, a term first coined by German botanist Andreas F. W. Schimper, who in 1898 first ventured into this unexpected, wonderful, and forbidding universe. The breath-taking beauty of the tropical rain forests is indescribable. It is impossible to capture on film or to convey in words what it is like to stand inside the heart of a tropical rain forest. Yet, the rain forests' majesty and richness are sadly in jeopardy as human intervention continues to destroy what nature has designed to exist forever.

(2)   Tropical rain forests have the unique distinction of occupying only 6 to 7 percent of the Earth's surface, but they nourish more than half of the Earth's plant and animal species. In this vast stretch of virtually unexplored territory, literally thousands of species of plant and animal life exist. Home to many varieties of amphibians, reptiles, insects, birds, and mammals, the tropical rain forests are a virtual Noah's ark of all creatures great and small.

(3)   Scientists believe some riches of the rain forests are yet to be discovered. In addition to finding new animal species, they continue to mine the many exotic plants that can yield untold benefits in developing new medicines for individuals with acute and chronic illnesses. In addition, scientists urge world leaders to take every measure possible to preserve the rain forests because of the many and varied plant species they contain that help to regulate the Earth's climate and ensure clean air.

(4)   Thus, when the rain forests are threatened by large industrial companies desiring to clear land for logging, farming, and mining projects, world citizens object and lobby dignitaries and business leaders to use caution in their desires to expand and grow. Both sides of this issue—those advocating the use of the rain forests for economic growth and gain and those advocating for the preservation of a natural reserve—are locked in a reasonable and vital discussion about the future use of one of (if not *the*) world's greatest natural resources. This debate, though, is never-ending and always exasperating. Each side—the environmentalists and the industrialists—claim that the other side is violating rules that serve to protect the environment from undue harm. As a result, long legal battles ensue, resulting in few if any reasonable compromises.

(5)   In some instances, though, the debate is almost futile. In 1950, rain forests covered about 8,700,000 square miles of the Earth's surface. Today, in the early twenty-first century, less than half of the original extent of the world's rain forests remain. In an area that once measured in practical terms the equivalent of nearly three-fourths of Africa, today stands vast regions—in places like Madagascar, Sumatra, and the Atlantic coast of Brazil—of arid, dry land.

(6)   Scientists estimate that deforestation—the ridding of the rain forests of valuable trees and foliage—eliminates from the Earth's surface about 7500 species per year, including the most valuable species on the planet, humankind. Millions of indigenous people, individuals who know little of the outside world or modern conveniences, make their homes in the rain forests. Explorers have discovered and recorded the comings and goings of such groups as the Yanomami of South Africa, the Dayaks of Southeast Asia, and the Pygmies of Central Africa. These people, the last of the earth's primitive tribes, make their living off this lush and forbidden land, and naturally, they have much to tell about using its natural resources for survival.

(7)   Fortunately, a number of governments and conservation organizations are working to preserve the rain forests. Organizations like the World Wildlife Fund and the Nature Conservancy are working with national and international government agencies to conserve rain forests. Their efforts include establishing protected lands, promoting conservation methods, and increasing public awareness. Specific measures include certifying that timber is harvested in a responsible manner and logging is in only designated and protected areas. To be sure, these are small steps, but with perseverance and common sense, the rain forests will continue as one of the Earth's most vital and precious resources.

116. The tone of this passage is best described as:

A. skeptical.
B. humorous.
C. sarcastic.
D. factual.

GO ON TO THE NEXT PAGE

117. Which of the following is a fact about tropical rain forests that is given in the first paragraph?

    A. Tropical rain forests are found near the equator.

    B. The breath-taking beauty of a tropical rain forest is indescribable.

    C. It is impossible to capture on film or to convey in words what it is like to stand inside the heart of a tropical rain forest.

    D. The rain forests' majesty and richness are sadly in jeopardy.

118. According to the passage, rain forests occupy what percent of the Earth's surface?

    A. less than 2 percent.

    B. 6 to 7 percent.

    C. 20 to 25 percent.

    D. over 50 percent.

119. This passage states that:

    A. deforestation of rain forests has resulted in the extinction of indigenous people.

    B. government agencies do little to preserve the rain forests.

    C. large industrial companies desiring to clear land for logging, farming, and mining threaten the rain forests.

    D. most of the species in the rain forest are insects.

120. In paragraph three the author uses the word *mine* in the context of:

    A. excavating from the Earth's soil.

    B. dissolving with chemicals.

    C. extracting from plants.

    D. supplying with new medicines.

121. Which of the statements about rain forests is neither stated nor implied in this passage?

    A. They provide safe havens for indigenous people.

    B. They provide natural resources for modern medicines.

    C. They provide unique treasures for self-defined explorers.

    D. They provide a rich laboratory for scientific investigation.

122. The primary purpose of this passage is to

    A. introduce rare rain forest plants and species.

    B. inform readers about the plight of the rain forests.

    C. argue the benefits of logging in the rain forests.

    D. underline the importance of scientific exploration.

123. According to this passage, all of the following are true except

    A. in 1950, rain forests covered about 8,700,000 square miles of the Earth's surface.

    B. rain forests nourish more than half of the world's plants and animals.

    C. today, less than half of the world's original rain forests remain.

    D. deforestation is a minor problem in today's rain forest environment.

124. According to this passage, millions of *indigenous* people live in the rain forests. *Indigenous* can best be defined as

    A. people who are transitory migrants on the land in which they live.

    B. people who own property on the land in which they live.

    C. people who are native to the land in which they live.

    D. people who work the land on which they live.

125. The author's claim that the "rain forests will continue as one of the Earth's most vital resources"

    A. is a non-objectionable, reasoned statement based on scant evidence.

    B. is a contradictory statement based on the passage's prior reasoning.

    C. is an objectionable remark that reveals the author's implicit bias.

    D. is a reasonable statement given the author's previous remarks.

Answer Key

General Knowledge Practice Test 1: English Language Skills

1. B	15. B	29. C
2. D	16. B	30. A
3. D	17. A	31. A
4. C	18. A	32. C
5. A	19. B	33. C
6. C	20. A	34. D
7. A	21. C	35. C
8. B	22. C	36. B
9. B	23. B	37. D
10. A	24. C	38. C
11. A	25. A	39. A
12. C	26. B	40. C
13. C	27. C	
14. B	28. B	

General Knowledge Practice Test 1: Mathematics

41. A	56. A	71. B
42. B	57. D	72. A
43. D	58. D	73. A
44. A	59. D	74. D
45. B	60. B	75. B
46. B	61. B	76. A
47. C	62. D	77. B
48. C	63. D	78. D
49. C	64. B	79. D
50. B	65. A	80. C
51. A	66. A	81. D
52. B	67. B	82. D
53. B	68. A	83. B
54. D	69. C	84. D
55. B	70. A	85. A

General Knowledge Practice Test 1: Reading

86. A	**100.** A	**114.** D
87. C	**101.** B	**115.** C
88. D	**102.** A	**116.** D
89. B	**103.** B	**117.** D
90. B	**104.** D	**118.** B
91. C	**105.** C	**119.** C
92. A	**106.** D	**120.** C
93. D	**107.** D	**121.** C
94. A	**108.** A	**122.** B
95. A	**109.** A	**123.** D
96. A	**110.** B	**124.** C
97. C	**111.** B	**125.** D
98. A	**112.** C	
99. B	**113.** A	

General Knowledge Practice Test 1: Essay Explanation

In this section of the examination, you were asked to prepare a written assignment on one of two topics.

Topic 1

Why I want to become a teacher

Topic 2

A person whom I admire

You were asked to write a 300- to 600-word response that would be well written, organized, and defined. You were also informed that your writing would be graded holistically, taking into consideration both mechanics and organization.

What follows are examples of a weak and strong response to both prompts.

Topic 1—Why I Want to Become a Teacher

Weak Response

Personally, I want to become a teacher because I like to teach and it seems fun. I enjoy working with young children and more so, the hours seem flexible and manageable. I once wanted to become a doctor, but I realized that the course work was much too difficult, so I decided on teaching instead. My love for young children made me switch and I am glad that I did. I have many good ideas for working with young children and I cannot wait to get started. I also don't know what class or grade I want to teach, but I do know that I don't want to teach the middle grades. I don't believe that I would have the patience or knowledge to work with teenagers. They seem like an real difficult group to work with. Still, I do know that I want to be a teacher and I will try my best to succeed.

Strong Response

Becoming a teacher has been a lifelong dream for me. I can think of no richer occupation for me to pursue than that of working with young children. As I achieve my goal, my life's ambition will become a dream come true. For embedded in my teaching will be the fulfillment of a mission that began as a young child, continued through my college years, and will culminate in my first real teaching position.

When I was a young child, I dreamed of becoming a teacher. I would line up my dolls in my playroom and pretend that I was their teacher. I would do everything that all my real teachers in school would do. I would teach lessons, walk them to specials, sit with them at lunch, and even take them on field trips. I would line my dolls up in my little red wagon—all 14 of them—and pull them along the sidewalk of my house. I would pretend we were taking a trip to the zoo or a museum. Like my real teachers in school, I would talk to my dolls, praising them when they did good work and scolding them when they misbehaved.

As I grew older, I became active in school, always nurturing my desire to teach and help others. In middle school, I became a peer counselor, helping other students with their problems and homework. I would work for hours before and after school with sixth and seventh graders who had trouble with their math and science homework since I was particularly good in those subjects. I would also help them solve problems and issues that they had with other children when they just needed someone to listen. In high school, I was active in the Future Teachers of America Organization, helping children in elementary schools with their assignments, and on occasion, teaching lessons for an entire classroom of children. In addition, I spent many hours in high school, volunteering my services in all sorts of organizations—from service clubs to student government—just learning how to become a better "people person."

Finally, during my college years, I started to fulfill my life-long ambition to become a teacher by majoring in elementary education. Attending the state university, I majored in education and minored in psychology, so now, when I do land a teaching job, I can combine my love for working with children with my desire to understand who they are as human beings. I was most able to put my knowledge to work during my final semester in college when I became a student teacher in a local elementary school. There, I was able to put all my knowledge and experience to work. Now, I feel better equipped to become a teacher for I have both the experience and credentials to succeed.

As stated, I love teaching, and I hope, soon, to land a wonderful teaching position in which I can contribute to the growth and development of young children. I want to return to my childhood days in which I played teacher with my dolls; only this time, I want to work with real children. I have already made an impact with my student peers and during my training years; now I want to make a difference in the real world of teaching.

Topic 2—A Person Whom I Admire

Weak Response

A person that I admire is my uncle. My uncle Ned has been with me since I was little boy and I was able to sit in his lap and listen to his fantastic stories about fishing. His idea of fun has always been to pretend to pull quarters out of my ear. When I was real young, I thought it was magic, but as I got older, I realized that he was just making it up. I really enjoy older people, especially someone I can look up to because you never know what good advice they are going to give you. My uncle and my grandfather always gave me good advice and I have always been eager to follow their smart wisdom. They taught me how to drive and what to study and how to do well in school and with girls. Yes, someone I admire is my uncle because he always helps me when I am in trouble. My uncle is also deaf which is an amazing in and of itself.

Strong Response

Admiration is a strong word that conjures up many meanings and implications. To admire someone is to not only appreciate someone for who they are, but to hope to emulate them for what they have become. When you admire parents or relatives, you are saying that you both love them and want to be like them. When you admire adults or friends, you are saying that you hope someday to be just like them, and that you hope that they, in turn, will teach you something about how they became who they are. Such is the admiration that I have for my uncle.

My Uncle Ned is a wonderful human being. He is not rich, famous, or especially talented. He does not play a musical instrument, excel in sports, or have the gift of speech. In fact, my Uncle Ned is deaf. Born with a congenital birth defect, my uncle can hardly hear (only high pitched sounds) and speak. He can lip read, and as a result, he has learned to conduct most of his conversations in sign language. He is very adept at signing most anything, and he can move at lightning speed when he is talking with someone who knows sign language as well as he does.

Uncle Ned is truly a remarkable person. Never one to be defeated, he has struggled since his birth to live a normal, everyday life. Attending public schools, he would seek the accommodations that the school would provide—teachers, tutors, special classes—and never once (so I am told) did he ever complain. Uncle Ned just took everything in stride, using his disability as an ability and not a liability. He would compensate for his deafness by working extra hard to make sure his assignments were done exceptionally well and that no one would think he was slacking off because he could not hear and barely could speak. Instead, he made sure, as his sister (my mother) tells me, that his teachers knew that he was really working and that he really cared.

Uncle Ned worked so hard and cared so much about his education that he, too, eventually became a teacher. Only this time, Uncle Ned devoted his teaching years to a special school for children who are just like him, hard of hearing and speaking. After getting his doctorate in education (I told you my uncle is special), he began what has become a nearly 30-year career teaching at Galludet University in Washington, D.C., one of the few institutions in higher education that is devoted solely to working with deaf and hard of hearing individuals. And it is there that my uncle has been able to give back to a new generation of students what he received in a public school setting.

Everyone admires somebody—a parent, a teacher, a friend. I have had the privilege of admiring someone who is not only a relative and a friend, but an inspiring role model for countless human beings who are both hearing and non-hearing, and he has truly inspired me above all. I feel very lucky to know my Uncle Ned who taught me not to try to be someone special, but to live like someone special.

General Knowledge Practice Test 1: English Language Skills Answers and Explanations

1. **B.** In this paragraph, the most logical sequence of sentences appears in Choice **B.** The paragraph reads best when sentences 3, 4, and 5 are rearranged to read sentences 4, 3, and 5.

2. **D.** Sentence 6 is the sentence LEAST relevant to this passage. The discussion of the automobile, although important to the overall discussion of transportation, does not belong in a paragraph whose sole discussion is about horses.

3. **D.** This paragraph already reads well. There is no need to rearrange the sentences in a different order.

4. **C.** Sentence 5 is the sentence LEAST relevant to this passage. The discussion of individuals who like engagement and wedding rings without precious stones is interesting but distracting to the paragraph's narrative.

5. **A.** The word *who's* should read *whose. Who's* is a contraction for the word *who is. Whose* is the possessive form of the word *who.* The other two words—*came* and *retrieve*—are spelled and used correctly.

6. **C.** The correct word choice is *except.* The word *accept* means *to take when offered.* The word *except* means *to exclude.* The other word choices—*at* and *summer*—are spelled and used correctly.

7. **A.** The correct word choice is "respectfully." All the other word choices are spelled and used correctly.

8. **B.** The correct word choice is *farther.* The word *further* is used to describe *abstract ideas.* The word *farther* is used to describe *concrete distance.* The other word choices—*fourth* and *than*—are spelled and used correctly.

9. **B.** The correct word choice is *could have.* The phrase *could of* is grammatically incorrect. *Could have* is the grammatically acceptable phrase. (*Should of* is also unacceptable.) The other word choices—*aunt* and *dessert*–are spelled and used correctly. Only capitalize the word *aunt* when you are naming a specific aunt, like *Aunt Betty.* The word *dessert* means the treat you eat after a meal. The word *desert* means the dry, sandy place with little or no plant life.

10. **A.** The correct word choice is *capital.* The word *capitol* means the building, The word *capital* means the city. The other word choices—*receive* and *their*—are spelled and used correctly.

11. **A.** The correct word is *weather.* The word *whether* implies a choice between two objects. The word *weather* refers to the climate. The other word choices—*admirably* and *congregants*—are spelled and used correctly.

12. **C.** The correct word is *proceeded.* The word *proceeded* means to 'venture forth' or 'go ahead.' The word *preceded* means to come before. The other word choices—*ineligible* and *everyone*—are spelled and used correctly.

13. **C.** The correct word is *than.* The word *than* is used when making a comparison between two objects. The word *then* implies a time frame. The other word choices—*certainly* and *board*—are spelled and used correctly in the sentence.

14. **B.** The correct word is *complement.* The word *complement* means to accompany, to match, or to complete something. The word *compliment* means to laud praise on someone. The other word choices—*exceptional* and *considerable*—are spelled and used correctly.

15. **B.** The correct phrase is *whether.* The word *whether* implies a choice between two objects. The phrase *as to whether* is not grammatically correct. The other word choices—*me* and *I*—are spelled and used correctly.

16. **B.** The correct word is *site.* The word *site* means a place or setting. The word *sight* refers to one's ability to see. The other word choices—*may* and *by*—are spelled and used correctly.

17. **A.** The sentence should be in the past tense, so *came* is the correct verb. The word *that* at **B** is correct because it introduces a restrictive clause. The comma at **C** is correct. Although you may see the omission of the comma before the coordinating conjunction *and,* the final comma in a series of three or more elements is never incorrect.

18. **A.** The word at **A** shows possession. The location belongs to the restaurant, so *restaurant* needs to be changed to *restaurant's*. The word *beach* at **B** is spelled correctly. The word *really* at **C** is an adverb modifying the adjective *romantic*, so it is correct.

19. **B.** A comma is needed at **B** to separate the introductory subordinate clause from the rest of the sentence. The word *tourists* at **A** does not show possession, so no apostrophe is needed. The word *than* at **C** is correctly used as a conjunction in a comparison. The word *then* is an adverb indicating time.

20. **A.** In this sentence, the word following the verb *felt* at **A** modifies the subject (a noun). The word *badly* is an adverb. It should not be used to modify a noun. The adjective *bad* should be used instead. The word *English* at **B** is a proper noun, so it should be capitalized. The title *superintendent* at **C** should not be capitalized. Titles are capitalized when they precede proper names, but as a rule are not capitalized when used alone.

21. **C.** The *West Indies* is the name of a specific place. The full name must be capitalized. The comma at **A** is needed to set off the nonrestrictive appositive. The word *explorer* at **B** is not a proper noun, so it should not be capitalized.

22. **C.** The past tense of *build* is *built*, not *builded*. The word *When* at **A** is correct and makes sense in the sentence. The comma at **B** is needed to separate the introductory subordinate clause from the rest of the sentence.

23. **B.** The word *between* is a preposition. The object of a preposition should be in the objective case. Change *I* at **B** to *me* to make the sentence grammatically correct. The sentence is in the present tense, so *am* at **A** is the correct verb. The word *that* at **C** is correct. It would be redundant to use *because* at C because the word *because* means *for the reason that*.

24. **C.** The underlined portion at **C** is the subject of the verb *can run* (which is understood) and, thus, should be in the subjective case. Change *them other athletes* to *those other athletes* to make the sentence grammatically correct. The pronoun *who* at **A** is correct because it is the subject of the subordinate clause it introduces. The word *faster* at **B** is the correct comparative form of the adverb *fast*.

25. **A.** The singular pronoun *it* is the subject of the verb at **A**, so change *don't* to *doesn't* to make the verb agree with its singular subject. No comma is needed at **B**. The second person pronoun *you* at **C** is correct. It would be incorrect to switch to the third person pronoun *one*.

26. **B.** The word at **B** should be spelled *mathematics*. The word *siblings* at **A** does not show possession, so no apostrophe is needed. The reflexive pronoun *myself* at **C** is used correctly to refer back to its antecedent *I*.

27. **C.** The plural noun *media* is the subject of the verb at **C,** so change *is* to *are* to make the verb agree with its plural subject. The possessive pronoun *their* at **A** is correct. The sentence is in the past tense, so *was* is the correct verb at **B**.

28. **B.** The past participle for the verb *to eat* is *eaten*. Note that "should of" in **A** and **C** is an error for "should have."

29. **C.** The tense of the verb in choice **C** relates logically to the verb in the main clause. The verb tenses in choices **A** and **B** do not.

30. **A.** The singular pronoun *Everyone* is the subject of the verb at **A,** so change *have enjoyed* to *has enjoyed* to make the verb agree with its singular subject. The plural form of *goldfish* at **B** is written correctly. The word *castle* at **C** is spelled correctly.

31. **A.** The word *Each* is the singular antecedent of the possessive pronoun at **A**. Use *his* instead of the plural pronoun *their* to refer to the singular antecedent *Each*. No comma is needed at **B**. The preposition *between* at **C** is correctly used to indicate a relationship involving two things. The preposition *among* is used when the relationship involves more than two elements.

32. **C.** Does *them* at **C** refer to *students* or *books*? Change *them* to *the books* to avoid ambiguity. No comma is needed at **A**. The word *organizations* at **B** does not show possession, so no apostrophe is needed.

33. **C.** In this sentence the words *studying, reading*, and *to write* are in parallel, but they do not have the same grammatical construction. You can correct this faulty parallelism by changing *to write* at **C** to *writing*. The word *middle* at **A** is not a proper noun, so it should not be capitalized. The word *grammar* at **B** is spelled correctly.

34. D. This sentence is correct as written. The word *quite* at **A** is spelled correctly and makes sense in the sentence. The possessive pronoun *his* at **B** is correct because *his* modifies the gerund *meddling*. The verb *personal* at **C** is spelled correctly and makes sense in the sentence.

35. C. The word at **C** is a noun, so *affect* should be changed to *effect* to make the sentence grammatically correct. The word *professors* at **A** does not show possession, so no apostrophe is needed. The singular verb *was* at **B** agrees with its singular subject *One*.

36. B. The word at **B** should be spelled *height*, not *heighth*. The sentence is in the past tense, so *measured* is the correct verb. No comma is needed at **C**.

37. D. This sentence is correct as written. The possessive word *Rose's* is punctuated correctly. The word *friend* at **B** is spelled correctly. At **C** the superlative form of *unusual* is *most unusual*, not *unusualest*.

38. C. All punctuation in sentence **C** is correct. Choice **A** is incorrect because it is a run-on sentence. It is two complete sentences connected by only a comma. Choices **B** and **D** are also run-on sentences. Each of these sentences is two complete sentences joined without a word to connect them or a proper punctuation mark to separate them.

39. A. All punctuation in Choice **A** is correct. In Choice **B,** the word *familys'* is incorrect. To form the possessive of a noun (either singular or plural) that does not end in *s*, add an apostrophe and *s*. Choice **C** is incorrect because it contains a fragment. (*Preferring to be hand-fed canned tuna.*) A comma is needed in Choice **D** to separate the introductory participial phrase from the rest of the sentence.

40. C. The modifiers in Choice **C** are placed correctly. The participial phrase *Rushing to finish the surprise dinner on time* modifies *Melissa,* the noun subject of the main clause of the sentence and should be close to it. In choices **B** and **D,** *Rushing to finish the surprise dinner on time* is separated from the noun *Melissa* resulting in ambiguity. The subordinate clause *that was rotten* modifies the noun *egg,* and should be close to it. In choices **A** and **B,** *that was rotten* seems to modify the noun *neighbor,* which clearly is not the intent of the writer.

General Knowledge Practice Test 1: Mathematics Answers and Explanations

41. A. The part of the total number of paintings purchased by the art connoisseur is $\frac{15}{25} = \frac{3}{5} = 0.6 = 60\%$. Choice **A** is the only choice that is <u>not</u> equivalent to $\frac{15}{25}$.

42. B. You need to separate $4\frac{1}{2}$ pounds into equal $\frac{3}{8}$ pound patties. Use division to separate a whole into equal parts. You want the units of your answer to be patties. Carry the units along in your computation, so that you can see that the answer works out to patties.

$4\frac{1}{2}$ pounds $\div \frac{3}{8} \frac{\text{pound}}{\text{pattie}} = \frac{9}{2}$ pounds $\times \frac{8}{3} \frac{\text{pattie}}{\text{pound}} = 12$ patties   The pounds "cancel out" when you multiply.

12 hamburger patties can be made, Choice **B.**

Did I answer the question? Yes, I found how many patties can be made. ✓

Is the answer stated in the correct units? Yes, the units are patties, which is correct. ✓

Choice **A** results if you multiply instead of divide. Choices **C** and **D** result if you divide $4\frac{1}{2}$ by $\frac{3}{8}$ incorrectly.

43. D. To simplify the expression $-9 + 36 \cdot 18 \div 3^2$, follow "<u>P</u>lease <u>E</u>xcuse <u>M</u>y <u>D</u>ear <u>A</u>unt <u>S</u>ally." The order of operations requires that any operations in parentheses be performed first. There are no parentheses in this expression, so the next step is to simplify any exponents. Since 3^2 is in exponential form, it should be performed first. It would be incorrect to perform $-9 + 36$ first (Choice **A**) because addition and subtraction, from left to right, are performed last when there are no parentheses indicating to do otherwise. It would be incorrect to perform $36 \cdot 18$ (Choice **B**) or $18 \div 3$ (Choice **C**) *first* because multiplication and division, from left to right, are performed after exponentiation, unless there are parentheses indicating to do otherwise.

44. A. Two steps are needed to solve the problem. First, subtract the older granddaughter's part from the whole. Then, divide what remains into four equal parts.

Step 1. The older granddaughter inherits $\frac{1}{3}$ of the land. Subtract to find the remaining part of the land:

$$1 - \frac{1}{3} = \frac{2}{3}$$

Step 2. The younger granddaughter and her three brothers equally share the remaining part of the land. Use division to separate $\frac{2}{3}$ into 4 equal parts:

$$\frac{2}{3} \div 4 = \frac{2}{3} \div \frac{4}{1} = \frac{\overset{1}{2}}{3} \times \frac{1}{\underset{2}{4}} = \frac{1}{6}$$

The younger granddaughter inherits $\frac{1}{6}$ of the land, Choice **A**.

Did I answer the question? Yes, I found the fraction of the land that the younger granddaughter inherits. ✓

Is the answer stated in the correct units? The answer is a fraction, so no units are needed. ✓

Choice **B** results of you fail to subtract the older daughter's part from the whole before dividing. Choice **C** results if you make a computation error in step 2. Choice **D** results if you fail to do step 2 after you complete step 1.

45. B. To find the change in temperature subtract:

35 °F – (–6 °F) = 35 °F + 6 °F = 41 °F. The temperature increased by 41 °F. Choice **A** results if you make the mistake of adding the temperatures algebraically, instead of subtracting them. Choice **C** results if you make a sign error. Choice **D** results if you mistakenly add the temperatures algebraically and make a sign error.

46. B. A number written in scientific notation is written as a product of two numbers: a number that is greater than or equal to 1, but less than 10, and a power of 10. Eliminate choices **A** and **C** because the first factor is greater than 10.

The number 108,200,000 is greater than 10, so the decimal point must be moved to the left to make the first factor greater than or equal to 1 but less than 10. If the decimal point is moved 8 places to the left, the first factor will be 1.082.

$$108,200,000 = 1.082000000 \times 10^{?} = 1.082 \times 10^{?}$$

Since the decimal point was moved to the left 8 places, the exponent for the power of 10 is 8. The exponent needs to be positive 8 so that when you convert back to the original number, the value is the same. The number 108,200,000 is written as 1.082×10^{8} in scientific notation, Choice **B.** You can check your answer by quickly performing the indicated multiplication.

$$1.082 \times 10^{8} = 1.082 \times 100,000,000 = 108,200,000.$$

Choices **A** and **C** result if you fail to make the first factor a number greater than or equal to 1, but less than 10. Choice **D** results if you incorrectly use a negative exponent on the power of 10. Negative exponents are used in scientific notation when you are writing very small numbers that are between 0 and 1. For example, 0.00000007 is 7×10^{-8} in scientific notation.

47. C. Label the diagram:

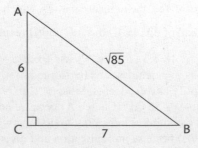

To approximate the value of $\sqrt{85}$, find two consecutive integers such that the square of the first integer is less than 85 and the square of the second integer is greater than 85. Since 9^2 is $81 < 85$ and 10^2 is $100 > 85$, the approximate value of $\sqrt{85}$ is between 9 and 10, Choice **C**. Choice **A** results if you mistakenly use the length of the legs of the right triangle to approximate $\sqrt{85}$. Choice **B** results if you underestimate $\sqrt{85}$. Choice **D** results if you mistakenly use the squares of the consecutive integers 9 and 10 to estimate $\sqrt{85}$.

48. C. Three steps are needed to solve the problem: First, find the number of overlimit minutes; next, find the cost of the overlimit minutes; and then, find the total charges by adding the cost of the overlimit minutes to the regular monthly charge.

Step 1. Subtract to find how many minutes of calls are over the 500 limit:

615 minutes – 500 minutes = 115 minutes

Step 2. Find the cost for the overlimit minutes by multiplying by $0.30:

115 minutes $\times$ $0.30/minute = $34.50

Step 3. Add the overlimit charges to the monthly charge:

$29.99 + $34.50 = $64.49.

Demetria's total charges for her cell phone calls last month are $64.49, Choice **C**.

Did I answer the question? Yes, I found Demetria's total charges for her cell phone last month. ✓

Is the answer stated in the correct units? Yes, the units are dollars, which is correct. ✓

Choice **A** does not include the overlimit charges. Choice **B** is the overlimit charges only. Choice **D** is the result of treating the 615 minutes as overlimit charges and not adding in the $29.99.

49. C. Two steps are needed to solve the problem: First, find the basketball player's height in feet. Then, find the difference between the basketball player's height and the height of the basketball hoop.

Step 1. Change the basketball player's height to feet:

The Mathematics Reference Sheet shows 3 feet = 36 inches. You can write this fact as $\frac{3 \text{ ft}}{36 \text{ in.}}$ and reduce to obtain $\frac{1 \text{ ft.}}{12 \text{ in.}}$ as one of your conversion fractions and $\frac{12 \text{ in.}}{1 \text{ ft}}$ as your other conversion fraction.

Write your measurement as a fraction with denominator 1 and let unit analysis tell you whether to multiply by $\frac{1 \text{ ft}}{12 \text{ in.}}$ or $\frac{12 \text{ in.}}{1 \text{ ft}}$. Since you want the inches to divide out, multiply by $\frac{1 \text{ ft}}{12 \text{ in.}}$.

$$\frac{75 \text{ in.}}{1} \times \frac{1 \text{ ft}}{12 \text{ in.}} = \frac{75 \text{ ft}}{12} = 6.25 \text{ feet}$$

Step 2. Subtract to find the difference between the basketball player's height and the height of the basketball hoop:

10 feet – 6.25 feet = 3.75 feet.

The distance in feet between the top of the player's head and the basketball hoop is 3.75 feet, Choice **C**.

Did I answer the question? Yes, I found the distance in feet between the top of the player's head and the basketball hoop. ✓

Is the answer stated in the correct units? Yes, the units are feet, which is correct. ✓

Choice **A** results if you use 1 foot = 10 inches, instead of 12 inches. Choice **B** results if you subtract incorrectly. Choice **D** results if you stop at Step 1 and incorrectly use the basketball player's height as your solution to the problem.

50. B. By glancing at the answer choices, you can see that to answer the question, you must add up the total number of hours and minutes, and then simplify the results, if needed. Three steps are needed to solve the problem:

Step 1. Add up the total time in hours and minutes:

> 1 hour, 44 minutes
> 2 hours, 32 minutes
> 3 hours, 76 minutes

Step 2. Change 76 minutes to hours and minutes:

The Mathematics Reference Sheet shows 1 hour = 60 minutes, so 76 minutes = 1 hour and 16 minutes.

Step 3. Add the 1 hour and 16 minutes to 3 hours.

> 3 hours, 76 minutes = 3 hours + 1 hour 16 minutes = 4 hours 16 minutes.

The total amount of time Carlos spent playing video games last weekend is 4 hours 16 minutes, Choice **B**.

Did I answer the question? Yes, I found the total amount of time Carlos spent playing video games last weekend. ✓

Is the answer stated in the correct units? Yes, the units are hours and minutes, which is correct. ✓

Choices **A** and **D** result if you add incorrectly in Step 3. Choice **C** occurs if you add incorrectly in Step 1.

51. A. First sketch a diagram to illustrate the problem:

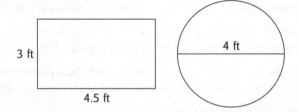

Three steps are needed to solve the problem: First, find the area of the rectangular table; next, find the area of the circular table; and then find the difference between the two areas.

Step 1. Find the area of the rectangular table:

The Mathematics Reference Sheet shows the formula for the area of a rectangle is $A = lw$.

$$A = lw = 4.5 \text{ ft} \cdot 3 \text{ ft} = 13.5 \text{ ft}^2$$

Step 2. Find the area of the circular table:

The Mathematics Reference Sheet shows the formula for the area of a circle is $A = \pi r^2$. You are given the diameter of the circular table is 4 feet. The radius is half the diameter, or 2 feet.

$$A = \pi r^2 = \pi(2 \text{ ft})^2 = 3.14(4 \text{ ft}^2) = 12.56 \text{ ft}^2$$

Step 3. Find the difference between the two areas:

> $13.5 \text{ ft}^2 - 12.56 \text{ ft}^2 = 0.94 \text{ ft}^2$.

The area of the circular table will be 0.94 ft² less than the area of the rectangular table.

Did I answer the question? Yes, I found how much less the area of the circular table will be than the area of the rectangular table. ✓

Is the answer stated in the correct units? Yes, the units are square feet, which is correct. ✓

Choice **B** is the area of the circular table, not the difference in the two areas. Choice **C** is the sum of the two areas, not the difference. Choice **D** results if you use 4 feet for the radius in finding the area of the circular table.

52. B. First, sketch a diagram to illustrate the problem:

$P = 50$ ft

$A = ?$ 7 ft

$l = ?$

The garden has a rectangular shape. The Mathematics Reference Sheet shows the formula for the area of a rectangle is $A = lw$. You are given that the width of the garden is 7 feet, but you do not know the length of the garden. You will need to find the length of the garden before you can find its area. Two steps are needed to solve the problem: First, find the length of the garden using the information given about its perimeter. Then, find the area of the garden using the formula, $A = lw$.

Step 1. Find the length of the garden:

The formula for the perimeter of a rectangle is $P = 2l + 2w$. The perimeter, P, is 50 feet. The width, w, is 7 feet. Let l equal the length of the rectangle in feet.

$P = 2l + 2w$	
$50 \text{ ft} = 2l + 2(7 \text{ ft})$	Substitute 50 ft for P and 7 ft for w. Solve for l, omitting the units for convenience.
$50 = 2l + 14$	Multiply $2(7) = 14$.
$50 - 14 = 2l + 14 - 14$	Subtract 14 from both sides of the equation.
$36 = 2l$	
$\dfrac{36}{2} = \dfrac{2l}{2}$	Divide both sides of the equation by 2.
$18 = l$	

The length of the rectangle is 18 feet.

Step 2. Find the area of the rectangular garden:

$A = lw = 18 \text{ ft} \cdot 7 \text{ ft} = 126 \text{ ft}^2$

The area of the garden is 126 ft^2, Choice **B.**

Did I answer the question? Yes, I found the area of the garden. ✓

Is the answer stated in the correct units? Yes, the units are square feet, which is correct. ✓

Choice **A** results if you stop at step 1 and incorrectly use your solution to the equation as the area of the garden. Choice **C** results if you mistakenly confuse perimeter with area. Choice **D** results if you incorrectly compute the area of the garden by multiplying 50 feet by 7 feet.

53. B. First, sketch a diagram to illustrate the problem:

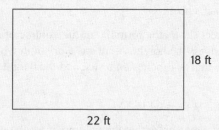

18 ft

22 ft

Square yards are units of area, so you will need to find the area of the carpet in square yards. Two steps are needed to solve the problem: First, convert the dimensions of the floor to yards. Next, find the area of the floor in square yards.

Step 1. Convert the dimensions of the floor to yards:

The Mathematics Reference Sheet shows 1 yard = 3 feet. You can write this fact as $\frac{3 \text{ ft}}{1 \text{ yd}}$ or as $\frac{1 \text{ yd}}{3 \text{ ft}}$.

Write your measurements as fractions with denominator 1 and let unit analysis tell you whether to multiply by $\frac{3 \text{ ft}}{1 \text{ yd}}$ or $\frac{1 \text{ yd}}{3 \text{ ft}}$. Since you want the feet to divide out, multiply by $\frac{1 \text{ yd}}{3 \text{ ft}}$.

$$\frac{22 \text{ ft}}{1} \times \frac{1 \text{ yd}}{3 \text{ ft}} = \frac{22 \text{ yd}}{3} = 7\frac{1}{3} \text{ yd}$$

$$\frac{18 \text{ ft}}{1} \times \frac{1 \text{ yd}}{3 \text{ ft}} = \frac{18 \text{ ft}}{3} = 6 \text{ yd}$$

Step 2. Find the area of the floor:

The Mathematics Reference Sheet shows the formula for the area of a rectangle is $A = lw$.

$$A = lw = 7\frac{1}{3} \text{ yd} \cdot 6 \text{ yd} = \frac{22 \text{ yd}}{3} \cdot 6 \text{ yd} = 44 \text{ yd}^2$$

At least 44 yd² of carpet are needed to cover the floor, Choice **B**.

Did I answer the question? Yes, I found how many square yards of carpet are needed to cover the floor. ✓

Is the answer stated in the correct units? Yes, the units are square yards, which is correct. ✓

Choice **A** results if you stop at Step 1 and incorrectly use your solution to the equation as the area of the garden. Choice **C** results if you mistakenly confuse perimeter with area. Choice **D** results if you incorrectly compute the area of the garden by multiplying 50 feet by 7 feet.

54. D. First, sketch a diagram to illustrate the problem:

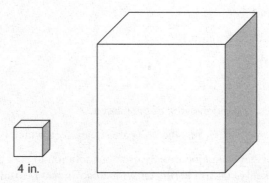

4 in.

Two steps are needed to solve the problem: First, find the volume of one 4-inch cube. Then, find the volume of the crate by multiplying the volume of one 4-inch cube by 81.

Step 1. Find the volume of one 4-inch cube:

The Mathematics Reference Sheet shows the formula for the volume of a prism is $V = Bh$, where B is the area of the base of the prism and h is the height. A cube is a prism in which all edges have the same length. A 4-inch cube has a square base that is 4 inches on a side and the height of the cube is 4 inches. The volume of the 4-inch cube is

$$V_{\text{cube}} = Bh = s \cdot s \cdot h = 4 \text{ in.} \cdot 4 \text{ in.} \cdot 4 \text{ in.} = 64 \text{ in.}^3$$

Tip: It might be easier for you to just memorize that the volume of a cube is $V = s^3$, where s is the length of an edge of the cube.

Step 2. Find the volume of the crate:

It takes 81 cubes to fill the crate, so the volume of the crate is

$V_{crate} = 81 \cdot$ (volume of one cube) $= 81 \cdot 64$ in.$^3 = 5184$ in.^{3}, Choice **D**.

Did I answer the question? Yes, I found the volume of the crate. ✓

Is the answer stated in the correct units? Yes, the units are cubic inches, which is correct. ✓

Choice **A** results if you stop at step 1 and mistakenly use the volume of one 4-inch cube as the volume of the crate. Choice **C** results if you mistakenly use the number of cubes in the crate as its volume in cubic inches. Choice **D** results if you make a computation error in step 2.

55. B. First, sketch a diagram to illustrate the problem:

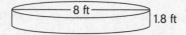

The Mathematics Reference Sheet shows the formula for the volume of a cylinder is $V = Bh$, where B is the area of the base of the cylinder and h is the height. The base of the cylinder is a circle. The Mathematics Reference Sheet shows the area of a circle is πr^2. The diameter of the cylinder is 8 feet. The radius of the circle is half the diameter, or 4 feet. The volume of the cylinder is

$V = Bh = \pi r^2 h = 3.14(4 \text{ ft})^2 \cdot 1.8 \text{ ft.} = 90.432 \text{ ft}^3$

The volume of the cube is approximately 90 ft^3, Choice **B**.

Choices **A** and **C** result if you use an incorrect formula for the volume of a cylinder. Choice **D** results if you make the error of using 8 feet, instead of 4 feet, as the radius of the cylinder's base.

56. A. First, sketch a diagram to illustrate the problem:

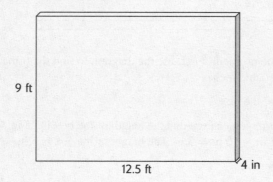

Cubic feet are units of volume. The amount of cement in the slab is equal to the volume of the slab, which is a rectangular prism. Two steps are needed to solve the problem: First, convert 4 inches to feet because the question asks for the number of cubic feet of cement. Then, find the volume of the slab in cubic feet.

Step 1: Convert 4 inches to feet:

The Mathematics Reference Sheet shows 3 feet = 36 inches. You can write this fact as $\frac{3 \text{ ft}}{36 \text{ in.}}$ and reduce to obtain $\frac{1 \text{ ft}}{12 \text{ in.}}$ as one of your conversion fractions and $\frac{12 \text{ in.}}{1 \text{ ft}}$ as your other conversion fraction.

Write your measurement as a fraction with denominator 1 and let unit analysis tell you whether to multiply by $\frac{1 \text{ ft}}{12 \text{ in.}}$ or $\frac{12 \text{ in.}}{1 \text{ ft}}$. Since you want the inches to divide out, multiply by $\frac{1 \text{ ft}}{12 \text{ in.}}$.

$\frac{4 \text{ in.}}{1} \times \frac{1 \text{ ft}}{12 \text{ in.}} = \frac{4 \text{ ft}}{12} = \frac{1}{3} \text{ ft}$

Step 2: Find the volume of the slab:

The Mathematics Reference Sheet shows the formula for the volume of a prism is $V = Bh$, where B is the area of the base of the prism and h is the height. The base of the prism is a rectangle. The Mathematics Reference Sheet shows the formula for the area of a rectangle is $A = lw$. The volume of the cement is

$$V = Bh = lw \cdot h = 12.5 \text{ ft} \cdot 9 \text{ ft} \cdot \frac{1}{3} \text{ ft} = 37.5 \text{ ft}^3$$

Tip: It might be easier for you to just memorize that the volume of a rectangular prism is $V = lwh$, where l is the length, w is the width, and h is the height of the rectangular prism.

There are 37.5 ft³ of cement in the slab, Choice **A.**

Did I answer the question? Yes, I found how many cubic feet of cement are in the slab. ✓

Is the answer stated in the correct units? Yes, the units are cubic feet, which is correct. ✓

Choice **B** results if you use an incorrect formula for the volume of a rectangular prism. Choice **C** results if you fail to change 4 inches to $\frac{1}{3}$ ft. Choice **D** results if you place the decimal point incorrectly when computing the volume.

57. D. Label the dimensions on the diagram:

5-inch squares are cut out on each corner.

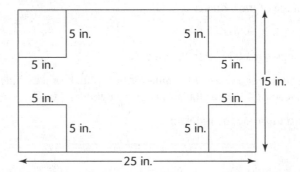

Two steps are need to solve the problem: First, use the diagram to find the dimensions of the box in inches. Next, find the volume of the box in cubic inches.

Step 1: Find the dimensions of the box.

From the preceding diagram, you can see that the length of the box is 25 in. –2(5 in.) = 25 in. – 10 in. = 15 in. The width of the box is 15 in. – 10 in. = 5 in. The height of the box is 5 in.

Step 2: Find the volume of the box:

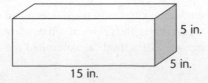

The box is a rectangular prism. The Mathematics Reference Sheet shows the formula for the volume of a prism is $V = Bh$, where B is the area of the base of the prism and h is the height. The base of the prism is a rectangle. The Mathematics Reference Sheet shows the formula for the area of a rectangle is $A = lw$. The volume of the box is

$$V = Bh = lw \cdot h = 15 \text{ in.} \cdot 5 \text{ in.} \cdot 5 \text{ in.} = 375 \text{ in.}^3$$

Tip: It might be easier for you to just memorize that the volume of a rectangular prism is $V = lwh$, where l is the length, w is the width, and h is the height of the rectangular prism.

The volume of the box is 375 in.³, Choice **D.**

Did I answer the question? Yes, I found the volume of the box. ✓

Is the answer stated in the correct units? Yes, the units are cubic inches, which is correct. ✓

The other choices result if you determine incorrect measurements for the dimensions of the box.

58. D. First, sketch a diagram to illustrate the problem. Of course, you can't draw it exactly to scale, but the sketch will help you "see" the situation:

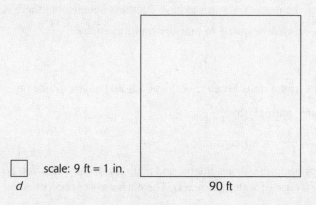

scale: 9 ft = 1 in.

d

90 ft

Let *d* = the distance between bases in the scale model. The scale model and the baseball diamond can be represented with two squares. The squares are similar figures, so the measurements of their corresponding sides are proportional. Write a proportion and solve it.

The ratio of the distance between bases in the actual baseball diamond to the distance between bases in the model is $\frac{9 \text{ ft}}{1 \text{ in.}}$.

$$\frac{\text{distance between bases of actual baseball diamond}}{\text{distance between bases in model}} = \frac{9 \text{ ft}}{1 \text{ in.}}$$

Plug in the values from your diagram. Be sure to check that the units match up correctly.

$$\frac{90 \text{ ft}}{d \, (\text{in.})} = \frac{9 \text{ ft}}{1 \text{ in.}}$$ Check: Both ratios have feet in the numerator and inches in the denominator.

For convenience, omit the units while you solve the proportion:

$$\frac{90}{d} = \frac{9}{1}$$

Multiply 90 by 1 and then divide by 9:

$$\frac{90 \times 1}{9} = 10 \text{ in.}$$

The distance between bases in the scale model is 10 inches, Choice **D.**

Did I answer the question? Yes, I found the distance between bases in the scale model. ✓

Is the answer stated in the correct units? Yes, the units are inches, which is correct. ✓

Choices **A** and **B** result if you make a computation error when solving the proportion. Choice **C** results if you set up the proportion incorrectly.

59. D. Three conversion facts from the Mathematics Reference Sheet are needed to solve the problem:

1 pint = 2 cups, 1 quart = 2 pints, and 1 gallon = 4 quarts. From these three facts, you get six conversion fractions:

$\frac{1 \text{ pt}}{2 \text{ c}}$ and $\frac{2 \text{ c}}{1 \text{ pt}}$, $\frac{1 \text{ qt}}{2 \text{ pt}}$ and $\frac{2 \text{ pt}}{1 \text{ qt}}$, and $\frac{1 \text{ gal}}{4 \text{ qt}}$ and $\frac{4 \text{ qt}}{1 \text{ gal}}$.

Write your measurement as a fraction with denominator 1 and let unit analysis tell you which conversion fractions to multiply by, keeping in mind that you want cups as your final units:

$\dfrac{5 \text{ gal}}{1} \times ?$ There are only two conversion fractions that involve gallons: $\dfrac{1 \text{ gal}}{4 \text{ qt}}$ and $\dfrac{4 \text{ qt}}{1 \text{ gal}}$. Since you want the gallons to divide out, multiply by $\dfrac{4 \text{ qt}}{1 \text{ gal}}$.

$\dfrac{5 \text{ gal}}{1} \times \dfrac{4 \text{ qt}}{1 \text{ gal}}$

This product has quarts as the units. You want to have cups as the units, but there is no conversion fraction that involves quarts and cups, so change quarts to pints by multiplying by $\dfrac{2 \text{ pt}}{1 \text{ qt}}$:

$\dfrac{5 \text{ gal}}{1} \times \dfrac{4 \text{ qt}}{1 \text{ gal}} \times \dfrac{2 \text{ pt}}{1 \text{ qt}}$

Now the product has pints as the units because both gallons and quarts divide out.

To change the pints to cups, multiply by $\dfrac{2 \text{ c}}{1 \text{ pt}}$:

$\dfrac{5 \text{ gal}}{1} \times \dfrac{4 \text{ qt}}{1 \text{ gal}} \times \dfrac{2 \text{ pt}}{1 \text{ qt}} \times \dfrac{2 \text{ c}}{1 \text{ pt}} = 80 \text{ cups}$

The final answer is in cups because gallons, quarts, and pints divide out when you do the multiplication. A 5-gallon container of water holds 80 cups of water, Choice **D.** The other answer choices occur if you use incorrect conversion facts or fractions.

60. **B. Method 1:** Use the conversion fact, 1 kilometer = 1000 meters, from the Mathematics Reference Sheet to obtain two conversion fractions: $\dfrac{1 \text{ km}}{1000 \text{ m}}$ and $\dfrac{1000 \text{ m}}{1 \text{ km}}$.

Write your measurement as a fraction with denominator 1 and let unit analysis tell you whether to multiply by $\dfrac{1 \text{ km}}{1000 \text{ m}}$ or $\dfrac{1000 \text{ m}}{1 \text{ km}}$. Since you want the meters to divide out, multiply by $\dfrac{1 \text{ km}}{1000 \text{ m}}$.

$\dfrac{12500 \text{ m}}{1} \times \dfrac{1 \text{ km}}{1000 \text{ m}} = \dfrac{12500 \text{ km}}{1000} = 12.5 \text{ km}$

Method 2: Use "**K**ing **H**enry **D**oesn't **U**sually **D**rink **C**hocolate **M**ilk," which is a mnemonic for remembering the following metric prefixes:

kilo-, hecto-, deca-, unit measurement, deci-, centi-, milli-

In this problem, the unit measurement is meters. You are going from meters to kilometers. Since to go from meters to kilometers you move left three times on the list above, you will divide by 10 three times to convert meters to kilometers. Of course, dividing by 10 three times is equivalent to dividing by 1000 one time. Therefore,

12 500 m = 12500 ÷ 1000 (3 moves) = 12.5 km

The runner ran 12.5 kilometers in the race, Choice **B.**

The other choices occur if you make a mistake in placing the decimal point in your answer.

61. **B.** Mark on the diagram. Draw a box at B to represent a right angle.

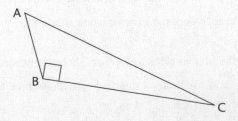

An obtuse angle measures more than 90° but less than 180°. The angle shown at B is greater than 90° but less than 180°. It is obtuse, Choice **B.** An acute angle measures more than 0° but less than 90°. The angles at A and C are acute (Choice **A**). A right angle (Choice **C**) measures 90°. No right angles are shown. A straight angle (Choice **D**) measures 180°. No straight angles are shown.

62. **D.** The sum of the measures of the three interior angles of a triangle always equals 180°. Check the answer choices to find the one that satisfies this requirement.

Checking **A:** 30° + 50° + 80° = 160° ≠ 180°, wrong.

Checking **B:** You should eliminate this choice by sight since 100° + 200° = 300° > 180°.

Checking **C:** 120° + 50° + 20° = 190° ≠ 180°, wrong.

Checking **D:** 40° + 50° + 90° = 180°, correct.

63. **D.** The Mathematics Reference Sheet shows the circumference of a circle is equal to the product of π and the diameter of the circle: $C = \pi d$. To find the diameter, plug in 48 inches for C and 3.14 for π and solve for d:

$C = \pi d$

48 in. = 3.14d

$\dfrac{48 \text{ in.}}{3.14} = \dfrac{3.14d}{3.14}$ Divide both sides of the equation by 3.14.

$\dfrac{48 \text{ in.}}{3.14} = d$, Choice **D.**

Choices **A** and **B** result if you solve the equation incorrectly. Choice **C** results if you use an incorrect formula for the circumference of a circle.

64. **B.** The coordinates of point P are (–3, 2). The x-coordinate of the new point is 5 units to the right of –3. The number 2 is 5 units to the right of –3. The x-coordinate of the new point is 2. The y-coordinate of point P is 2. The y-coordinate of the new point is 6 units down from point P. The number –4 is 6 units down from 2. The y-coordinate of the new point is –4. The coordinates of the new point are (2, –4), Choice **B.** Choice **A** occurs if you calculate the new y-coordinate incorrectly. Choice **C** occurs if you calculate both new coordinates incorrectly. Choice **D** occurs if you calculate the x-coordinate incorrectly.

65. **A.** Examine the diagram. Note that $AB//DC$ means AB is parallel to DC and $AD//BC$ means AD is parallel to BC.

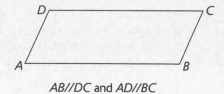

AB//DC and AD//BC

A parallelogram is a quadrilateral that has opposite sides parallel. The figure shown is a parallelogram, Choice **A.** Choices **B** and **C** are incorrect because rectangles and squares are parallelograms that have four right interior angles. The angles in the figure shown are not right angles. Choice **D** is incorrect because a trapezoid is a quadrilateral in which only one pair of opposite sides is parallel.

66. **A.** A figure has a horizontal line of symmetry if it can be folded horizontally into two congruent halves. A figure has a vertical line of symmetry if it can be folded vertically into two congruent halves. The letter **H** is the only letter shown that has both a vertical and a horizontal line of symmetry, Choice **A.** The choices **B** and **C** are incorrect because the letters **A** and **W** have vertical lines of symmetry, but not horizontal lines of symmetry. Choice **D** is incorrect because the letter **N** does not have a line of symmetry.

67. B. First, sketch a diagram to illustrate the problem:

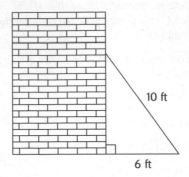

Since the ladder and the wall of the building form a right triangle, use the Pythagorean Theorem to find the length of the missing side. Let *b* represent the distance from the base of the wall to the top of the ladder. This distance is the length of the missing leg of the right triangle. The length (10 feet) of the ladder is the length of the hypotenuse, *c*, of the right triangle. The length of the known leg, *a*, of the triangle is 6 feet. Substitute these values into the Pythagorean Theorem, omitting the units for convenience:

$$a^2 + b^2 = c^2$$

$$6^2 + b^2 = 10^2$$

$$36 + b^2 = 100$$

$$36 + b^2 - 36 = 100 - 36 \qquad \text{Subtract 36 from both sides.}$$

$$b^2 = 64$$

$$\sqrt{b^2} = \sqrt{64} \qquad \text{Take the square root of both sides.}$$

$$b = 8 \text{ feet.}$$

The ladder reaches 8 feet up the wall, Choice **B.**

Did I answer the question? Yes, I found how high up the side of the building the ladder reaches. ✓

Is the answer stated in the correct units? Yes, the units are feet, which is correct. ✓

Choice **A** results if you mistakenly decide to solve the problem by finding the difference between the lengths of the hypotenuse and the known leg to find the length of the missing leg. Choice **B** results if you mistakenly use the length of the hypotenuse as the length of the unknown leg. Choice **D** results if you mistakenly decide to solve the problem by adding the lengths of the hypotenuse and known leg to find the length of the missing leg.

68. A. Mark on the diagram.

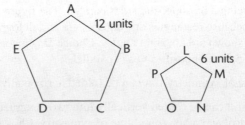

Since *ABCDE* and *LMNOP* are regular pentagons, they are similar figures. In similar figures corresponding sides are proportional. The ratio of proportionality of the sides of *ABCDE* to *LMNOP* is $\dfrac{12 \text{ units}}{6 \text{ units}} = \dfrac{2}{1}$. In other words, the length of each side of *ABCDE* is twice the length of its corresponding side in *LMNOP*. The scale factor is 2. Therefore, the ratio of the perimeter of *ABCDE* to *LMNOP* = $\dfrac{5(12 \text{ units})}{5(6 \text{ units})} = \dfrac{12}{6} = \dfrac{2}{1}$ or 2:1, Choice **A.**

69. C. First, sketch a diagram to illustrate the problem:

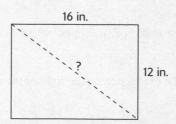

The television screen can be modeled by a 16 inch by 12 inch rectangle. The diagonal divides the rectangle into two right triangles, with legs 16 inches and 12 inches in length. The diagonal is opposite the right angle, so it is the hypotenuse of the right triangle. Use the Pythagorean Theorem to find the length of the diagonal. Let c represent the diagonal. Substitute 16 inches for a and 12 inches for b into the formula and solve for c:

$$a^2 + b^2 = c^2$$
$$(16 \text{ in})^2 + (12 \text{in})^2 = c^2$$
$$256 \text{ in}^2 + 144 \text{ in}^2 = 400 \text{ in}^2$$
$$400 \text{ in}^2 = c^2$$
$$= \sqrt{400 \text{ in}^2} = \sqrt{c^2}$$
$$20 \text{ in.} = c$$

The size of the television is 20 inches, Choice **C**.

Did I answer the question? Yes, I found the size of the television. ✓

Is the answer stated in the correct units? Yes, the units are inches, which is correct. ✓

Choice **A** is the incorrect result of using the width of the television as its size. Choice **B** is the incorrect result of using the length of the television as its size. Choice **D** is the incorrect result of using the sum of the length and width of the television as its size.

70. A. To solve the problem, you must answer the question: 108 is r% of 120?

Method 1: To solve the problem, identify the elements of the percent problem, plug the values into the percent proportion, and solve the proportion:

Step 1. Identify the elements.

$$r = ?$$
$$\text{part} = 108$$
$$\text{whole} = 120$$

Step 2. Plug into the percent proportion (omitting the units for convenience).

$$\frac{r}{100} = \frac{108}{120}$$

Step 3. Solve the proportion (omitting the units for convenience).

Multiply 108 by 100 (a cross product you can calculate), and then divide by 120 (the numerical term you didn't use):

$$r = \frac{108 \times 100}{120} = 90, \quad \frac{90}{100} = 90\%$$

Of the 120 fans at the game, 90% were players' parents, Choice **A**.

Did I answer the question? Yes, I found the percent of the fans who were players' parents. ✓

Is the answer stated in the correct units? No units are needed for the answer. ✓

Method 2: Write an equation and solve it:

Let $R = r\%$

$108 = R$ times 120   Hint: The word "of" is "times" when it occurs between two numbers.

$108 = R120$

For convenience, you should rewrite the expression on the right of the equation as $120R$:

$108 = 120R$

You are solving for R, so divide both sides of the equation by 120, the coefficient of R:

$$\frac{108}{120} = \frac{120r}{120}$$

$$0.9 = R$$

Change 0.9 to a percent by moving the decimal point two places to the right and adding a percent sign:

$R = 90\%$, Choice **A.**

Choices **A** and **D** result if you make a decimal point mistake. Choice **C** is the percent of fans who were not players' parents.

71. **B.** Mark on the diagram. Draw a line segment connecting the points $T(5, -2)$ and $U(3, 2)$. Mark the midpoint of the line segment.

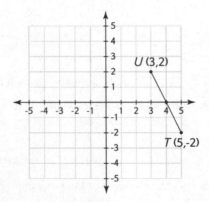

The Mathematics Reference Sheet gives the formula for the midpoint between two points (x_1, y_1) and (x_2, y_2) as $\left(\frac{x_1 + x_2}{2}, \frac{y_1 + y_2}{2}\right)$. To find the midpoint between $(5, -2)$ and $(3, 2)$, let $x_1 = 5$, $y_1 = -2$, $x_2 = 3$, and $y_2 = 2$. Then plug into the formula:

$$\left(\frac{x_1 + x_2}{2}, \frac{y_1 + y_2}{2}\right) = \left(\frac{5 + 3}{2}, \frac{-2 + 2}{2}\right) = \left(\frac{8}{2}, \frac{0}{2}\right) = (4, 0)$$

The midpoint between the points T and U has coordinates $(4, 0)$, Choice **B.** Choice **A** results if you switch the x and y values. Choices **C** and **D** result if you make an error in computing the coordinates for the midpoint.

72. **A.** Substitute into the expression, being sure to enclose the substituted values in parentheses:

$x - y = (-5) - (-13) = -5 + 13 = 8$, Choice **A.**

Choice **B** occurs if you make a sign error. Choices **C** and **D** result if you deal with the subtraction incorrectly.

73. A. Mark on the diagram. Draw a line segment connecting the points $R(2, -2)$ and $S(3, 4)$.

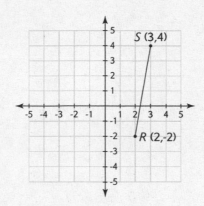

The Mathematics Reference Sheet gives the formula for the distance between two points (x_1, y_1) and (x_2, y_2) as $\sqrt{(x_2 - x_1)^2 + (y_2 - y_1)^2}$. To find the distance between $(2, -2)$ and $(3, 4)$ let $x_1 = 2$, $y_1 = -2$, $x_2 = 3$, and $y_2 = 4$. Then plug into the formula:

$$\sqrt{(x_2 - x_1)^2 + (y_2 - y_1)^2} = \sqrt{(2-3)^2 + (-2-4)^2} = \sqrt{(-1)^2 + (-6)^2} = \sqrt{1 + 36} = \sqrt{37}$$

The distance between the points R and S is $\sqrt{37}$ units, Choice **A**. Choices **B, C,** and **D** result if you make a computation error.

74. D. The expression 4 less than 5 times x is written symbolically as $5x - 4$. The sentence 4 less than $5x$ is 6 is written symbolically as $5x - 4 = 6$, Choice **D**. Choice **A** is incorrect because $4 - 5x$ is 5 times x less than 4, not 4 less than 5 times x. Choice **B** is incorrect because $4x - 5$ is 5 less than 4 times x, not 4 less than 5 times x. Choice **C** occurs if you make a simplification error.

75. B. $-2x - 5 = 3x + 15$

$-2x - 5 - 3x = 3x + 15 - 3x$ Subtract $3x$ from both sides of the equation.

$-5x - 5 = 15$

$-5x - 5 + 5 = 15 + 5$ Add 5 to both sides of the equation.

$-5x = 20$

$\dfrac{-5x}{-5} = \dfrac{20}{-5}$ Divide both sides of the equation by -5.

$x = -4$, Choice **B**.

Check your answer by substituting -4 for x into the equation:

$-2x - 5 = 3x + 15$

$-2(-4) - 5 \overset{?}{=} 3(-4) + 15$

$8 - 5 \overset{?}{=} -12 + 15$

$3 \overset{\checkmark}{=} 3$

Choice **A** is incorrect because substituting -20 for x in the equation gives:

$-2x - 5 = 3x + 15$

$-2(-20) - 5 \overset{?}{=} 3(-20) + 15$

$40 - 5 \overset{?}{=} -60 + 15$

$35 \neq -45$

Choice **C** is incorrect because substituting 2 for x in the equation gives:

$$-2x - 5 = 3x + 15$$
$$-2(2) - 5 \stackrel{?}{=} 3(2) + 15$$
$$-4 - 5 \stackrel{?}{=} 6 + 15$$
$$-9 \neq 21$$

Choice **D** is incorrect because substituting 4 for x in the equation gives:

$$-2x - 5 = 3x + 15$$
$$-2(4) - 5 \stackrel{?}{=} 3(4) + 15$$
$$-8 - 5 \stackrel{?}{=} 12 + 15$$
$$-13 \neq 27$$

Another way to work this problem is to check the answer choices, rather than solve the equation—a smart test-taking strategy for multiple-choice math tests. Substitute each answer choice into the equation and whichever choice makes the equation a true statement is the correct response.

76. A. To determine which ordered pair satisfies the system, you will need to find the ordered pair that makes *both* equations true. Check each ordered pair by substituting the x and y values into the two equations, being careful to enclose the substituted values in parentheses.

Checking **A:** $x + 2y = (5) + 2(-3) = 5 + -6 = -1$. ✓. Since $(5,-3)$ works in the first equation, try it in the second equation. $3x - 4y = 3(5) - 4(-3) = 15 + 12 = 27$ ✓. Choice **A** is the correct response because the ordered pair $(5,-3)$ makes both equations true.

It is not necessary to check the other choices since you know that Choice **A** is the correct response.

Choice **B** is incorrect because $x + 2y = (-3) + 2(-5) = -3 + -10 = -13 \neq -1$.

Choice **C** is incorrect because $x + 2y = (-5) + 2(3) = -5 + 6 = 1 \neq -1$.

Choice **D** is incorrect because $x + 2y = (3) + 2(5) = 3 + 10 = 13 \neq -1$.

77. B. Mark on the diagram. Draw a line connecting the points $T(4, -3)$ and $U(1, 2)$.

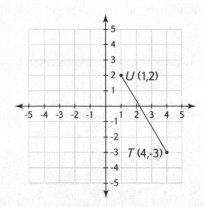

The Mathematics Reference Sheet gives the formula for the slope of the line between two points (x_1, y_1) and (x_2, y_2) as *slope of line* $= \frac{y_2 - y_1}{x_2 - x_1}$. To find the slope of the line between $(4, -3)$ and $(1, 2)$, let $x_1 = 4$, $y_1 = -3$, $x_2 = 1$, and $y_2 = 2$. Then plug into the formula:

$$\frac{y_2 - y_1}{x_2 - x_1} = \frac{2 - (-3)}{1 - 4} = \frac{2 + 3}{-3} = \frac{5}{-3} = \frac{2 + 3}{-3} = -\frac{5}{3}, \text{ Choice } \mathbf{B}.$$

Choice **A** occurs if you make the mistake of putting the difference in the x values in the numerator and the difference in the y values in the denominator. Choice **C** results if you subtract incorrectly. Choice **D** results if you make a sign error.

78. D. Rewrite the expression using parentheses for x:

$$3(\ )^3 - (\ )^2 + 5$$

Plug 2 inside the parentheses and evaluate, being sure to follow PE(MD)(AS):

$$3(2)^3 - (2)^2 + 5 = 3 \cdot 8 - 4 + 5 = \quad \text{There are no operations to do in parentheses, so first do the exponentiation.}$$

Hint: The term $3(2)^3$ is not 6^3. Also, do not square the $-$ sign in $-(2)^2$. Remember, an exponent applies only to the number immediately to its left.

$$= 24 - 4 + 5 = \quad \text{Next, do multiplication and division, from left to right.}$$

$$= 25 \quad \text{Finally, do addition and subtraction, from left to right.}$$

Thus, $3(2)^3 - (2)^2 + 5 = 25$, Choice **D**.

Choice **A** occurs if you incorrectly evaluate by squaring the $-$ sign before $(2)^2$ and multiplying 3 times 2 in $3(2)^3$ before applying the exponent. Choice **B** occurs if you make the mistake of multiplying 3 times 2 in $3(2)^3$ before applying the exponent. Choice **C** occurs if you square the $-$ sign before $(2)^2$.

79. D. Solve $4(x - 8) = 24$

$$4x - 32 = 24 \quad \text{Use the distributive property to remove parentheses. Be sure to multiply the 8 by 4, too.}$$

$$4x - 32 + 32 = 24 + 32 \quad \text{Add 32 to both sides of the equation.}$$

$$4x = 56$$

$$\frac{4x}{4} = \frac{56}{4} \quad \text{Divide both sides of the equation by 4.}$$

$$x = 14, \text{Choice } \mathbf{D}.$$

Choice **A** results if you subtract 32 from both sides of $4x - 32 = 24$, instead of adding 32. Choice **B** results if you fail to remove the parentheses correctly and you make a subtraction error. Choice **C** results if you obtain $4x - 8$ when removing the parentheses in $4(x - 8)$, instead of $4x - 32$.

80. C. Mark on the diagram.

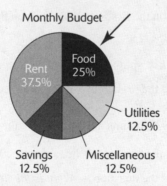

From the pie chart, you can see that 25% of the monthly salary is budgeted for food. To answer the question, you must find 25% of $2800.

Method 1: Identify the elements of the percent problem, plug the values into the percent proportion, and solve the proportion:

Step 1. Identify the elements.

$$r = 25$$

$$\text{part} = ?$$

$$\text{whole} = \$2800$$

Step 2. Plug into the percent proportion (omitting the units for convenience).

$$\frac{25}{100} = \frac{x}{2800}$$

Step 3. Solve the proportion (omitting the units for convenience).

Multiply 25 times 2800 (a cross product you can calculate), and then divide by 100 (the numerical term you didn't use):

$$\frac{25 \times 2800}{100} = \$700$$

The amount budgeted for food is \$700, Choice **C.**

Did I answer the question? Yes, I found the amount budgeted for food. ✓

Is the answer stated in the correct units? Yes, the units are dollars, which is correct. ✓

Method 2: Change 25% to a decimal fraction or common fraction and multiply:

25% of \$2800 = 0.25 × \$2800 = \$700.00

$$25\% \text{ of } \$2800 = \frac{1}{4} \times \$2800 = \frac{\$2800}{4} = \$700$$

Choice **A** results if you make a calculation error. Choice **B** results if you solve the problem incorrectly by finding 12.5% of \$2800. Choice **C** results if you solve the problem incorrectly by finding 25% of \$2800.

81. D. You should eliminate Choice **C** immediately because probabilities cannot be greater than 1. Probabilities are always greater than or equal to 0 and less than or equal to 1. The outcome of the first spin has no effect on the outcome of the second spin. Therefore, this is a compound event made up of two independent events. To find the probability of spinning red on the first spin and green on the second spin, multiply the probabilities of these two events: P(red) · P(green).

First, calculate the probability of spinning red on the first spin. There are four red sections on the spinner, out of a total of 10 sections: P(red) = $\frac{4}{10}$

There is one green section on the spinner, out of a total of 10 sections: P(green) = $\frac{1}{10}$

To find the probability of spinning red on the first spin and green on the second spin, multiply the probabilities:

P(red) · P(green) = $\frac{4}{10} \cdot \frac{1}{10} = \frac{4}{100} = \frac{1}{25}$.

The probability of spinning red on the first spin and green on the second spin is $\frac{1}{25}$, Choice **D.**

Did I answer the question? Yes, I found the probability of spinning red on the first spin and green on the second spin. ✓

Is the answer stated in the correct units? No units are required for the answer. ✓

Choices **A** and **B** result if you multiply the two probabilities incorrectly.

82. D. Read the problem carefully. What is the question?—*What is the lowest grade the student can make on the fourth test and still receive a B in the course?* Devise a plan. The average of the student's four test grades must be at least 80. This means the sum of the four test grades divided by 4 must be at least 80.

Method 1. You can find the answer by writing and solving an equation.

Let *x* = the lowest grade the student can make on the fourth test and still have at least an 80 average.

$$\frac{\text{sum of 4 test grades}}{4} = \frac{78 + 91 + 75 + x}{4}$$

Solve $\frac{78 + 91 + 75 + x}{4} = 80$ for *x*

$$\frac{244 + x}{4} = 80 \qquad\qquad \text{Simplify the numerator.}$$

$\frac{4}{1} \cdot \frac{244 + x}{4} = 80 \cdot \frac{4}{1}$ Multiply both sides of the equation by 4 to remove the fraction.

$244 + x = 320$

$244 + x - 244 = 320 - 244$ Subtract 244 from both sides of the equation.

$x = 76$

The lowest grade that will yield an average of at least 80 is 76, Choice **D**.

Did I answer the question? Yes, I found the lowest grade the student can make on the fourth test and still receive a B in the course. ✓

Is the answer stated in the correct units? No units are needed for the answer. ✓

Method 2: Another way to work this problem is to check the answer choices—a smart test-taking strategy for multiple-choice math tests. However, be careful with this problem. Because you have to find the *lowest* test score that will work, you must check all the answer choices even if you find an answer choice that gives an average in the 80s.

Checking **A**: $\dfrac{\text{sum of 4 test grades}}{4} = \dfrac{78 + 91 + 75 + 99}{4} = 85.75$

Checking **B**: $\dfrac{\text{sum of 4 test grades}}{4} = \dfrac{78 + 91 + 75 + 82}{4} = 81.5$

Checking **C**: $\dfrac{\text{sum of 4 test grades}}{4} = \dfrac{78 + 91 + 75 + 80}{4} = 81.0$

Checking **D**: $\dfrac{\text{sum of 4 test grades}}{4} = \dfrac{78 + 91 + 75 + 76}{4} = 80.0$, correct because 76 is the *lowest* grade needed.

The other answer choices are too high.

83. **B.** In an ordered set of numbers, the median is the middle number if there is a middle number; otherwise, the median is the arithmetic average of the two middle numbers. First, put the running times in order from smallest to largest:

61 s, 63 s, 64 s, 64 s, 66 s, 68 s, 69 s, 73 s

Since there is no single middle number, average the two running times, 64 s and 66 s, that are in the middle of the list:

$\dfrac{64 + 66}{2} = \dfrac{130}{2} = 65$.

Mario's median running time is 65 s, Choice **B**.

Did I answer the question? Yes, I found Mario's median running time. ✓

Is the answer stated in the correct units? Yes, the units are seconds, which is correct. ✓

Choice **A** is the mode running time. Choice **C** is the mean running time. Choice **D** results if you forget to put the running times in order first.

84. **D.** This problem is a counting problem. First, decide on how many tasks are involved. The students have three tasks to perform. The first task is to choose a sandwich. After that task, the second task is to select a drink. After that, the third task is to make a chip selection. The number of ways each task can occur does not depend on the outcome of the other tasks. To find the possible combinations for the three tasks, multiply the number of ways the first task can occur by the number of ways the second task can occur by the number of ways the third task can occur:

(number of ways students can select a sandwich) · (number of ways students can select a drink) · (number of ways students can make a chip selection) = $4 \cdot 2 \cdot 3 = 24$ ways.

The students can select from 24 different combinations of sandwiches, drinks, and chips for lunch, Choice **D**.

Did I answer the question? Yes, I found the number of possible combinations that the students can choose from for lunch. ✓

Is the answer stated in the correct units? No units are required for the answer. ✓

Choice **A** is the number of combination of sandwiches and drinks without including the chip selection. Choice **B** occurs if you add the number of ways each task can occur, instead of multiplying. Choice **C** occurs if you multiply incorrectly.

85. A. Check each answer choice to determine which statement is true.

Checking **A:** To decide which set of grades has greater variability, you can look at the range of the two sets. The range of a set of data equals the greatest value minus the least value in the set. The range in the English class is $92 - 56 = 36$. The range in the French class is $84 - 75 = 9$. Since $36 > 9$, Choice **A** is a correct statement.

You would not have to continue checking since you know that **A** is true.

Checking **B:** This choice is incorrect because 9 is not greater than 36.

Checking **C:** You have to calculate the means in the two classes.

The mean in the English class is

$$\frac{75 + 89 + 67 + 56 + 92}{5} = \frac{379}{5} = 75.8$$

The mean in the French class is

$$\frac{75 + 78 + 83 + 84 + 80 + 77}{6} = \frac{477}{6} = 79.5$$

Choice **C** is incorrect because the mean in the English class is not higher than the mean in the French class.

Checking **D:** This choice is incorrect because the means in the two classes are not equal.

General Knowledge Practice Test 1: Reading Skills Answers and Explanations

86. A. Choice **A** is correct. This passage is focused on the topic of *appropriate literature for young readers*. Choice **B** is incorrect because this topic is too general to describe the focus of this passage. Choice **C** is incorrect because it disagrees with the intent of the passage, which is to point out that young people should be encouraged to read books written specifically for young readers. Choice **D** is incorrect because this topic is too narrow to describe the focus of this passage.

87. C. This passage states that teenagers *need to escape from their everyday lives* (Choice **C**). This information is given in the last sentence of the third paragraph. None of the other answer choices are stated in this passage.

88. D. In the first paragraph, the word *travail* most nearly means *tribulation* (Choice **D**), a trial of one's ability to overcome adversity. The words in the other answer choices do not mean the same as the word *travail*.

89. B. The main idea of the third paragraph is given by the statement in Choice **B:** *Many good books written for young readers are available*. The information in Choice **A** is given in the last sentence of the third paragraph, but it is not the main idea of the paragraph. The statement in Choice **C** could be inferred from the second sentence of the third paragraph — particularly, when considered in the context of the whole passage — however, it is not the main idea of the third paragraph. The statement in Choice **D** disagrees with the last sentence of paragraph three, so it is not the main idea of the paragraph.

90. B. According to this passage, Judy Blume is the author of *Are You There God?* (Choice **B**) The other answer choices are incorrect because according to this passage, Paula Danziger is the author of *The Cat Ate My Gymsuit* (Choice **A**), S. E. Hinton is the author of *The* Outsiders (Choice **C**), and Robert Cormier is the author of *The Chocolate War* (Choice **D**).

91. C. According to the passage, the one way in which teenagers can be motivated to read is to provide them with high-interest, young adult novels. This is the main idea of this reading passage. Choice **A** is incorrect because the author emphatically states that introducing non-readers to only classical literature can be counter-productive. Choice **B** is incorrect. Although the author mentions television watching as a high interest for young people, the author does not advocate television watching as a substitute for reading. Choice **D** is incorrect because the author does not discuss the value of providing teenagers with nonfiction.

92. A. As used in the third paragraph, the phrase "escapist fare cloaked in realistic language" best describes *fiction books*. The author of this passage is advocating that young people read books that allow them to escape into both real and imaginary worlds filled with characters and language that is intimately familiar to their own lives. Of all the choices, *fiction books* is the best choice. Choice **B,** non fiction books, is not considered "escapist fare" because nonfiction books are considered stories about actual persons, places, or events. Choice **C,** textbooks, is not considered escapist fare, nor is Choice **D,** autobiographies. Both are incorrect choices.

93. D. The tone of this passage can best be described as *subjective.* The author provides a passionate, yet practical argument for the use of young adult literature with adolescents. Choice **A** is incorrect because the author's tone is not caustic, meaning biting and harsh. Choice **B** is incorrect because the author's tone is not optimistic, but instead, expresses a point of view. Choice **C** is incorrect because the author is not objective, meaning he is without opinion and provides a reasoned argument for both sides of this issue.

94. A. The main idea of the passage is best expressed in the sentence *young adults should be given literature that speaks to their developmental interests.* Clearly, the main idea of this narrative is how adolescents should be reading books that deal with issues and characters that relate to their age and interests. Choice **B** is incorrect because the author does not imply that the purpose of literature for young people is only to inspire good citizenship. Choice **C** is incorrect because the author does not say that young people should read books that discuss traditional family values. Choice **D** is incorrect because the author does not say young people should only read books that are universally recognized as good books.

95. A. The relationship between the two sentences in the second paragraph ("To entice young people. . . , Well intentioned as these informed advocates are . . . ") is that the second sentence clearly expands upon the material presented in the first. Choice **B** is incorrect because the second sentence clarifies the first and does not contradict it. Choice **C** is incorrect because the second sentence does not illustrate the first by providing clear examples of what young adult literature is—the names of specific examples, and so on. Choice **D** is incorrect because the second sentence does not ignore the first, but clarifies it.

96. A. A statement that is implied in the first paragraph is the statement given in Choice **A:** *Religion is an important part of people's lives.* The reader can infer this statement from the third sentence (*For the first two questions, the reasons for humankind's existence and its noble purpose, people of all races and creeds have turned to religion.*) and fourth sentence (*There, amidst ancient myths and modern realities, individuals have found great comfort and joy in the teachings and practices of many of the world's most ancient and revered religious traditions.*) of the first paragraph. The other answer choices are not supported by the information given in the first paragraph.

97. C. An opinion expressed in this passage is the statement given in Choice **C:** *We are fortunate to live in an age of intense exploration.* The word *fortunate* is a judgment word reflecting the author's opinion about living in an age of intense exploration. The word *intense* to describe the level of space exploration might also be debatable. Choice **A** is a statement of fact given in the second sentence of the third paragraph. Choice **B** is a statement of fact given in the third sentence of the third paragraph. Choice **D** is a statement of fact given in the second sentence of the last paragraph.

98. A. In the second paragraph, the word *unprecedented*, meaning unmatched or never achieved before, most nearly means *unparalleled* (Choice **A**). The words in the other answer choices have a meaning opposite to that of *unprecedented.*

99. B. The Challenger disaster occurred in *January of 1986* (Choice **B**). This information is given in the second sentence of the last paragraph. The dates in the other answer choices are incorrect.

100. A. According to information given in this passage, *people seek answers to the reasons for humankind's existence* (Choice **A**). This information is given in the first paragraph of the passage. Choices **B** and **C** are incorrect because, even though these are true statements, this information is not given in the passage. Tip: Do not select answer choices based on your personal knowledge that goes beyond the information given in the passage. Choice **D** is incorrect because it disagrees with information given in the last paragraph.

101. B. In this narrative, the author speaks *of two shuttle disasters.* They occurred in 1986 and 2003. Choices **A, C,** and **D** are incorrect.

102. A. Since the dawn of time, individuals have been fascinated with exploration because of *mankind's natural inquisitiveness about the universe*. This piece speaks directly about the desire of human beings to explore the vast reaches of the universe—earth, sea, and outer space—simply because it is there. Choice **B** is incorrect because the narrative does not address the need for individuals to become powerful world leaders and rule vast stretches of the universe. Choice **C** is incorrect because this narrative addresses just the opposite, mankind's desire to connect with others in the quest to understand and explore. Choice **D** is incorrect because the narrative does not address mankind's need to bring civilization to the uncivilized universe.

103. B. The author would probably agree that *exploring unknown regions of the world is necessary for human development*. The thrust of this piece is how discovering the riches of the world is part of the human desire to understand the world. Choice **A** is incorrect because the author stresses that scientific exploration is anything but risk-free; instead, it is filled with real and ever-present dangers. Choice **C** is incorrect because individuals feel the urge to explore all the time and not just in times of trouble or despair. Choice **D** is incorrect because searching for the unknown is the province of all, regardless of wealth, status, or ambition.

104. D. In this narrative, the following statement is NOT stated: *Tragedy has extinguished America's exploratory spirit*. In fact, as the narrative mentions, tragedy, such as the shuttle disasters, has only fueled America's interest to continue on the path of space exploration. Choice **A** is incorrect because the narrative specifically implies that today for many once undreamed-of inventions and events, the unimaginable has become reality. Choice **B** is incorrect because the narrative does imply that space exploration has had a positive impact in America. Choice **C** is incorrect because this narrative does imply that America is a leader in space exploration.

105. C. The word or phrase when substituted for "Instead" in the fifth paragraph that would maintain the same relationship between the last two sentences is the word *rather*. *Rather* is a word that means the same as *instead* or *besides*. Choice **A** is incorrect because the world *therefore* implies a concluding remark to follow the sentence before. Choice **B** is incorrect because the words *in addition* imply that that the sentence which follows is an added thought or conclusion to the preceding sentence. Choice **D** is incorrect because the word *obviously* implies something that is understood by many and, in this narrative's section, the logical conclusion to this paragraph is not something generally assumed.

106. D. According to this passage Maria Montessori was born in *Italy* in 1870 (Choice **D**). The other answer choices do not give the correct country of Montessori's birth.

107. D. A statement that is implied in this passage is the statement given in Choice **D**: *Maria Montessori was well-educated*. Although this statement is not explicitly stated in this passage, from the first sentence of the second paragraph, which states that Montessori had a "strong academic record" and that she became "the first female certified physician in Italy," the reader can infer that Montessori was well-educated. Choice **A** is incorrect because the statement in this answer choice disagrees with the third sentence of the first paragraph. Choice **B** is incorrect because the statement in this answer choice disagrees with the information given in the second paragraph. Choice **C** is incorrect because it disagrees with Montessori's ideas about teaching children given in this passage.

108. A. An opinion about Maria Montessori expressed in this passage is the statement given in Choice **A**: *She revolutionized the teaching profession*. The word *revolutionized* is a judgment word reflecting the author's opinion about Montessori's impact on the teaching profession. Choice **B** is a statement of fact given in the first sentence of the third paragraph. Choice **C** is a statement of fact derived from information given in the third and fourth sentences of the fourth paragraph. Choice **D** is a statement of fact given in the first sentence of the last paragraph.

109. A. In the third sentence of the sixth paragraph, this passage states that Maria Montessori *advocated age-appropriate learning activities* (Choice **A**). Choices **B** and **C** are incorrect because these answer choices disagree with information is given in the passage. Choice **D** is incorrect because the first sentence of the last paragraph tells you that Montessori was *nominated* for the Nobel Peace Prize in 1951, but the passage does not tell you that she actually *won* the Nobel Peace Prize in that year.

110. B. According to the third sentence of the sixth paragraph, Maria Montessori's teaching ideas *gained attention world-wide during her lifetime* (Choice **B**). Choice **A** is incorrect because this statement is neither stated nor implied by the passage. Choice **C** is incorrect because it disagrees with information given in the first sentence of the last paragraph. Choice **D** is incorrect because there is no information in the passage to support it.

111. B. According to this passage, the best word to describe Maria Montessori is *progressive*. As this passage both implies and states, Maria Montessori was a woman who clearly accomplished goals that were unheard of by a woman in the early twentieth century. She was a true revolutionary leader. Choice **A** is incorrect because Maria Montessori was anything but *passive*; *passive* implies not reacting to the events or ideas that are happening around you. Choice **C** is incorrect because there is no indication in this passage that Maria Montessori was *cynical* or sharply negative. Choice **D** is incorrect because although Maria Montessori was *active*, the best word to describe her behavior from the list presented is the word *progressive*, meaning forward thinking.

112. C. According to this passage, Maria Montessori revolutionized the education profession because *she respected the emotional experiences that young people brought to their learning*. As mentioned in the narrative, Montessori was a strong advocate for nurturing children's emotional well-being and made it an intimate part of their learning. Choice **A** is incorrect because this passage is more concerned with emotional rather than academic needs. Choice **B** is incorrect, because in this passage there is no mention of Montessori's stand on the need for standardized assessment in order to understand the academic or subject matter knowledge of young children. Choice **D** is incorrect because even though Montessori would have been a strong advocate for individualized reading preferences, there is no mention of this interest or desire in this passage.

113. A. According to this passage, Maria Montessori's philosophy is *learning by doing ordinary work*. This passage mentions that Montessori was interested in the ordinary everyday lives of young children and incorporating these activities into their learning. Choice **B** is incorrect because no mention is made of learning by memorization. Choice **C** is incorrect because no mention is made of learning by objectives. Choice **D** is incorrect because no mention is made of learning by competition.

114. D. According to the ideas in this passage, the choice that best demonstrates active, involved learners who are capable of making independent choices, is a seven-year-old playing dress-up enthusiastically. The joyous enthusiasm indicates a free-spirit and a emotionally-healthy child. Choices **A, B,** and **C** imply young people who are operating under distress and without free choice, something Montessori would not have advocated.

115. C. As used in the fifth paragraph, the word *self-reliance* most nearly means *autonomous*. *Self-reliance* means an ability to rely on no one but oneself to accomplish one's stated goals. Choice **A,** dependence, implies just the opposite—to rely on someone else to achieve one's objective. Choice **B,** persistence, implies that one is aggressive toward achieving one's desire, but not necessarily self-reliance or solely in control. Choice **D,** caution, implies to be hesitant about achieving one's goals, which does not mean the same as being actively involved in achieving one's objectives independently.

116. D. The tone of this passage is best described as *factual* (Choice **D**). The author does not show a disbelieving, skeptical tone (Choice **A**); an amusing, humorous tone (Choice **B**); or a mocking, sarcastic tone (Choice **C**).

117. D. A statement that is a fact about tropical rain forests that is given in the first paragraph is the statement in Choice **A:** *Tropical rain forests are found near the equator*. The statements in the other answer choices are statements of opinion by the author.

118. B. In the first sentence of the second paragraph, this passage states that rain forests occupy only *6 to 7 percent of the Earth's surface* (Choice **B**). The percents in the other answer choices are either too small or too great.

119. C. In the first sentence of the fourth paragraph, this passage states *that large industrial companies desiring to clear land for logging, farming, and mining threaten the rain forests* (Choice **C**). Choice **A** is incorrect because, although from information given in the sixth paragraph, you might assume that the statement in Choice **A** is accurate; this passage does not state this information. Choice **B** is incorrect the statement in this answer choice disagree with information is given in the last paragraph. Choice **D** is incorrect because, even though this is a true fact that you, perhaps, know, this information is not given in the passage. Remember, do not select answer choices based on your personal knowledge that goes beyond the information given in the passage.

120. C. In paragraph three the author uses the word *mine* in the context of *extracting from plants* (Choice **C**). The author is describing the extraction of substances from plants. Choice **A** is incorrect because the word *mine* is not used in the sense of digging in the Earth. Choice **C** is incorrect because no mention is made of chemicals in the paragraph. Choice **D** is incorrect because, while mining might help increase the supply of new medicines, the verb *to mine* does not mean *to supply*.

121. C. A statement about rain forests that is neither stated nor implied in this passage is *They provide unique treasures for self-defined explorers.* Although this passage mentions the many treasures to be found in the rain forests, this passage does not advocate the use of the rain forests as a place to explore and to retrieve for personal gain. Indeed, this passage advocates the opposite—that the rain forest be a place for all to enjoy and that any riches to be found in these regions, be shared and regulated by overseeing partners and organizations. The statements in choices **A, B,** and **D** are stated or implied in the passage. The rain forests do provide a safe haven for indigenous people, serve as a prime source for modern medicines, and act as a rich resource for scientific exploration.

122. B. The primary purpose of this passage is to *inform readers about the plight of the rain forests.* This piece speaks in a detailed voice about the natural beauty of the world's rain forests and how commercial interests threaten to destroy this lush and rich vegetative community. Choice **A** is incorrect because although this passage does mention that rare plants and species are found in the rain forests, this is not the primary purpose of this passage. This passage speaks in an advocacy voice for the preservation of the rain forests. Choice **C** is not correct because, if anything, this piece speaks to the obvious side effects of unprotected and indiscriminate logging of the rain forests. Instead, this piece calls for a more responsible approach toward logging in the rain forests. Choice **D** is incorrect because although this piece does underline the importance of scientific exploration in the rain forests, this passage concentrates on how the rain forests can contribute to society in a multitude of ways besides scientific discovery.

123. D. Deforestation is a major, not a minor, problem in today's rain forest environment. All the rest of the statements are true.

124. C. According to this passage, the millions of *indigenous* people who live in the rain forests are called by the word *indigenous* because they *are native to the land in which they live. Indigenous* is a term that defines a group of people who inhabit a land long before they are discovered by others; they belong to the land because they were born there and usually are not prepared to live anywhere else. Choice **A** is incorrect because *indigenous* implies permanent residents and not transitory migrants who are known to travel from place to place seeking work and shelter. Choice **B** is incorrect because *indigenous* people do not own, in the economic sense, the property on which they live; instead, they own the land because they were born to the land and have lived there for all their natural lives. Choice **D** is incorrect because although *indigenous* people do work the land on which they live, that and that alone does not make them an indigenous people. Inhabiting for a long time on the land in which they work and live makes them an *indigenous* people to their home in the rain forests.

125. D. The author's claim that "the rainforests will continue as one of the earth's most vital resources" *is a reasonable statement given the previous remarks.* The author provides a realistic, yet hopeful presentation of the facts surrounding the preservation of the rain forests and their chance for continual renewal despite many competing, often self-serving interests. Choice **A** is incorrect because the author's non-objectionable, reasoned statement is based on evidence, not, as the answer states, a flimsy, unsubstantiated response. Choice **B** is incorrect because the author's optimistic statement is perfectly aligned with the passage's remarks, and is not contradictory to the author's thesis or subsequent narrative. Choice **C** is incorrect because the author's optimistic remarks are not objectionable or biased, but a reasonable corollary given the thrust of this author's remarks about the condition and continuation of the world's rain forests.

Answer Sheet for FTCE General Knowledge Practice Test 2

(Remove This Sheet and Use It To Mark Your Answers)

Diagnostic General Knowledge Test: Essay

Write your essay on lined paper.

General Knowledge Test: English Language Skills

1 Ⓐ Ⓑ Ⓒ Ⓓ	11 Ⓐ Ⓑ Ⓒ Ⓓ	21 Ⓐ Ⓑ Ⓒ Ⓓ	31 Ⓐ Ⓑ Ⓒ Ⓓ
2 Ⓐ Ⓑ Ⓒ Ⓓ	12 Ⓐ Ⓑ Ⓒ Ⓓ	22 Ⓐ Ⓑ Ⓒ Ⓓ	32 Ⓐ Ⓑ Ⓒ Ⓓ
3 Ⓐ Ⓑ Ⓒ Ⓓ	13 Ⓐ Ⓑ Ⓒ Ⓓ	23 Ⓐ Ⓑ Ⓒ Ⓓ	33 Ⓐ Ⓑ Ⓒ Ⓓ
4 Ⓐ Ⓑ Ⓒ Ⓓ	14 Ⓐ Ⓑ Ⓒ Ⓓ	24 Ⓐ Ⓑ Ⓒ Ⓓ	34 Ⓐ Ⓑ Ⓒ Ⓓ
5 Ⓐ Ⓑ Ⓒ Ⓓ	15 Ⓐ Ⓑ Ⓒ Ⓓ	25 Ⓐ Ⓑ Ⓒ Ⓓ	35 Ⓐ Ⓑ Ⓒ Ⓓ
6 Ⓐ Ⓑ Ⓒ Ⓓ	16 Ⓐ Ⓑ Ⓒ Ⓓ	26 Ⓐ Ⓑ Ⓒ Ⓓ	36 Ⓐ Ⓑ Ⓒ Ⓓ
7 Ⓐ Ⓑ Ⓒ Ⓓ	17 Ⓐ Ⓑ Ⓒ Ⓓ	27 Ⓐ Ⓑ Ⓒ Ⓓ	37 Ⓐ Ⓑ Ⓒ Ⓓ
8 Ⓐ Ⓑ Ⓒ Ⓓ	18 Ⓐ Ⓑ Ⓒ Ⓓ	28 Ⓐ Ⓑ Ⓒ Ⓓ	38 Ⓐ Ⓑ Ⓒ Ⓓ
9 Ⓐ Ⓑ Ⓒ Ⓓ	19 Ⓐ Ⓑ Ⓒ Ⓓ	29 Ⓐ Ⓑ Ⓒ Ⓓ	39 Ⓐ Ⓑ Ⓒ Ⓓ
10 Ⓐ Ⓑ Ⓒ Ⓓ	20 Ⓐ Ⓑ Ⓒ Ⓓ	30 Ⓐ Ⓑ Ⓒ Ⓓ	40 Ⓐ Ⓑ Ⓒ Ⓓ

General Knowledge Test: Mathematics

41 Ⓐ Ⓑ Ⓒ Ⓓ	51 Ⓐ Ⓑ Ⓒ Ⓓ	61 Ⓐ Ⓑ Ⓒ Ⓓ	71 Ⓐ Ⓑ Ⓒ Ⓓ	81 Ⓐ Ⓑ Ⓒ Ⓓ
42 Ⓐ Ⓑ Ⓒ Ⓓ	52 Ⓐ Ⓑ Ⓒ Ⓓ	62 Ⓐ Ⓑ Ⓒ Ⓓ	72 Ⓐ Ⓑ Ⓒ Ⓓ	82 Ⓐ Ⓑ Ⓒ Ⓓ
43 Ⓐ Ⓑ Ⓒ Ⓓ	53 Ⓐ Ⓑ Ⓒ Ⓓ	63 Ⓐ Ⓑ Ⓒ Ⓓ	73 Ⓐ Ⓑ Ⓒ Ⓓ	83 Ⓐ Ⓑ Ⓒ Ⓓ
44 Ⓐ Ⓑ Ⓒ Ⓓ	54 Ⓐ Ⓑ Ⓒ Ⓓ	64 Ⓐ Ⓑ Ⓒ Ⓓ	74 Ⓐ Ⓑ Ⓒ Ⓓ	84 Ⓐ Ⓑ Ⓒ Ⓓ
45 Ⓐ Ⓑ Ⓒ Ⓓ	55 Ⓐ Ⓑ Ⓒ Ⓓ	65 Ⓐ Ⓑ Ⓒ Ⓓ	75 Ⓐ Ⓑ Ⓒ Ⓓ	85 Ⓐ Ⓑ Ⓒ Ⓓ
46 Ⓐ Ⓑ Ⓒ Ⓓ	56 Ⓐ Ⓑ Ⓒ Ⓓ	66 Ⓐ Ⓑ Ⓒ Ⓓ	76 Ⓐ Ⓑ Ⓒ Ⓓ	
47 Ⓐ Ⓑ Ⓒ Ⓓ	57 Ⓐ Ⓑ Ⓒ Ⓓ	67 Ⓐ Ⓑ Ⓒ Ⓓ	77 Ⓐ Ⓑ Ⓒ Ⓓ	
48 Ⓐ Ⓑ Ⓒ Ⓓ	58 Ⓐ Ⓑ Ⓒ Ⓓ	68 Ⓐ Ⓑ Ⓒ Ⓓ	78 Ⓐ Ⓑ Ⓒ Ⓓ	
49 Ⓐ Ⓑ Ⓒ Ⓓ	59 Ⓐ Ⓑ Ⓒ Ⓓ	69 Ⓐ Ⓑ Ⓒ Ⓓ	79 Ⓐ Ⓑ Ⓒ Ⓓ	
50 Ⓐ Ⓑ Ⓒ Ⓓ	60 Ⓐ Ⓑ Ⓒ Ⓓ	70 Ⓐ Ⓑ Ⓒ Ⓓ	80 Ⓐ Ⓑ Ⓒ Ⓓ	

General Knowledge Test: Reading

86 Ⓐ Ⓑ Ⓒ Ⓓ	96 Ⓐ Ⓑ Ⓒ Ⓓ	106 Ⓐ Ⓑ Ⓒ Ⓓ	116 Ⓐ Ⓑ Ⓒ Ⓓ	126 Ⓐ Ⓑ Ⓒ Ⓓ
87 Ⓐ Ⓑ Ⓒ Ⓓ	97 Ⓐ Ⓑ Ⓒ Ⓓ	107 Ⓐ Ⓑ Ⓒ Ⓓ	117 Ⓐ Ⓑ Ⓒ Ⓓ	
88 Ⓐ Ⓑ Ⓒ Ⓓ	98 Ⓐ Ⓑ Ⓒ Ⓓ	108 Ⓐ Ⓑ Ⓒ Ⓓ	118 Ⓐ Ⓑ Ⓒ Ⓓ	
89 Ⓐ Ⓑ Ⓒ Ⓓ	99 Ⓐ Ⓑ Ⓒ Ⓓ	109 Ⓐ Ⓑ Ⓒ Ⓓ	119 Ⓐ Ⓑ Ⓒ Ⓓ	
90 Ⓐ Ⓑ Ⓒ Ⓓ	100 Ⓐ Ⓑ Ⓒ Ⓓ	110 Ⓐ Ⓑ Ⓒ Ⓓ	120 Ⓐ Ⓑ Ⓒ Ⓓ	
91 Ⓐ Ⓑ Ⓒ Ⓓ	101 Ⓐ Ⓑ Ⓒ Ⓓ	111 Ⓐ Ⓑ Ⓒ Ⓓ	121 Ⓐ Ⓑ Ⓒ Ⓓ	
92 Ⓐ Ⓑ Ⓒ Ⓓ	102 Ⓐ Ⓑ Ⓒ Ⓓ	112 Ⓐ Ⓑ Ⓒ Ⓓ	122 Ⓐ Ⓑ Ⓒ Ⓓ	
93 Ⓐ Ⓑ Ⓒ Ⓓ	103 Ⓐ Ⓑ Ⓒ Ⓓ	113 Ⓐ Ⓑ Ⓒ Ⓓ	123 Ⓐ Ⓑ Ⓒ Ⓓ	
94 Ⓐ Ⓑ Ⓒ Ⓓ	104 Ⓐ Ⓑ Ⓒ Ⓓ	114 Ⓐ Ⓑ Ⓒ Ⓓ	124 Ⓐ Ⓑ Ⓒ Ⓓ	
95 Ⓐ Ⓑ Ⓒ Ⓓ	105 Ⓐ Ⓑ Ⓒ Ⓓ	115 Ⓐ Ⓑ Ⓒ Ⓓ	125 Ⓐ Ⓑ Ⓒ Ⓓ	

CUT HERE

General Knowledge Practice Test 2: Essay

This section of the examination involves a written assignment. You are asked to prepare a written response for *one of the two topics* presented below. Select one of these two topics and prepare a 300- to 600-word response. Be sure to read both topics very carefully to make sure that you understand the topic for which you are preparing a written response. Use your allotted time to plan, write, review, and edit what you have written for the assignment.

Topic 1

What are your favorite hobbies?

Topic 2

A historical figure who changed the world

Be sure to read the two topics again before attempting to write your response. Remember to write your answer on the space provided in the examination booklet. Your answer also must be on only one of the topics presented, and it must answer the complete topic.

Your essay is graded holistically, meaning only one score is assigned for your writing—taking into consideration both mechanics and organization. *You are not scored on the nature of the content or opinions expressed in your work.* Instead, you are graded on your ability to write complete sentences, to express and support your opinions, and to organize your work.

At least two evaluators will review your work and assign it a score. Special attention is paid to the following specific indicators of good writing:

- Does your writing demonstrate a strong definitive purpose?
- Is there a clear thesis or statement of a main idea?
- Are your ideas organized?
- Do you support your thesis with clear details?
- Are effective transitions present?
- Do you demonstrate an effective use of language?
- Are a variety of sentence patterns present?
- Is there a consistent point of view?
- Are the conventions of standard American English used?

Before you begin, be sure you plan what you want to say. Organize your thoughts and carefully construct your ideas. This should be your original work, written in your own hand, and in your own voice.

As you write your piece, you may cross out or add information as necessary. Although handwriting does not count, be sure to be legible in your response.

General Knowledge Practice Test 2: English Language Skills

Directions: For items 1 and 2, read the entire passage carefully and then answer the questions. Please note that intentional errors have been included in this passage. This passage is designed to measure your identification of logical order and irrelevant sentences in a written passage.

The passage reads as follows:

(1) The outside shell is one of the most important parts of an organism. (2) Shells grow on the outside of living things. (3) Many plants and animals, from tiny nuts to huge alligators, have a shell to protect them at least one time in their life cycles. (4) Some shells are as tiny as a grain of sand. (5) Many people collect shells as a hobby. (6) Shells also vary in color, helping to protect the organism inside from possible predators. (7) They also serve as a necessary protection from the elements. (8) Plants and animals with shells are usually the most vulnerable of living things without their shells. (9) The shell functions as protective outerwear. (10) Shells are nature's way of protecting creatures that otherwise would likely perish.

1. Select the arrangement of sentences 1, 2, and 3 that provides the most logical sequence of ideas and supporting details in the paragraph. If no change is needed, select Choice **A.**

   A. The outside shell is one of the most important parts of an organism. Shells grow on the outside of living things. Many plants and animals, from tiny nuts to huge alligators, have a shell to protect them at least one time in their life cycles.

   B. Shells grow on the outside of living things. The outside shell is one of the most important parts of an organism. Many plants and animals, from tiny nuts to huge alligators, have a shell to protect them at least one time in their life cycles.

   C. Many plants and animals, from tiny nuts to huge alligators, have a shell to protect them at least one time in their life cycles. Shells grow on the outside of living things. The outside shell is one of the most important parts of an organism.

   D. The outside shell is one of the most important parts of an organism. Many plants and animals, from tiny nuts to huge alligators, have a shell to protect them at least one time in their life cycles. Shells grow on the outside of living things.

2. Which numbered sentence is LEAST relevant to the passage?

   A. Sentence 3
   B. Sentence 4
   C. Sentence 5
   D. Sentence 6

The passage reads as follows:

(1) Students must learn to function in schools where the main language is English, not their home language. (2) Today, most urban school districts have an amalgamation of students who speak different languages. (3) Families from all over the world settle in primarily large metropolitan school districts and bring with them their languages, culture, and customs. (4) Learning in a new language is a difficult and serious concern for all involved—teachers, parents, and students. (5) Steps are being taken by school districts to ensure that all eager and eligible learners can participate in classroom lessons. (6) Faced with a diverse population of learners, teachers must learn to adapt their lessons. (7) They must take special courses to learn how to work with students whose first language is not English. (8) Also, administrators must rethink discipline policies for students who are unfamiliar with American lifestyle and traditional norms. (9) These measures should help ensure success for students who speak English as a second language. (10) With the burgeoning ethnic population in our nation's cities, new specialty foods are being introduced into society.

3. Select the arrangement of sentences 1, 2, and 3 that provides the most logical sequence of ideas and supporting details in the paragraph. If no change is needed, select Choice **A**.

A. Students must learn to function in schools where the main language is English, not their home language. Today, most urban school districts have an amalgamation of students who speak different languages. Families from all over the world settle in primarily large metropolitan school districts and bring with them their languages, culture, and customs.

B. Families from all over the world settle in primarily large metropolitan school districts and bring with them their languages, culture, and customs. Students must learn to function in schools where the main language is English, not their home language. Today, most urban school districts have an amalgamation of students who speak different languages.

C. Today, most urban school districts have an amalgamation of students who speak different languages. Families from all over the world settle in primarily large metropolitan school districts and bring with them their languages, culture, and customs. Students must learn to function in schools where the main language is English, not their home language.

D. Students must learn to function in schools where the main language is English, not their home language. Families from all over the world settle in primarily large metropolitan school districts and bring with them their languages, culture, and customs. Today, most urban school districts have an amalgamation of students who speak different languages.

4. Which numbered sentence is LEAST relevant to the passage?

A. Sentence 7
B. Sentence 8
C. Sentence 9
D. Sentence 10

GO ON TO THE NEXT PAGE

309

Directions: For questions 5–34, select the answer choice that corrects an error in the underlined portion. If there is no error, choose **D** indicating "No change is necessary."

5. All the actors, <u>accept</u> Martha and John, were
   [A]

   <u>allowed</u> <u>to eat</u> in the cafeteria.
   [B]   [C]

   A. except
   B. aloud
   C. to have eaten
   D. No change is necessary.

6. The children on the school bus <u>are wearing</u> brand
   [A]

   <u>new</u> t-shirts from <u>Coach Henderson</u>.
   [B]   [C]

   A. was wearing
   B. knew
   C. coach Henderson
   D. No change is necessary.

7. We encouraged our visitors <u>too</u> <u>formally</u>
   [A]   [B]

   introduce <u>themselves</u> to our neighbors.
   [C]

   A. to
   B. formerly
   C. theirselves
   D. No change is necessary.

8. After school, I <u>read</u> my <u>french</u> textbook to
   [A]   [B]

   prepare for <u>tomorrow's</u> quiz.
   [C]

   A. red
   B. French
   C. tommorrow
   D. No change is necessary.

9. Repeatedly, the cheerleaders <u>have went</u> to the
   [A]

   <u>all-American</u> championship to represent <u>their</u>
   [B]   [C]

   high school.

   A. have gone
   B. all-american
   C. there
   D. No change is necessary.

10. Police officer Lance Jones <u>sat</u> <u>among</u> Janice and
    [A]   [B]

    me at the <u>awards</u> ceremony.
    [C]

    A. set
    B. between
    C. Awards
    D. No change is necessary.

11. Mark is <u>deep</u> in love with Maria despite <u>their</u>
    [A]   [B]

    <u>considerable differences</u> in age and interest.
    [C]

    A. deeply
    B. there
    C. considerably different
    D. No change is necessary.

12. After the umpire cried <u>fowl</u>, all my teammates
    [A]

    protested <u>loudly</u> in <u>disbelief</u>.
    [B]   [C]

    A. foul
    B. loud
    C. disbelieve
    D. No change is necessary.

13. Unfortunately, the tennis team had lost more
    [A]   [B]
    tournaments then they ever had before.
                    [C]

    A. Unfortunate
    B. have
    C. than
    D. No change is necessary.

14. My uncle's surprising musical talents masks
                   [A]   [B]
    his inability to read.
    [C]

    A. surprisingly
    B. mask
    C. his own
    D. No change is necessary.

15. Among the three sisters, only me and Nancy
    [A]   [B]
    are tall.
        [C]

    A. Between
    B. Nancy and I
    C. the tallest
    D. No change is necessary.

16. Despite the harsh reign, we found a dry space
                         [A]   [B]
    to eat our lunch.
       [C]

    A. rain
    B. had found
    C. ate
    D. No change is necessary.

17. The students, who seldom were consulted about
        [A]   [B]
    issues by the administration, quickly seen they
                                          [C]
    must speak up about the injustice of the situation.

    A. students'
    B. whom
    C. saw
    D. No change is necessary.

18. The teacher was explaining to the class that
                                              [A]
    scientists are really careful when they take
                   [B]   [C]
    measurements.

    A. how
    B. real
    C. he or she
    D. No change is necessary.

19. When the students performed the experiment they
    [A]   [B]   [C]
    were amazed that the liquid turned a dazzling

    green.

    A. Whenever
    B. students'
    C. experiment, they
    D. No change is necessary.

20. Dustin is happy that his new cell phone number
                [A]
    is more easier to remember than was his previous
       [B]   [C]
    number.

    A. happier
    B. easier
    C. remember, than
    D. No change is necessary.

21. The boys' mother asked them whether they felt

    badly about breaking her new Tiffany lamp when
    [A]   [B]
    they were playing with the ball in the house.
         [C]

    A. bad
    B. tiffany
    C. was
    D. No change is necessary.

GO ON TO THE NEXT PAGE

311

22. Last November Ms. Villa's <u>history</u> class <u>went</u> on
    [A]   [B]
    a field trip to Washington, D.C., the nation's

    <u>capitol</u>.
    [C]

    A.   History
    B.   had went
    C.   capital
    D.   No change is necessary.

23. The <u>girls'</u> mother asked them to water the
    [A]

    <u>plants and</u> feed the dog after they finished <u>there</u>
    [B]   [C]
    homework.

    A.   girl's
    B.   plants, and
    C.   their
    D.   No change is necessary.

24. <u>When</u> they arrived at the mall, the children
    [A]

    <u>had run</u> into the toy store to find the most recent
    [B]

    edition of <u>their</u> favorite trading cards.
               [C]

    A.   Whenever
    B.   ran
    C.   thier
    D.   No change is necessary.

25. It is hard for me to believe that we <u>cannot</u> resolve
                                          [A]

    the problems between you and <u>I</u> after all these
                                  [B]

    <u>years</u> of trying.
    [C]

    A.   can not
    B.   me
    C.   years'
    D.   No change is necessary.

26. My daughter and my son <u>are</u> both taller than <u>me</u>,
                            [A]   [B]
    but they still mind what I <u>say when</u> I correct their
                                [C]
    behavior.

    A.   were
    B.   I
    C.   say, when
    D.   No change is necessary.

27. I was anxious during my first semester at the new

    <u>school because</u> the <u>principal</u> told me she would
    [A]   [B]

    be strict with <u>whomever</u> broke the rules.
                    [C]

    A.   school, because
    B.   principle
    C.   whoever
    D.   No change is necessary.

28. Only one of the contestants <u>who</u> participated in
                                 [A]

    the race <u>want</u> the winner to be disqualified for
              [B]

    being <u>too</u> young.
          [C]

    A.   which
    B.   wants
    C.   to
    D.   No change is necessary.

29. Just before Caleb <u>left, he</u> told me he <u>didn't</u> think
                       [A]   [B]

    he did very <u>good</u> on his geometry test.
                [C]

    A.   left he
    B.   don't
    C.   well
    D.   No change is necessary.

30. <u>Me</u> graduating from college <u>has</u> been a dream of
[A]   [B]

      my parents, neither of <u>whom</u> ever finished high
                        [C]

      school.

    A. My
    B. have
    C. who
    D. No change is necessary.

31. The contributors to the fundraiser were pleased

      to <u>see that</u> every one of the children <u>were</u>
         [A]   [B]

      wearing a <u>brand new</u> outfit.
             [C]

    A. see, that
    B. was
    C. brand-new
    D. No change is necessary.

32. The <u>couple's</u> teenage sons had outgrown their
           [A]

      board <u>games, so</u> the couple donated <u>them</u> to the
            [B]   [C]

      local charter school.

    A. couples'
    B. games so
    C. the board games
    D. No change is necessary.

33. Donna, <u>who</u> never seeks recognition, <u>recieved</u>
           [A]   [B]

      the outstanding teacher <u>award in</u> her school
                        [C]

      this year.

    A. whom
    B. received
    C. award, in
    D. No change is necessary.

34. Austin, Ricardo's <u>most nicest</u> <u>friend,</u> comes over
                [A]   [B]

      to Ricardo's house <u>every day</u> after school to play.
                     [C]

    A. nicest
    B. freind
    C. everyday
    D. No change is necessary.

For questions 35–37, select the correct response for the underlined word.

35. When you meet the two girls, you will find it
      difficult to tell which one is <u>oldest</u>.

    A. the oldest
    B. older
    C. more old
    D. No change is necessary.

36. Because the students were going to be gone all
      day on the field trip to the park, they <u>should have</u>
      <u>took</u> a lunch.

    A. should of took
    B. should have taken
    C. should of taken
    D. No change is necessary.

37. As the sun <u>sets</u>, the horizon glowed a bright
      orange.

    A. had set
    B. has been setting
    C. set
    D. No change is necessary.

GO ON TO THE NEXT PAGE

For questions 38–40, select the best response.

38. Choose the option that is punctuated correctly.

    A. When you broke your promise, I was extremely upset, I hope that I will be able to trust you in the future.

    B. When you broke your promise I was extremely upset I hope that I will be able to trust you in the future.

    C. When you broke your promise, I was extremely upset. I hope that I will be able to trust you in the future.

    D. When you broke your promise I was extremely upset. I hope that I will be able to trust you in the future.

39. Choose the option that is punctuated correctly.

    A. Having been raised in our household from a puppy, our family's trusted canine is a spoiled pooch.

    B. Having been raised in our household from a puppy, our familys' trusted canine is a spoiled pooch.

    C. Having been raised in our household from a puppy. Our family's trusted canine is a spoiled pooch.

    D. Having been raised in our household from a puppy our family's trusted canine is a spoiled pooch.

40. Choose the sentence in which the modifiers are placed correctly.

    A. Driving through the neighborhood, the woman waved to a child playing with his dog on the sidewalk.

    B. Playing with his dog on the sidewalk, the woman waved to a child driving through the neighborhood.

    C. The woman waved to a child playing with his dog on the sidewalk driving through the neighborhood.

    D. The woman waved to a child driving through the neighborhood playing on the sidewalk with his dog.

IF YOU FINISH BEFORE TIME IS CALLED, CHECK YOUR WORK ON THIS SECTION ONLY. DO NOT WORK ON ANY OTHER SECTION IN THE TEST.

General Knowledge Practice Test 2: Mathematics

Mathematics Reference Sheet

Area

Triangle

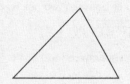

$A = \frac{1}{2} bh$

Rectangle

$A = lw$

Trapezoid

$A = \frac{1}{2} h (b_1 + b_2)$

Parallelogram

$A = bh$

Key	
b = base	d = diameter
h = height	r = radius
l = length	A = area
w = width	C = circumference
S.A. = surface area	V = volume
	B = area of base
Use π = 3.14 or $\frac{22}{7}$	

Circle

$A = \pi r^2$
$C = \pi d = 2\pi r$

Surface Area

1. Surface area of a prism or pyramid = the sum of the areas of all faces of the figure.

2. Surface area of a cylinder = the sum of the two bases + its rectangular wrap.

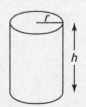

$S.\,A. = 2(\pi r^2) + 2(\pi r)h$

3. Surface area of a sphere: $S.A. = 4\pi r^2$

Volume

1. Volume of a prism or cylinder equals (Area of the Base) times (height): $V = Bh$

2. Volume of a pyramid or cone equals $\frac{1}{3}$ times (Area of the Base) times (height): $V = \frac{1}{3} Bh$

3. Volume of a sphere: $V = \frac{4}{3} \pi r^3$

CUT HERE

Mathematics Reference Sheet, continued

Pythagorean Theorem: $a^2 + b^2 = c^2$

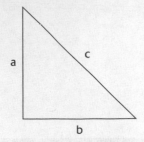

Given a line containing points

(x_1, y_1) and (x_2, y_2)

• Slope of line $= \dfrac{y_2 - y_1}{x_2 - x_1}$

• Distance between two points $=$

$$\sqrt{\left(x_2 - x_1\right)^2 + \left(y_2 - y_1\right)^2}$$

• Midpoint between two points $=$

$$\left(\dfrac{x_1 + x_2}{2}, \dfrac{y_1 + y_2}{2} \right)$$

Simple Interest Formula: $I = prt$

$I =$ simple interest, $p =$ principal

$r =$ rate, $t =$ time

Distance Formula: $d = rt$

$d =$ distance, $r =$ rate, $t =$ time

Conversions	
1 yard = 3 feet = 36 inches	1 cup = 8 fluid ounces
1 mile = 1,760 yards = 5,280 feet	1 pint = 2 cups
1 acre = 43,560 square feet	1 quart = 2 pints
1 hour = 60 minutes	1 gallon = 4 quarts
1 minute = 60 seconds	1 pound = 16 ounces
	1 ton = 2,000 pounds
1 liter = 1000 milliliters = 1000 cubic centiliters	
1 meter = 100 centimeters = 1000 millimeters	
1 kilometer = 1000 meters	
1 gram = 1000 milligrams	
1 kilogram = 1000 grams	

Note: Metric numbers with four digits are written without a comma (e.g., 2543 grams).

For metric numbers with more than four digits, a space is used instead of a comma (e.g., 24 300 liters).

CUT HERE

Directions: Read each question and select the best answer choice.

41. Find the greatest common factor of 30 and 45?

A. 2
B. 3
C. 5
D. 15

42. In scientific notation, the distance from Venus to the Sun is approximately 1.082×10^8 kilometers. How is this distance expressed in standard notation?

A. 10 820 000 000 km
B. 1 082 000 000 km
C. 108 200 000 km
D. 0.00000001082 km

43. The length of the diagonal of a rectangular bedroom is $\sqrt{164}$ feet. This length is:

A. between 6 ft and 7 ft.
B. between 12 ft and 13 ft.
C. between 42 ft and 43 ft.
D. between 81 ft and 82 ft.

44. Simplify $7 + 3(4^2) - 8$.

A. 23
B. 32
C. 47
D. 152

GO ON TO THE NEXT PAGE

45. How is the product $2 \times 2 \times 5 \times 5 \times 5$ expressed in exponential notation?

    A. $2^2 \times 5^3$

    B. 10^5

    C. $2^5 \times 5^2$

    D. 4×15

46. Justin bought a souvenir while vacationing in Texas where the sales tax rate is $8\frac{1}{4}\%$. What is this tax rate expressed as a decimal?

    A. 8.25

    B. 0.825

    C. 0.0825

    D. 0.0814

47. The following Fahrenheit temperatures were the lowest recorded in February for the past five years in a particular city.

$$2°, 0°, -6°, 4°, -8°$$

Which list shows the temperatures in order from coldest to warmest?

    A. $0°, 2°, 4°, -6°, -8°$

    B. $4°, 2°, 0°, -6°, -8°$

    C. $-6°, -8°, 0°, 2°, 4°$

    D. $-8°, -6°, 0°, 2°, 4°$

48. If 30% of a monthly salary of $2400 is budgeted for rent, how much money is budgeted for rent?

    A. $72

    B. $168

    C. $720

    D. $1680

49. A runner ran a 1500-meters race. How many kilometers did the runner run in the race?

    A.   1.5 kilometers

    B.   15 kilometers

    C.   150 kilometers

    D.   1 500 000 kilometers

50. What is the temperature to the nearest degree?

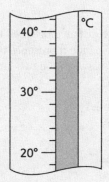

    A.   33°

    B.   35°

    C.   36°

    D.   34°

51. What is the perimeter of a rectangle that measures 12 inches by 10 inches?

    A.   22 in.

    B.   44 in.

    C.   60 in.

    D.   120 in.

52. If a circular flower garden has a diameter of 3 feet, what is the approximate area of the garden?

    A. 4.71 ft^2

    B. 7.065 ft^2

    C. 28.26 ft^2

    D. 9.42 ft^2

53. How many cubic feet of cement are in a rectangular cement slab that is 0.5 feet thick and measures 20 feet long and 10 feet wide?

    A. 100 ft^3

    B. 30.5 ft^3

    C. 300 ft^3

    D. 1000 ft^3

General Knowledge Practice Test 2

GO ON TO THE NEXT PAGE

54. A box that has the shape of a cube and measures 10 cm on a side is cut open to form the flattened figure shown here.

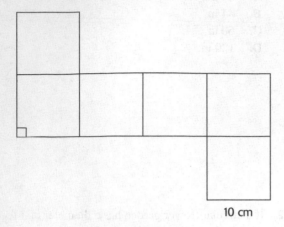

10 cm

What is the surface area of the box?

A. 30 cm²
B. 100 cm²
C. 600 cm²
D. 3600 cm²

55. A car travels 221 miles in 3 hours 15 minutes. How many miles per hour did the car travel?

A. 165.75 mph
B. 70.1 mph
C. 73.7 mph
D. 68 mph

56. A nutrition expert recommends that healthy adults drink 64 ounces of water each day. At this rate, how many gallons of water will be consumed in a week by a person who follows the recommendation?

A. 0.5 gallons
B. 3.5 gallons
C. 14 gallons
D. 16 gallons

57. On a map, the distance between two landmarks is 9.5 inches. If ½ inch represents 10 miles, how far, in miles, is it between the two landmarks (to the nearest mile)?

A. 0.475 miles
B. 19 miles
C. 85 miles
D. 190 miles

58. How much will it cost, without including tax, to carpet a large classroom that measures 18 feet by 15 feet if the cost of the carpet, including installation, is $25.75 per square yard?

A. $30.00
B. $772.50
C. $2317.50
D. $6952.50

59. Which of the following is the most specific name for the figure shown here?

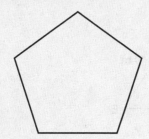

A. pentagon
B. rhombus
C. hexagon
D. trapezoid

60. A length of cable is attached to the top of a 16-foot pole. The cable is anchored 12 feet from the base of the pole. What is the length of the cable?

A. 20 feet
B. 28 feet
C. 200 feet
D. 400 feet

61. A square is also a:

A. cube.
B. prism.
C. rhombus.
D. trapezoid.

GO ON TO THE NEXT PAGE

62. Which of the following figures contains a correctly drawn line of symmetry?

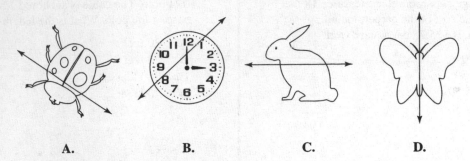

A.   B.   C.   D.

63. In the drawing shown, right triangle ABC is similar to right triangle DEF. What is the length of the hypotenuse in triangle ABC?

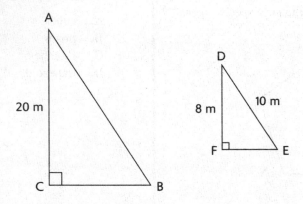

- A.   4 meters
- B.   25 meters
- C.   28 meters
- D.   30 meters

64. Which figure below contains an obtuse angle?

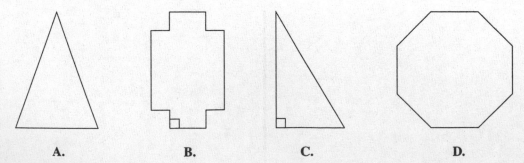

A.   B.   C.   D.

65. Trapezoid A' on the grid that follows represents what kind of transformation of trapezoid A?

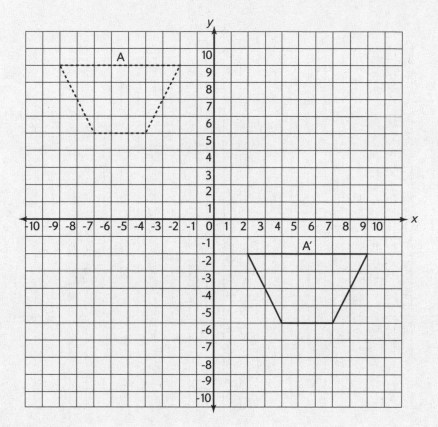

A. translation
B. reflection
C. rotation
D. dilation

GO ON TO THE NEXT PAGE

66. Which point has coordinates (−8, 3)?

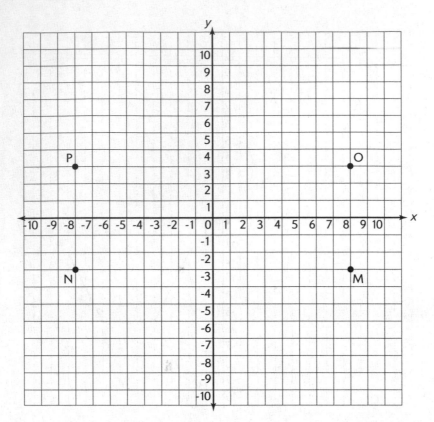

A. M
B. N
C. O
D. P

67. Find the slope of the line that passes through the points (−4, 1) and (2, 3).

A. −3

B. $-\frac{1}{3}$

C. $\frac{1}{3}$

D. 3

68. Find the missing number in the following sequence.

$$2, \underline{\hspace{1cm}}, 8, -16, 32$$

   A.   −4
   B.   4
   C.   5
   D.   −6

69. The area of a trapezoid is $A = \frac{1}{2}h(b_1 + b_2)$ where h is the height of the trapezoid and b_1 and b_2 are the lengths of its two bases. Translate the expression $\frac{1}{2}h(b_1 + b_2)$ into words.

   A.   one-half the product of h times b_1 plus b_2
   B.   the product of one-half the height times b_1 plus b_2
   C.   one-half the height times one-half the sum of the bases
   D.   the sum of b_1 and b_2 times one-half of h

70. Simplify $4 + 2(3x + 1)$

   A. $12x$
   B. $6x + 5$
   C. $6x + 6$
   D. $18x + 6$

71. If $x = 10$ and $y = -4$, then $x - y$ has what value?

   A.   −14
   B.   −6
   C.   6
   D.   14

GO ON TO THE NEXT PAGE

72. Solve for x

$$3(x-6) = 21$$

A. 1
B. 5
C. 9
D. 13

73. Determine which of the following ordered pairs satisfies the given system.

$$2x - y = -7$$
$$x + 3y = -7$$

A. $(-4, -1)$
B. $(-4, 1)$
C. $(4, -1)$
D. $(4, 1)$

74. If $x = -5$, which of the following statements is true?

A. $\frac{1}{x} > -x$
B. $3x < 2x$
C. $-x < 0$
D. $x - 6 > x + 6$

75. Solve $-2x + 5 < 7$

A. $x < -1$
B. $x < -6$
C. $x > -1$
D. $x > -6$

76. Find the missing number in the following sequence.

$$15, \_\_\_\_, -5, -15, -25$$

A. −5
B. 5
C. 25
D. 45

77. The graph that follows represents the monthly average low and high temperatures in the city of Townville for 4 months of the year. In which month was the difference in the average low and high temperatures the greatest?

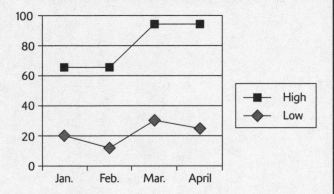

A. January
B. February
C. March
D. April

78. Given are students' scores on a history test. What is the median of the set of scores?

Student	Score
A	96
B	42
C	56
D	88
E	69
F	73
G	67
H	88

A. 71
B. 72
C. 72.375
D. 88

79. Given is a box of 50 colored marbles containing 20 blue, 10 red, 14 green, and 6 yellow. If a person picks out a single marble from the box without looking, what is the probability that it will be a yellow marble?

A. $\frac{2}{5}$

B. $\frac{7}{25}$

C. $\frac{1}{5}$

D. $\frac{3}{25}$

GO ON TO THE NEXT PAGE

80. A girl is making a sandwich for lunch. She has a choice of three kinds of bread (white, whole wheat, and rye bread) and four sandwich fillings (ham, turkey, sliced beef, and pimiento cheese). How many different sandwiches can she make if she chooses one type of bread and one kind of sandwich filling?

   A. 7
   B. 9
   C. 12
   D. 16

81. A library surveys 200 young readers to ask what kind of books they read most often from among adventure, nature, science fiction, and biography or historical books? The results are recorded in the pie graph shown that follows. According to the graph, how many young readers surveyed read science fiction books most often?

Book Type Survey

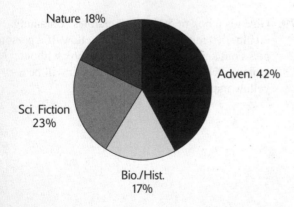

   A. 34
   B. 36
   C. 46
   D. 84

82. A student received the following grades on six science quizzes: 100, 96, 70, 96, 86, and 80. What is the range of the student's grades?

   A. 30
   B. 88
   C. 91
   D. 96

83. Which of the following sets of prices has a median of $10.24?

   A. $10.29, $9.87, $11.99, $8.45, $10.60, $10.25
   B. $7.50, $12.98, $8.25, $10.89, $11.05, $10.67
   C. $11.98, $10.50, $9.98, $8.50, $12.95, $9.98
   D. $11.05, $12.98, $8.25, $10.89, $7.50, $10.67

84. Which of the following sets of scores has a mode of 87?

    A. 90, 87, 96, 96, 87, 96

    B. 99, 87, 93, 94, 87, 90

    C. 91, 92, 89, 97, 84, 84

    D. 92, 91, 85, 87, 88, 95

85. A box contains tiles numbered 1 through 40. If a person picks out a single tile from the box without looking, what is the probability that the number on the tile will be a prime number?

    A. $\dfrac{1}{4}$

    B. $\dfrac{3}{10}$

    C. $\dfrac{13}{40}$

    D. $\dfrac{27}{40}$

IF YOU FINISH BEFORE TIME IS CALLED, CHECK YOUR WORK ON THIS SECTION ONLY. DO NOT WORK ON ANY OTHER SECTION IN THE TEST.

General Knowledge Practice Test 2: Reading

Directions: Please read the following passages carefully. Each passage in this section is followed by questions based on the passage's content. After reading each passage, answer the questions by choosing the best answer from among the four choices given. Be sure to base your answers on what is *implied* or *stated* in the passage.

Passage 1

Baseball: America's National Pastime

(1)   It is often said that if you want to know the spirit of America, all you have to do is to know the role of baseball in American life. Loved by millions, played by thousands, baseball, since its first introduction into American life, has become the hallmark of all that is good and right about our country. Unlike football or basketball, baseball evokes a bygone era of American independence, openness, and renewal. Perhaps because it is played outside in the fresh air and beneath America's clear blue skies, or perhaps because it is such a civil and simple game, it evokes nostalgia and happiness whenever people, young and old alike, gather to watch this home-grown sport played out on our nation's amateur and professional fields.

(2)   Patterned after a game in England, baseball has its roots in America's colonies. Early settlers played "rounders," a game that involved hitting a ball with a bat and advancing around bases. One big difference from the traditional English rounders, though, in this early colonial game is that players were counted out when another threw the ball and hit the man advancing. The practice was known as "plugging," or "soaking" runners. Fortunately, this practice of literally "striking" people was changed to a simple "tagging" of people, thereby beginning the game of baseball as we know it today. In fact, by the mid 1800s, baseball was played in America, pretty much as it is played today—a baseball diamond, two teams, three outs, nine innings, and whichever team has the most runs batted in, wins.

(3)   Although myth has it that Abner Doubleday invented modern baseball, it is most often credited to Alexander Cartwright, a New York City sportsman. In 1845, he started a club, "The Knickerbocker Base Ball Club of New York," whose sole purpose was to play baseball. Beginning with a dream and a desire, Cartwright wrote many of the rules that baseball follows today. Shortly after Cartwright's New York team was formed, others followed. Ironically enough, the Civil War (1861–1865) helped spread baseball across the United States. For recreation, Union troops played the game to the amusement of onlookers from both sides of America's great conflict. After the war, Northerners and Southerners were playing this popular game, and gradually, its popularity grew from state to state.

(4)   With popularity came commercialism, and soon baseball became a professional sport. Major American cities—Boston, New York, Philadelphia, Detroit, and others—sported a major league baseball club to rival competing teams. Americans, eager to watch this new sport and cheer their respective home teams, began flocking to makeshift baseball stadiums in the early 1900s, ensuring the success of the country's first professional sports franchise system.

(5)   Success meant more competition. Fans followed their favorite teams, hoping for championship seasons. Soon, star players became local and national heroes and baseball enthusiasts knew the statistics of every player. Baseball became America's national pastime. With each passing game, teams and their players added more to its historical lore and contemporary allure.

(6)   Of all of America's obsessions, baseball is one of pure passion. To fans of the game, nothing exemplifies more America's spirit, independence, and competitiveness than an exciting game of baseball. And, nothing has come along to replace the feeling of sitting outdoors, soaking in the warm summer sun, and enjoying a favorite team at play in a leisurely and orderly game of ball. Perhaps, that is why baseball has so long endured.

86. This passage states that:

    A. baseball should be played outside and on grass.

    B. "plugging" is not a part of modern baseball.

    C. Abner Doubleday invented baseball.

    D. Alexander Cartwright was an American patriot.

87. According to this passage, "rounders" is a game that:

    A. was imported from England.

    B. had nine innings.

    C. was played by Civil War soldiers.

    D. was never popular in America.

88. In the first paragraph, the word *evokes* most nearly means:

    A. deters.

    B. entices.

    C. projects.

    D. elicits.

89. According to this passage, the Knickerbockers baseball club was formed in:

    A. Boston.

    B. Detroit.

    C. New York.

    D. Philadelphia.

90. Which of the following is an opinion expressed in this passage?

    A. Early settlers played "rounders."

    B. Andrew Cartwright wrote many of the rules that baseball follows today.

    C. Professional baseball teams were formed by the 1900s.

    D. Baseball has become the hallmark of all that is good and right about our country.

91. According to the passage, why is baseball considered America's favorite pastime?

    A. It provides interested individuals with a casual diversion.

    B. It engages sports enthusiasts in a fast-paced, spectator sport.

    C. It is played casually without rules.

    D. It occurs at a leisurely pace in a pastoral setting.

92. As said in the final paragraph, the word *exemplifies* best means:

    A. to define by definition

    B. to illustrate by example

    C. to organize by listing

    D. to delineate by detailing

93. The narrative style of this passage can best be described as:

    A. derisive.

    B. cynical.

    C. subjective.

    D. pessimistic.

94. Which sentence best states a main idea of this passage?

    A. Baseball is a sport that is elitist in tone and style.

    B. Baseball evokes an era of a simpler life and pace.

    C. Baseball reflects the simplicity of all competitive sports.

    D. Baseball inspires youngsters to become competitive athletes.

95. Identify the relationship between the following three sentences in the final paragraph.

"Of all of America's obsessions, baseball is one of pure passion. To fans of the game, nothing exemplifies America's spirit, independence, and competitiveness than an exciting game of baseball. And, nothing has come along to replace the feeling of sitting outdoors, soaking in the warm summer sun, and enjoying a favorite team at play in a leisurely and orderly game of ball."

The second and third sentences:

    A. dispute the first sentence.

    B. contradict the first sentence.

    C. explain the first sentence.

    D. ignore the first sentence.

GO ON TO THE NEXT PAGE

Passage 2

Learning to Dance: One Person's Lament

(1)   Do you know how to dance? I mean, really dance? Most people know how to shake, rattle, and roll, and many can do a pretty good imitation of an individual in the "throes of a demonic possession," but very few of us can actually dance. We might know how to twist and shout, but how many of us can cha-cha, rhumba, or waltz?

(2)   I know I can't. I have (to repeat a time-honored phrase) two left feet, and have tried on numerous occasions to learn to really dance, but have always ended up in the arms of someone desperate enough to be kind, but not quite assertive enough to say, "Stick to walking." I know that at parties and weddings, I kick up my heels at the first sound of the music striking a familiar chord, hoping that I'll finally be able to show the world the new Fred Astaire, Gene Kelly, or John Travolta. Instead, the world inevitably witnesses a disappointing version of a cross between a bouncing Muppet and a jolly Barney. Not a pretty sight.

(3)   Dancing, to be sure, is among the oldest of human art forms. It has always been the most human and most immediate form of self-expression. Ancient rituals were (and still are to this day) celebrated in dance, as the dance symbolizes a form of prayer. Dancing for rain, good fortune, fertility of crops, and for success in war or hunting was common. Often, elaborate costumes and props were incorporated in these highly ritualistic endeavors as well.

(4)   Ritualistic dancing eventually gave rise to social dancing. Instead of being used to strengthen religious connections, dancing became the prime means for "social bonding" as people gathered for celebrations and used their love for movement and song to unite their heads and hearts. Social dancing became the mechanism through which individuals discovered common bonds and together affirmed their sense of common identity or belonging.

(5)   As dance evolved, it naturally took on a life of its own. Soon, formal dancing emerged. In formal dancing, the steps involved are more complicated in design than dancing that is self-willed and free-wheeling. Instead of simple and impulsive movements, the participants learn exact steps that require time, diligence, and a certain special nimbleness to master.

(6)   I have never had the patience to master formal moves, but I envy all who really know "how to dance"—those who have perfected both the art and skill of masterful movement to music and who can "cha-cha" and "tango" expertly. Blessed with the gift of mimicry, these strong and able dancers rival professional athletes in their dexterity, agility, and nimbleness. Indeed, their expertise lies in making the difficult and strenuous look easy and joyous. In this way, the universal language of dance invites its watchers and participants—even those as seemingly hopeless as I—to engage in activity that is part seduction, part mystery, and part unifier, and that expresses the whole range of human emotions. Now, if only I could really cha-cha!

96. According to this passage, the author believes that dancing:

A.   is detrimental to one's health and well-being.

B.   is always free-willed and free-wheeling.

C.   is a waste of time and energy.

D.   is a joyous expression of movement to music.

97. The author's claim that "I have two left feet" (paragraph 2) is:

A.   questionable because of the author's love for dance.

B.   a narrative technique to engage the reader.

C.   full proof that the author dislikes dancing.

D.   an argumentative style to disarm the reader.

98. This passage is an example of:

A.   a narrative portrayal of a positive experience.

B.   a cynical perspective on the human condition.

C.   a valedictory speech regarding a dying art form.

D.   a descriptive narration of an obscure obsession.

99. In the sixth paragraph, the phrase "blessed with the gift of mimicry" best means:

A.   being able to deceive.

B.   being able to reinvent.

C.   being able to imitate.

D.   being able to circumvent.

100. According to this narrative, dancing is universally enjoyed because:

    A. it is an ancient and mysterious ritual.
    B. it speaks to human emotions.
    C. it is compelling and consequential.
    D. it revels in the known and factual.

101. Which of the following statements is implied in the first paragraph?

    A. Most people know how to shake, rattle, and roll.
    B. The waltz is an easy dance to master.
    C. The cha-cha, rhumba, and waltz are types of dances.
    D. Few people can actually dance.

102. Which of the following is an opinion expressed in this passage?

    A. Ancient rituals were celebrated in dance.
    B. Ritualistic dancing gave rise to social dancing.
    C. Dancing has always been the most human form of self-expression.
    D. In formal dancing, the participants learn exact steps.

103. In the second paragraph, the word *assertive* most nearly means:

    A. hesitant.
    B. ambiguous.
    C. bold.
    D. inhibited.

104. This passage states that:

    A. Gene Kelly was a good dancer.
    B. Ritualistic dancing is no longer practiced.
    C. Dancing is an art form.
    D. Only expert dancers can learn to cha-cha.

105. According to information given in this passage:

    A. people have an inborn desire to want to learn to dance.
    B. ritualistic dancing is very similar to social dancing.
    C. Native Americans performed ritualistic dances for success in hunting.
    D. formal dancing is difficult and strenuous.

Passage 3

Directions: Read the following passage and answer questions 106–115.

Jean Piaget: The Beginning of Educational Thought

(1)   Some wonder just how the study of educational thought really began. Most scholars credit the work of Swiss psychologist Jean Piaget (1896–1980) with the creation of modern educational thought. It was Piaget's seminal studies on the thought processes of children that paved the way for everything that has come since in this field of study.

(2)   Piaget's major contribution to the history of human thought and the study of cognitive science is that he believed that children pass through four periods of mental development. Each period, he believed, lasted for a specified period of time and must be followed in a designated order. His feelings were that this defined order accounted for why young children perceived the world as they do and why they make their respective choices. Piaget's work is seminal to understanding modern child development and integral to defining his subsequent impact on everything that followed his early findings.

(3)   Piaget's four stages of mental development are the *sensorimotor period* (birth to 2 years old), the *preoperational period* (2 to 7 years old), the *period of concrete operations* (7 to 11 years old), and the *period of formal operations* (11 to 15 years old). Each stage has its own defined characteristics, and each must be lived or traversed in the chronological order in which it appears. The *sensorimotor period* is the time when infants and toddlers obtain their basic knowledge of the world through their senses. Next, the *preoperational period* is when young children develop such skills as language and drawing ability. In the period of *concrete operations*, older children begin to think logically. Gradually, they begin to take on the ability to organize their knowledge, classify objects, and do thought problems. Finally, during the period of *formal operations*, young people or teenagers begin to think conceptually, applying rational and abstract reasoning to their burgeoning thought processes. Piaget knew, though, that if young children got stuck in a particular stage of mental development, their world would be forever defined by that mental stage. Thus, if young people gradually grow into the final developmental stage—the *period of formal operations*—they, more than likely, will be forever secured a bright and promising intellectual

GO ON TO THE NEXT PAGE

future. To be stuck in an earlier stage, though, means a life of limited intellectual abilities.

(4)   Before we discuss Piaget's work any further, it is best to know his life. Born in 1896 in Neufchatel, Switzerland, Jean Piaget was soon recognized by his family, teachers, and peers as an exceptionally bright and inquisitive child. Not satisfied with simple explanations, Piaget spent hours researching whatever scientific principle or theory fancied his interest. In fact, at the age of 10 (or some say 11), his innate curiosity and deep-seated drive led him to publish his first scientific paper on an albino sparrow. This was followed by a number of articles on mollusks at the age of 15.

(5)   Naturally, this precocious child excelled in school, and by 1918, at the early age of 22, he received his doctorate in the natural sciences. Not content to just know the physical world, Piaget began studying psychology, hoping to uncover the mysteries of the human mind. Retreating in 1921 to the world-famed Institute J. J. Rousseau in Geneva, Piaget embarked on a career that eventually led to his breakthrough discoveries in human cognition. From 1933 to 1971, Piaget served as the co-director of this famed institute and as the director of the International Bureau of Education (1929–1967). Always busy and engaged, Piaget was also a professor of psychology at the University of Geneva from 1929 until his death in 1980, at age 94.

(6)   Piaget's most significant contribution to the world of scientific thought about human cognition is that he studied young children, primarily his own children–Jacqueline, Lucienne, and Laurent. From infancy to their language acquisition, Piaget recorded their every move and nuance, crystallizing his observations into his renowned scientific theories. And his lasting contribution, though commonplace today, was radical for its time—that children think differently than adults. Both a qualitative and a quantitative researcher, Piaget studied human growth and development from a holistic perspective, always trying to integrate disparate elements of information into a cohesive and recognizable human whole. His research on how knowledge grows systematically, that it is a progressive construction of logically embedded structures superseding one another, transformed the manner in which psychologists think of young people. No longer are they thought of as miniature adults. Instead, Piaget's seminal work recognized that children's logic and modes of thinking were entirely their own. His thinking radically transformed the world of cognitive science and led to the formation of the field of developmental psychology. Simply, by studying his own children, Piaget introduced us to the world of all children.

106. In this narrative, the author describes Piaget as:

A. a curious and prodigious thinker.

B. an effete intellectual and disciplinarian.

C. a raucous and caustic intellectual.

D. a cautious and solitary scientist.

107. As our thinking about human cognition has evolved, one principle, according to this passage, has remained constant:

A. Human beings need to reconcile the absurd.

B. Human beings need to understand the misunderstood.

C. Human beings need to develop in defined stages.

D. Human beings need to rediscover ancient truths.

108. The author would probably agree that:

A. developmental psychology has its origins in ritualistic thinking.

B. studying cognitive thinking reveals human behavior patterns.

C. understanding abstract thinking parallels nutritional habits.

D. searching for the unknown is the providence of only religious thinkers.

109. In the narrative, which of the following statements is NOT stated?

A. Psychology is the study of human developmental growth patterns.

B. Piaget's developmental theories were the result of a small sample size.

C. Developmental thinking can be classified into specified age groups.

D. Cognitive psychology relies on the suspension of disbelief.

110. In the fifth paragraph, the phrase, "Not content to just know the physical world," implies that Piaget:

A. was a literal scientific researcher.

B. understood only the human body.

C. engaged in quantitative research.

D. intended to explore mental functions.

111. According to this passage Jean Piaget was born in:

    A. France.

    B. England.

    C. Italy.

    D. Switzerland.

112. Which of the following is the topic of the second paragraph?

    A. Piaget's four stages of mental development.

    B. Piaget's views on teaching and learning.

    C. Piaget's ideas about rational thought.

    D. Piaget's theories on how infants perceive the world.

113. Which of the following is an opinion about Jean Piaget expressed in this passage?

    A. His work is seminal to understanding modern child development.

    B. He received a doctorate degree in natural sciences.

    C. He studied his own children.

    D. He published his first paper before he was 12 years old.

114. This passage states that Jean Piaget:

    A. advocated developmentally-appropriate learning activities.

    B. made breakthrough discoveries in human cognition.

    C. received a number of honorary degrees in his lifetime.

    D. died before his theories were generally accepted.

115. The tone of this passage is best described as:

    A. doubtful.

    B. mocking.

    C. persuasive.

    D. serious.

Passage 4

Directions: Read the following passage and answer questions 116–125.

Whales: A Special Species Indeed

(1) Many people think whales are a type of fish because whales live in the water. Whales, however, are not fish; they are mammals and have much in common with human beings. It is hard to believe, but it is true. Whales, monkeys, dogs, and people all belong to the same class, and like these mammals, whales have a highly developed brain and are among the most behaviorally complex of all animals.

(2) Whales differ from fish in multiple ways. First, whales have different tails than fish. Fish tails are vertical—they move sideways; whale tails are horizontal—they move up and down. Second, fish breathe through gills, taking in dissolved oxygen from water. Whales, on the other hand, have lungs and must come to the surface to breathe. But, for some whales, the trip to the surface for some oxygen can be delayed quite a while; in fact, the sperm whale can hold its breath for up to two hours.

(3) Gestation and birth are another example of how fish and whales differ. Fish lay eggs and do not feed their offspring. Whales, though, have the "mothering instinct" of mammals—like apes, dogs, cats—they give birth to live young and proceed to feed them with milk from their mother's body. Fish are detached from their offspring; whereas, for a whale, the mothering instinct remains strong throughout its lifetime.

(4) Another major difference between fish and whales is that fish are *cold-blooded* and whales are *warm-blooded*. As a cold-blooded creature, fish body temperature changes with the water's temperature. When the water is cold, the fish are cold. Whales, however, remain warm regardless of the temperature of the surrounding water.

(5) Adaptation has played a major role in the evolving of the whale species. Yes, they are considered mammals, but unlike most mammals, they do not have much hair, nor do they have legs or much neck mobility. Through centuries of change and adaptability, whales have developed streamlined, compact, and compressed body frames that allow them to carry enormous weight and still manage to swim through the sea with great ease. In fact, scientists believe their front legs developed into flippers, allowing them to steer and keep their balance.

GO ON TO THE NEXT PAGE

(6)   Today, many whales are an endangered species, and some, especially the blue and humpback, are in danger of extinction because of unregulated hunting. For years, whalers were permitted to kill whales, like the blue and humpback, for their meat and byproducts. The result is that whales of all kinds slowly disappeared from our oceans. Yet, thanks to environmental laws and public awareness, the significance of whales as one of the oldest and most distinct species is readily recognized by scientists and citizens alike. Once again, whales populate our oceans and add to our knowledge about this most unique of sea mammals.

116. One thing that this narrative makes clear is that whales have more in common with:

    A. mammals than fish.

    B. reptiles than mammals.

    C. amphibians than fish.

    D. fish than mammals.

117. According to the passage, whales are a unique species in the animal kingdom because:

    A. whales are indigenous only to the northern hemisphere.

    B. whales can carry enormous weight without much effort.

    C. whales are nonmaternal and indifferent to their offspring.

    D. whales rely on protective fish clans for self-preservation.

118. The author of this passage implies that whales are:

    A. timid.

    B. aggressive.

    C. intelligent.

    D. unintelligent.

119. Which of the following statements can be inferred from the passage?

    A. Whales are creatures who have experienced successful adaptations.

    B. Whales are ponderous creatures with a sluggish metabolism.

    C. Whales are a species timid in scale and singular in design.

    D. Whales are an anomaly on the scale of biological diversity.

120. In the fifth paragraph, the word "adaptation" can best be defined as:

    A. modification.

    B. skillfulness.

    C. awareness.

    D. immutability.

121. The tone of this passage is best described as:

    A. skeptical.

    B. humorous.

    C. sarcastic.

    D. factual.

122. Which of the following is a fact about whales that is given in this passage?

    A. Whales are a type of fish.

    B. Whales have lungs.

    C. The blue whale is extinct.

    D. Blubber comes from whales.

123. Which of the following statements about whales is implied in this passage?

    A. They are cold-blooded creatures.

    B. They cannot take in oxygen when underwater.

    C. They have gills.

    D. They have nothing in common with humans.

124. This passage states that the sperm whale can hold its breath for:

    A. no more than 30 minutes.

    B. up to 2 hours.

    C. at least 3 hours.

    D. well over 4 hours.

125. According to the passage:

    A. whales are the world's largest animal.

    B. whales nurture their young.

    C. whales have difficulty swimming.

    D. whales are of little concern to environmentalists.

Answer Key

General Knowledge Practice Test 2: English Language Skills

1. B	15. B	29. C
2. C	16. A	30. A
3. C	17. C	31. B
4. D	18. D	32. C
5. A	19. C	33. B
6. D	20. B	34. A
7. A	21. A	35. B
8. B	22. C	36. B
9. A	23. C	37. C
10. B	24. B	38. C
11. A	25. B	39. A
12. A	26. B	40. A
13. C	27. C	
14. B	28. B	

General Knowledge Practice Test 2: Mathematics

41. D	56. B	71. D
42. C	57. D	72. D
43. B	58. B	73. A
44. C	59. A	74. B
45. A	60. A	75. C
46. C	61. C	76. B
47. D	62. D	77. D
48. C	63. B	78. A
49. A	64. D	79. D
50. C	65. A	80. C
51. B	66. D	81. C
52. B	67. C	82. A
53. A	68. A	83. C
54. C	69. D	84. B
55. D	70. C	85. B

General Knowledge Practice Test 2: Reading

86. B	100. B	114. B
87. A	101. C	115. D
88. D	102. C	116. A
89. C	103. C	117. B
90. D	104. C	118. C
91. D	105. D	119. A
92. B	106. A	120. A
93. C	107. C	121. D
94. B	108. B	122. B
95. C	109. D	123. B
96. D	110. D	124. B
97. B	111. D	125. B
98. A	112. A	
99. C	113. A	

General Knowledge Practice Test 2: Essay Explanation

In this section of the examination, you were asked to prepare a written assignment on one of two topics.

Topic 1

What are your favorite hobbies?

Topic 2

A historical figure who changed the world

You were asked to write a 300- to 600-word response that would be well-written, organized, and defined. You were also informed that your writing would be graded holistically, taking into consideration both mechanics and organization.

What follows are examples of a weak and strong response to both prompts.

Topic 1–What Are Your Favorite Hobbies?

Weak Response

My favorite hobbies are many. In fact, I have so many favorite hobbies that I have difficulty listing them all in one sitting. I like to swim, read, play tennis, and even collect stamps. I know that stamp collecting is not a very popular hobby anymore, but I really like it, I really do! Don't you? I also like bike riding. In fact, I think bike riding is my favorite thing to do. I just love going out on a sunny afternoon, feeling the brisk cool air at my back and just letting myself go on my bicycle. I ride everywhere, smiling at all I meet and waving to all who I see. Then, when I am really anxious, I love to do crossword puzzles. Thinking real hard about the right word calms me down and gets my juices flowing. I have to stop and think about what word would fit in a particular space—and that requires great skill. But, then again, sometimes I just give up and just sit and stare into space, and that's fun too.

Strong Response

Human beings can be many things. They can be parents, friends, lovers, workers, caregivers, cooks, handymen, and tired souls. Yet, despite our various roles, the one that we often enjoy the most is the one we do when often, no one is looking. This is the role that we call our hobby. We find an activity that just tickles our fancy and despite everything—bills, problems, and even illness—we find time to pursue our enjoyment. I know. I have three hobbies that I enjoy no matter what.

First, I enjoy reading. For me, reading is a luxury that I try to enjoy at every opportunity. Wherever I go, I carry something to read. Sometimes, it is a book that I just can't put down—so when no one is looking, or there is a lull at work, I sneak in a few seconds to read just a little bit more of what I am presently enjoying. And there is no limit to my reading preferences. I enjoy everything from mysteries to political biographies. I find each fascinating and intriguing. Each genre—comedy, mystery, romance, thriller, and biography—provides a new insight into the human condition and, of course, whets my appetite for more.

Second, I enjoy eating. Now, I know eating is not considered a typical hobby, but when you are a connoisseur of fine food like I am, then eating is considered your hobby. Often, my wife and I will go miles just to try out a new restaurant—no matter how obscure or famous it might portend to be. We enjoy trying new dishes—comparing our culinary adventures to climbing Mount Everest or floating down the Nile—you never know what to expect. Sometimes, we hit a real gem with great dishes, breads, and wines. Other times, well, let's just say, we don't finish our plates. But, despite all, I never tire of eating.

Third, I enjoy laughing. Laughing, you say? Is laughing really a hobby? It is if you laugh like I do. I laugh loud and long and hard. And I constantly look for things to amuse me. I enjoy good jokes (preferably clean and clever), funny books, musical comedies, and silly movies. Each—when done well—tickles my ribs like nothing else possible. Does that mean that I don't like sad things? Sure, I do, but I figure, why cry when laughing is so much more pleasurable, and besides, it is harder to execute. Making someone laugh—even a pushover like me—is a skill in and of itself.

Thus, my hobbies are personal and unique. While many adults enjoy tennis and jogging, I prefer reading, eating, and laughing. I know that I won't end up looking like Arnold Schwarzenegger, but, I will have fun pursuing my passion—just like him. And what more could you ask?

Topic 2—A Historical Figure Who Changed the World

Weak Response

To be sure, there are many historical figure who have had a major impact on world events. Everyone from four start general to great explorers have impacted the way the world events have and continue to unfold. No person, though, in my mind, has had a greater impact on world events than Franklin Delano Roosevelt. Elected to an unprecedented four terms in political office, Roosevelt literally changed the face of the globe with his far-reaching goals and programs. He lifted—singlehandedly—people out of poverty and defeated Nazism with one fell swoop. His reach is felt to this day as his political programs and ideas are still being implemented in the halls of American government and foreign countries. His far-reaching social programs were just the tonic needed for a downtrodden and desperate American people. And his great courage to defeat a world wide enemy despite his own personal pain and hardship is much to be admired. Indeed, he is a truly remarkable historical figure.

Strong Response

President Franklin D. Roosevelt is truly a historical figure who changed the world. The only president to be elected to four consecutive terms in office, Roosevelt led the United States through its worst depression and its worst war. In his personal life, he showed courage and great strength of character in overcoming hardships. Stricken by polio in mid-life, he refused to give up his career of public service. In fact, even after being stricken with polio, Roosevelt was elected to the Presidency. It was this strength of determination in the face of insurmountable difficulty and pain that helped him to successfully lead the country through very difficult times.

In the prime of his life, Roosevelt became paralyzed from the waist down. Polio left him immobile, but not downtrodden. For the rest of his life, he fought desperately to overcome his disability and from the comfort of his wheelchair, he continued his political career. He loved public service and relished the attention that it brought him. He also wanted to prove to himself and the world that any hardship could be overcome with sheer determination. With this in mind, he ran for public office. He was elected governor of New York, and then later became President of the United States.

When Roosevelt became President, America was experiencing an unprecedented social upheaval; a serious economic depression was occurring and millions of people were unemployed. Immediately, Roosevelt and his administration began the difficult work of trying to solve the country's social and economic problems. Quickly, he set up numerous government agencies to provide relief for the jobless and to stabilize the country's economy. He also supplied banks in good financial condition with money so that they would reopen and return the country to a healthy financial condition. Finally, he passed laws to protect the investments of those who held stocks and bonds. All these actions were taken to ensure the economic viability of a country and a people who were desperate for help.

At the beginning of Roosevelt's third term in office, the United States entered the Second World War. Shortly after the attack of the Japanese on Pearl Harbor, Roosevelt declared war on Japan. Three days later, Germany and Italy declared war on the United States. America then declared war on those countries. Under Roosevelt's leadership, the United States together with its allies prevailed over the enemy. America's citizens firmly supported Roosevelt during the difficult war years, but unfortunately, he was never to see the final victory. He died suddenly at his favorite spa for the treatment for his polio, Warm Spring, Georgia, just before the surrender of the German army.

Truly, Roosevelt was a remarkable historical figure. Despite crippling pain, he managed to achieve political greatness and monumental significance by imposing his own physical and intellectual will onto the American people. Overcoming tremendous odds both at home and abroad, Roosevelt raised the economic conditions of the American people while simultaneously liberating the world from oppression and tyranny. In so doing, he changed the course of history and demonstrated the power of the human spirit.

General Knowledge Practice Test 2: English Language Skills Answers and Explanations

1. **B.** Choice **B** provides the most logical sequence of ideas and supporting details in this paragraph, Choices **A**, **C**, and **D** do not represent a logical arrangement of the possible sentence combinations.

2. **C.** Choice **C** is the sentence *least relevant to the passage.* The passage is discussing shells as a protective covering, nothing about collecting them.

3. **C.** Choice **C** provides the most logical sequence of ideas and supporting details in the paragraph. Choices **A**, **B**, and **D** do not represent a logical arrangement of the possible sentence combinations.

4. **D.** Choice **D** is the sentence *least relevant to the passage.* The passage is discussing the challenge of language diversity in schools, not ethnic foods.

5. **A.** The word *accept* is used incorrectly in this sentence. The correct choice is *except* or Choice **A**. The word *accept* means to receive something from another person. The word *except* means "everything but. . ."; it is an indication that something is not included in the general whole. The word *allowed* is the correct spelling and used properly. The verb *to eat* is also the proper usage.

6. **D.** No change is necessary. The sentence is correct as written.

7. **A.** The word *too* is used incorrectly in this sentence. The correct choice is *to* or Choice **A**. The word *too* means also or "in addition." The word *to* is a preposition used to connect two thoughts together in a sentence. The words *formally* and *themselves* are both the correct word choices for this sentence.

8. **B.** The word *french* is presented incorrectly in this sentence. The correct choice is *French* or Choice **B**. A language—English, Spanish, German, and so on—is considered a proper noun and, hence, is capitalized. The words *read* and *tomorrow* are spelled and used correctly in this sentence.

9. **A.** *Have went* is incorrect. The correct choice is *have gone* (Choice **A**). The word *all-American* is properly capitalized as America is a proper noun. The word *their* is properly used as a possessive pronoun.

10. **B.** The word *among* is used incorrectly in this sentence. The correct choice is *between* or Choice **B**. *Among* is used when you are talking about three or more objects; *between* is used when you are referring to only two objects. The verb form *sat* is correctly used in this sentence. The word *awards* does not require capitalization.

11. **A.** The word *deep* is used incorrectly in this sentence. The correct choice is *deeply* or Choice **B**. The word deep is used here as an adverb and, thus, should be spelled *deeply*. The word *their* is the correct word choice because it is showing possession. The phrase *considerable differences* is an appropriate word choice for this sentence.

12. **A.** The word *fowl* is the wrong word choice in this sentence. The correct choice is *foul* or Choice **A**. The word *fowl* is another word for bird. The word *foul* refers to a penalty for "going out of bounds" in a game of play. The word *loudly* is an adverb modifying protested and is used correctly in this sentence. The word *disbelief* means hard to believe and is spelled correctly.

13. **C.** The word *then* is the wrong word choice in this sentence. The correct word choice is *than* or Choice **C**. The word *than* is used when making a comparison, as is the case in this sentence. The word *then* refers to time and/or direction. In this sentence, the word *unfortunately* is used correctly to modify the action of the tennis team. The verb form, *had*, is used correctly in this sentence as written.

14. **B.** The word *masks* is the wrong word choice in this sentence. The correct word choice is *mask* or Choice **B**. The word *mask* is used because the subject of the sentence is *talents,* and in subject-verb agreement, plural nouns take singular verbs. In this sentence, the word *surprising* is used correctly to modify the noun *talents.* The possessive form, *his,* is used correctly in this sentence as written.

15. **B.** The phrase *me and Nancy* is the wrong choice for this sentence. The correct choice is *Nancy and I* or Choice **B**. When used as the subject of a sentence, you always write *the person's name and I.* The word *among* is the correct word choice because it refers to more than two sisters. The word *tall* is correct as used in this sentence.

16. **A.** The word *reign* is used incorrectly in this sentence. The correct choice is *rain* or Choice **A.** The verb *found* is used correctly in this sentence. Similarly, the verb *eat* is used correctly in this sentence.

17. **C.** The sentence should be in the past tense, so *saw* is the correct verb at **C.** Keep in mind that the verb *seen* cannot stand alone; it requires an auxiliary verb. The word *students* at **A** docs not show possession, so no apostrophe is needed. The word *who* at **B** is correct because it serves as the subject of the nonrestrictive clause it introduces.

18. **D.** The word *that* at **A** introducing the subordinate clause, which identifies what is being talked about, is correct. The word *really* at **B** is also correct because it is an adverb modifying the adjective *careful*. The plural pronoun *they* at **C** is correct because it agrees with its antecedent *scientists*.

19. **C.** A comma is needed at **C** to separate the introductory subordinate clause from the rest of the sentence. The word *when* at **A** is correct and makes sense in the sentence. The word *students* at **B** does not show possession, so no apostrophe is needed.

20. **B.** The phrase *more easier* at **B** is a faulty comparison of two things. The correct comparative form of *easy* is *easier*, which makes Choice **B** correct. The word *happy* at **A** is correct because it is an adjective referring to one thing. Placing a comma at **C** would be incorrect.

21. **A.** In this sentence, the word following the verb *felt* at **A** modifies its subject, the pronoun *they*. The word *badly* is an adverb, however, and should not be used to modify a pronoun. The adjective *bad* should be used instead. The word *Tiffany* at **B** is a proper noun, so it should be capitalized. The plural verb *were* at **C** agrees with its plural subject *they*.

22. **C.** The word *capitol* refers to a building, not to a city. Change *capitol* to *capital* (Choice **C**), which refers to a seat of government, to make the sentence grammatically correct. The word *history* at **A** is not a proper noun, so it should not be capitalized. The sentence is in the past tense, so *went* is the correct verb at **B.**

23. **C.** The word *there* at **C** should be changed to the plural third person pronoun *their* (Choice **C**) to make the sentence grammatically correct. The possessive form *girls'* of the plural noun *girls* at **A** is correctly formed. To form the possessive of a plural noun that ends in *s*, add an apostrophe after the *s*. Inserting a comma at **B** would be incorrect. No comma should be placed between two items joined by the word *and*.

24. **B.** The sentence is in the past tense; *ran* (Choice **B**) is the correct verb instead of *had run* at **B.** The word *when* at **A** is correct and makes sense in the sentence. The word *their* at **C** is spelled correctly.

25. **B.** The word *between* is a preposition. The object of a preposition should be in the objective case. Change *I* at **B** to *me* to make the sentence grammatically correct. The word *cannot* at **A** is spelled correctly. The word *years* at **C** is not showing ownership, so it should not be in the possessive case.

26. **B.** The word at **B** is the subject of the verb *am* (which is understood) and thus, should be in the subjective case. Change *me* to *I* to make the sentence grammatically correct. The sentence is in the present tense, so *are* at **A** is correct. Inserting a comma at **C** would be incorrect.

27. **C.** The word at **C** should be in the subjective case because it is the subject of the subordinate clause it introduces. Change *whomever* to *whoever* (Choice **C**) to make the sentence grammatically correct. Inserting a comma at **A** would be incorrect. The word *principal,* referring to the person who is the building supervisor of the school, at **B** is correct.

28. **B.** The singular pronoun *one* is the subject of the verb at **B,** so change *want* to *wants* (Choice **B**) to make the verb agree with its singular subject. The relative pronoun *who* at **A** is correct because it is the subject of the relative clause it introduces. The word *too* at **C** is spelled correctly.

29. **C.** The word *good* at **C** modifies the verb *did,* so it should be an adverb. Change *good* to *well* (Choice **C**) to make the sentence grammatically correct. The comma at **A** following the introductory clause is correct. The verb *didn't* at **B** agrees with its singular subject *he*.

30. **A.** The pronoun at **A** modifies the gerund *graduating*, which is the subject of the main clause; hence you should use the possessive pronoun *My* (Choice **A**) instead of *Me* to make the sentence grammatically correct. The singular verb *has* at **B** agrees with its singular subject *graduating*. The relative pronoun *whom* at **C** is the object of the preposition *of*, so it should be in the objective case.

31. **B.** The singular pronoun *one* is the subject of the verb at **B,** so change *were* to *was* to make the verb agree with its singular subject. Inserting a comma at **A** would be incorrect. No hyphen is needed at **C.**

32. **C.** Does *them* at **C** refer to *sons* or *board games*? Change *them* to *the board games* to avoid ambiguity. The word *couple's* at **A** is the correct possessive form of *couple*. The comma at **B** is needed to separate the two independent clauses.

33. **B.** The word at **B** should be spelled *received*. The relative pronoun *who* at **A** is correct because it is the subject of the clause it introduces. Inserting a comma at **C** would be incorrect.

34. **A.** At **A** the superlative form of *nice* is *nicest*, not *most nicest*. The word *friend* at **B** is spelled correctly. The noun phrase *every day* at **C** should not be replaced with the adjective *everyday*, which means "common" or "used daily."

35. **B.** The correct comparative form of *old* is *older*. The comparative form is used when two things are compared.

36. **B.** The past participle for the verb *to take* is *taken*. Note that "should of" in **A** and **C** is an error for "should have."

37. **C.** The tense of the verb in Choice **C** relates logically to the verb in the main clause because both verbs are in the past tense. The verb tenses in choices **A** and **B** do not relate logically to the verb in the main clause.

38. **C.** All punctuation in Choice **C** is correct. Choice **A** is incorrect because it is a run-on sentence. It is two complete sentences connected by only a comma. Choice **B** is also a run-on sentence. It is two complete sentences joined without a word to connect them or a proper punctuation mark to separate them. The first sentence in Choice **D** needs a comma after the word *promise*.

39. **A.** All punctuation in Choice **A** is correct. In Choice **B,** the word *familys'* is incorrect. To form the possessive of a noun (either singular or plural) that does not end in *s*, add an apostrophe and *s*. Choice **C** is incorrect because it contains a fragment. (*Having been raised in our household from a puppy.*) A comma is needed in Choice **D** to separate the introductory participial phrase from the rest of the sentence.

40. **A.** The modifiers in sentence A are placed correctly. The participial phrase *driving through the neighborhood* modifies *woman* and should be close to it. In choices **B** and **C,** *driving through the neighborhood* is separated from the noun *woman,* resulting in ambiguity. Additionally, the participial phrase *playing with his dog* modifies the noun *child* and should be close to it. In Choice **D** the participial phrase *playing with his dog* is separated from the noun *child,* resulting in ambiguity.

General Knowledge Practice Test 2: Mathematics Answers and Explanations

41. **D.** The greatest common factor of 30 and 45 is the largest number that will divide into both 30 and 45 evenly. The numbers that will divide evenly into 30 are 1, 2, 3, 5, 6, 10, 15, and 30. The numbers that will divide evenly into 45 are 1, 3, 5, 9, 15, and 45. Looking at the two sets of divisors, you can see that 15 is the largest number that will divide into both 30 and 45 evenly. Thus, GCF (30, 45) = 15. Choice **A** is incorrect because 2 is not a common factor between 30 and 45. Choices **B** and **C** are incorrect because 3 and 5 are common factors of 30 and 45, but both are less than 15, so neither is the greatest common factor.

42. **C.** $1.082 \times 10^8 = 1.082 \times 100,000,000 = 108,200,000$, which is equivalent to moving the decimal point 8 places to the right. Choice **A** is the result of moving the decimal point 10 places to the right. Choice **B** is the result of moving the decimal point 9 places to the right. Choice **D** is the result of moving the decimal point 8 places to the left.

43. **B.** To approximate the value of $\sqrt{164}$, find two consecutive integers such that the square of the first integer is less than 164 and the square of the second integer is greater than 164. Since 12^2 is $144 < 164$ and 13^2 is $169 > 164$, the approximate value of $\sqrt{164}$ is between 12 and 13, Choice **B**. Choice **A** results if you mistakenly separate 164 into $16 + 4$, take the square roots of these two numbers, and then add to obtain 6. Choice **C** results if you divide 164 by 4 to obtain 42. Choice **D** results if you divide 164 by 2 to obtain 81.

44. C. To simplify the expression $7 + 3(4^2) - 8$, follow the order of operations using the mnemonic "<u>P</u>lease <u>E</u>xcuse <u>M</u>y <u>D</u>ear <u>A</u>unt <u>S</u>ally."

$$7 + 3(4^2) - 8 = 7 + 3(16) - 8 \qquad \text{First, do the exponentiation inside the parentheses.}$$

$$= 7 + 48 - 8 \qquad \text{Next, multiply.}$$

$$= 47, \text{ Choice } \mathbf{C} \qquad \text{Finally, add and subtract from left to right.}$$

Choice **A** results if you evaluate 4^2 incorrectly as $4 \times 2 = 8$. Choice **B** results if you add and subtract before multiplying. Choice **D** results if, after you do the exponentiation in the first step, you continue by simplifying from left to right without regard for the order of operations.

45. A. Expressed in exponential notation, the product $2 \times 2 \times 5 \times 5 \times 5$ is $2^2 \times 5^3$ (Choice **A**), which indicates 2 factors of 2 and 3 factors of 5. Choice **B** indicates 5 factors of 10. Choice **C** indicates 5 factors of 2 and 2 factors of 5. Choice **D** is not in exponential notation, nor is it equivalent to $2 \times 2 \times 5 \times 5 \times 5$.

46. C. To change $8\frac{1}{4}\%$ to a decimal, first rewrite it as 8.25%. Then move the decimal point two places to the left and drop the percent sign to obtain 0.0825. Choices **A** and **B** result if you drop the percent sign, but fail to move the decimal point two places to the left. Choice **D** results if you convert 8¼ to a decimal representation incorrectly.

47. D. To list the temperatures in order from coldest to warmest, list them in order from lowest to highest. Start with the positive temperatures: $2° < 4°$. You know that $0°$ is less than the positive temperatures and greater than the negative temperatures, so you have this: negative temperatures $< 0° < 2° < 4°$. To compare $-6°$ and $-8°$, sketch a number line.

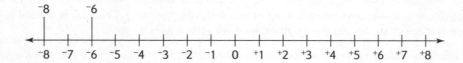

From the number line, you can see that -6 is greater than -8 because it lies to the right of -8, so you end up with $-8° < -6° < 0° < 2° < 4°$, Choice **D**. Choice **A** results if you list the temperatures in order as if all were nonnegative. Choice **B** results if you list the temperatures from warmest to coldest. Choice **C** results if you make the mistake of thinking $-6° < -8°$.

48. C. To find the amount budgeted for rent, you will need to answer the question: what is 30% of $2400?

Method 1: To solve the problem, identify the elements of the percent problem, plug the values into the percent proportion, and solve the proportion:

Step 1. Identify the elements.

$$r = 30$$

$$\text{part} = ?$$

$$\text{whole} = \$2400$$

Step 2. Plug into the percent proportion (omitting the units for convenience).

$$\frac{r}{100} = \frac{\text{part}}{\text{whole}}$$

$$\frac{30}{100} = \frac{x}{\$2400}$$

Step 3. Solve the proportion (omitting the units for convenience).

$$30 \times 2400 \qquad \text{Find a cross product you can calculate. You don't know the value of } x, \text{ so the only cross product you can calculate is 30 times 2400.}$$

$$x = \frac{30 \times 2400}{100} \qquad \text{Divide by 100, the numerical term you didn't use.}$$

$$x = \$720$$

The amount budgeted for rent is $720, Choice **C**.

Did I answer the question? Yes, I found the amount budgeted for rent. ✓

Is the answer stated in the correct units? Yes, the units are dollars, which is correct. ✓

Method 2: Change 30% to a decimal fraction or common fraction and multiply:

$$30\% \text{ of } \$2400 = 0.30 \times \$2400 = \$720.00$$

$$\text{or } 30\% \text{ of } \$2400 = \frac{3}{10} \times \$2400 = 3 \times \$240 = \$720$$

Choice **A** results if you make a decimal point error. Choice **B** results if you solve the problem incorrectly by finding 70% of $2400, and you make a decimal point error. Choice **D** results if you solve the problem incorrectly by finding 70% of $2400.

49. **A.** Use the conversion fact, 1 kilometer = 1000 meters, from the Mathematics Reference Sheet to obtain two conversion fractions: $\frac{1 \text{ km}}{1000 \text{ m}}$ and $\frac{1000 \text{ m}}{1 \text{ km}}$.

Write your measurement as a fraction with denominator 1 and let unit analysis tell you whether to multiply by $\frac{1 \text{ km}}{1000 \text{ m}}$ or $\frac{1000 \text{ m}}{1 \text{ km}}$. Since you want the meters to divide out, multiply by $\frac{1 \text{ km}}{1000 \text{ m}}$.

$$\frac{1500 \text{ m}}{1} \times \frac{1 \text{ km}}{1000 \text{ m}} = \frac{1500 \text{ km}}{1000} = 1.5 \text{ km}$$

The runner ran 1.5 kilometers in the race, Choice **A**.

Choices **B** and **C** occur if you make a mistake in placing the decimal point in your answer. Choice **D** results if you multiply by 1000 to convert.

50. **C.** The thermometer is reading between 30° and 40°. The difference between these two points is $40° - 30° = 10°$. It takes five marks to go from 30° up to 40°. Divide the difference between the two points by 5: $10° \div 5 = 2°$. Therefore, each mark on the thermometer represents 2°. The thermometer is reading 3 marks or 6° above 30°, which is 36°F (Choice **C**). Choice **A** results if you mistakenly determine that each mark represents 1°. Choice **B** results if you mistakenly determine that the reading is at 35°. Choice **D** results if you read down from 40° instead of up from 30°.

51. **B.** First, sketch a diagram to illustrate the problem:

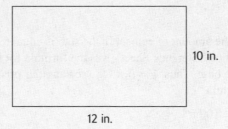

The perimeter of a figure is the distance around it. To find the perimeter of the rectangle, plug into the following formula.

$$P = 2l + 2w = 2(12 \text{ in.}) + 2(10 \text{ in.}) = 24 \text{ in.} + 20 \text{ in.} = 44 \text{ in.}, \text{ Choice } \mathbf{B}.$$

Did I answer the question? Yes, I found the perimeter of the rectangle. ✓

Is the answer stated in the correct units? Yes, the units are inches, which is correct. ✓

Choice **A** results if you fail to multiply each dimension by 2. Choice **C** results if you use an incorrect formula. Choice **D** results if you find the area instead of the perimeter, and you disregard that the units do not work out to be inches when you make this mistake.

52. B. First, sketch a diagram to illustrate the problem.

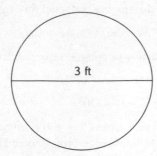

3 ft

The Mathematics Reference Sheet gives the formula of a circle as $A = \pi r^2$. To find the area of the circular garden, find the radius, and then plug in to the formula.

Step 1. The radius is half the diameter = 3 ft ÷ 2 = 1.5 ft.

Step 2. Plug into the formula, using $\pi = 3.14$.

$A = \pi r^2 = A = 3.14(1.5 \text{ ft})^2 = 3.14(2.25 \text{ ft}^2) = 7.065 \text{ ft}^2.$

The area of the circular garden is 7.065 ft^2, Choice **B.**

Did I answer the question? Yes, I found the area of the circular garden. ✓

Is the answer stated in the correct units? Yes, the units are square feet, which is correct. ✓

Choice **A** results if you find the radius but do not square it. Choice **C** results if you use the diameter in the area formula instead of the radius. Choice **D** results if you find the circumference instead of the area, and you disregard that the units do not work out to be square feet when you make this mistake.

53. A. First, sketch a diagram to illustrate the problem:

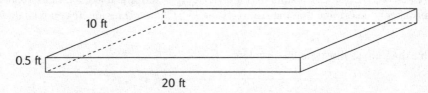

10 ft

0.5 ft

20 ft

Cubic feet are units of volume. The amount of cement in the slab is equal to the volume of the slab, which is a rectangular prism. The Mathematics Reference Sheet gives the formula for the volume of a rectangular prism as $V = Bh$, where B is the area of the base. Thus, $V = lwh$ for a rectangular prism. To find the amount of cement, plug the dimensions into the formula.

$V = lwh = 20 \text{ ft} \cdot 10 \text{ ft} \cdot 0.5 \text{ ft} = 100 \text{ ft}^3$

There are 100 ft^3 of cement in the slab, Choice **A.**

Did I answer the question? Yes, I found how many cubic feet of cement are in the slab. ✓

Is the answer stated in the correct units? Yes, the units are cubic feet, which is correct. ✓

Choice **B** results if you add the dimensions instead of multiplying. Choice **C** results if you multiply the volume by 3. Choice **D** results if you place the decimal point incorrectly when computing the volume.

54. C. The surface area of a cube is the sum of the areas of the faces of the cube. The cube in this problem has six congruent faces, each of which is a 10-cm square. To find the surface area of the cube, multiply 6 times the area of one face.

Surface Area = $6 \times (10 \text{ cm})^2 = 6 \times 100 \text{ cm}^2 = 600 \text{ cm}^2$

The surface area of the 10-cm cube is 600 cm^2, Choice **C.**

Did I answer the question? Yes, I found the surface area of the cube. ✓

Is the answer stated in the correct units? Yes, the units are square centimeters, which is correct. ✓

Choice **A** results if you add the dimensions instead of multiplying. Choice **B** is the area of only one of the six faces. Choice **D** results if you multiply 6×10 before squaring.

55. D. To solve this problem requires two steps. First, convert 3 hours 15 minutes to hours. Then, divide 221 miles by the result.

Step 1. Convert 3 hours 15 minutes to hours. The Mathematics Reference Sheet shows the conversion fact, 1 hour = 60 minutes, which yields two conversion fractions: $\frac{1 \text{ h}}{60 \text{ min}}$ and $\frac{60 \text{ min}}{1 \text{ h}}$.

Write 15 minutes as a fraction with denominator 1 and let unit analysis tell you whether to multiply by $\frac{1 \text{ h}}{60 \text{ min}}$ or $\frac{60 \text{ min}}{1 \text{ h}}$. Since you want the minutes to divide out, multiply by $\frac{1 \text{ h}}{60 \text{ min}}$.

$$\frac{15 \text{ min}}{1} \times \frac{1 \text{ h}}{60 \text{ min}} = \frac{15 \text{ h}}{60} = \frac{1}{4} \text{ h or } 0.25 \text{ h. Thus, 3 hours 15 minutes} = 3.25 \text{ hours.}$$

Step 2. To obtain miles per hour, divide 221 miles by 3.25 hours $= \frac{221 \text{ mi}}{3.25 \text{ h}} = 68$ mph

The car traveled at the rate of 68 mph, Choice **D**.

Did I answer the question? Yes, I found the rate of travel in miles per hour. ✓

Is the answer stated in the correct units? Yes, the units are miles per hour, which is correct. ✓

Choice **A** results if you divide incorrectly. Choices **B** and **C** result if you convert 3 hours, 15 minutes to hours incorrectly.

56. B. To determine how many gallons are consumed per week, find how many gallons are consumed per day. Then multiply the result by 7 days per week $\left(\frac{7 \text{ d}}{\text{wk}}\right)$.

Step 1. Find how many gallons are consumed per day.

The Mathematics Reference Sheet provides the following information.

1 cup = 8 fluid ounces

1 pint = 2 cups

1 quart = 2 pints

1 gallon = 4 quarts

These conversion facts yield 8 conversion fractions: $\frac{1 \text{ c}}{8 \text{ oz}}$ and $\frac{8 \text{ oz}}{1 \text{ c}}$, $\frac{1 \text{ pt}}{2 \text{ c}}$ and $\frac{2 \text{ c}}{1 \text{ pt}}$, $\frac{1 \text{ qt}}{2 \text{ pt}}$ and $\frac{2 \text{ pt}}{1 \text{ qt}}$, $\frac{1 \text{ gal}}{4 \text{ qt}}$ and $\frac{4 \text{ qt}}{1 \text{ gal}}$. Write 64 ounces per day as a fraction. Then, using unit analysis, multiply a "chain" of conversion fractions that will result in gallons as the final unit.

$$\frac{64 \text{ oz}}{\text{day}} \times \frac{1 \text{ c}}{8 \text{ oz}} \times \frac{1 \text{ pt}}{2 \text{ c}} \times \frac{1 \text{ qt}}{2 \text{ pt}} \times \frac{1 \text{ gal}}{4 \text{ qt}} = \frac{0.5 \text{ gal}}{\text{day}}$$

Step 2. Multiply by 7 days per week $\left(\frac{7 \text{ d}}{\text{wk}}\right)$.

$$\frac{0.5 \text{ gal}}{\text{day}} \times \frac{7 \text{ d}}{\text{wk}} = \frac{3.5 \text{ gal}}{\text{wk}}$$

The person will consume 3.5 gallons of water per week, Choice **B**.

Did I answer the question? Yes, I found the number of gallons consumed per week. ✓

Is the answer stated in the correct units? Yes, the units are gallons per week, which is correct. ✓

Choice **A** results if you fail to multiply by 7 days per week. Choices **C** and **D** result if you convert 64 ounces to gallons incorrectly by omitting one or more of the conversion fractions.

57. D. This problem is a proportion problem involving a map scale. To solve the problem, determine the ratios being compared, being sure to compare corresponding quantities in the same order; write a proportion using the two ratios; and use cross products to solve the proportion.

Step 1. Determine the ratios being compared.

Let d be the actual distance in miles between the two landmarks. The first sentence gives the first ratio: $\dfrac{d\,(\text{in miles})}{9.5 \text{ in.}}$. The second sentence gives you the second ratio: $\dfrac{10 \text{ miles}}{\frac{1}{2} \text{ in.}}$. (Notice, you put miles in the numerator in the second ratio because you have miles in the numerator in the first ratio.)

Step 2. Write a proportion using the two ratios.

$$\frac{d\,(\text{in miles})}{9.5 \text{ in.}} = \frac{10 \text{ miles}}{\frac{1}{2} \text{ in.}}$$

For ease of calculation, change $\frac{1}{2}$ to 0.5.

$$\frac{d\,(\text{in miles})}{9.5 \text{ in.}} = \frac{10 \text{ miles}}{0.5 \text{ in.}}$$

Step 3. Use cross products to solve the proportion (omitting the units for convenience).

9.5×10 Find a cross product you can calculate. You don't know the value of d, so the only cross product you can calculate is 9.5 times 10.

$d = \dfrac{9.5 \times 10}{0.5}$ Divide by 0.5, the numerical term you didn't use.

Key the calculation into the calculator like this: $9.5 \times 10 \div 0.5 = 190$

$d = 190$ miles, Choice **D**

Did I answer the question? Yes, I found the actual distance in miles between the two landmarks. ✓

Is the answer stated in the correct units? Yes, the units are miles, which is correct. ✓

Choice **A** results if you set up the proportion incorrectly. Choice **B** results if you make a mistake in placing the decimal point in the answer. Choice **C** results if you deal with the $\frac{1}{2}$ in the proportion incorrectly.

58. B. First, sketch a diagram to illustrate the problem:

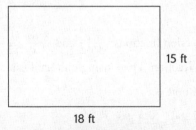

Square yards are units of area. The number of square yards of carpet needed will be the area of the rectangular room. The Mathematics Reference Sheet gives the formula for the area of a rectangle as $A = lw$. The cost of the carpet is $25.75 per square yard. You will need to find the area of the room in square yards. To find the cost of the carpet will take three steps: First, convert the dimensions of the room to yards; next, find the area of the room in square yards; then, multiply the number of square yards by the cost per square yard.

Step 1. Convert the dimensions of the room to yards.

The Mathematics Reference Sheet shows 1 yard = 3 feet. This conversion fact yields two conversion fractions: $\frac{1 \text{ yd}}{3 \text{ ft}}$ and $\frac{3 \text{ ft}}{1 \text{ yd}}$. Write each dimension as a fraction with denominator 1, and let unit analysis tell you which conversion fraction to use. Since you want the feet to divide out use $\frac{1 \text{ yd}}{3 \text{ ft}}$.

$$\frac{\overset{6}{\cancel{18}} \ \cancel{ft}}{1} \times \frac{1 \text{ yd}}{\underset{1}{\cancel{3}} \ \cancel{ft}} = 6 \text{ yd}$$

$$\frac{\overset{5}{\cancel{15}} \ \cancel{ft}}{1} \times \frac{1 \text{ yd}}{\underset{1}{\cancel{3}} \ \cancel{ft}} = 5 \text{ yd}$$

Step 2. Find the area of the room in square yards. Plug into the formula.

$A = lw = 6 \text{ yd} \cdot 5 \text{ yd} = 30 \text{ yd}^2$

Step 3. Multiply the number of square yards by the cost per square yard.

$$30 \ \cancel{yd}^2 \times \frac{\$25.75}{\cancel{yd}^2} = \$772.50$$

Not including tax, it will cost $772.50 to carpet the room, Choice **B**.

Did I answer the question? Yes, I found the cost of carpeting the room. ✓

Is the answer stated in the correct units? Yes, the units are dollars, which is correct. ✓

Choice **A** results if you fail to multiply by the cost of the carpet, and you disregard that the units do not work out to be dollars when you make this mistake. Choice **C** results if you find the area in square feet and divide this result by 3 to convert to square yards. This approach is incorrect because $1 \text{ yd}^2 = 3 \text{ ft} \times 3 \text{ ft} = 9 \text{ ft}^2$, not 3 ft^2. Choice **D** is the result of finding the area in square feet and then multiplying by the cost per square yard.

59. A. The figure is a polygon that has five sides, so it is a pentagon. Choice **B** is incorrect because a rhombus is a parallelogram that four congruent sides. Choice **C** is incorrect because a hexagon is a polygon that has exactly six sides. Choice **D** is incorrect because a trapezoid is a quadrilateral that has exactly one pair of opposite sides parallel.

60. A. First, sketch a diagram to illustrate the problem:

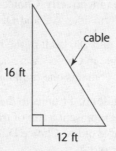

The pole and the cable form a right triangle. From the diagram, you can see that the length of the cable is the hypotenuse of the right triangle that has legs of 16 feet and 12 feet. Plug into the formula:

$c = \text{hypotenuse} = ?$, $a = 16 \text{ ft}$, and $b = 12 \text{ ft}$

$c^2 = a^2 + b^2 = (16 \text{ ft})^2 + (12 \text{ ft})^2 = 256 \text{ ft}^2 + 144 \text{ ft}^2 = 400 \text{ ft}^2$

To solve this equation, you must think of a number that multiplies by itself to give 400. From the list of square roots given in the section titled "Numeration and Operations" in Chapter 4, you know that $\sqrt{400} = 20$, so $c = 20 \text{ ft}$. The length of the cable is 20 feet, Choice **A.**

Did I answer the question? Yes, I found the length of the cable. ✓

Is the answer stated in the correct units? Yes, the units are feet, which is correct. ✓

Choice **B** results if you mistakenly decide to solve the problem by adding the lengths of the two legs to find the length of the hypotenuse. Choice **C** results if you make the mistake of dividing 400 by 2 to find its square root. Choice **D** results if you fail to find the square root of 400.

61. **C.** A square is a parallelogram that has four congruent sides and four right angles. A rhombus is a parallelogram that has four congruent sides. Therefore, a square is a special type of rhombus that has four right angles. Choices **A** and **B** are incorrect because cubes and prisms are three-dimensional figures, but a square is a two-dimensional figure. Choice **D** is incorrect because a trapezoid has exactly one pair of opposite sides parallel, but a square has two pairs of opposite sides parallel.

62. **D.** Only the figure for Choice **D** has a correctly drawn line of symmetry that cuts the figure into two congruent halves. The lines in the figures for choices **A, B,** and **C** do not cut the figures into two congruent halves.

63. **B.** The corresponding sides of similar triangles are proportional. Side $\overline{AB}$ is the hypotenuse of triangle ABC. Its corresponding side is $\overline{DE}$, which is the hypotenuse of triangle DEF. The corresponding side for side $\overline{AC}$ is $\overline{DF}$. Let h = length of $\overline{AB}$. Set up the proportion and solve it.

$$\frac{\text{length of } \overline{AB}}{\text{length of } \overline{DE}} = \frac{\text{length of } \overline{AC}}{\text{length of } \overline{DF}}$$ *Hint:* Made sure you keep corresponding sides in the same order.

$$\frac{h}{10 \text{ m}} = \frac{20 \text{ m}}{8 \text{ m}}$$

Use cross products to solve the proportion (omitting the units for convenience).

10×20 Find a cross product you can calculate. You don't know the value of h, so the only cross product you can calculate is 10 times 20.

$h = \frac{10 \times 20}{8}$ Divide by 8, the numerical term you didn't use.

Key the calculation into the calculator like this: $10 \times 20 \div 8 = 25$

$h = 25$ meters

Did I answer the question? Yes, I found the length of the hypotenuse of triangle ABC. ✓

Is the answer stated in the correct units? Yes, the units are meters, which is correct. ✓

Choice **A** results if you set up the proportion incorrectly. Choice **C** results if you add the lengths of sides $\overline{AC}$ and $\overline{DF}$. Choice **D** results if you add the lengths of sides $\overline{AC}$ and $\overline{DF}$.

64. **D.** An obtuse angle measures between 90° and 180°. All of the interior angles of the octagon in Choice **D** are obtuse angles. All of the angles in the triangle in Choice **A** are acute angles. All of the angles in Choice **B** are right angles. The right triangle in Choice **C** contains one right angle and two acute angles.

65. **A.** Trapezoid A' represents a translation (slide) of 11 units to the right and 11 units down of trapezoid A. Choice **B** is incorrect because trapezoid A' does not represent a flip of trapezoid A. Choice **C** is incorrect because trapezoid A' does not represent a turn of trapezoid A. Choice **D** is incorrect because trapezoid A' does not represent an enlarging or shrinking of trapezoid A.

66. **D.** The point P is located 8 units to the left and 3 units up from the origin, so it has coordinates (–8,3). Choice **A** is incorrect because point M is located at (8,–3). Choice **B** is incorrect because point N is located at (–8,–3). Choice **C** is incorrect because point O is located at (8, 3).

67. C.

Step 1. Sketch a diagram and label it.

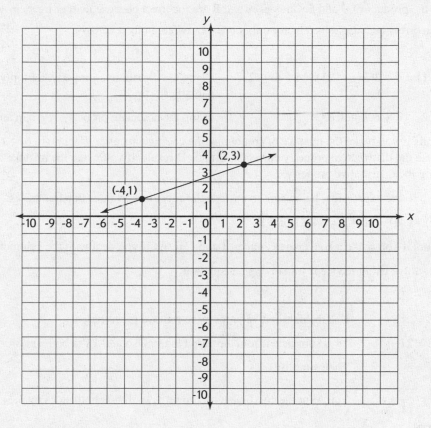

Step 2. Specify (x_1, y_1) and (x_2, y_2).

Let $(x_1, y_1) = (-4, 1)$ and $(x_2, y_2) = (2, 3)$. Then $x_1 = -4$, $y_1 = 1$, $x_2 = 2$, and $y_2 = 3$.

Step 3. Plug into the formula. (*Hint:* Enclose negative values in parentheses.)

$$\text{Slope of line} = \frac{y_2 - y_1}{x_2 - x_1} = \frac{3 - 1}{2 - (-4)} = \frac{3 - 1}{2 + 4} = \frac{2}{6} = \frac{1}{3}$$

The line through the points $(-4, 1)$ and $(2, 3)$ has slope $\frac{1}{3}$, Choice **C.**

Choice **A** results if you invert the slope formula and make a sign error. Choice **B** results if you make a sign error. Choice **D** results if you invert the slope formula.

68. A. Check for an arithmetic sequence by subtracting consecutive terms listed from the terms that follow them.

$-16 - 8 = -24$

$32 - (-16) = 32 + 16 = 48$

No common difference found. Next, check for a geometric sequence by dividing consecutive terms listed by the terms that follow them.

$-16 \div 8 = -2$

$32 \div -16 = -2$

You get -2 as the quotient both times, so the sequence is geometric with a common quotient of -2. Multiply 2 by -2 (the common quotient) to obtain the missing term: $2 \times -2 = -4$, Choice **A.**

Choice **B** results if you multiply 2×-2 incorrectly. Choice **C** results if you mistakenly conclude that the next number is halfway between 2 and 8. Choice **D** results if you mistakenly conclude the sequence is arithmetic with a common difference of -8.

69. D. This expression is a product of three terms: $\frac{1}{2}$, h, and $(b_1 + b_2)$. Notice that the sum $b_1 + b_2$ is in parentheses, so it must be treated as a quantity. Using the order of operations, this sum would be computed first, and then multiplied by the product of $\frac{1}{2}$ and h. Choices **A** and **B** are incorrect because neither treats $b_1 + b_2$ as a quantity. Choice **C** is incorrect because $\frac{1}{2}$ is a factor only once, not twice, in the expression.

70. C.

$4 + 2(3x + 1) = 4 + 2(3x) + 2(1) = 4 + 6x + 2$	Using the distributive property, multiply each term in the parentheses by 2.
$= 6x + 4 + 2 = 6x + 6$, Choice **C**	Using the associate property, regroup and simplify.

Choice **A** results if you make the mistake of combining the coefficients after you obtain $6x + 6$. Choice **B** results if you fail to use the distributive property correctly. Choice **D** results if you make the mistake of adding 4 and 2 before applying the distributive property.

71. D. Substitute into the expression, being sure to enclose the substituted values in parentheses:

$x - y = (10) - (-4) = 10 + 4 = 14$, Choice **D**.

Choice **A** occurs if you make a sign error. Choices **B** and **C** result if you deal with the subtraction incorrectly.

72. D. Method 1. Solve using the steps for solving an equation.

Solve $3(x - 6) = 21$

$3x - 18 = 21$	Use the distributive property to remove parentheses.
$3x - 18 + 18 = 21 + 18$	18 is subtracted from the variable term, so add 18 to both sides of the equation.
$3x = 39$	Then simplify.
$\dfrac{3x}{3} = \dfrac{39}{3}$	You want the coefficient of x to be 1, so divide both sides by 3.
$x = 13$	

Choice **A** results if you subtract 18 from both sides instead of adding 18. Choices **B** and **C** result if you fail to use the distributive property correctly.

Method 2. Check each answer choice by plugging the value into the equation.

Checking **A:** $3(x - 6) = 3(1 - 6) = 3(-5) = -15 \neq 21$. Choice **A** is incorrect because $x = 1$ does not satisfy $3(x - 6) = 21$.

Checking **B:** $3(x - 6) = 3(5 - 6) = 3(-1) = -3 \neq 21$. Choice **B** is incorrect because $x = 5$ does not satisfy $3(x - 6) = 21$.

Checking **C:** $3(x - 6) = 3(9 - 6) = 3(3) = 9 \neq 21$. Choice **C** is incorrect because $x = 9$ does not satisfy $3(x - 6) = 21$.

Checking **D:** $3(x - 6) = 3(13 - 6) = 3(7) = 21\checkmark$. Choice **D** is correct because $x = 13$ makes $3(x - 6) = 21$ true.

73. A. To determine which ordered pair satisfies the system, you will need to find the ordered pair that satisfies *both* equations. Check each ordered pair by plugging the x and y values into the two equations, being careful to enclose in parentheses the values you put in.

Checking **A:** $2x - y = 2(-4) - (-1) = -8 + 1 = -7\checkmark$.

Since $(-4, -1)$ works in the first equation, try it in the second equation. $x + 3y = (-4) + 3(-1) = -4 + -3 = -7 \checkmark$. Choice **A** is correct because the ordered pair $(-4, -1)$ satisfies both equations in the system.

In a test situation, you should go on to the next question since you have obtained the correct answer. Here are the other checks.

Checking **B:** $2x - y = 2(-4) - (1) = -8 + -1 = -9 \neq -7$. Choice **B** is incorrect because $(-4, 1)$ does not satisfy $2x - y = -7$.

Checking **C:** $2x - y = 2(4) - (-1) = 8 + 1 = 9 \neq -7$. Choice **C** is incorrect because $(4, -1)$ does not satisfy $2x - y = -7$.

Checking **D:** $2x - y = 2(4) - (1) = 8 + -1 = 7 \neq -7$. Choice **D** is incorrect because $(4, 1)$ does not satisfy $2x - y = -7$.

74. B. Check each response by replacing x with -5 in the statement.

Checking **A:** When $x = -5$, $\frac{1}{x} > -x$ becomes $\frac{1}{-5} > -(-5)$. Simplifying both sides, this statement is $-\frac{1}{5} > 5$, which is false because 5 is to the right of $-\frac{1}{5}$ on the number line.

Checking **B:** When $x = -5$, $3x < 2x$ becomes $3(-5) < 2(-5)$. Simplifying both sides, this statement is $-15 < -10$, which is true because -10 is to the right of -15 on the number line.

In a test situation, you should go on to the next question since you have obtained the correct answer.

Checking the remaining choices, you would find:

Checking **C:** When $x = -5$, $-x < 0$ becomes $-(-5) < 0$. Simplifying both sides, this statement is $5 < 0$, which is false because 5 is to the right of 0 on the number line.

Checking **D:** When $x = -5$, $x - 6 > x + 6$ becomes $(-5) - 6 > (-5) + 6$. Simplifying both sides, this statement is $-11 > 1$, which is false because 1 is to the right of -11 on the number line.

75. C.

$$-2x + 5 < 7$$

$-2x + 5 - 5 < 7 - 5$ 5 is added to the variable term, so subtract 5 from both sides of the inequality. Then simplify.

$x > \dfrac{2}{-2}$ You want the coefficient of x to be 1, so divide both sides by -2 and reverse the inequality because you divided both sides by a negative number.

$x > -1,$ Choice **C**

Choice **B** results if you add 5 to both sides of the inequality, instead of subtracting 5. Choice **A** results if you fail to reverse the inequality. Choice **D** results if you add 5 to both sides of the inequality, instead of subtracting 5, and you fail to reverse the inequality.

76. B. Check for an arithmetic sequence by subtracting consecutive terms listed from the terms that follow them.

$$-15 - (-5) = -15 + 5 = -10$$

$$-25 - (-15) = -25 + 15 = -10$$

You get -10 as the common difference both times, so the sequence is arithmetic with a difference of -10. Add -10 to 15 to obtain the missing term: $15 + -10 = 5$, Choice **B**.

Choice **A** results if you make a sign error. Choice **C** results if you add 10, instead of -10, as the common difference. Choice **D** results if you mistakenly conclude the sequence is geometric with a common quotient of 3.

77. D. From the graph, you can see that the greatest gap between the average low and high temperature lines occurs in April, Choice **D**. The gaps for choices **A, B,** and **C** are not as great.

78. A. To find the median, do the following:

Step 1: Put the numbers in order from least to greatest.

42, 56, 67, 69, 73, 88, 88, 96

Step 2: Find the middle number. The median is the average of the two middle numbers, 69 and 73.

The median $= \dfrac{69 + 73}{2} = 71$

Choice **B** results if you fail to order the scores and mistakenly decide to average 56 and 88 to find the median. Choice **C** is the mean, not the median. Choice **D** is the mode, not the median.

79. **D.** This problem is a probability problem. To solve the problem, find the number of total outcomes possible, find the number of favorable outcomes, and then plug into the probability formula.

There are 50 total possible outcomes. There are 6 favorable outcomes. The probability of drawing a yellow marble is $\text{P}\left(\text{yellow}\right) = \dfrac{\text{number of favorable outcomes}}{\text{number of total outcomes possible}} = \dfrac{\text{number of yellow marbles}}{\text{total number of marbles}} = \dfrac{6}{50} = \dfrac{3}{25}.$

Did I answer the question? Yes, I found the probability of drawing a yellow marble from the box. ✓

Is the answer stated in the correct units? No units are required for the answer. ✓

Choice **A** is the probability of drawing a blue marble. Choice **B** is the probability of drawing a green marble. Choice **C** is the probability of drawing a red marble.

80. **C.** This problem is a counting problem. To solve the problem, multiply the number of ways the girl can select a bread by the number of ways she can select a sandwich filling.

number of ways to select a bread	×	number of ways to select a sandwich filling	=	total number of possible sandwiches
3		4		12

Did I answer the question? Yes, I found the number of possible sandwiches. ✓

Is the answer stated in the correct units? No units are required for the answer. ✓

Choice **A** results if you add, instead of multiply, in the problem. Choices **B** and **D** result if you count or compute incorrectly.

81. **C.** From the pie chart, you can see that 23% of the young readers surveyed responded they read science fiction books most often. To answer the question, you must find 23% of 200.

Method 1: To solve the problem, identify the elements of the percent problem, plug the values into the percent proportion, and solve the proportion:

Step 1. Identify the elements.

$r = 23$

part $= ?$

whole $= 200$

Step 2. Plug into the percent proportion (omitting the units for convenience).

$\dfrac{r}{100} = \dfrac{\text{part}}{\text{whole}}$

$\dfrac{23}{100} = \dfrac{x}{200}$

Step 3. Solve the proportion (omitting the units for convenience).

23×200	Find a cross product you can calculate. You don't know the value of x, so the only cross product you can calculate is 23 times 200.
$x = \dfrac{23 \times 200}{100}$	Divide by 100, the numerical term you didn't use.
$x = 46$ readers	

The number of young readers surveyed who responded they read science fiction books most often is 46, Choice **C**.

Did I answer the question? Yes, I found the number of young readers surveyed who responded they read science fiction books most often. ✓

Is the answer stated in the correct units? Yes, the units are readers, which is correct. ✓

Method 2: Change 23% to a decimal fraction or common fraction and multiply:

23% of 200 = $0.23 \times 200 = 46$

23% of 200 = $\frac{23}{100} \times 200 = 23 \times 2 = 46$

Choice **A** is the number of young readers surveyed who responded they read biography or historical books most often. Choice **B** is the number of young readers surveyed who responded they read nature books most often. Choice **D** is the number of young readers surveyed who responded they read adventure books most often.

82. A. The range is the difference between the greatest and the least score.

range = greatest score – least score = $100 - 70 = 30$, Choice **A**

Choice **B** is the mean score, not the range. Choice **C** is the median score, not the range. Choice **D** is the mode score, not the range.

83. C. To answer the question, find the median for each answer choice.

Choice **A:** $10.29, $9.87, $11.99, $8.45, $10.60, $10.25

Step 1: Put the prices in order from least to greatest.

$8.45, $9.87, $10.25, $10.29, $10.60, $11.99

Step 2: Since there are six values, the median is the average of the two middle values, $10.25 and $10.29. You can eliminate **A** at this point because you can see that the average of these two prices is greater than $10.24. Just so you know, the median = $\frac{\$10.25 + \$10.89}{2} = \$10.78$

Choice **B:** $7.50, $12.98, $8.25, $10.89, $11.05, $10.67

Step 1: Put the prices in order from least to greatest.

$7.50, $8.25, $10.67, $10.89, $11.05, $12.98

Step 2: Since there are six values, the median is the average of the two middle values, $10.67 and $10.89. You can eliminate **B** at this point because you can see that the average of these two prices is greater than $10.24. Just so you know, the median = $\frac{\$10.67 + \$10.89}{2} = \$10.78$

Choice **C:** $11.98, $10.50, $9.98, $8.50, $12.95, $9.98

Step 1: Put the prices in order from least to greatest.

$8.50, $9.98, $9.98, $10.50, $11.98, $12.95

Step 2: Since there are six values, the median is the average of the two middle values, $9.98 and $10.50.

median = $\frac{\$9.98 + \$10.50}{2} = \$10.24$. Choice **C** is the correct response.

In a test situation, you should go on to the next question since you have obtained the correct answer. Just so you know, the median for Choice **D** is $10.11.

84. B. To answer the question, find the mode for each answer choice.

Choice **A** is incorrect. The mode is 96 because it occurs three times.

Choice **B** is correct: The mode is 87 because it occurs two times.

Choice **C** is incorrect. The mode is 84 because it occurs two times.

Choice **D** is incorrect. There is no mode because each score occurs the same number of times.

85. B. This is a probability problem. To solve the problem, find the number of total outcomes possible, find the number of favorable outcomes, and then plug into the probability formula.

There are 40 total possible outcomes. The primes between 1 and 40 are 2, 3, 5, 7, 11, 13, 17, 19, 23, 29, 31, and 37. There are 12 favorable outcomes. The probability of drawing a tile numbered with a prime number is

$$P(\text{prime}) = \frac{\text{number of favorable outcomes}}{\text{number of total outcomes possible}} = \frac{\text{number of prime} - \text{numbered tiles}}{\text{total number of tiles}} = \frac{12}{40} = \frac{3}{10}$$

Did I answer the question? Yes, I found the probability of drawing a prime-numbered tile. ✓

Is the answer stated in the correct units? No units are required for the answer. ✓

Choice **A** is the result of mistakenly determining that there are 10 favorable outcomes. Choice **C** is the result of including 1 as a prime number. The number 1 is neither prime nor composite. Choice **D** is the probability of drawing a composite-numbered tile.

General Knowledge Practice Test 2: Reading Skills Answers and Explanations

86. B. This passage states that *"plugging" is not a part of modern baseball* (Choice **B**). This information is given in the second paragraph. None of the other answer choices are stated in this passage.

87. A. According to this passage, rounders is a game that *was imported from England.* (Choice **A**). Although this information is not stated explicitly in this passage, it can be inferred from the information given in the second paragraph. The other answer choices are not supported by the passage.

88. D. In the first paragraph, the word *evokes* most nearly means *elicits* (Choice **D**), to draw forth. The words in the other answer choices do not mean the same as the word *elicits*.

89. C. According to this passage, the Knickerbockers baseball club was formed in *New York* (Choice **C**). The cities in the other answer choices are incorrect locations.

90. D. An opinion expressed in this passage is the statement given in Choice **D**: *Baseball has become the hallmark of all that is good and right about our country.* The description of baseball as *the hallmark of all that is good and right about our country* is a view, not a fact, expressed by the author, reflecting the author's opinion about baseball. Choice **A** is a statement of fact given in the second sentence of the second paragraph. Choice **B** is a statement of fact given in the last sentence of the third paragraph. Choice **C** is a statement of fact that can be determined from the information given in the fourth paragraph.

91. D. According to the passage, baseball is considered America's pastime because *it occurs at a leisurely pace in a pastoral setting.* Remember, the question reads "according to this passage," and this reference to "baseball and its natural allure to wide open spaces," is exactly the description the reader needs to select Choice **D**. Choice **A** is incorrect because as the passage implies, baseball certainly does more than provide interested individuals with more than a "casual diversion." It provides a dramatic confrontation of a competitive sport in which fans can cheer for their respective teams and watch the game leisurely unfold before them. Choice **B** is incorrect because it is not supported by the passage. Choice **C** is incorrect because the passage indicates baseball has rules.

92. B. As used in the final paragraph, the word *exemplifies* best means *to illustrate by example*. The author of this passage provides vivid metaphors to illustrate how baseball symbolizes America's spirit. Choice **A** is incorrect because the word *exemplifies* does not mean "to define by explanation." Choice **C** is incorrect because the word *exemplifies* does not mean "to organize by listing." Choice **D** is incorrect because the word *exemplifies* does not mean "to delineate by detailing."

93. C. The narrative style of this passage can best be described as *subjective*. The author provides a passionate, yet practical analysis of the reason that baseball is regarded as America's favorite pastime. Choice **A** is incorrect because the author is not derisive, meaning antagonistic and degrading. Choice **B** is incorrect because the author is not cynical, but instead presents a realistic picture of why baseball is so endeared by millions of fans. Choice **D** is incorrect because the author is not pessimistic about the future of baseball; instead, the author is realistic and fair in his assessment of it as a spectator sport.

94. B. The sentence that best states a main idea of this passage is *baseball evokes an era of a simpler life and pace.* Baseball is a leisurely sport, and this passage reflects this ease and calm. Choice **A** is incorrect because baseball is not a sport that is elitist in tone and style. Choice **C** is incorrect because the passage describes baseball as simple in design and pace. Choice **D** is incorrect because although watching professional baseball might inspire youngsters to become competitive athletes, this thought is not expressed in this narrative about baseball.

95. C. In the final paragraph, the second and third sentences *explain the first sentence.* The two sentences that follow the first sentence explain by illustration what the author means by *Of all of America's obsessions, baseball is one of pure passion.* Choice **A** is incorrect because the second and third sentences do not dispute or disagree with the first sentence, and do not modify it. Choice **B** is incorrect because the second and third sentences support the first sentence. Choice **D** is incorrect because the second and third sentences relate to the first sentence, and do not ignore it.

96. D. The author of this passage believes that dancing *is a joyous expression of movement to music.* The passage demonstrates the author's fondness for dancing as a form of self-expression. Choice **A** is incorrect because the passage does not portray dancing as detrimental to one's health and well-being. Choice **B** is incorrect because the author says that formal dancing is not self-willed and free-wheeling. Choice **C** is incorrect because nowhere does the author imply that dancing is a waste of time and energy.

97. B. The author's claim that "I have two left feet," is clearly *a narrative technique to engage the reader.* The author uses the technique of self-deprecating humor to lure the reader into his discussion of dance and the many forms it has taken throughout and even before human history. Choice **A** is incorrect because even though the author loves to dance, he may truly be what he says he is: a bad dancer. Choice **C** is incorrect because the self-deprecating humor is no indication that the author does not like dance; indeed, it is an indication of the contrary. Choice **D** is incorrect because the author does not engage in an argumentative style; instead, he uses self-deprecating style to entice and tease the reader into his discussion about his love for dance.

98. A. This passage is an example of *a narrative portrayal of a positive experience.* The author writes in a clear and optimistic voice about the power of dance to transform the lives of all who participate in it or observe it. Choice **B** is incorrect because the author does not provide a cynical perspective on the human condition in this passage. Choice **C** is incorrect because the author does not see dance as a dying art form—it is something that lives from generation to generation—and thus, this narrative is not a valedictory speech . Choice **D** is incorrect because the author believes that dancing is universally enjoyed and thus, is not an obscure obsession.

99. C. In the sixth paragraph, the phrase *blessed with the gift of mimicry* best means *being able to imitate.* Choices **A, B,** and **D** are incorrect meanings of the word *mimicry* and, thus, are inappropriate choices.

100. B. According to this narrative, dancing is universally enjoyed because *it speaks to human emotions.* Choice **A** is incorrect because even though some types of dance may be part of ancient and mysterious rituals, there are other dance forms that are not. Choice **C** is incorrect because although dancing can be compelling, it certainly does not have to be consequential, and is not universally enjoyed as thus. Choice **D** is incorrect because, if anything, dancing revels in the imaginative and unreal, and not usually the known and the factual.

101. C. A statement that is implied in the first paragraph is the statement given in Choice **C**: *The cha-cha, rhumba, and waltz are types of dance.* The author never states explicitly that these are types of dances, but the reader can draw this conclusion based on the topic of the paragraph. Even though you may disagree with the statements in choices **A** and **D,** these statements are explicit in the first paragraph. The statement given in Choice **B** is neither stated nor implied in the first paragraph.

102. C. An opinion expressed in this passage is the statement given in Choice **C**: *Dancing has always been the most human form of self-expression.* The description of dancing as *the most human form of self-expression* is a view, not a fact, expressed by the author, reflecting the author's opinion about dancing. Choice **A** is a statement of fact given in the third sentence of the third paragraph. Choice **B** is a statement of fact given in the first sentence of the fourth paragraph. Choice **D** is a statement of fact given in the last sentence of the fifth paragraph.

103. C. In the second paragraph, the word *assertive*, meaning aggressively self-confident, most nearly means *bold* (Choice **C**). The words in the other answer choices have a meaning opposite to that of *assertive.*

104. **C.** This passage states that *dancing is an art form*. This information is given in the first sentence of the third paragraph. The statement in Choice **A** is implied, but not stated, in the second paragraph. Choice **B** disagrees with the third sentence of the third paragraph. Choice **D** is implied, but not stated in the first paragraph.

105. **D.** According to information given in this passage, formal dancing is difficult and strenuous (Choice **D**). This determination can be inferred from the third sentence in the last paragraph "their [referring to those who do formal dancing] expertise lies in making the difficult and strenuous look easy and joyous." Choices **A** and **B** are not supported by the passage. Neither is Choice **C** supported by the passage. Even though this is a true statement, this information is not given in the passage. Tip: Do not select answer choices based on your personal knowledge that goes beyond the information given in the passage.

106. **A.** In this narrative, the author speaks of Piaget as *a curious and prodigious thinker*. As the narrative indicates, from a very early age, Piaget showed signs of the intense intellectual curiosity that served him well all his life. Choice **B** implies that Piaget was an effete intellectual and disciplinarian; the narration mentions nothing of the sort. Choice **C** defines Piaget as a raucous and caustic intellectual; again, there is nothing in the narrative that implies this distinction toward Piaget. Finally, Choice **D** states that Piaget was a secretive and solitary scientist, and all indications from the narrative are that Piaget was not author of these.

107. **C.** As our thinking about human cognition has evolved, one principle, according to the passage, has remained constant—*Human beings need to develop in defined stages*. Piaget was one of the first cognitive psychologists to define human development as a series of well-defined stages of growth and maturity. Each stage defined a different thinking process and learning perspective. Choice **A** is incorrect because although human beings do sometimes have to reconcile the absurdity of many events, this does not underline the constancy of human development and growth as expressed in this passage. Choice **B** is incorrect because again, human beings do not need to understand the "misunderstood" as a universal principle of growth and learning, nor is this theory discussed in this passage. Choice **D** is incorrect because this is not mentioned in the central thesis of this passage.

108. **B.** The author would probably agree that *studying cognitive thinking reveals human behavior patterns*. The thrust of this piece is how Piaget's discovery of cognitive thinking led him to define human behavior into recognizable patterns of development. None of the other answer choices are supported by this passage.

109. **D.** In this narrative, the following statement is NOT stated: *cognitive psychology relies on the suspension of disbelief*. In fact, as the narrative mentions, cognitive psychology relies on validated truths or things that you can actually see. Choice **A** is incorrect because the narrative specifically implies that psychology is the study of the mind and its mental and emotional processes. Choice **B** is incorrect because Piaget's developmental theories were the result of a small sample size. Choice **C** is incorrect because developmental thinking can be classified into specified age groups.

110. **D.** In the fifth paragraph, the phrase, *Not content to know just the physical world,* implies that Piaget *intended to explore mental functions*. The paragraph goes on to discuss Piaget's pursuit of psychology. Choice **A** is incorrect because Piaget was much more than a literal or "just the facts" scientific researcher. Choice **B** is incorrect because Piaget understood more than the human body when he explained his theories. Choice **C** is incorrect because Piaget engaged in more than quantitative or "numbers only" research; instead, he relied on qualitative or observed characteristics as well.

111. **D.** According to this passage Jean Piaget was born in *Switzerland* in 1896 (Choice **D**). The other answer choices do not give the correct country of Piaget's birth.

112. **A.** The topic of the second paragraph is *Piaget's four stages of mental development* (Choice **A**). The topic in Choice **B** is too broad to describe the information in the second paragraph. The topics in choices **C** and **D** are too narrow to describe the information in the second paragraph.

113. **A.** An opinion about Jean Piaget expressed in this passage is the statement given in Choice **A**: *His work is seminal to understanding modern child development*. The word *seminal* is a judgment word reflecting the author's opinion about Piaget's impact on the field of child development. Choice **B** is a statement of fact given in the first sentence of the fifth paragraph. Choice **C** is a statement of fact given in the first sentence of the sixth paragraph. Choice **D** is a statement of fact established by the fourth sentence of the fourth paragraph.

114. B. In the third sentence of the fifth paragraph, this passage states that Jean Piaget embarked on a career that led to *breakthrough discoveries in human cognition* (Choice **B**). Choices **A** and **C** are incorrect because, although these are true statements (as you may know), this information is not given in this passage. Remember, you must not select answer choices based on your personal knowledge that goes beyond the information given in the passage. Choice **D** is not supported by the passage.

115. D. The tone of this passage is best described as *serious* (Choice **D**). The author does not show a disbelieving, doubtful tone (Choice **A**); a sarcastic, mocking tone (Choice **B**); or a convincing, persuasive tone (Choice **C**).

116. A. One thing that this narrative makes clear is that whales have more in common with *mammals than fish*. The central thesis of this passage is how whales belong to the mammal class, although most people think of them as fish. Choice **B** is incorrect because whales are not reptiles. Choice **C** is incorrect because whales are not amphibians. Choice **D** is incorrect because, as said, whales are not fish.

117. B. According to this passage, whales are a unique species in the animal kingdom because *whales can carry enormous weight without much effort*. They are the largest sea creatures, yet their bodies are structured so that they can glide through the ocean without much difficulty or effort. Choice **A** is incorrect because the passage makes no mention of this. Choice **C** is incorrect because whales are very maternal and, like all mammals, nurture their offspring. Choice **D** is incorrect because the passage makes no mention of this.

118. C. The author of this passage implies that whales are intelligent. The author of this passage states that whales have a higly developed brain from which can be inferred that they are intelligent. Choices **A, B,** and **D** are not supported by the passage.

119. A. After reading this passage, the following statement can be inferred as true: *whales are creatures who have experienced successful adaptations*. Clearly, this passage implies that the adaptability of whales throughout the ages has contributed to its long history as the largest and most impressive of all sea creatures. The other answer choices are not supported by the passage.

120. A. In the fifth paragraph, the word *adaptation* can best be defined as *modification*. As the passage states, whales have grown into the successful creatures they are because their bodies have adapted to life in the sea. The other answer choices are not accurate definitions for *adaptation*.

121. D. The tone of this passage is best described as *factual* (Choice **D**). The author does not show a disbelieving, skeptical tone (Choice **A**); an amusing, humorous tone (Choice **B**); or a mocking, sarcastic tone (Choice **C**).

122. B. A statement that is a fact about whales that is given in the first paragraph is the statement in Choice **B**: *Whales have lungs*. The statements in choices **A** and **C** disagree with information given in the passage. Neither is Choice **C** supported by the passage. Even though this is a true statement, this information is not given in the passage. Tip: Do not select answer choices based on your personal knowledge that goes beyond the information given in the passage.

123. B. A statement about whales that is implied in this passage is given in Choice **B**: *They cannot take in oxygen when underwater*. This statement can be inferred from the third sentence, which states that fish can take in dissolved oxygen from water and the fourth sentence, which states that whales must come to the surface to breathe, of the second paragraph. The statements about whales given in the other answer choices disagree with information given in this passage.

124. B. In the last sentence of the second paragraph, this passage states that *the sperm whale can hold its breath for up to two hours* (Choice **B**). The timeframes given in the other answer choices disagree with information in this passage.

125. B. According to information given in the third paragraph of this passage, *whales nurture their young* (Choice **B**). Choice **A** is a true statement, but this information is not given in this passage. As stated earlier, do not select answer choices based on your personal knowledge that goes beyond the information given in the passage. Choice **C** is incorrect because it disagrees with the third sentence of the fifth paragraph. Choice **D** is incorrect because it disagrees with information given in the first paragraph.